Emyl Jenkins'
APPRAISAL
BOOK

Emyl Jenkins' APPRAISAL BOOK

Identifying, Understanding, and Valuing Your Treasures

Three Rivers Press
New York

Drawings courtesy Hickory Chair Company, page 7; Hudson-Belk, pages 9, 145, 146, 159; Reed and Barton, page 130. Photographs courtesy Weschler's Auction Gallery, pages 8, 212 (top), 214; Savoia and Fromm Auction Services, page 218; Henry J. Young Jewelers, page 10; Richard A. Bourne Company, pages 201, 204 (bottom), 210, 212 (bottom); David and Linda Arman, pages 204 (top), 205; North Carolina Department of History, pages 242, 243.

Portions of this book first appeared in *Why You're Richer Than You Think* by Emyl Jenkins, copyright © 1982 by Emyl Jenkins

Published by Three Rivers Press, a division of Crown Publishers, Inc., 201 East 50th Street, New York, New York 10022
Member of the Crown Publishing Group.

Originally published in hardcover by Crown Publishers, Inc., 1982.

Random House, Inc. New York, Toronto, London, Sydney, Auckland.

http://www.randomhouse.com/

Three Rivers Press and colophon are trademarks of Crown Publishers, Inc.

Printed in the United States of America

ISBN 0-517-88434-8

10 9 8 7 6 5 4

For Macon Riddle,
whose idea of fun is, "Let's go antiquing!"

CONTENTS

FOREWORD

Let's face it: modern life is complicated. It's bad enough that we can't fix most of the gadgets around the house if they break. But what happens if we lose them—and our silver and our pictures and our you-name-its—in a fire or a burglary?

There are rules. The IRS has rules. The insurance companies have rules. The police have rules.

None of them wants sob stories. They want hard, cold, detailed information. Pictures. Lists. Marks. Sizes. Values.

The time to get all that information, of course, is before the disaster. But how and where?

Appraisal. That's where.

Can you do it yourself? Yes, but . . .

This book will help. Pictures and lists of reference works and periodicals will get you in the ballpark. But if you own more than a carpetbag full of possessions you probably need a professional appraisal.

What kind of appraisal? As I said, things are complicated. There are at least three kinds of appraisals and you don't want to get them mixed up. If the IRS finds your deceased grandmother's insurance appraisal, for instance, your estate tax bill will jump, but if you give the insurance company her estate appraisal, you won't be able to replace half her things.

What kind of appraiser? Real estate appraisers have to be certified by state boards, but not one personal property appraiser is certified by any state board. Some so-called appraisers are really dealers who would rather buy your valuables than tell you what they are worth.

Look, it's a jungle out there in personal property land. *Emyl Jenkins' Appraisal Book* is just the sharp edge that may help you cut your way out of it.

SAMUEL PENNINGTON
Editor, *Maine Antiques Digest*

Part One

WHY YOUR POSSESSIONS ARE VALUABLE

WARNING!
I Know More About
What's in Your House
Than You Do!

For years, I spent more time in other people's homes than I did in my own.

I know where wealthy collectors hide their silver.

I have appraised priceless antiques that even museum curators have never seen.

And I have seen fakes that the owners bought as rare antiques supposedly worth thousands of dollars.

I save insurance companies hundreds of thousands of dollars by helping them uncover false and fraudulent claims.

And I work for individuals, people like you, helping them, after burglaries, fires, and moving disasters, to recover insurance money that they had given up hope of ever collecting.

I have checked out mansions and cottages, dusty attics and cluttered basements, all over the United States and, according to at least one man, broken hearts when I have told people that their silver was plated, not sterling, and that the "antique" was an old reproduction, not a period piece.

In short, I know more about your personal property and what it is worth than you do. And, let me warn you, so do most thieves!

The crime rate is rising incredibly today. This, combined with the continually increasing value of all personal property—antique and new—means the time has come when you must know what you own. No longer can you sit back and think, The robbers won't hit my house or I'm safe from fire. I know from firsthand experience that disasters can happen to anyone.

This book is a direct outgrowth of my day-to-day work. I have learned that not only do most people not know the value of their personal property, they do not even know what they own.

Would you buy a $30,000 car without knowing its make or getting insurance for it? Would you leave the car unattended on a dark street with its motor running and the keys in the ignition?

Of course not.

Such superior-quality reproductions as the Rhode Island desk and bookcase and Philadelphia Queen Anne armchair in the Winterthur Collection by the Kindel Company of Grand Rapids, Michigan, provide the connoisseur with an opportunity to have faithfully measured and detailed copies of museum-quality pieces in his home. The quality shows up in both the pieces and the price. **Photograph courtesy Kindel**

Yet you leave your house, apartment, or condominium filled with thousands of dollars' worth of silver, jewelry, antiques, expensive furniture—literally all your worldly goods—without knowing what you have and, often, are grossly underinsured.

Rather than spend your time trying to outwit the thieves, why not take the time to become your own detective and learn about your many treasures? Bob Volpe, the well-known New York Police Department "art cop," observed that thieves spend twenty-four hours a day thinking about hiding places, but you spend only a few minutes trying to outsmart these professionals before leaving on a trip or vacation. Why should you be surprised that your "hidden" treasures are so often stolen?

Though theft is a concern of most of us today, there are other reasons to learn more about your personal property. Not the least of these is the fun you'll have discovering exactly what some little piece is, how old it is, where it came from, and what it's worth.

Every day I receive countless letters and phone calls all asking the same questions. Oh, the objects are different and the reasons for wanting to know vary, but basically everyone wants to know . . .

> **What** is it?
> **How old** is it?
> **Where** did it come from?

and always . . .   What's it **worth?**

Now I want to come into your home and show you why you should be more aware of your antiques, silver, china, furniture, collections, old and new, even those treasures hidden away or packed in storage. Based on my experience as an appraiser, I can honestly tell you, you're richer than you think!

You've taken what you live with for granted long enough. This book is written for you. It is designed to help you get your house in order. If you follow the guidelines provided here, you may protect yourself from losing thousands of dollars, or you may uncover objects worth thousands of dollars that you might have discarded without a second thought!

You will learn:

- *How to correctly identify objects.* Hints on where to look and what to look for, as well as makers' marks and labels, will help turn you into an instant expert.
- *Whether an object truly is an antique or collectible.* By learning how to detect the "real," you will also learn how to identify reproductions and fakes. You'll not only learn about the items you own, you'll also become a more astute shopper!
- *How to make your own inventory.* I describe a simple step-by-step procedure that you can follow in making your own inventory or appraisal. This is the same method professional appraisers use.
- *How and why antiques and personal property are increasing in value today.* The phenomenal rise in values has led to heavy investing in antiques. Is this wise? If you are going to invest, what should you buy?

What is overpriced? What about the quality of today's manufactured furniture? How do you protect what you already own? What kind and how much insurance do you need? These and other urgent questions are answered here.

- *When and how to seek professional appraisal help if you need it.* You will learn what an appraiser can and cannot do for you. Learn who and what a certified appraiser is. Learn how to keep down appraisal fees and what to expect from appraisal services.
- *How and when to sell and donate antiques and other objects of personal property.* Almost every person must decide sometime what to do with "all these things." You may be cleaning out a parent's or grandparent's dwelling, moving from one place to another, moving a child into his or her own apartment or home, separating objects in a divorce, or just spring cleaning. Regardless of the reason, you don't want to make mistakes that you'll regret later.

You live with your belongings. You love them and cherish the memories they hold for you. You anticipate passing on these treasured possessions to the next generation—and the next—as a token of your taste and appreciation of beauty. I have written this book because I, too, share your love and concern for silver, good furniture, and fine china. Take my book and use it in your own home to protect your treasures, your investments, and your peace of mind.

1

Why Your Possessions Are Valuable

If you are like the majority of people I work with, you have no idea how much your personal property has risen in value. Don't feel guilty; neither do many museum curators, insurance professionals, and other experts who should know. But the police know.

One officer told me that one of the biggest surprises victims of jewelry robberies get is when they learn the current cost of an old high school ring—usually one the owner hasn't worn in years! A ring bought for only $35 or $50 years ago today easily costs $250 to $500 new. And even if your ring were stolen and you chose not to replace it, its sale value for meltdown gold content alone is probably in the $60 to $80 range. You wouldn't consciously throw $60 or $80 away, would you?

If you are over fifty years old, you set up housekeeping in an era when a sterling silver teaspoon cost $3 to $5 and a good reproduction chair $10 to $20. The cost of buying a new sterling silver spoon today is $50 to $80, and a comparable new chair costs $450 to $700.

Often I find that people in the sixty- to eighty-age group simply do not believe me. Maybe you've had a similar experience if you've tried to convince your parents that they need better insurance coverage. I can't even get my own mother to face the reality of how much personal property bought in the late 1930s costs now.

"How can you say that it would cost $1,500 to replace my four-poster bed when the entire bedroom suite only cost $180 when we bought it?" she asks.

In reality this same bedroom suite—bed, dressing table, stool, mirror, chest of drawers, and bedside table—would cost at least $4,000 to buy today.

Proof? If you, your parents, or your grandparents saved any catalogs from early housekeeping days, you'll have firsthand proof of the cost *then*. And it only takes a glance at the newspaper or a magazine advertisement to learn today's prices *now*. The reprints of many catalogs, from Sears, Roebuck & Co. to the Wallace Nutting General Catalogue, make us all long for "the good old days," at least for shopping.

In case you, like my mother, are skeptical, here are a few items typical of those you probably own and what they cost at an earlier time and their replacement cost today.

Furniture

Many homes will have a traditional reproduction bedroom suite, usually mahogany, walnut, or cherry and by one of the better American furniture manufacturers. The style may be Chippendale, Queen Anne, Federal, or even French Provincial, but regardless of the style, the increase in its replacement cost over just the past twenty-five to thirty years can be quite an eye-opener.

A bedroom suite of comparable style, quality, and materials in 1962 and 1995:

	1962	1995
Four-poster bed	$ 160.00	$1,500.00
Bedside table	75.00	525.00
Four-drawer chest	275.00	1,200.00
Five-drawer chest	375.00	1,700.00
Vanity and bench	225.00	1,800.00
Total	$1,100.00	$6,725.00

One major change between 1962 and 1995 is the presence of the discount stores. Even if the pieces are purchased at a generous discount in 1995, the replacement cost would be in the $4,000 range.

Silver

In today's "sale"- and "discount"-oriented world, it is important that you realize that the "suggested retail prices" published by the silver manufacturing companies are inflated values, and that the retailers and discount houses price the silver far below the "silver retail prices." The values given here and throughout this book are realistic replacement prices.

Two silver flatware patterns that are as popular in the 1990s as they were in the 1930s and 1960s are "Chantilly" (by Gorham) and "Repoussé" (by Kirk). Even though you may have a different pattern, you can use these figures as an indication of the cost of replacing silver flatware sets with patterns that are still currently available.

"Chantilly"	1968	1995
Teaspoon	$ 9.00	$ 88.00
Place fork	13.50	108.00
Place knife	12.00	76.00
Salad fork	11.50	98.00
Butter spreader	8.00	71.00
Soup spoon	11.25	102.00
Ice tea spoon	11.25	88.00
Tablespoon	22.00	195.00
Pickle fork	10.25	86.00
Cold meat fork	22.00	196.00
Sugar spoon	13.25	98.00
Gravy ladle	22.00	196.00
Butter server	13.25	71.00

A place setting for eight—teaspoon, knife, fork, salad fork, butter spreader, soup spoon, and ice tea spoon—with six serving pieces in 1968 cost $714.75; today, twenty-seven years later, the replacement cost would be $5,890.00. That's an 824 percent increase.

The next chart shows the change that evolved from yet another generation, 1938. A couple selecting Repoussé as their wedding silver in 1938 celebrated their fiftieth wedding anniversary in 1988. Many younger people now have their parents' or grandparents' silver that was originally purchased in the 1930s.

"Repoussé"	1938	1995
Teaspoon	$1.35	$78.00
Place fork	2.75	109.00
Place knife	2.25	72.00
Salad fork	1.75	78.00
Butter spreader	1.50	62.00
Soup spoon	1.75	98.00
Ice tea spoon	2.00	98.00
Tablespoon	3.50	180.00
Pickle fork	1.50	78.00
Cold meat fork	3.25	156.00
Sugar spoon	1.75	92.00
Gravy ladle	3.75	196.00
Butter server	2.50	86.00

A place setting for eight—teaspoon, knife, fork, salad fork, butter spreader, soup spoon, and ice tea spoon—plus six serving pieces in 1938 cost $123.05; today, the replacement cost is $5,548.00. That's a 4,508.7 percent increase.

We'll talk about insurance later. But just in case you're one of those people who complains, "I can't afford to insure my personal property," stop and take a second look at the figures for sterling silver. Ask yourself, "How many knives, forks, and spoons do I have?" If you have eight of each, you'll need to spend around $2,000 to $2,200 to replace these twenty-four pieces if they're stolen. You can't afford the insurance? In some states you can insure $5,000 worth of silver for less than the cost of *one teaspoon*!

China

Fine china and crystal have always been expensive, but you may not realize that the prices have increased proportionally as much as silver. Following are samples of popular china patterns and what they cost then and now.

"Autumn" (*Lenox*)	1977	1995
Dinner plate	$ 22.50	$ 61.00
Salad plate	16.85	44.00
Bread and butter plate	11.65	31.00
Cup and saucer	34.50	92.00
Five-piece place setting	85.50	228.00
Fruit bowl	20.10	69.00
Soup bowl	28.00	84.00
Total	$133.60	$381.00

This represents a 285.2 percent increase in eighteen years.

"Marlborough Sprays" (*Spode*)	1965	1995
Dinner plate	$ 5.50	$ 20.00
Salad plate	4.25	15.00
Bread and butter plate	3.25	10.00
Cup and saucer	5.75	25.00
Five-piece place setting	18.75	70.00
Fruit dish	3.20	16.00
Soup bowl	4.20	28.00
Total	$26.15	$114.00

This represents a 435.9 percent increase in thirty years.

Crystal

The names of crystal patterns are not as easily remembered as china patterns, plus there is no place on the goblet to write the name. Further, many patterns are no longer made. For these reasons, the following tables are of a more general nature than those for silver and china, but the message is the same: the cost to replace fine crystal may far exceed your guesstimate.

Simple gold rim	1978	1995
Single goblet	$ 8.75	$ 39.00
Set of 24 goblets	$210.00	$936.00

This represents a 445.7 percent increase in seventeen years.

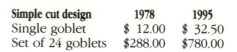

Simple cut design	1978	1995
Single goblet	$ 12.00	$ 32.50
Set of 24 goblets	$288.00	$780.00

This represents a 270.8 percent increase in seventeen years.

Elaborate cut design	1978	1995
Single goblet	$ 9.25	$ 39.50
Set of 24 goblets	$222.00	$948.00

This represents a 427 percent increase in seventeen years.

But just in case you have crystal by the very well known crystal manufacturer Waterford, you may find the following comparison quite interesting.

Waterford "Lismore"	1962	1995
Single goblet	$ 3.25	$ 49.50
Set of 24 goblets	$78.00	$1188.00

In thirty-three years a Waterford "Lismore" goblet has increased 1,523 percent!

Is it little wonder that we wish *now* we had bought more *then*?

The Price Is Right, or Why Personal Property Is So Valuable Today

So, you see, inflation affects everything, and personal property is no exception—antiques, silver, furniture, china, carpeting, draperies, lighting, linens, books. Many older householders are not aware of the value of their property because they haven't bought any major pieces of furniture or added to their silver or china in the last five, ten, or even fifteen years. It has been during these years that price increases have become so rampant. Most china, crystal, silver, and furniture companies now update (a polite word for increase) their price lists at least twice a year.

When people are totally unaware of the *new value* for personal property and have an appraisal made, the appraiser's word is often doubted. I had such an experience a few years ago when I appraised a Hepplewhite lady's desk dating from the 1920s. The piece certainly was not an antique, but it was attractive and could be used in any room in a house or small apartment. However, it was also a manufactured piece identical to literally hundreds of other desks made during that time. You could only classify it as a good reproduction—nice used furniture. When I appraised the piece at $350, the owner was visibly stunned. "This is surely *too high*," she insisted.

Once clients question the value an appraiser puts on a piece, you know that they are thinking, If she is so far off on *that* piece, what about the other pieces?

There were two possibilities for my client. She could call in another appraiser. Or she could shop around and check the cost of another desk similar to or exactly like hers. At my suggestion, this is what she decided to do. A couple of weeks later she called.

"Remember my desk?" she asked. "Well, I shopped around—and frankly

I didn't find a single desk that was as nice as mine, and they were all $300 or $400! Don't you want to raise the value a little?"

The truth is, if you're not in the marketplace, you just don't know the prices, to say nothing of what's "hot." That incident took place about seven or eight years ago. Today I would appraise the desk not at $350, but at around $850. Why? Good-quality manufactured reproduction furniture is one of the hottest items around these days. In fact, later on there's an entire section on the topic under the furniture part of this book.

Though you may be astounded at some of the figures you've just read and assume that inflation is the basis for the rise in both the cost and value of not-so-old personal property, there are actually several reasons the spiral continues upward—some obvious, others more subtle.

Quality

Quality is undoubtedly one of the most obvious reasons many people prefer the old to the new. To maintain high quality in manufacturing today, prices have to rise. This rise is passed on to you, the customer; thus, the very high quality reproduction secretary that cost $2,500 in 1973, or $6,500 in 1983, costs you $20,000 today.

But there's another side to quality. Because many people can't or won't pay $20,000 for a secretary, a number of manufacturers are substituting cheaper materials in currently manufactured pieces. There are some obvious changes almost anyone who looks at the usual piece of new furniture today can see.

Look at the interior of a drawer, for example. How is it joined to the front? Are those nails? Previously, they used to use dovetails—mortises and tenons that locked the pieces together.

No, wait—those aren't nails, those are staples!

And what about the drawer bottoms?

Wood? No.

Plywood? No.

Chipboard or composition board? Yes.

If you've looked at moderately priced new furniture lately, you've probably already observed these concessions to cost. But, after all, who sees the inside of a drawer?

What's going on on the outside? I spoke to a furniture dealer whose lines include Henredon, Baker, and Heritage, as well as Thomasville, Drexel, and other well-known manufacturers. "There's been plastic introduced even in some of the fine lines," he explained. Moldings around the edges of tables and decorative touches, such as brackets connecting tabletops and the legs, are two examples he showed me.

"What does this do to repairing a piece of furniture once it breaks?" I asked, remembering my children's shattered plastic toys—particularly my daughter's plastic dollhouse furniture of a few years back.

"In the case of a corner bracket, there's no problem. You just get another one and stick it on. But when the plastic edge molding gets chipped or damaged, you've got a real problem."

He then went on to explain other cost-cutting procedures, one of which will be particularly offensive to the lovers of good woods and beautiful grains. Some companies are engraving grains onto blond boards. The result is a particle board with a nice-looking oak grain printed on it.

And what happens to it when it gets damaged? Well, he told me about the time one of his workers was putting a bedroom suite together and his hammer slipped. A huge hunk was knocked out of the nightstand, and they were left with a gaping hole in the piece. This would not have happened had the piece been made out of good, hard, solid oak.

Let this be a warning to you in buying new furniture today. Ask if the piece is wood or "wood-grained." Take notice of furniture ads that use such descriptions as "mahogany veneer on hardwood" or "cherry solids."

If you look at a piece of furniture made even as recently as the 1950s or 1960s and compare it with those made today, you will notice some real differences.

One antiques dealer I know keeps a brand-new Chippendale-style desk in stock just to use to show the difference in finish, materials, and overall look. "That one desk sells more antiques than all the salesmanship in the world," he told me.

Why Early Attic Looks So Good

This is why so many antiques dealers today are buying the fine old reproductions and selling them in their shops—not as antiques, but as good-quality reproduction pieces with high prices. The dealers are recognizing the quality of the old reproductions, pieces like those you have in your home. These old "early attic" reproductions are gaining new respectability and higher price tags.

Another reason dealers are upscaling the value of these old reproductions is scarcity. When you can't get an eighteenth-century lowboy, but your customers want a lowboy, what are you going to do? Sell them a nineteenth-century or even early-twentieth-century lowboy. Whether or not the antiques dealer sells the nineteenth-century lowboy for what it is—a nineteenth-century piece—or tries to pass it off as an eighteenth-century piece is something I'll deal with later.

Everyone agrees—more people want antiques or antique look-alikes than ever before. It's the old supply-and-demand story. Our country has not been racked by war for over one hundred years. Generally, over the last one hundred years, the quality of life has improved greatly. The middle class has grown substantially. How do you show your prosperity? By the house you live in and the furnishings you choose to have around you. If you already had these in your family, you have held on to them. If you are self-made, you seek what others have—symbols of the past. Add to this the potential investment quality value of antiques today, and the result is—everyone wants them.

This unprecedented demand has antiques dealers all singing the same sad song. "I can't replace my stock when I sell it," they moan. "If I am lucky enough even to find a . . . Tiffany lamp . . . lowboy . . . Ming vase . . . Georgian tea service, or Windsor chair [whatever he or she is looking for] . . . I'll probably have to pay as much for it *wholesale* as what I sold my last one for."

Who doesn't want a good-quality secretary? Secretaries are utilitarian as well as attractive. But when an eighteenth-century secretary is beyond your financial means, a later reproduction secretary may be the answer. But that's what your sister thinks and your next-door neighbor as well. Quite obviously, the prices of these pieces are rapidly increasing. Photograph courtesy Weschler's Auction Gallery

The sterling silver cigarette urn, once an inexpensive accessory found on cocktail tables in apartments and fine homes, and as suitable for small flowers as cigarettes, is no longer being made today. Photograph courtesy Reed and Barton

What does this mean to you, the owner of these pieces the antiques dealers want? Your possessions are worth more than you think, and if you ever need to replace them, you might be in for a long and expensive search.

While this may be true of antiques, you think, I don't need to worry. None of my things are old. They're only ten, twenty years old. Well, you've just read how both inflation and quality affect value. But there's more news, and it's not good—even items that you expect to be able to replace are no longer available, especially in silver.

A clear example of the cutback in production can be seen by comparing one silver company's price list for sterling silver hollowware—teapots, goblets, children's cups, letter openers, and so forth. The 1975 list had 228 items. In 1981, prices were given for 95 of these items. Next to the 133 other items was one word—"Discontinued." The companies just aren't making what they used to.

Also, when considering replacement of silver items, remember the tremendous meltdown that occurred in the early months of 1980, when silver prices reached $30, $40, and $50 an ounce. The result is that there just is not as much silver for sale in antiques shops as there was. And when you find the piece you're looking for, you may have to pay more for it because of its new scarcity.

Mention silver and images of the dining room table and sideboard or buffet adorned with lovely silver follow. These images are one of the more subtle reasons prices continue to rise.

Look through a 1940s, 1950s, or even 1960s cookbook and what do you see? Mostly recipes and a few pictures of food—food served simply on a nondescript plate or still on the baking sheet or casserole dish. Look at a 1980s or 1990s cookbook and what do you see? A New England cherry drop-leaf table spread with tea cakes and pastries in a variety of English and American nineteenth- and twentieth-century sterling silver and silver-plated baskets and trays. In the background is an antique secretary bookcase filled with nineteenth-century hand-painted oyster plates. And on the floor is a colorful hooked rug.

Pick up most 1940s, 1950s, or 1960s flower-arranging books and you'll find numerous drawings illustrating the line, proportion, and texture. Pick up any newly published flower-arranging book today and you'll see beautiful color photographs of a perennial garden with a terra-cotta garden ornament in the foreground and a handcrafted, Chippendale-style, lattice-backed settee in the background.

Put simply, we want the "total look" today. In New Orleans one of the most successful antiques shops in the French Quarter is Lucullens, a charming store specializing in culinary antiques, from French copper roasting pans to fine Georgian silver wine coasters.

Walk into the foyer of any luxury hotel in America today and you'll find flowers, whether real or silk, in a porcelain or brass container.

The presentation of food and flowers, two statements of our appreciation of the finer things in life, is enhanced through the use of fine and beautiful objects, whether antique or new.

When the English turn-of-the-century teapot with a cracked spout can no longer be used for pouring tea, it is now perfect for the bouquet of daisies for the tea table. Furthermore, you can be sure this little gem won't be thrown out as it once might have been. Today you'll find it in a tag sale or at the flea market, but with a $5 to $25 price tag on it!

And when the teapot is in perfect condition and can be used for serving tea or just to decorate a tea table similar to those pictured in one of the many popular decorator or life-style magazines, it will cost more than it did only a few years ago.

Items for Every Taste

The wealth of beautiful decorating and life-style books and magazines has heightened our appreciation of the many treasures of material culture. Period rooms at Colonial Williamsburg, Winterthur, the Metropolitan Museum of Art—to mention only three of our best-known museums—have enhanced our awareness of faithfully coordinating styles, fabrics, and accessories. Offsetting this trend is the eclectic school of decorating that makes it possible to display a rainbow of pastel Depression glass from the 1930s on a sophisticated, inlaid mahogany Hepplewhite-style sideboard. In a world where anything goes, being able to pick and choose your own style from the endless variety of items created by talented craftsmen and designers throughout the many civilizations of the world is a mark of independence.

There's another subtle reason for wanting these lovely objects. As our lives become more and more dependent on microchips, computers, and high technology, both in the work force and in our daily lives, we look for reassurance and comfort in objects that speak of a less competitive, more leisurely life-style. Obviously antiques and collectibles from twenty, fifty, one hundred, and even two hundred years ago appeal to our longing to be in touch with an earlier, less hurried time.

Our "things" have become an extension of ourselves, our personalities, our tastes, and our appreciation for quality and the fine things of life. As one person told me, "In today's world, my things have become my old friends that I can depend on."

There's another reason people are willing to pay more for these treasures from the past—this one with an ironic twist. As everything costs more—food, travel, entertainment, clothes, and so on—and the stock market bounces about, some people are looking around and saying, "It costs $100 for four people to have dinner in a cozy, not elegant restaurant. A simple shirtwaist dress costs $125. My 'great stock' has just lost five points. Why should I spend all my money on goods that are consumable, disposable, and uncertain? I want to buy something that lasts and from which I can receive continued enjoyment."

This line of thinking has led people with some disposable income to buying antiques and collectibles *now*. This means more demand for a limited number of available items. And so the price for the chest, plate, bowl, or painting increases.

The 1920s and 1930s taste leaned heavily toward Early American antiques, from Colonial gateleg tables to the higher-style Queen Anne highboy. These fine reproductions pictured in the 1930 Baker Furniture Company catalog are now finding a niche in the 1980s market-place.

Antiques dealers are selling more to the twenty-five-to-forty age group whose attitudes seems to be "Buy now." Add to that the reasoning, "If I *don't* buy it now, it's going to cost *more* next year, or the next, or the next," and you understand another of the many different facets affecting personal property and antiques values today.

Nostalgia and Sentiment

These are not all new ideas formed by the yuppie generation. Americans have always loved reminders of our romantic past. But greater interest in our country's history began building around the mid-1960s with the celebration of the Civil War centennial. Momentum gained with the 1976 bicentennial and most recently the 1987 constitutional bicentennial. The one-hundredth-year celebration of the great Columbian Exposition in 1993 created even more interest and excitement for the decorative arts of the 1893 era.

There have been other times when Americans glorified their country's past. After the 1876 centennial celebration, Pennsylvania (especially Philadelphia) furniture became the rage—as was all eighteenth-century formal Chippendale furniture. As a result, late-nineteenth-century cabinetmakers turned out Chippendale chairs, Chippendale lowboys, and Chippendale secretaries, all copied from the original eighteenth-century pieces. The trained eye can distinguish these nineteenth-century pieces from the eighteenth-century originals.

Some fifty years later, coinciding with the one hundred and fiftieth anniversary of the Revolution in 1926, there was another rebirth of interest in American antiques. (The first American Wing of the Metropolitan Museum of Art opened two years before.) During the 1920s, however, the public wanted "Colonial" or "Pilgrim" furniture in addition to the more formal pieces. This demand was met by reproductions of Windsor chairs, gateleg tables, Welsh dressers, and joint stools, as well as formal Queen Anne, Chippendale, and Federal pieces. There were numerous fine companies making reproductions at that time—Margolis, Charack, even names still familiar to us today, like Baker and Kittinger. But perhaps best known was Wallace Nutting, the famous collector, writer, and artist, who also made reproductions. In 1930, in the Supreme Edition of the *Wallace Nutting General Catalogue*, Wallace Nutting wrote, "A broker whose office was furnished by me said he believed the prestige derived from the equipment of his office would pay for it [the furniture] in three months. Anyhow, he died rich.

"Shrewd businessmen have told me that pieces bearing my name will soon be coveted by collectors. The thought did not originate with me. Think it over."

If you had parents or grandparents who followed Nutting's advice, you may well be sitting, literally, on what is now a valuable collector's item. The Windsor bow-back side chair that Nutting sold in 1932 for $30 can now fetch $800, and the Windsor fan-back armchair, which sold between $50 and $60, can now bring $1,500 and up.

"But if only my grandmother had bought a true, fine antique Windsor

bow-back side chair, it might be worth $2,000 today," you may moan. Yes, but not everyone has always loved "old things." In fact, many of our grandmothers threw away *their* grandmothers' furniture and accessories. I have found this particularly true in the South around the turn of the century.

In the southern states the 1860s brought great loss of personal property. After the Civil War, hard times followed for many years.

But economic conditions improved around the turn of the century, and for the next twenty-five years, people had the money to buy new furniture. So they often discarded those pieces from the 1830s, 1840s, and 1850s, the "old things" they had used out of necessity, and, to demonstrate their new economic security, replaced them with new items.

And why not throw the old away? In 1910 a piece of furniture that had been made in 1850 was not considered an antique, but just old, used furniture.

In the 1990s the piece from the 1850s looks good to us. After all, it's almost 150 years old by now—an antique. Furthermore, now that we are more economically secure we like to point with pride to furniture our great-great-grandparents had. It would be quite different if we had our great-great-grandparents' pieces because we couldn't afford anything new. Instead, today we have a new generation eager to buy *with pride* those exact same pieces Grandmother threw away.

The New Antiques—Collectibles—and Their Rapid Rise

What Grandmother did not realize when she threw away all of those "old things" was that she was making the remaining items from the nineteenth century rare or hard to get for later generations. At the same time, our population has increased. Thus, there are more people wanting the remaining pieces. What happens when the demand forces the price beyond reasonable reach or when the supply dries up?

When the Reynolds family of Reynolds Tobacco wealth furnished Reynolda House in the 1920s and 1930s era, they mainly chose fine reproduction furniture—both in earlier styles and adaptive comfortable seating pieces— to combine with true period pieces.

Victorian chairs like this one were not even true antiques in the first half of the twentieth century. Today Victorian pieces are the topic of articles and books, and the prices are rising. Photograph courtesy Weschler's Auction Gallery

Many fine pieces were discarded in the early twentieth century in favor of manufactured pieces in the latest fashion. Painted bedroom suites with attached mirrors became especially popular. This is a Carrollton piece from about 1916.

When the first situation occurs, the buyer looks around to see what she can afford. When it is difficult to buy an eighteenth-century Queen Anne chair for under $2,000, but you can buy a Victorian chair for $500, the Victorian chair is quickly snatched up as a substitute.

When the supply of pieces from a particular time or in a particular style dries up, the collector looks for something else to collect. If you have collected antiques yourself, you've had the experience of watching whatever you collect continually become harder to find.

Full Circle

Just in case you still believe that an item has to be an antique to be valuable and therefore your twentieth-century pieces can't be worth much, you're in for a real eye-opener!

Could *anybody really want* your 1965 reproduction Italian-style cane-back chair in the attic? "We've moved out of Spanish Provincial into an American traditional look," one furniture dealer told me a few years ago. "I'm beginning to see more interest in Mediterranean styles and French Provincial furniture," another furniture dealer told me recently. Can Mediterranean possibly be coming back?

For whatever reason—quality, yearning, nostalgia, eye appeal, inflation—the fact is, almost every fashion has a rebirth at some time. The wonderful thing is that someone seems to like every style today! No longer are we hung up on American Colonial or Duncan Phyfe. There's room for every taste.

It is hard to know which comes first, a renewed interest in crafts—handmade quilts, hand-thrown pottery, hand-wrought metal pieces; accessories—the mass-produced textiles, vases, bowls, candlesticks; or the furniture of a given time. But styles and eras do become "hot," and as the demand increases and the supply dwindles, prices go up.

At the moment there is renewed interest in the Arts and Crafts movement of the 1905–1920 era, new interest in the Art Deco era of the 1930s, and even pioneer collecting of vintage pieces from the 1950s! Just to whet your appetite for what lies ahead, here are some items and their prices that might surprise you if you haven't been following the marketplace closely.

A Gustav Stickley "knock-down" settle sold for $36,300 at Skinner's Auction Gallery in April 1987.

An early twentieth-century ebonized mahogany writing cabinet by Charles Rennie MacKintosh sold for $1.18 million at Christie's London gallery in 1994.

A Frank Lloyd Wright dining room ensemble sold to Thomas S. Monaghan, founder and president of Domino's Pizza, for $1.6 million.

Meanwhile, more "mundane" pieces from the same eras are no longer going to the thrift shop.

An Art Deco door stop of a running greyhound recently sold for $45.

An unsigned brass-and-copper four-piece desk set sold for $125 in a tag sale.

A lady's writing desk with accompanying chair, oak, and of the "generic"

Arts and Crafts type, sold the first day in a consignment shop for $450.

A black-and-pink 1950s "dimestore"-quality coffeepot, sugar, and creamer sold for $25 in a yard sale.

The Thrill of the Chase

The fun of it all is that before *everyone* knows what's hot, these and similar pieces are found in country flea markets and international auction house salesrooms alike. If you are fortunate enough to own such treasures, they can be sold for high prices in the right market. And if you have a quick eye and good memory, you may be able to uncover the sleeper everyone else passes by.

Soon, however, the collecting public becomes aware of these items. And when the public wants an item badly enough to *compete* for it, especially

The Arts and Crafts furniture from the 1905–1920 era is once again highly desirable after being out of favor for many years. The quality varies widely, but even unlabeled and unattributable pieces are selling for more than you might imagine. Photograph courtesy D. J. Puffert, Arts and Crafts Shop, Sausalito, California

when the supply is limited—either because not many were ever made or because those that were made have been discarded—the price goes up.

The collecting public realizes that there will never be any more Mission furniture or any more nineteenth-century Haviland Limoges china or any more brilliant cut glass that equals the old in quality and styling. When the public buys, the items become harder to obtain, and the prices soar upward. Once the market for the items is established, scholars come out of the woodwork. Books are written, price guides appear, magazine articles glamorize the pieces, and soon everyone wants to collect the "new antiques."

Furthermore, remember that production cutbacks by manufacturers are leaving empty spots in gift shops and department stores, and the public is returning to antiques shops and auction houses to buy the items it can no longer find in retail stores.

So if you look around you, what do you find in your home? Most people have a hodgepodge of personal property. There are the new items you have bought, mixed in with gifts and pieces you have inherited from one side of the family or the other, and more bric-a-brac than you can possibly display at one time, much less remember. Clearly they are worth a great deal more than you realized.

Up to this point we've spoken mostly of treasures from our own generation and those of our parents, grandparents, and maybe a few great-grandparents—those "new" items received as gifts or bought in the twentieth century. What about the *true* antiques—those pieces from the eighteenth and early nineteenth centuries? The facts and figures are truly mind-boggling.

You may have read or heard about these astounding record prices:

- **$12.1 million,** the record for American furniture sold at an auction, paid for the Nicholas Brown secretary bookcase, eighteenth century. (Christie's)
- **$198,000,** for a sampler, this one embroidered by ten-year-old "Ruthy Rogers," c. 1780 (Skinner's)
- **$107,000,** for an arcade machine for testing strength, c. 1894. (Sotheby's)

But what about other objects, those items that do not break records but certainly sell for much more money than you might expect if you're not "in the marketplace"? Here is just a random citing of some items sold over the past few years. These are not *rare, unique,* or *museum quality.* They are items found in homes across the country that, for one reason or another, have been sold in the billion-dollar American antiques market.

- An attractive tiger maple frame with mirror, c. 1850: **$550**
- A 14½-inch walnut steeple clock made by Jerome & Co. in New Haven, Connecticut, c. 1840: **$400**
- A sampler signed "Lucy Nichols, Aged eleven in the year 1800" with alphabet, verse, and floral border: **$2,250**
- A nineteenth-century Gaudy Welsh teapot with colorful butterfly decoration: **$10,000**

Frankart, Inc., 225 Fifth Avenue, New York, advertised "Flower Vase No. F612— Aesthetic dancing figure holds a removable glass vase of transparent green, canary, or amber. Height over all 12½ inches" in the 1930– 1931 catalog for $10. Savoia and Fromm Auction Services, South Cairo, New York, sold one in 1987 for $385.

Supply and demand was as much a reason for buying a reproduction in the 1910s, 1920s, and 1930s as it is today. This ad for the Stickley line of Early American furniture ran in the May 1928 House & Garden.

- A pair of Federal brass andirons, probably New York State, c. 1810: **$1,200**
- An eight-piece Victorian painted bedroom suite from Philadelphia, c. 1850: **$30,800**
- A Currier and Ives print of "The American Game of Baseball": **$44,000**

When prices like these are paid for objects that are frequently found in shops, auctions, and tag sales, it becomes clear that there are many collectors vying for those very items you, your mother, or your grandmother may have stored away, not realizing their potential worth. Just a room full of "antiques" can quickly add up to thousands of dollars, as every country—or city— auctioneer will tell you!

But Before You Get Carried Away—Things Are Seldom As They Seem

A few years ago the antiques world waited breathlessly to learn *who* would buy an eighteenth-century Philadelphia Chippendale tea table and *how much* it would sell for. Rumors were that it would break the $1 million mark. When the last bid was in and the hammer fell, true to the rumors, Christie's had sold the first piece of American furniture for over $1 million. In the weeks that followed, scores of photographs of "eighteenth-century Philadelphia Chippendale tea tables" flooded into Christie's Americana department, sent by eager owners who believed they owned a table "just like" the $1 million one. Some of the tables were indeed eighteenth-century Philadelphia Chippendale tea tables, but none was as finely carved, as well proportioned, or of the same $1 million quality as *the* table. But most were either late-nineteenth- or early-twentieth-century reproduction tables—some even with the manufacturer's label or mark still present.

Which leads to another point, and if you learn only one lesson from this book, learn this one. It may make you a great deal of money—or it may save you a great deal of money.

Always look for a mark—first.

The scene was a large antiques extravaganza with dealers from across the country. The collector spied a charming little chamberstick and asked to see it. The first thing the wise collector did was to look for a mark. When he saw a sunburst, he immediately recognized it as the mark of Matthew Boulton, a well-known English silversmith. Next he looked at the price tag: $75. Realizing that this was quite a steal (he was prepared to pay several hundred dollars for the piece) and thinking the dealer had missed the mark, he pointed it out. (Few people would ever do this.)

"Oh," replied the dealer, "most people don't ever look for a mark."

"That's *all* I look for," he replied as he paid her the $75.

The moral of the story is simple, but one you should always remember. *Knowing what you're looking at* is the key to making money or losing money in the antiques and collectibles world.

Meanwhile, the possibility of finding hidden treasures leads the *unknowing* public to dream that any object can or might be a rare and valuable one. But it is the person who *knows* who finds the treasure.

A friend of mine passing a mall antiques show spied a delightful hooked rug. She hadn't expected to spot anything she would be interested in (after

They are both tilt-top Chippendale piecrust tables. But the one below is a Kittinger reproduction from their 1928 catalog, and the one below right sold at Christie's in 1986 for just over $1 million. Photograph below right courtesy Christie's

all, antiques displayed in front of a Baskin-Robbins ice-cream parlor tend to lose their charm). But the rug had kittens on it, was colorful and "cute" and well priced. Still she hesitated—until she got home that afternoon and began thumbing through the *Antiques* magazine that had arrived in the day's mail. There she saw the same hooked rug illustrated as part of the Henry Ford Museum collection in Dearborn, Michigan. Needless to say, she returned immediately and bought the rug—quite a discovery for an afternoon's shopping.

The Truth About $1 Million Objects

Yes, $1 million objects do exist—sometimes in the least expected places—and sometimes they can even go undetected by experts. A sixteenth-century religious painting by Carracci that slipped by one prestigious auction house with an appraised value of $720 was later auctioned for $1.5 million by another house.

But so are some items thought to be $1 million pieces worth only a pittance. The important point to remember is that the whole spectrum of antiques and collectibles truly epitomizes a double-edged sword. Pieces you wouldn't give a second glance or thought to may be rare, important, and truly valuable, while the item you cherish most and believe is extremely rare and valuable simply may not be. By keeping your eyes open and increasing your knowledge, you will be able to make these distinctions.

If you only learn one lesson from this book, learn this: always look for a mark, first! It may make you a great deal of money—or it may save you a great deal of money. **Photograph by Jon Zachary**

2

Putting First Things First:
Do You Know What You Own?

Today, on every hand, you're being told how to go out and invest in gold, silver, antiques, and collectibles. Flea markets, antiques shops, and auction galleries are springing up as quickly as investment advisers. Price lists and guides cover every conceivable subject from Barbie dolls to barbed wire and American Chippendale highboys to Beatles' memorabilia.

But wait. Before you become an expert in carnival glass or Mission furniture, before you invest in gold stocks or a bombé secretary, look around you. What are you overlooking?

Do you know the value of what you already own? When was the last time you counted your silver forks? Did your neighbor ever return the tablecloth she borrowed? How much would it cost to replace your living room rug today?

Consider your wedding presents, those souvenirs you bought on trips, the gifts you've received over the years, the furniture you bought five, ten, or even thirty years ago, the pieces you inherited and have always cherished.

Do you know what you've got? Take my word for it. You've already got quite an investment right in your own home.

So you have a serving plate just like this, too! But is it sterling silver or silver plate? And how much would it cost you to replace it today? Photograph courtesy Reed & Barton

The Chest Test

Start right now. Pick up paper and pencil and take the chest test.

Choose any place in your home where you store or hide an assortment of household items—linen, china, or crystal accessories, pieces of silver you seldom use, jewelry, candlesticks, trivets. . . . Usually the place is a chest in your dining room, living room, or foyer. But you may use the bottom of a corner cupboard, a sideboard, or credenza, even a trunk or blanket chest. If you're an impeccably organized person, or if you wish to be really hard on yourself, choose the attic or basement. Do not select a chest or closet where you store only clothes.

Now that you have the specific place in mind, begin listing, from memory, the items you have stored there. In other words, make an inventory of everything in the chest, cupboard, or trunk.

"I can't do that" or "That's ridiculous, I can't remember everything," you complain.

But what if, instead of beginning to read this book, you had just opened your front door to discover that your house or apartment had been burglarized? What if you had just received a call that your house had burned?

The first thing you have to do after a loss of personal property is to list what you have lost. Otherwise you cannot (1) help the police look for your property, (2) file a claim with your insurance company, or (3) claim your property if it is recovered. Knowing that sooner or later you are going to have to know what you own, bite the bullet, plunge in, and take the chest test.

Simply start making a list of the items stored in the place you have selected. Once you have finished making your list, go to the chest and check your accuracy.

What You Did and Did Not Find

If you are like the majority of people who have taken this chest test, you have found that you left off many items stored in your chest. And what about the items on your list that you thought were in the chest but weren't there?

Chances are, like most people, you have put your belongings away carelessly, often cramming extras into a drawer or cupboard at the last minute before guests arrived or in an attempt to straighten up a little. "I'll go back and see about that later," you said to yourself, but "later" may be weeks, months, even years away, and meanwhile you forget where you put your things or that they even exist.

For a firsthand comment on how easy it is to forget even those pieces you store right at your fingertips, ask any painter what he hears when people unload their storage cabinets.

"There's Grandmother's plate, the one with flowers. I looked all over for it last Christmas, and it was right under my nose all along."

Or, "Look at these candlesticks! I forgot I even had them. They're black." Then, turning over the tarnished candlesticks, the owner exclaims, "Sterling. I didn't know that."

That last comment tells you that not only do you forget what you have and where you last put your things, you also don't really know what you have. Sterling or plated candlesticks? What if they had been stolen? Worth $50 or $500?

And that plate you were looking for—it had flowers on it, but were they daisies or forget-me-nots? Knowing something like that can make a difference between getting it back or giving it up.

So often we take the pieces we live with day in and day out for granted. Many coin silver cups given as birth and christening presents are thought to be silver plate because they are not marked "Sterling." Isn't it time for you to take a more careful look at your treasures from the past? Photograph courtesy North Carolina Division of Archives and History

Even if you are a collector, could you accurately describe your items if something happened to them? Are other pieces of your china collection stored away? Quickly now, how many plates have scalloped edges and how many don't? When you buy pieces one at a time, it is easy to forget the minute details of pieces purchased years ago. Photograph courtesy Garth's Auctions

Don't Think You Can Rely on Your Memory

When you took the chest test, if you found that you did not remember even half of what you'd hidden or stored away, don't despair. You are not alone. In fact, you are only normal.

A while back, *Time* magazine reported on memory studies made by psychologist Elizabeth Loftus. The article explained that most people could not even make the correct identification of articles they see and handle every day. *Time* featured fifteen slightly different sketches from which the reader was to select the correct face of a penny. Nobody at our house got it right.

Ms. Loftus commented that people have poor recall because they haven't observed objects carefully in the first place. That observation comes as no surprise to the appraiser. I wish I could receive a bonus every time I point out a feature about a desk or tray that the owners never have noticed.

Once, while looking at a silver service, I made a casual comment that the two pots did not match. One had a flower design and the other a grapevine design. The amazed owner said, "I've never seen that, and I've polished this set for thirty-five years."

One insurance executive told me that his favorite trick is to blindfold a client in the client's own living room and ask the person to name everything in it.

"They always miss at least twenty percent," he said, "and that's the living room, where everything is out and visible!" (If the property in the house were worth $80,000 and it was destroyed, you'd be out at least $16,000 without an inventory!)

In my work I am often called in after a disaster to try to help the victims and the insurance company reach a decision about the value of the property for a monetary settlement. Many times the dialogue goes something like this:

APPRAISER: What furniture was in the dining room prior to the fire?

WIFE: Let's see now. There was a table and chairs . . .

APPRAISER: How many chairs?

WIFE: Eight. No, wait . . . there were ten. I stored two extra chairs up in the attic. The room only holds eight chairs.

HUSBAND: No, dear, you're wrong. There weren't ten chairs, there were twelve. Remember, you used the other armchair in the guest bedroom. I distinctly remember putting three chairs in the attic.

(At this point I write down, "Eight, ten, or twelve dining room chairs.")

APPRAISER: Can you tell me what you paid for the chairs?

WIFE: Well, we didn't really buy them. Joe's sister had inherited them from her husband's aunt, but she couldn't use them, so when Joe's mother died, we traded them bedroom furniture for the chairs. I guess you'd say that we sort of inherited them.

APPRAISER: What style were they?

WIFE: Well, they went up in the back like this. . . . (lots of hand gestures)

APPRAISER: What about the legs? Were they straight or were they curved?

WIFE: Yes.

APPRAISER: Which? Straight or curved?

WIFE: They were . . . What were they, Joe?

An exaggeration? Hardly. And this is furniture, big, bulky wooden furniture, about which I'm trying to get a description. You should hear the description of crystal and china patterns. If you can't describe it, how can you put a value on it?

When You Do Remember . . . Five Years Later

Insurance companies are plagued with calls from clients who, two, five, or even ten years after they have settled a personal property loss claim, remember items they forgot to report at the time of a robbery or disaster. What can they do?

The law varies from state to state as to when the statute of limitations on such an insurance claim expires. Usually policies state that the owner has one year in which to change and add to his initial claim. However, some states allow up to six years for reopening or adjusting a claim. So if you have suffered a recent loss of personal property and, while reading this book, discover additional losses, check with your state insurance commissioner's office to find out your rights for adjusting your claim if the need arises.

Cheating Yourself

It is never easy to lose personal property. But I can assure you from my experience of working with people who have suffered such losses that those who knew what they had and who had adequate insurance took the loss much better than those who felt they were cheated because they couldn't remember what they had.

Sometimes they blame the insurance company. "My agent should have made me compile a list." Without a list, you can't remember what you owned. Ask anyone in a police crime prevention unit. "The best cure is an ounce of prevention," one officer told me. Without a list, people don't know what they're missing, especially items they don't use every day.

"You know the cut glass pitcher sitting out on the buffet?" the officer asked parenthetically. "You didn't remember it when you made out the list. Then, four weeks after the robbery, you want to use the pitcher. You go to the buffet to get it and it's gone. Too late."

The Room Test

The room test is a particularly good one to give a family member whom you're trying to persuade to update his or her insurance, make an inventory, or have an appraisal made. Give it to your parents, for example. (A lot of my calls come from young couples who want to force their parents or aunts or grandparents to have an appraisal made.)

Or, if you've been trying to convince your husband that all the bric-a-brac around the house was a good investment and not just a dust-gathering collection, give him this test.

If you find your husband seated on a comfortable chair in the den where there are bookcases or shelves decorated with candlesticks, porcelain, or pewter figurines, wooden carvings, books, and other items, ask him to tell you what is on the shelf behind him. Or ask him to name all the pieces of furniture in the living room or dining room and then tell you what accessories are placed around on the tables—lamps, ashtrays, vases, and so on—and what pictures are hanging on the wall.

(If he, or your parents, or aunt, or child, whoever is taking this test, gets a perfect score, then give him the job of making out the inventory that you need!)

Women Die, Too

In all the talk about husbands dying, the fact that women die, too, is often overlooked. But who has usually taken a primary interest in the furnishings and personal property in a home? A woman. And if she dies first, her husband often is totally unaware of the value of the property in his house.

I remember doing an appraisal for a man in his mid-fifties who was suddenly widowed. His concern was that the house, now empty during the day, might be broken into.

The blue-and-white platter stored in the bottom of your corner cupboard. You've been told it's valuable, but is it? Could you substantiate your claim? And anyway, how can you find out how old and valuable it is? Isn't it time you learn the answers to these questions? Photograph courtesy David and Linda Arman

"I haven't any idea what is in this house," he explained to me. "I don't know what's in the drawers, or how valuable anything is. But I do know that my children would kill me if something happened to these things. They loved their mother and treasure her belongings."

As it turned out, there were many fine pieces and valuable paintings. When my client received his appraisal he was amazed at the total value.

"As far as the artwork goes," he said, "if someone had offered me fifty dollars for the lot, I would have sold it to him and then thrown in a piece of silver to make sure he wasn't getting cheated. I never really looked at it."

The Next Step

Just for fun, list all the furniture and accessories in one room—obviously not the room you are in—from memory. (Most people's jaws drop when they hear the "memory" part.) To really test yourself, while you're making this list try adding some description to the items. Does the Victorian table in your basement that you've been meaning to refinish have a rectangular top or a square top? What shape are its legs? How many drawers are there in that pine chest in your son's or daughter's room? Describe the scene of a painting or picture in your living room. If you can't describe it in words, you might try drawing it.

Now go one step further. What is the table worth today? What would it cost to replace the pine chest or picture in your living room? And, incidentally, do you know how much insurance you have on all of your personal property?

My point really is a simple one. Everyone wants to know, "What's it worth?" But before you know this, you must first know what you own. In almost every home where I've made an appraisal I've found unknown and often forgotten treasures. One client even found her "lost" demitasse set when we were going through her attic. If you've lived in a home for more than ten years, I can almost guarantee that you have stored a few items away and simply forgotten about them. And if you have broken up a parent's or grandparent's home and had to hurriedly move possessions into your home, you may well have some real treasures hidden away in a trunk or box.

A young couple was being transferred from one part of the country to another, and the husband's company was willing to pay for an appraisal before the move. Having completed the appraisal of the more valuable and fragile pieces, I was leaving through the garage door when I spied a black bowl perched precariously between a soccer ball and some garden tools. "I must include that bowl on your breakables list," I commented. The wife didn't even know what bowl I was referring to. When I showed her the black San Ildefonson pottery bowl and the "Maria" signature, she replied, "I wasn't even going to take it with me. My husband's aunt died a few years ago, and we just packed up a lot of things and brought them here with us. It's been on that shelf since I unpacked. It's a miracle it hasn't gotten broken." If it had, an $800 piece of American material culture would have been lost forever.

3

What You Need to Know About Grandmother

As an appraiser I know all about grandmothers. You see, I've never had a client yet who didn't have at least two grandmothers, and usually by the time I've finished the appraisal I may even know about the grandmothers' grandmothers!

The wonderful thing about grandmothers is that they bought, bought, bought. The bad thing about grandmothers is that, when they died, family legend turned all their purchases into instant antiques.

If your grandmothers, like mine, were born in the 1880s, or approximately a hundred years ago, gifts they were given at birth are antiques. (According to the United States Director of Customs, an item becomes an antique when it reaches one hundred years of age.) But when was your grandmother actually gathering her personal property?

First there were the drawings, dance cards, and memorabilia she saved as a schoolgirl—her mementos. Then there were her wedding presents, and they gave some lavish presents in those days—sets of sterling silver oyster forks and pearl-handled fruit knives. But lavish doesn't mean antique, and even if your grandmother who was born in 1880 was a child bride and married in 1896, her wedding presents, even the ones from Tiffany's, aren't true antiques—yet.

After the wedding, the babies—your mother or father, aunts and uncles— began arriving. Families came sooner and were larger in those days. Thus, for the next few years your grandmother probably did not add too many precious possessions to her collection. (However, if she saved a Quaker Oats box, a Theodore Roosevelt campaign button, and the front-page story of Lindbergh's landing, you can cash in on her pack-rat habits.)

Actually, your grandmother was probably making her most expensive and tasteful purchases between the 1920s and 1950s. And, as my own parents keep reminding me, in the middle of those years there was the Great Depression.

Yet the comment I hear so often when I'm making appraisals is, "I know you want to see my lamp, silver, rocking chair [whatever]. . . . It is a very old and valuable antique. It was my grandmother's."

Please don't misunderstand me. I share your love for your grandmother's treasures. In fact, I even expect to be a grandmother myself one day, and I hope my grandchildren will revere me and the treasures I am collecting—

many made in the 1990s, incidentally. But no matter how much my grandchildren brag, it will be in the 2090s before my new Chinese panda bear rug is an antique.

Even if your grandmother or even great-grandmother did not live in the eighteenth century, many of her mementos may be highly sought after collectibles in the 1980s. **Photographs courtesy Mid-Hudson Galleries**

Your Grandmother Did Not Live in the Eighteenth Century

Just as the 2090s are a long way into the future, so was the eighteenth century a long time in the past. The chances that you had a grandmother who lived in the eighteenth century are extremely slim.

Let's hypothesize that you were born in 1900. If your mother was forty years old when you were born, she would have been born in 1860. If her mother, your grandmother, was forty years old when your mother was born, your grandmother would have been born in 1820. This calculation is stretching each generation from its usual twenty-five-year span to forty years. Furthermore, most women in the nineteenth century had their children in their earlier years—their teens and twenties. Thus the chances of having a grandmother who was born over 180 years ago are extremely rare.

But because your grandmother or even great-grandmother lived much later, don't suddenly do a spring cleaning of all her possessions. A whole new field has emerged on the antique horizon: the "collectible."

You will see the difference between antiques and collectibles later. But at this point I want you to realize that some of the items you may have thought were true antiques because they did belong to your grandmother may not be as old as you thought. However, this does not mean that they are not valuable. In fact, it will probably cost you more to replace your grandmother's 1905 Chantilly teaspoon than to replace your great-grandmother's 1850 coin silver teaspoon!

Another problem with grandmothers is that they pass on family legends. Now, family legends are grand. They bring history to life. They make heroes out of black sheep and silk purses out of sow's ears. Some family legends are accurate, but sadly, many are not. Often inaccuracies that occur in many family legends as they pass from one person to another result from the "number jumble"—1900 becomes 1800, 1876 becomes 1846, 1806, and, eventually, 1776.

The truth is, antiques can be dated by the materials used, their style, the marks they bear, and even scientific evidence. But as long as sentimental attachment is placed on any item, all the facts are dismissed as irrelevant, even by rational people.

Two comments I constantly hear from my clients exemplify this irrational thinking.

1. "This vase can't be replaced. It belonged to my great-aunt Maude, and it is the only one I've ever seen like it."
2. "This table is priceless. You won't even be able to appraise it. President

You know the Queen Anne highboy was in your grandmother's home. But did she say 1927, 1897, or 1797? The number jumble occurs quite unintentionally when family stories are passed down but not written down. The clues throughout this book will help you learn the truth about family heirlooms. Photograph courtesy Weschler's Auction Gallery

Fillmore visited our old home place and signed an important document on this table."

To these comments I say:

- Any piece can be replaced.
- Everything has its price.

Antiques Are Not Born Old

Before you burn this book for its heritical content (you might save it—it will be an antique one day), let me confess that I have made statements like those about my own possessions. To me, what I have is more precious than what you have, just as your treasures are more precious to you. This is human nature, and thank goodness for it.

It is family sentiment that preserves many of our antiques for the next generation. Antiques are not born old. They were all new at one time. Family pride and sentiment—emotional attachment to material things—have preserved the craftsmanship and styles of an earlier time. These heirlooms have now passed into your hands. You want to keep them and pass them on to the next generation, and so you should. This is commendable and gives each generation a knowledge of an earlier life-style and age.

The Truth About Replacement

But as for antiques being irreplaceable, this simply is not true. A walk through any antiques mall or down New York City's Second Avenue turns up literally thousands of duplicates. The most often heard comment in any restoration or historical society museum is, "My aunt, grandmother, mother-in-law [whomever] had one *just like that.* I wonder whatever happened to it?" Granted, some items are one of a kind. A sampler stitched by a schoolgirl, custom-made jewelry, an initialed dower chest—these were all individualized by the person who made them. But so is your home, once you live in it and give it your special touch. Yet, if you have to, you can and do find another home to take its place for shelter and protection.

What is important is that you correctly identify your treasures and learn their history and value so that, should anything happen to them, you will have sufficient coverage to replace them if you wish. I have stated it many times, but never have I had a client who, if a prized object was lost, did not take the loss better when she received compensation for her loss.

Daniel Webster's Pewter Goblet—Made in Sweden

The stories of mistaken family legends could be a book in itself. In particular I remember examining a pewter goblet that was marked on the bottom "Made in Sweden," which identified the piece as dating after 1914. (Daniel Webster died in 1852).

Then there was the wicker rocking chair, which the owner insisted was at least 350 years old since it had come over on the *Mayflower*. (Wicker rocking chairs like his were unknown in 1621—this one dated from the 1870s.)

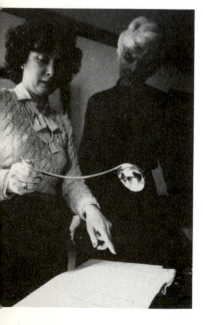

By turning to the right source, you can learn accurate information about the many family heirlooms you have wondered about for years. Photograph by Jon Zachary

Objects do not lie. You must first learn the W's.
> **What** is it?
> **When** was it made?
> **Where** was it made?
> **Who** made it?

in order to know
> **Why** it is
> **Worth** its value.

My point is to educate you, not to discourage you. The quality of each piece speaks for itself. Enjoy the family stories and pass them on. But unless there is documentation—specific dates of marriage, birth, or death that coincide with the family story or, better yet, actual inventories or bills of sale—take the stories with a grain of salt. You must even be cautious about handwritten hearsay stories that could have been jumbled fifty, one hundred, or even more years before they were actually written down.

The Appraiser's Rule of Thumb

From my experience in other people's homes I have my own rule of thumb, which I pass on to my clients.

Expect to find that the piece you consider most valuable may have only minimum monetary value. And be prepared to learn that a piece you probably would give to the first friend who asked for it may be very valuable indeed.

Provenance: What It Really Means

Often I am told that an item is priceless or at least extremely valuable because it has had some association with a famous person. The fancy word commonly used in the antiques world to describe this situation even *sounds* expensive, "provenance."

Provenance simply means the source or origin, or who owned the piece at one time. Provenance is also established when a piece is displayed in a museum or sold at an auction. Provenance is a word that rolls off museum curators' tongues and is frequently used in describing pieces sold at Sotheby's and Christie's.

But provenance does not always mean profit. In fact, provenance can be compared to "George Washington slept here." You can hang the sign anywhere, but without documentation it doesn't mean much. Every piece you own has a provenance. Its provenance may begin with you, or it may go back in your family, or someone else's family, for several generations. The only time you can cash in on provenance, or prior ownership, is when the owner himself was of substantial note and when there is documentation.

Even when provenance is established, the value of the piece lies ultimately in its own merit—in other words, in how good the piece itself is. Take as an example a client, now deceased, who owned a collection of German crinoline figurines. As an international entertainer, her name evoked mem-

The appraiser's rule of thumb—be prepared to learn that the piece you consider most valuable may have only minimum monetary value, and be prepared to learn that a piece you'd probably give away or toss out may be very valuable indeed. Many people have tossed out stoneware crocks found in damp basements, thinking they were of no value, and kept a chipped Haviland cup and saucer from the corner cupboard in the belief it was very valuable. The crock is the valuable object. Photograph courtesy Vicki and Bruce Waasdorp

No, these are not eighteenth-century American blockfront chests. The one above may have been bought by your mother or grandmother. Photograph courtesy Weschler's Auction Gallery

You may purchase the Kindel Winterthur reproduction pictured above right. The point is that the use of fine materials and the superior quality of both these chests will assure their continued value for future generations.

ories of movies and television to three generations. But because her figurines were neither terribly old nor rare, their value was limited. However, when they were sold as her property, the figurines found eager buyers who paid more money for them because they were hers. Without the association of her famous name, however, the figurines would have sold for much less.

On the other hand, another of my clients owns an extremely rare sterling silver cake basket made in London by Paul de Lamerie in 1742. Other baskets by de Lamerie in the same style and motif have sold at international auction houses. My client is not famous. But if his cake basket were sold at auction right now, it probably would fetch considerably more than $100,000.

Quality is the ultimate determinant of value.

So before you dash out and declare your piece as one of a kind, dating from the eighteenth century and touched by George Washington, look at the facts and the dates. See if they match. Remember that, in the end, it is not who touched or even who owned a piece but what the piece is and how well it was made that determines its value.

Part Two

WHY YOU NEED TO KNOW WHAT YOUR POSSESSIONS ARE WORTH

4

Times When You Need to Know What You Own and What It Is Worth

There are three, and possibly four, times in your life when you will need to know what you own and what it is worth.

The first time is when you buy insurance to protect your personal property. Everyone needs some kind of household insurance for day-to-day protection, and if you move you will need additional coverage while your property is in transit. The information I share in chapter 5 is not intended to be the last word in insurance advice, but it is designed to guide you toward knowing about possible options and to alert you as to why you must analyze your insurance needs.

The second time you need to know your property values is when you are faced with a catastrophe. Unfortunately, everyone seems prone to misfortune these days. A burglary is the most usual loss, but fire can be even more devastating. Chapter 6 alerts you to the problems that owners of personal property face and how they can prepare ahead of time for the problems these catastrophes bring.

The third time you need to know about your personal property is when you either wish to sell or donate property, or when property must be divided for estate purposes. In these instances, the Internal Revenue Service publishes guidelines. Chapter 7 deals with appraisals for estate purposes, and chapter 8 discusses appraisals for donation purposes.

Finally, there is divorce. Personal property is often a bone of contention between couples. Knowing what you own and its value can be essential in divorce settlements. Chapter 9 deals with this problem.

5

Insurance:
Before It's Too Late

HOME IS WHERE THE HEART IS—AND THE "MONEY," TOO

Stop for a minute and think of everything in your home. Clothing, furniture, tools, pictures, lawn equipment, jewelry, electronic and entertainment equipment, rugs and carpets, appliances, silver, bed and table linens, cooking utensils, crystal and glass, sporting equipment, books, musical instruments, photographic equipment, toys, perhaps office or work-related equipment—the list is endless.

Realize, too, that your house is where you keep all of your personal property—probably worth more than your cash wealth—in a very small, concentrated area. A thief moves quickly from dining room to living room and on to the bedroom, gathering silver, jewelry, and other objects as he goes. Fire jumps from curtains to sofas to rugs and spreads rapidly across a roof or along wiring. Tornadoes flatten an entire city block in a matter of seconds.

Now, consider for a moment that, if you are a homeowner, the total value of everything in your house may well equal or even surpass the value of your house itself.

This was not always true. Up until the recent spiraling of household property and antiques values, the external dwelling was considered substantially more valuable than the contents of the house. So just what kind and how much personal property insurance do you need?

Your Personal Property Insurance and You

You are the one who must ultimately decide *what kind* and *how much*. And because there really isn't much information about personal property lines readily available, you may find that learning about personal property can be difficult. After you read this chapter and assess your personal needs, together you and your insurance agent should be able to arrive at the best policy or policies for you and your treasures.

The policies are available. In fact, you can choose among numerous types of policies—standard "actual cash value" policies, replacement value endorsements, "all risk" policies, "automatic coverage escalators," tenants insurance, unscheduled coverage policies, scheduled-itemized coverage, personal articles or inland marine floaters, fine arts floaters, even customized policies. But you should know that unscheduled coverage policies, once a standard of the insurance industry, are becoming more difficult to obtain— just another reason you need to get a handle on your valuable personal property today. And, if your assets are in the seven-figure category, your agent will probably want to discuss a tailor-made customized policy, the kind usually written through Lloyds of London. But only *you* know what you own and what your needs are.

The Impersonal Approach to Personal Property Insurance

Personal property insurance coverage is quite unlike your life insurance and hospitalization policies. Ed McMahon, Dennis James, and other celebrities are each personally interested in your health, well-being, and life insurance policies. But who cares about your personal property—those items you inherited from your family or friends, the pieces you saved to be able to purchase, the property that surrounds you and is used both for necessity and pleasure? Well, I do and you do, but who else?

As one young woman told me pointedly, "Every insurance agent in town called me about my life insurance. They all wanted to come out to the house and see me. But when I tried to get insurance on my antiques and personal property, a secretary asked me *over the phone* how much I wanted to write the policy for!"

The Other Side of the Story

But wait. Give the insurance industry its due. What about those pamphlets, brochures, and booklets the casualty insurance companies put out telling you about your personal property insurance? Not only do they inform you about the policies available, they provide invaluable, free information about how to protect your home from fire and theft, how to make an inventory of your property, and how to locate an appraiser to value your possessions.

So what's the problem?

Of course there are many problems, but some are particularly noteworthy.

Stumbling Blocks to Good Personal Property Insurance

The first problem is inherent in personal property. It is just that—property. It is not your health, your life, or a relative's life. It can be replaced in kind, whereas no human life, once lost, can ever be replaced. As a result, personal property insurance sometimes just isn't taken seriously.

Everyone understands the devastation of the death of a loved one, but it is virtually impossible to empathize with another person's loss of his sterling silver, diamond rings, or valued collection. Granted, we talk about sentimental value, heirlooms, irreplaceable handcrafted items and works of art, but deep down we know these can be replaced.

So isn't it a little bit ironic that we try to insure that which we cannot replace and are slack in insuring that which we can replace!

The Stepchild of the Industry

A second problem results from the second-place standing personal property insurance has in the insurance industry today. As one executive said, "It's a stepchild." Or, as another executive confessed, his company is only interested in insuring low-end property where they collect the premiums but seldom have to pay any claims. Though there is some evidence this stepchild attitude may be changing, it still prevails among most insurance companies. Even among those companies that have identified the potential market in personal property lines, little help is given to sales agents. "We're telling our agents to go out and tap this market, but it's really up to them," admitted one large national casualty company spokesperson.

Agents Are Not Antiques Appraisers

As a result, few agents, both those who sell the policies and those who settle the claims, are well trained in or knowledgeable about personal property. But, once again, this is understandable. Insurance agents are educated in insurance, not antiques, collectibles, and personal property. Anyway, there is so much to know about personal property.

I have been slightly amused when listening to the woeful tales of victims of personal property losses who are maligning an insurance agent because he or she "didn't know the value of my grandmother's priceless Handel lamp!" Would the victim have known about Handel lamps if his grandmother hadn't owned one? I doubt it. So we might want to be a little tolerant of the agent for not knowing about a particular item of personal property.

Insurance Companies Have Problems, Too

In my years of appraising I have been involved in more false and erroneous claims than I wish to remember. The astute adjuster watches for "red flags" that suggest errors in the claim. In fire claims, for example, are there more pieces of furniture listed than could possibly have fitted into the dwelling? In cases of robbery, do the items listed far exceed the value of insurance the insured was carrying? Is there clear evidence of a robbery and was it reported to the police immediately? And then there are the times when the adjuster has that gut feeling that the claim is in error but can't put his finger on why.

An adjuster called me in just such an instance. Would I go with him to question the insured about the property that had been lost in a fire? There were a couple of listings that really disturbed him. One was the claim for a wicker rocking chair for $1,000, and the other was for a quilt for $2,500. Once

I had the list in hand, I also picked up several other discrepancies in values, so I agreed to work on the case. We drove out into the country and met with the insured, her attorney, and her son.

"How do you know your wicker rocker was worth $1,000?" I asked. The insured had seen one, not as good, for sale in an antiques shop for $400, so she figured hers was worth $1,000 at least.

"And about the quilt?" I inquired. Well, one night she was listening to a call-in radio program. Someone had called in and described a quilt. The guest appraiser had said that the caller's quilt would be worth at least $1,000, so the insured looked at hers and decided it would be worth $2,500.

Throughout this dialogue two people said nothing—the attorney and the son. Close to the end of our session, however, I came to this listing:

> Leather-bound books. *One Hundred Greatest Masterpieces of American Literature*. Franklin Mint. $50 each. Total loss $5,000.

"Whose books were these?" I inquired.

"Oh, those were Harold's [not the son's real name]," the mother replied. "He just loves to read great literature."

At this point I directed my questions to Harold. Harold, it seems, was unemployed. He had managed to graduate from high school and had held a variety of jobs, but none of them had lasted long.

"What were some of the titles of the masterworks?" I asked.

When Harold couldn't recall any of the titles, his mother tried—also without much luck.

"You mean to tell me that you don't remember the names of books that cost you $35 apiece, and you say are now worth $50 each?"

"Ah, well, we didn't buy the whole set. We started buying them—then dropped them," was the stammered reply. That dialogue set off a full investigation. The total loss was eventually disclaimed, and the insurance company did not have to pay a single penny.

But for every false claim filed, there are one hundred claims where the victim is being false to himself because he did not know what he lost or how valuable his property was.

Realizing this, you hold the key to dealing with the final problem. As owner of your personal property, you have the responsibility of properly and accurately protecting and insuring your treasures. The problem repeatedly cited by insurance professionals is simple: the owner didn't know what he had or what it was worth—until something happened to it.

It Won't Happen to Me

Even if your next-door neighbor's house has been burglarized, your across-the-street neighbor's house has been struck by lightning, and your back-door neighbor's house has burned down, you simply don't think any of those things will happen to you. And maybe they won't. We all certainly hope not, but claims for large losses of silver, jewelry, rugs, antiques, and electronic equipment come into insurance companies on a daily basis. These claims are the reason adjusters are putting the burden of proof of ownership on the insured when a loss is filed. And well they should, to keep the rest of our premiums from going up to cover the payoff of false claims.

Once Again, It All Comes Back to You

Because you *do* care about your personal property and want to protect it, how, then, do you find the policy that is best suited to your individual needs? After asking this direct question to at least six representatives of national insurance companies, I have the answer. Each insurance spokesperson replied to the question in a slightly different way, but the conclusion was always the same. In a nutshell, you, the insuree, have to take the initiative.

How to Avoid Being a Dissatisfied Policy Holder

It is the lack of knowledge about both your own property and the many personal property insurance policies available to you that leads to dissatisfaction, I was told by a major insurance company. Whether you follow the advice to contact an independent insurance agent who can shop around for the best policy at the best (lowest) premium or you elect a direct carrier (Nationwide, Allstate, and so on), you must first know what you've got and what it is worth.

The customers most apt to be dissatisfied with claim settlements are those who do not have the replacement value endorsement to their homeowner's policies. This dissatisfaction results when they find out, after the loss, how much it costs to replace their lost property, something they hadn't investigated *before* purchasing their insurance policy. If they had known the value and told their insurance agent their requirements before the loss, they could have gotten the correct coverage.

To keep *you* from being that dissatisfied customer, here is some basic information you need to know about the three most popular personal property policies.

Remember that each state's insurance industry is regulated by an insurance commissioner's office, and insurance policies, as well as premiums, will vary from state to state.

The 50 Percent Standard Policy—Is It Enough?

The standard homeowner's policy is based on the cost of your property at the time of a loss, less any depreciation resulting from age and condition. The cash amount you receive is determined by subtracting depreciation from the amount it would cost to replace the item.

To see how this works, let's use the example of your five-year-old green side-by-side refrigerator with automatic ice maker. A comparable refrigerator would cost $850 today. The life expectancy of a refrigerator is about twenty years, so with the standard homeowner's policy you would figure a 25 percent depreciation for its five years. Your settlement from the insurance company should be about $638, minus your deductible.

But what about the pine blanket chest you paid $250 for ten years ago? It certainly has not depreciated in value. To this antique, a few years add to both its patina and its value. Furthermore it has no "life expectancy." Your pine blanket chest has a value today of $625.

So as you begin to realize how much money it would take to replace your possessions today, you need to ask yourself: Does a "standard policy" really provide enough coverage? Remember—standard policies are usually written on 50 percent of the value of the external dwelling. Thus, if your home has a value of, say, $150,000 (to use a round figure), your personal property will be insured for $75,000. Though that sounds like a lot of money, a quick survey of the replacement cost of your antiques, reproductions, books, electronic and entertainment equipment, clothes, collections, china, kitchen and laundry appliances, rugs, lamps, bric-a-brac, and other items may exceed that lump sum.

In addition, the items under the standard policy are covered only for "named perils," and the standard deductible is $250. Thus, if you wish to insure your collection of Haviland china against breakage (not a "named peril") or your $150 small ivory figurine (whose value falls below your $250 deductible), the standard policy is not for you.

Many years ago the standard policy provided good, adequate insurance coverage. But that was before personal property values began to escalate as a result of both inflation and wider-spread collecting and before families accumulated as much personal property as we do today. Current standard personal property policies provide only minimum protection.

The Replacement Value Endorsement—A Major Breakthrough

The replacement value endorsement, in most states, increases the coverage on your household contents from the standard 50 to 70 percent, 80 percent, or even more of the value of your dwelling. Many carriers today are allowing the insured to select the percentage coverage they wish to choose. Furthermore, the depreciation factor of your personal property is eliminated when you purchase the replacement value endorsement.

If you have this coverage and your five-year-old refrigerator is crushed when the runaway leaf truck tears through your kitchen, you will receive, not a settlement for $638, but a comparable new, side-by-side refrigerator with automatic ice maker (and probably in peach instead of green). And of course the blanket chest will also be fully covered for its full $650 replacement cost if it is destroyed or damaged beyond repair. (Remember, the deductible is always applicable.)

But having *only* the replacement value endorsement may not be adequate coverage if you have a substantial collection of antiques, fine arts, or collectibles that are rapidly increasing in value.

Imagine that you inherited a group of Arts and Crafts furniture from your grandparents fifteen years ago. You wanted to discard it all but for sentimental reasons stored it in your basement instead. Fifteen years ago the Gustav Stickley settle and two reclining armchairs were probably worth no more than $300 for the set and the Limbert bookcase was worth $150. Today the Stickley parlor set has a value of $20,000–$25,000, and the bookcase can easily be sold for $1,500—and you'd have to pay $2,000 to $4,000 for one in the Arts and Crafts specialty gallery.

So the protection of your personal property comes back to *you*. Only if you know what you own and what it's worth can you adequately insure your antiques. A replacement value endorsement probably would have covered the bulk of your household personal contents, but you would not have recovered the additional $20,000–$30,000 you lost when the Arts and Crafts furniture was destroyed.

Unless, however, you have had the Arts and Crafts furniture appraised, now know its value, and have . . .

Personal Articles Floater

. . . an inland marine or personal articles floater.

According to Louis Korecki, assistant director in product management at Travelers, the personal articles or inland marine floater should be seriously considered by anyone with personal property of substantial value. These floaters can provide all-risk coverage and guarantee an agreed-upon amount to be paid by the insurance company for the items covered by the floater. But once again, it is up to you to have an accurate handle on the value of your property. If you insure a prized antique for only $6,000 on such a floater and it is really worth $20,000, you can only receive the $6,000 value as stated on the floater. A few companies have tried to incorporate an automatic inflation escalator on these floaters, but because of the variables in the antiques and collectibles market, Korecki suggests that these escalators may not be accurate indicators of value.

Other Facts to Discuss with Your Agent

Now that you are a little more familiar with these three most common types of policies, you need to be aware of two other factors that can influence the type of policy you and your agent determine best suits your needs.

Limitations

Regardless of what kind of policy you decide on, there are many exclusions and at least six limitations you need to know about. These vary from state to state, and the maximum compensation allowed also varies, so ask your agent for specifics about the following:
- coins, currency, and stamps (both new and collections)
- deeds, securities, travel tickets, and passports
- certain recreational property, boats, outboard motors, boat trailers, and the like

- jewelry, gems, watches, and furs
- metals—silver, gold, pewter
- guns and gun collections

If you have a sizable investment in any of these areas, you will be grossly underinsured with a common policy, as the maximum compensation on almost all these items ranges from $100 to $1,000 in most states.

Depreciation

Another limitation that sometimes appears on the replacement value policy states that the company's liability will not exceed four times the actual cash value of the depreciated cost of the item. In other words, let's say you lost an expensive television that is now several years old but would cost $850 to replace. However, the actual cash value of the TV, due to the depreciation applied to limited-life terms, is only $100. In keeping with the replacement value policy language, the total amount you can expect from your insurance is four times the cash value, or $400, leaving you $450 short of its true replacement value for an identical product.

I personally think that, for the money, the replacement value endorsement offers the best coverage for your personal property. It is certainly better than the standard policy. If you have valuable antiques or extensive collections or feel that your belongings are particularly susceptible to loss, you will want to consider combining the replacement policy with an all-risk floater policy for maximum protection.

But don't walk into any policy "blind." Take the time to read the "replacement cost" on your endorsement. It will read something like this:

> "Replacement Cost" means the cost, at the time of the loss, of a new article identical to the one damaged, destroyed, or stolen. When the identical article is no longer manufactured or is not available, replacement cost shall mean the cost of a new article similar to that damaged or destroyed and which is of comparable quality and usefulness.

As always, there are limitations and loopholes on the amount the insurance company is going to pay in replacing your possessions. Insurance companies still have the option to repair or replace items lost rather than making a cash settlement. I am finding that more and more insurance companies are choosing to replace possessions for the clients in lieu of a cash settlement, especially when the possessions lost are still manufactured today. Or, if the insurance company can buy the item or items for less money than the individual, if he takes a cash settlement, the individual must accept the lower replacement cost settlement available to the insurance company rather than the higher cost he would have to pay for the item.

One insurance agent told me that, when his clients lose expensive camera equipment, it is usually replaced by mail, within a few days' time. The adjuster calls in an order to a discount house, and the camera, lens, or whatever is shipped to the owner. Thus, if you entered your camera equipment for $3,000 but the insurance company only paid $2,500 to replace it, you may feel you were cheated.

This replacement value policy can create a problem for the policy owner when prices decline, as in the well-known case of silver. If your silver was appraised when silver prices were at their highest—$200 and more for a single fork—but your silver was stolen after silver prices fell, and the insurance company replaced your forks for only $65 each, you may feel doubly robbed.

"I was paying the premium for a $200 fork, not a $65 fork," you complain.

To avoid such problems you should consult your agent whenever a large price change occurs—either up or down—on items you have insured. But remember, it is your responsibility to follow the market—not your insurance agent's or your appraiser's. They simply cannot remember every client's possessions, nor should you expect them to.

Whose Hands?

Let's see now—the standard policy, the replacement value endorsement, the additional personal property floater. Which is best suited to your needs? And remember, these are only three among many insurance options.

But, armed with this primer on the fundamentals of personal property insurance, you should now be better equipped to talk to your insurance agent about adequately covering your personal property. Remember, the policies are there, but until you assess your personal needs you cannot expect your insurance agent, no matter how professional he or she is, to write the perfect policy for you. Your personal property insurance is in *your* hands.

When You Need to File a Claim

By the time you have completed reading this book, you will undoubtedly either have prepared your own inventory or sought outside assistance. Then, if anything happens to your property, you will be well armed for any claims you must prepare. But what happens when a claim must be made without benefit of a written inventory, appraisal, or substantiating photographs?

My advice is—do your homework, be prepared, and tell the truth. The two major points you will have to establish are (1) what you lost, and (2) proof that you owned it.

To make it easier, here is what you need to know:
- What you lost. Give the item a proper name.
- How many of each item listed you lost.
- A description of each item—size, material, age, and condition.
- Purchase date and original cost, if known.
- What you consider a fair value for the item today.

Most insurance companies provide forms in the event of a loss. Though the specific format will vary from company to company, the following example is fairly typical.

Item	Description	Date Acquired	Original Cost	Current Value
1 chair	Mahogany side chair with floral needlepoint seat	1972	Inherited	$550
7 salad forks	Sterling silver ornate shell pattern by Gorham. Monogrammed "MBB."	1938	Mother's silver	$125
Picture	Watercolor. Scene of Venice. Matted. Gold and black wooden frame.	1985	$150 plus frame	$600

Do Your Homework

Always take the time to prepare your claim form fully and accurately. For example, you may wonder why you should provide the original cost. Actually the original cost provides two clues: 1) it helps to establish the quality (quality is often reflected in cost), and 2) it serves as a check against original bills of sale. So my advice is to take this task seriously.

One reason insurance adjusters take so long to settle personal property claims is that they themselves do not know the value of personal property! I can promise that if you will present a well-documented and prepared claim, in addition to the skeleton list required by the company, your claim will more likely be settled quickly, and you will probably be pleased with the settlement.

Avoiding Disappointments

If you are providing your own values, be sure that the sources you use are accurate. Don't use the value of a solid cherry bedroom suite as the price for a mahogany veneer dining room suite. Or if you need to seek outside advice to assist you in preparing your claim, be certain the person you select is knowledgeable in the field. In chapter 28 you will learn who appraisers are and how to find them. But a preliminary word of caution—there are scores of people claiming to be experts whose advice is not worth the time of day. Completing an insurance claim form to get your money is serious business. Just because you have a piece of paper with a value on it signed by an appraiser does not mean that this value will be accepted by the insurance company.

Establishing Proof of Ownership

Once you have your list compiled, you next need to establish proof of ownership. Of course if you have made up your list ahead of time, the proof of ownership will have been established. But if not, you must now gather the information the best you can.

- Collect all bills of sale, canceled checks, any sort of receipt that can establish proof of ownership and at the same time jar your memory. For example, finding the receipt for one item will often help you remember that you bought another item from the same store.

- Gather together prints of all interior photographs that you, relatives, or friends have taken of your family. Backgrounds in family pictures often contain many material objects you can identify as lost.
- Ask others—family members, neighbors, visitors, anyone who can help—to recall objects they remember in your home. They can also serve as witnesses to the fact that you owned specific objects, if necessary.
- Contact store clerks who sold you items to help arrive at a fair replacement price to accompany the claim. This also establishes the fact that you actually owned the items involved.
- As an alternative to photographs, especially in the case of fire or other destruction of property where photographs might also have been destroyed, find pictures in magazines and books as similar as possible to the items you have lost. You can even draw rough sketches that will help the adjuster or appraiser assist you in arriving at a fair dollar settlement.

Remember the couple in the second chapter who didn't even remember how many chairs they had, much less what they looked like? I repeat, do your homework before submitting your claim.

The Double Check

At the same time, expect the insurance adjuster or investigator to double-check your sources and claims. I recall one case in particular where the owners voluntarily told me where they had purchased their furniture and how much they had paid for it at the time. They lived in a fairly small suburban town where people all knew one another. Just as routine procedure I called the furniture store and asked for verification.

"Did the Joneses buy an oak bedroom suite from you in 1976?" I inquired. The store's records showed that they had. "And would you remember the general price range of the suite? Would it have cost $1,200 or more like $5,000 at the time?" I asked.

"Oh, they couldn't have bought anything that expensive," replied the store owner. "They paid their bills on time, but they did not buy expensive furniture."

I looked back to double-check the figure the Joneses had submitted on their insurance claim for replacing the suite. It was $5,000. Whether the figure was arrived at out of ignorance or intent to deceive, or whether it was just a mistake, had a more accurate figure of $1,800 or $2,000 for a 1981 replacement value been given, the embarrassment that followed could have been avoided.

These double checks are also protection to keep insurance fraud to a minimum. A colleague's remarkable memory helped crack one such case.

When silver was at its height in 1980–81, silver theft was rampant. Jerry Young, a jeweler friend, and I often worked together, going through the stacks of claims that came in almost daily. One such claim was accompanied by clear, almost professional-quality photographs. Each piece listed on the claim form was numbered in the photographs. We were able to whiz through the claim and commented on how we wished everyone had such good records and would take the time to do such a thorough job in filling out the claim forms.

Five years later I got a call from Jerry. "Remember that picture-perfect silver claim we got back in 1981? Well, I'm sitting here looking at the same pictures sent in by a different insurance company and a different client."

A proper investigation ended that claim. But not all insurance claims involve theft, fire, or natural disasters.

So You're Going to Move

When a family moves, it's high stress time. As moving costs go up, more people are trying to save money by doing it themselves, an exhausting process.

Obviously, the way to get around all of this is to hire professional packers to come in and take care of everything. The problems that result are also obvious. You have complained about them yourself. The packing wasn't properly done. Your most prized possessions were thrown into a truck. The box of crystal had a heavy brass ashtray on the top and arrived with only the ashtray intact.

Then there is always the possibility that the boxes and crates will never arrive. Remember the horror stories about the box that was left behind and the time your neighbors received someone else's china instead of their own? Anyway, all boxes and crates look alike.

Everyone knows the case where the owners had packed one group of boxes to be picked up by a charity and another group of boxes to be moved to their new home. You know what happened. The charity ended up with the family's good china, and when the family unpacked what they thought was going to be their best china, they found the other set of china that had been intended for the charity. The question is, Can you afford the high risk of moving without knowing what you own?

Moving losses are much like robbery or fire losses. It is those objects you do not use on a day-to-day basis but often treasure most and want to pass on to the next generation that you may not miss for a long time. One reason you do not use them is that they're antiques, family pieces, or valuable, and you're trying to keep them in pristine condition for your children.

One of my clients did not miss her mother's cut glass lemonade pitcher until several months after she was finally settled in her home and decided to go antiquing. While browsing in an antiques shop she saw a cut glass lemonade pitcher identical to hers. Naturally she began to wonder where she had put hers when she unpacked. Next she realized that she did not remember unpacking the pitcher at all. A thorough search of the cabinets and closets revealed nothing. Then she realized there were other pieces she hadn't seen since she had unpacked.

She began looking for the things she remembered packing in the same box with the pitcher. None of these appeared. By now my client was distraught. She went back to the antiques shop where she had seen the pitcher. There she began finding other heirlooms that she recognized as her own—including her grandfather's baby cup with his name and birth date engraved on it!

Yes, she got them back. She bought them back.

Breakage is, of course, a high-risk chance in moving. Scratches and dents are facts of life, as are splintered chair legs and even totally demolished chests and secretaries.

I have been involved in moving claims where vans have been wrecked, and even one in which a van was "lost" for almost a month. (Who pays for furniture rental while you wait for yours to be found?) In fact, some of my most bizarre cases have come from moving claims.

I was driving down Interstate 85 early one spring morning when suddenly, in the opposite lane, I saw a charred and burned moving van abandoned along the side of the road. Who could have anticipated that a moving van on an interstate highway would catch fire?

I did not know when the fire had occurred, but I could see that the truck was deserted with only orange cones and some burned-out flares to mark it off. Had the contents of the truck also been burned, or, if they survived, how long had they been left on the truck, unattended, unguarded, and unprotected? I wondered. Later that afternoon, as I returned along the same highway, there was another moving van, and the objects from the burned van were being loaded onto the second truck.

Don't get me wrong. I have nothing against moving companies. I've moved several times myself without incident, and I even highly recommend several movers I've dealt with who handle each piece of your property as if it were their own. But if you are anticipating a move, you have an urgent reason for making an inventory of your personal property. Accidental loss, breakage, theft, depreciating damage—these are only some of the risks involved in moving today.

6

Theft and Fire

What You Need to Know About Burglaries

In approximately a third of the break-ins in America, the burglar gains unlawful entry without using force.

Personal property and art crime is second only to narcotics crimes.

These are typical headlines that appear in every newspaper across the country daily:

THREE FBI IMPOSTERS SOUGHT IN JEWEL THEFT

SERVICE TRUCK YIELDS LOOT

THIEVES FIND CHURCH ITEMS IRRESISTIBLE

STOLEN GOODS ARE VALUED AT $4 MILLION

Chances are, a family member or neighbor of yours has been robbed recently. But both you and I know it's not going to happen to us. Or do we?

The chances are roughly one in ten that you will be the victim of a personal property burglary or robbery. But until theft hits close to home, most of us are going to ignore the possibility. I can best illustrate this point by telling you what happened to my friend the insurance agent. Mind you, he is an insurance agent who tells other people to have appraisals made. In fact, he often called asking me to make appraisals for clients.

But he never asked me to make one of *his* property.

Furthermore, this insurance agent invested in antiques. Every time he bought a new piece his dealer would warn, "Have your collection appraised. It has greatly increased in value over the years."

Then one Christmas his brother's house was broken into and robbed. When his brother had difficulty collecting his insurance because he couldn't remember everything he owned, had no proof of ownership for many of the stolen items, and had no idea of the current value of his lost possessions, the insurance agent panicked. He called me to appraise his collection.

"I just never thought it could happen to me. Now I know it can," he said.

What the Thieves Left

The tales of robberies are as unbelievable as fiction, yet they happen every day. One of the most incredible stories happened in my own neighborhood and almost got my very respectable husband into a great deal of trouble.

One Saturday morning my husband had so much work left from having been out of town most of the week that he decided to get up very early and go into the office. At the end of our street he noticed a large pile of rugs lying by the mailbox.

They look like Orientals, he thought, but why would Mrs. Coley be throwing away her Oriental rugs? They must just be copies, he reasoned. After all, it wasn't even light. Then he stopped.

Wait! he thought. If Emyl comes by later and sees them, she's bound to pick them up and drag them home. I'll load them in the trunk of my car and take them down to the Goodwill pickup. Naw . . . that'll take too much time. I'll just hope Emyl sleeps late this morning, he decided, and drove on past.

When Mrs. Coley's across-the-street neighbor went into the kitchen sometime later that morning to cook breakfast, she saw the pile of rugs by the mailbox. But she knew what my husband didn't know: Mrs. Coley was out of town.

The thieves had already taken the silver, jewelry, and easily transportable items but had left the rugs on the street, intending to come back and pick them up.

Yet another startling story happened in our quiet community when a van, disguised as a Salvation Army truck, pulled into the driveway and stole silver, paintings, crystal, even items of furniture while the family was on vacation. Dealing with victims of such burglaries can be most difficult, but this case I will always remember fondly because of the wife's indomitable spirit.

When we were discussing the items that had been stolen, she confessed, "One thing has really bothered me ever since the crime. I'd always cherished this dear little chair," she said, pointing out a sweet mid-Victorian side chair. "Now every time I walk past it I look at it and think, Ump! You must not have been so fine after all!"

Repeat Performances

Repeat robberies have also increased at an alarming rate. Once the robbers learn how to gain entry into a home and discover where things are kept, they return, knowing the job will be easier the second time.

One woman who was robbed decided that since she lived alone she did not want the responsibility of worrying about her antiques—the ones the robbers had left—anymore. She packed up a couple of boxes of china and drove to a reputable shop where she had bought antiques in the past. She explained her situation and offered her china for sale. The shop owner was happy to purchase it. Excited over her good fortune, she told him about some brass candlesticks and sterling silver she had at home that she would also sell. Yes, he'd buy those, too. She drove straight home to get them. A while later the dealer received a call from her. She was sorry she couldn't sell him the other pieces. While she was at his shop her home had been robbed—again.

This raises the question of what happens to stolen property. Usually it is sold almost immediately at flea markets or to antiques dealers, at auctions, to scrap metal dealers, to fences, to receivers. It is hawked on street corners, sold at fine uptown galleries, shipped out of state, across the country, and out of the country. But seldom does it find its way back to the original owner.

Why can't people recover their stolen property? There are two major reasons. The first will make you indignant. The second should make you get on with an inventory.

The first reason is that the police usually do not know enough about the nature of the stolen property to recover it effectively. How can a policeman trained in law enforcement know how to identify a Tiffany lamp, a Paul Storr tea urn, or a set of Belter furniture? These are the high rollers, the items worth $10,000, $15,000, $25,000, and more. But the same problem— identifying an Imari bowl worth $250, a Georg Jensen fork worth $175, or a set of Lenox china worth $1,200—hinders the recovery of personal property taken from your home and mine.

One detective, an expert on art property, told me, "When someone reports the loss of a rug, the police may be thinking $19.95 a yard, not $6,000 for an Oriental; when someone reports a stolen lamp, the police may be thinking $29.95, but if it is a Tiffany worth $15,000 . . ."

Raymond Kendall, of the famous international police organization Interpol, admits, "We know that ninety-nine percent of police officers have absolutely no special knowledge of 'cultural property' at all."

The second reason people cannot recover their stolen property is lack of sufficient proof of ownership and inability to adequately describe personal property to identify it for retrieval.

The following story told by Robert Volpe, the art and antiquities expert on the New York City police force, illustrates the problem better than any other I could tell.

According to Volpe, a fence who specialized in toasters, TVs, tape decks, and the like was offered a statue by a thief. At first the fence was going to turn it away, but the fence's girlfriend saw it and liked it, so the fence bought it for her. Word got out that the fence's girlfriend liked antiques and art. Soon thieves began bringing the fence pictures and silver and the like. Naturally the fence found where he could sell these antiques, but he also found that he liked these things, too. He became a collector. Eventually the fence was caught, and when the police went to arrest him they found a house laden with antiques—Tiffany lamps in every room, including the bathroom, Oriental rugs on the floor, Georgian silver in the kitchen cabinets! It was a fine display.

Now, the amazing thing is that at this point the fence admitted to the police that he was almost relieved he had been caught. He had come to love and treasure his collection so much that he worried some dumb thief would come in and steal all his precious pieces and not know what he was stealing!

The police put the stolen items on display, and thousands of people viewed the property in hopes of finding their missing goods.

But, says Volpe, few people could positively identify pieces and reclaim them. Either they didn't have police reports to back up their claims, or several individuals claimed the same piece. Others just couldn't be sure that the pieces were really theirs.

At this point the fence himself showed up and claimed everything in the room.

"It's mine," he declared. "You, the police, are my witness that I was in possession of these things because you were there . . . you saw all this in my house."

Furthermore, the fence could properly identify the pieces. He had cataloged and photographed all of them. (Incidentally, thieves and fences photograph pieces so they can show what they have to offer.) In short, he had proof that the stolen goods were his.

But as the public is becoming more attuned to the value of their personal property, so are the courts turning in more convictions of personal property burglars. Being able to positively identify the objects as yours remains the key to a successful conviction. Have you ever thought how difficult it would be to prove that a set of Chantilly or Old Master flatware is really yours?

One client was told by the police she would never see her Tiffany flatware again. She had inherited the set from her mother-in-law, and her first memory of seeing the set was when her future husband invited her to dinner at his house. As she started to put the first bite in her mouth, she stabbed herself with the fork. She discovered the outside tine was bent, and when she inherited the set she always put that fork at her place when she was entertaining.

A couple of years after the silver had been stolen she walked into a local antiques show and found herself looking at her own silver, still in its original case with her mother-in-law's initials on the brass plaque! She left quickly so as not to create suspicion, walked to the phone, and called the police.

When the police arrived they wanted to know how she could positively identify the silver as hers. When she mentioned the plaque and initials, she was told she could have seen them.

"Okay, there's one dinner fork with an outside bent tine," she said.

When the police officer found the fork near the bottom of the stack, he began to believe her story.

Knowing little peculiarities and distinctions about our things can be a valuable source of information.

With the increasing incidences of personal property crimes and our heightened awareness of the need to police our own neighborhoods, local community watches have been established in many areas. Checklists are distributed by police and sheriff's offices. But if you do not follow their guidelines, you are not protecting yourself fully.

Our Life-Style

I do all these things, you think. But do you?

"I can walk around my local area in Paris and see shutters down, mail left out, and all the visible signs that people are away," says Raymond Kendall of Interpol. "You can find out who is away just by driving through a neighborhood. Or you can do as one burglar I know did. He read names and addresses off luggage tags at the airport to compile a list of victims."

"It is our everyday contacts with life that expose us to the criminal element," says Robert Volpe. "We allow everyone into our homes today—repair people, service people of all kinds. Sometimes a person who has been in your home innocently talks to the wrong person. He'll say, 'Wow, you gotta see the house I went into to pick up the diapers today!' in the hearing of the wrong person.

"And that's not all," Volpe continues. "You can see thieves shopping along Madison Avenue—and they go shopping in neighborhoods, too. There are some individuals who are only spotters. They're the ones who haven't the courage to go into someone's home. But they spot a victim and sell the information. The problem is, a lot of individuals do not think of themselves as collectors. They have things in their homes that they do not even realize are valuable collectibles or antiques. But the thief is aware of it. And to make matters worse, these are the individuals who are not properly insured and whose homes often are not properly secured."

Fire—Ashes Blacken Your Memory

Any loss of personal property is devastating. But fire is perhaps the most traumatic of all experiences. You may have barely escaped with your life. You may lose not only your home, but records of your personal property, even your inventory or appraisal and photographs that could have served as proof of ownership. A thief seldom takes such items.

Yet the problems that result from fire losses are the same as those that occur after a theft. You must know what you lost.

Generally, when working with fire victims adjusters tend to be a little more lenient in demanding proof of ownership on each item. Furthermore, some of the limitations cited in chapter 5 ("Insurance: Before It's Too Late") apply only to theft losses and *not* to fire losses. Although this is good news for the consumer, unfortunately so much has usually been lost in a total fire that the victim, bound by the coverage he had, is underinsured and thus can never be compensated for his entire loss.

Unusual events can occur in the course of a house fire. When the firemen arrived on the scene of a fire in a large, seventy-five-year-old home in a well-to-do neighborhood, they found the curving hallways an impediment to getting the hoses to the source of the fire. In trying to wield the hoses through an interior hallway, the firemen inadvertently knocked over a large nineteenth-century English breakfront filled with glass and china.

Though the owners were most understanding, the task of sifting through the broken glass and porcelain to try to reconstruct the contents of the breakfront was very difficult for the wife. In the back of her mind I am sure she wondered if the breakage could have been avoided. We were matching pieces of porcelain much as you would match together pieces of a jigsaw puzzle. I had assembled a charming blue-and-white nineteenth-century teapot and pieces of what could have been either four or six handleless cups and saucers. When I asked the owner how many she had, she looked at the grouping blankly and said, "I don't know. I've never seen that before in my entire life. Where did it come from?"

Ashes, whether real or psychological, really do blacken your memory after a fire.

Where to Keep Your List

"I had a list and photographs, but they were lost in the fire," I've been told.

"I had an appraisal of my silver made, but I kept it in the silver box, and when the thieves took the box they took my appraisal."

When I ask audiences around the country where you should keep your inventory, appraisal, or photographs, I hear in great unison: "In the safe deposit box!"

No!

First, always have *two* copies of your inventory, appraisal, videotape, photographs, or whatever. Keep one where you think it is safe and can get your hands on it quickly if you need to under normal circumstances—no burglary, fire, or the like. This may be a fairly obvious place—a locked drawer at home or the office, a home safe, or even a safe deposit box. But the second copy—the one you want to get to in an emergency . . .

Put this copy in an envelope and label it "Property Belonging to [your name]." Then give this sealed envelope to your most trusted friend or relative and have that person place the envelope in *his* or *her* safe deposit box. This way, if something happens (as in the case of a fire) and you cannot locate your key in the rubble, or your safe deposit key is stolen in a burglary—and I've seen that happen—you can still get a copy of important lists quickly.

Furthermore, there can be a significant difference between an insurance and an estate appraisal. An insurance appraisal left in an owner's safe deposit box might mistakenly be used in an estate inventory when the contents of the box are inventoried by the clerk of court in beginning the probate process.

Also remember that most appraisers retain a copy of your appraisal if you have a professional appraisal made.

You may never be the victim of a burglary or fire. But why not use the principle of preventive medicine—take the time now and make an inventory . . . and hope you'll never need it.

7

Estates:
The Objects May Be More Important Than Valuable

First, let me go on record as saying that in most estates much too much attention is given to the unfounded fear of having to pay estate taxes on personal property and not enough attention is given to the objects in the estate itself. After each talk I give, someone from the audience rushes up and says, "I can't believe the things I gave away when I was settling my aunt's estate a few years ago!"

Second, you should know that estate values are *not* insurance replacement values.

When an Estate Needs an Appraiser's Services

An appraisal is needed if the property in the estate must be divided equally among several heirs or if the estate's fair market value is large enough to require a federal estate tax report. Each state has its own laws for state death tax reports, but at this point in time federal law allows an exemption of $600,000.

On the other hand, if the value is under the estate tax threshold, if there is only one beneficiary, or if all items are specifically bequeathed, then there is no reason for an appraisal to be made for the benefit of the heir or heirs. An appraisal is most useful when several heirs are named but there are no specific bequests in the will and the property is to be divided equally among them. Usually in such circumstances no one can agree on what equals what, so an appraiser who has no sentimental attachment or monetary interest in any of the property can prepare an unbiased appraisal from which the heirs can then work.

Even without family spats, questions still arise:

- What should I keep?
- Can I sell these things?
- Should I donate these antiques?

And always the bottom-line question is:

- Is my inheritance valuable?

These are all valid questions. Think for just a moment: each time an object is sold at auction, in a flea market, in a gallery, at an antiques show, or in a tag sale, it either was or one day will be part of someone's estate.

When I make an estate *division* appraisal, realizing that some heirs will keep their pieces but others will sell or donate them, I use the same format as when preparing an estate *tax* appraisal and provide fair market values. I tell the heirs that if I sign my name to the appraisal for scrutiny by the IRS, they can be assured that the values I provide are fair to all involved.

Heirs should also know that if an estate's property is going to be sold, either through an auction or tag sale shortly after a death, there is no reason to have the estate appraised for tax purposes. As long as the sale of the property is legitimately transacted (at arm's length and with all parties knowing the relevant facts, according to the IRS), the sale prices will stand as the fair market value of the estate.

And what if nothing is to be sold? My experience has shown that tax attorneys and executors are now looking more closely at the total value of an estate to see if the property is indeed valuable.

"I used to just pass on estates that had the usual amount of silver flatware, good china and crystal, some nice antiques and furniture, but no fine art collections or jewelry, stamp or coin collections," one tax attorney told me. "But now that all values have jumped so high, I'm taking a second look at personal property in estates. I'd say I'm taking a more cautious approach."

In other words, though the government allows a liberal amount of money to pass from one generation to the next before taxes are imposed, gone are the days when a man could die leaving hundreds of thousands of dollars in real estate, stocks, and bonds and the attorney would list the value of his personal property at $500 or $1,000.

Another reason for the tax attorney to be cautious is IRS Regulation §20.2031-6(b), which states that if personal effects articles having a total value in excess of $3,000 exist in an estate (jewelry, furs, artwork, coin and stamp collections, silver, and so on are cited as possible examples), then an appraisal shall be submitted with the return.

Thus, to learn the value of estate property, as well as to be sure no unknown treasures are discarded, many attorneys and executors are now electing to have professional appraisals made.

Choosing an Appraiser for Estate Purposes

If an estate appraisal is needed, be extremely cautious in your choice of an appraiser. There are appraisers with self-serving interests who will offer to make an estate appraisal contingent upon the amount of taxes they save the estate. Equally as bad are those who charge a percentage of the total amount of the estate's value. They may be tempted to appraise used furniture at full retail prices just to increase their paychecks—which brings us to the question: What are estate values, anyway?

In the simplest layman's terms, an estate value is how much money an item will sell for to generate cash for the deceased's estate.

This next story explains all about estate values and points up the many problems that can beset estate appraisals when the heirs know nothing about the deceased's property.

Many years ago a very popular hostess who was noted for her passion for pink was given a large pink swan vase as a gift. Two of her friends had bought the swan at a local estate auction for ten dollars. The friends often joked about how happy the auctioneer must have been to have had more than one bidder run this obviously ten-cent-store item up to an exorbitant ten dollars. But they were determined to buy the swan to give as a joke to their favorite hostess.

The swan became the focal point of every party. Sometimes it was used as a centerpiece with flowers floating in it. Other times it was filled with greenery and pink and silver Christmas balls. Over the years one wing became chipped and one foot got cracked, but no party was held without the ubiquitous pink swan.

Some twenty years later the hostess died, and only six weeks later her husband died unexpectedly. No provision had been made for such a quick succession of deaths, and the only heir, a daughter, had to pay double tax on all of the jointly owned property—even the cracked and chipped swan. When the appraiser valued the swan he knew nothing of the story. The ten-dollar swan was valued at $125, or $250 for the double taxation.

Three years later the daughter began disposing of part of the personal property left by her parents. She looked over the appraisal, saw the swan listed at $125, and packed it into the "sell" box.

The dealer who took the estate items on consignment really didn't want the swan, but he took it as part of a total lot. Everything sold—everything but the pink swan.

Eighteen months later, in desperation, the dealer sold the chipped and cracked swan for $15 just to get rid of it. He advised the daughter of his action and handed her a check for the swan, minus his commission of 33⅓ percent. Her check was for $10—the same amount the swan had brought some twenty-two years earlier.

The IRS actually tries to keep such outrageous errors from occurring in estate evaluations by stating guidelines for estate appraisal valuations. This is the wording used by the IRS, which all good appraisers can quote: "The fair market value of the decedent's household and personal effects is the price at which a willing buyer would sell to a willing seller, neither being under any compulsion to buy or to sell and both having reasonable knowledge of relevant facts."

Estate Values Are *Not* Replacement Values

Many heirs worry about the value of used or secondhand property in estates. "You're going to put those in low, aren't you?" they ask almost pleadingly. There is no other way that an honest appraiser can appraise a piece of used furniture that has no value as an antique.

For example, take an undistinguished upholstered lounge chair that has not been recovered in fifteen years. Even at full retail price, its value would be modest, for you would find such a chair for sale only at a tag sale or in a flea market or at a Salvation Army store. The top retail price for that used lounge chair would be $25 to $50.

"But I couldn't go out and buy a new chair like that for $50," you say.

No, but you are not buying a new chair. You are buying a used piece and paying its retail value—$25 to $50. Once you own the chair and have spent $350 to have it reupholstered, then if you wish to insure it for its replacement value—say, $400—that's a different matter.

But what about the twenty-five-year-old good- but not exceptional-quality mahogany secretary in perfect condition? This piece would be suitable for sale in a decorator's shop or antiques store that also sells reproductions. Its value would not be that of a new piece today because those shops must sell the "old reproduction" pieces below the cost of a new piece in order to move them.

The secretary could easily be sold for anywhere from $800 in a tag sale to $2,500 in an interior decorator's shop. Once again, then, the estate value of the secretary could reasonably be stated to be $800, but its replacement value for insurance purposes could be placed at $2,500, or approximately three times its estate value.

A true antique, however, would be even closer to its full and ultimate value because it would sell for what it is—an antique—under all circumstances. Thus an eighteenth-century walnut chest of drawers that would sell locally for $3,000 to any one of several buyers, whether at auction, tag sale, or private sale, would be stated as having an estate value of $3,000.

Ultimately the attorney, executor, or heirs will determine what needs to be appraised in an estate, based on the size and bequeaths of the will. But you should know that no one, the IRS least of all, expects every kitchen and bathroom article to be counted and valued individually in an estate. Obviously furniture, silver collections, and large vehicles are included in an appraisal.

What happens when there is an estate where one classification of objects or a collection is much more significant than the rest of the property? What do you do when the deceased had a library of first editions, but everything else was the usual household contents? At this point you will want to call in a book specialist to work along with the general household appraiser both for tax purposes and for the fair division of the estate.

What you want to guard against, however, is hiring two or more appraisers who do not see eye to eye in how to value estate property. I was once involved in an estate appraisal where one appraiser in an entire team of appraisers assigned values totally out of line with the rest of our figures. This created a discrepancy in the appraisal, the value of the estate, and the tax basis. Consistency is important in estate appraisal when more than one appraiser is hired.

Don't Forget the Objects

Of foremost importance is remembering to search out the objects. Few children know, or have been shown, all their parents' things unless the parents have had their children's help in moving to a smaller or retirement residence.

Why do you think unscrupulous dealers, auctioneers, appraisers, and even trust officers like to get into an estate before the children have had a chance to sort things out? This is one reason you must be so careful in selecting the knowledgeable and honorable professional in estate situations.

Once, when working with a very honorable young woman sent by a bank to help me sort through a tremendous estate, I was brought a box of jar bottoms and cracked china.

"Is it okay if I throw these broken things out?" she asked. "And here are a couple of things that look like tops to something, but I can't find the bottoms," she said, holding up a pair of Oriental brass hand mirrors that later netted the estate $1,200.

Where You May Find Some Treasures

There is a section on basements and attics later which you should read if you're involved in cleaning out or sorting through an estate. But the one area I find most consistently overlooked when relatives are cleaning out a home in an estate is the accumulation of old flower-arranging materials and vases, usually stored in boxes in the kitchen, pantry, attic, basement, or even garage. More times than I can count I've found signed pieces by Steuben, Tiffany, Rookwood, and Lalique (the more expensive names), as well as Roseville, Hull, and Heisey (more modest names), in among florist and dimestore pieces. Usually these boxes go straight into the garbage or to the Goodwill store without even a second glance. That's money out the door.

Don't forget the flower vases! This signed and dated 1915 acorn-and-leaf decorated Van Briggle pottery vase sold for $245 at a Savoia and Fromm auction sale.

Protecting an Estate—Beforehand

While discussing estates, it seems appropriate to touch upon a related topic that concerns me these days—the antiques and property belonging to the elderly, who may not know the value of their pieces.

No one is left more open to prey and chicanery than the elderly, especially when they are living alone and have no one to protect or advise them. I have seen the sad results of these situations when preparing estate appraisals after a death.

Not long ago, at the request of an attorney, I went to an expensive resort area to prepare the estate appraisal of a woman who had no direct heirs. Her extensive estate had numerous tax problems, but the attorney wanted to distribute the now unprotected valuable personal property to the benefactors as quickly as possible.

The treasures were wonderful! She had inherited fine antiques from her family, and with her husband she had made many choice purchases over the years. There was a $25,000 New England highboy, a $15,000 Maryland sideboard, fine oil paintings mounting into the six figures—and these were all estate, not replacement, values. In a few drawers I found old Tiffany bills of sale, and I was looking forward to seeing the silver she had both inherited and bought. But when I opened the drawer where the flatware was kept, I found it empty, except for two objects: an inexpensive silver-plated salad serving set and a magnifying glass—the same magnifying glass the employees in the home had used to identify the sterling silver before they "borrowed" it. "And I was worried about something happening to the property *now*," the attorney remarked.

What if she had not been so wealthy? These days many people are selling their personal property to be able to maintain health care in their later years.

If you are responsible for an older relative or person who does live alone, it might be wise to make an inventory of that person's personal property and take the time to discuss with him or her the potential worth of the property and why it should not be carelessly sold or given away.

Your Own Estate

Estate planning is a phenomenon of the 1980s, and if you go to elaborate means to list your true investments, your stocks, bonds, CDs, real estate, IRA, and so on, but ignore your personal property, you may be both overlooking property of value and setting your family up for some of the problems I've recounted. And who knows what treasures you may have inherited and not known about all these years? What will happen to those items in *your* estate?

And as I was writing this book, a true "fairy tale" was transpiring.

When an older couple was considering moving into a smaller home, the "cleaner-upper" husband finally convinced his "pack-rat" wife to discard some items stored away in drawers and cabinets. One piece, a hand-embroidered silk needlework picture, was on its way to the church bazaar until the wife (probably not truly willing to part with it) decided to ask a museum curator if the museum would be interested in it. The picture was practically identical in subject with another at the museum, but hers was signed and dated on the back and helped authenticate the museum's picture. Furthermore, when I was asked to appraise the picture for the donor's taxes, a little research turned up another similar picture that had sold only a few months earlier for $20,900! No, these discoveries don't happen every day, but each time one does, I reflect sadly, "Wonder what treasures were discarded in someone's estate today?"

Many appraisers today have word-processing programs and computerized systems that make it easy to provide both an *insurance* valuation and an *estate* valuation merely by changing values and running the document twice. If you are having a professional appraisal prepared for insurance purposes, ask the appraiser what it would cost to have an estate appraisal run at the same time. Hopefully you won't need it anytime soon, but once you can see the potential estate values of your items, you may be able to more equitably divide your property among your heirs. This way you may decide that you really should leave Susie the silver service *and* the corner cupboard if John is going to get the secretary and the dining room table.

But money aside, speaking personally now, not as an appraiser but as someone who has observed people's reactions to inheriting property, I have a little advice for you.

Over the years I've been touched when someone has shown me some object, whether a cut glass pitcher, a modest diamond ring, a silver bowl, or a rocking chair, and said lovingly, "I know this isn't very valuable, but I do cherish it. It was given to me on my sixteenth birthday [or when I was married, or when our first child was born, or whenever]." This person is speaking about a generous act, giving something you love to a person you believe will enjoy and receive pleasure from the object for yet another lifetime.

In contrast with this, I've observed the frustration, bewilderment, and distress that often exist when I'm called in by someone who has just inherited an entire estate. Disorder reigns. Valuable jewelry is mixed in with costume pieces, linen is tossed out of drawers, furniture is in random array, and the heir has a plea in her voice when she asks, "What am I going to do with all this stuff?"

So my advice is, take the time now, when you can make purposeful, meaningful decisions, to plan for the disposal of your personal property the same way you have of your investment property. You have no idea how much pleasure you can derive from knowing that those who appreciate your taste and love for beautiful things will have these cherished mementos from you.

8

Gifts, Taxes, and Your Good Intentions

Mention the IRS and hearts stop beating. Domineering men become timid pussycats and Milquetoast types turn into raging lions. This chapter is meant to soothe your concerns that the IRS will come after you if you donate gifts of antiques and personal property to charitable organizations.

True, it is more difficult than ever before to "give things away" if you're going to take a tax credit for them, because there are forms and papers that must be completed, signed (sometimes by several people), and submitted with your taxes. But the task is not impossible.

Historically there are many reasons the IRS has imposed new rules and even red tape upon well-intentioned donors who wish to make contributions of antiques to charitable institutions. Unfortunately, there have been several well-publicized instances of gifts of personal property and antiques that have been grossly overappraised. Had these gifts slipped by the IRS, the donor would have benefited from an excessive tax break.

The IRS recently released information that several groups of donated items with a claimed tax donation value of $3,291,000 were determined to have a value of $1,200,700 when reviewed and valued by the Art Advisory Panel, a group of independent experts selected by the IRS. That is a difference of over $2,000,000. We all know that the amount of taxes you and I, as citizens, must pay is determined by how much tax is collected. When an exaggerated tax deduction is allowed, you and I are going to pay more taxes while the donor is going to get the unfair deduction.

So, to the question I am often asked—"Why has the IRS made it so difficult to give away gifts?"—the answer must be, "To protect the public coffers."

Who Pays for the Appraisal

You will find that, if you wish to make a gift "in kind" (an object rather than money, stocks, or bonds), you will be required to have the object appraised. But why can't the museum professionals—the curators, in particular—appraise the items you wish to donate, thereby saving you the expense of having an appraisal made? you may wonder. The IRS has uncovered cases where employees of charitable organizations have overvalued items to make the donor "feel good," as well as to enhance the number of "valuable" donations received under their leadership.

The Appraiser's Responsibility

As a result of these and other unethical practices, the IRS requires that the appraisal be made by a disinterested party, generally expected to be a qualified appraiser. Further, the IRS requires the appraiser to take more responsibility for the value actually assigned donated gifts of antiques and personal property than in the past. If an item is deemed overappraised by a specific percentage, the appraiser is subject to fines and may be barred from preparing other appraisals for the IRS.

The real key to avoiding trouble with the IRS in matters of donating personal property is finding a reputable and knowledgeable appraiser who is an expert about both the property to be valued and the IRS forms and regulations.

Donation Value = Fair Market Value

After reading chapter 7 on estate taxes, you should have a grasp of the meaning of "fair market value" and thus understand how the appraiser approaches valuing gifts for estate tax purposes. The rules of fair market value also apply when an appraiser evaluates property for donation purposes.

For example, the illustration of the lounge chair that would be appraised for tax purposes at $25 to $50 would have that same value range for donation purposes. The IRS will disallow an appraised value of $450, its replacement cost, for donation purposes. The fair market value rule prevents a donor from falsely declaring that a ten-year-old color TV worth $50 can be donated to a local charity at a tax write-off of a brand-new color TV costing $595.

To determine the fair market value of an antique, an appraiser must establish what prices other items similar in age, style, quality, and condition to the one in question have sold for recently and document his value with specific evidence.

The form that you, as a donor of personal property with an appraised fair market value of over $500, will need to file with your taxes is IRS Form 8283. These are available by calling the IRS office or through your CPA or other financial adviser. If the property you are donating exceeds $5,000, Form 8283 must be signed by you, a representative of the receiving institution, and the appraiser who established the fair market value of the donated property. You need to know that failure to file the completed form, along with the required appraisal, may lead to a disallowance of the claimed deduction.

The best source you can use for understanding the current status of the individual donor, collector, and/or investor and the IRS is *The ARTnews Guide to Tax Benefits* by Robert S. Persky. This book explains in readable layman's terms the rules and regulations surrounding donations that are usually offered up in legal jargon. Further, the guide shows how you can benefit or suffer from the Internal Revenue Code's provisions and your individual tax bracket. Persky's purpose is to explain how, through understanding tax laws and identifying your status under the law, the collector can make informed decisions on acquiring antiques and art and then administering and maintaining the collection.

Other materials that are invaluable in understanding the IRS definitions and regulations affecting donation of personal property for a tax benefit are IRS publications 526, *Charitable Contributions,* and 561, *Determining the Value of Donated Property.*

Interestingly, despite the paperwork involved, to say nothing of the trouble of finding an appraiser and the expense of having the appraisal made, I have never had a client decide to make a gift of antiques or personal property to a museum, historical society, college, or other charitable organization based on the amount of taxes he has or has not saved. Once you understand that it is for your protection against fraud and personal property, art, and antiques tax scams that these rules and regulations exist, you should fear them no longer.

9

Divorce:
What You May Leave
Behind

Each attorney I have spoken to about personal property in separations and divorces has the same advice: Get personal property division agreed upon at the start. This advice is usually followed by each attorney's favorite story about his client's amicable division of property and how it all turned out—thirteen lawsuits later!

The division of personal property in divorce suits can be so unpleasant that many appraisers will not even take these cases. And I know from experience that settlement of personal property can be the *final* settlement to be made.

A lawyer friend was casually walking through the courthouse one day when he saw a judge who looked even more distraught and harried than usual.

"A tough one, eh?" he asked.

"They're fighting over who's going to get the Tupperware!" the judge exclaimed incredulously.

Tea for One

In one instance, both parties agreed to divide the property according to my values—they just couldn't decide who was going to get what. (Remember, the attorneys' meters are ticking all this time.) After days of squabbling in the wife's attorney's office, they came to the last item—a group of six teacups and saucers. The couple argued about these cups and saucers for a full half hour. Finally the exasperated attorney called in the husband's attorney to complete the negotiations. Later, when the attorneys told me the story, I vividly recalled the cups and saucers. Not only were they not valuable—they were ugly as well!

What You Leave Behind

Because women generally know more about the objects in their homes, husbands can unwittingly surrender large sums of money by giving up all the personal property in the house. A lawyer friend who specializes in divorce cases says most men will settle for the compact disk player (to use while courting the new girlfriend) until they find out how much plates and glasses and towels cost. Then they want to renegotiate the entire property settlement.

And a wife can be just as profligate if she carelessly leaves property behind without determining its true value. Of all the divorce proceedings I've been involved in, one stands out in my mind.

The year was 1980, and silver was hovering in the $45 to $47 per ounce range. The husband, knowing how badly his soon-to-be-ex-wife treasured the sterling silver flatware they had received as wedding gifts, made a trip to the local jeweler. He came home with the "suggested retail price list." He laid the price list out on the dining room table and then counted out the silver—eight spoons, six forks, nine salad forks, and so forth. He then showed his wife the silver's replacement cost. "You take $5,000 worth of silver flatware and I'll take $5,000 worth of IBM stock. That will be fair," he reasoned.

Luckily the wife's attorney insisted that a quick, inexpensive net worth appraisal (what the property would *sell* for) of their joint property be prepared, otherwise we all know what would have happened. Silver took a nosedive to a low of under $5 per ounce, while IBM stock, selling at around 60 in 1980, climbed steadily to a high of 175⅞ in 1987.

The best way to avoid such unpleasantness at a difficult time? Keep a log, several divorce attorneys have suggested. As more couples sign prenuptial agreements, they should keep a simple log of purchases, gifts, and inheritance. Later I will give examples of how to make an inventory. To keep ownership of objects straight, a simple notation of "whose it is" can be made on the inventory.

Each state has its own laws governing division of property in divorce. However, for the protection of both parties, when valuable personal property is involved, an objective appraiser's services can be invaluable.

Part Three

HOW YOU CAN MAKE YOUR OWN INVENTORY OR APPRAISAL

10

Getting Started:
What You Need to Know

The life-style magazines have made decorations and antiques "sexy." But inventorying your things is best described as a "task" and to some it is often "drudgery."

Yet almost every day someone says to me, "What an exciting and interesting job you have" or "I want to do what you do" or "I wish I knew all you know." Rather than dreading the job ahead, why not approach it with good humor and a spirit of adventure? Remember, you're going to become a "detective of the decorative arts."

The Pitfalls and How to Avoid Them

But I must admit that not everyone will approach this task with my attitude.

"I've been meaning to call you for years," began my client. "But somehow, every time I thought about dragging out all that silver and china, I couldn't face it. Now my neighbors on both sides have been robbed. Can you come over this afternoon?"

Sound familiar? If so, don't despair. (Don't call, either, if you expect to find

You're about to become a "detective of the decorative arts." A thorough investigation of your own property will make you a more discerning and knowledgeable shopper. Photograph by Jon Zachary

an appraiser available "this afternoon." Today most appraisers are booked for weeks, even months, in advance.)

Most people just don't want to do the work involved in making a proper inventory. The majority start out without a scheme or plan, thinking that it will take only a short while to complete the list. Naturally, an hour later, when they realize they have more than they thought they did, or have stopped to search for an item they suddenly remembered but can't find, they are frustrated and ready to quit. You can avoid these frustrations by planning ahead.

Inventory Your Belongings—Don't Polish Them

Mary was smart. She knew it was going to take a lot of time to make her own inventory. She began on a snowy Monday morning. After the children left for school, she put a sheet on the dining room table and opened her silver drawer. She hadn't used her silver for two months—since Christmas—and she had been rushed when she'd put it away. Her silver was gold from tarnish, so instead of putting it out on the table, she took it straight to the kitchen and began polishing the knives and forks. When the children got home she was still polishing trays and goblets. She hadn't even begun her inventory.

To avoid this problem, which happens rather frequently, be determined to proceed with the job at hand. Save the polishing and cleaning or washing for later.

Another solution, if you're a compulsive cleaner, is to wait until you do your spring or fall cleaning. If you routinely rearrange linen closets or wash all your crystal, plan to make your inventory while you're doing that job anyway—if you think the burglars will wait for you.

The Pitfall of "Lost" Things

Before you start, be prepared to discover that you've lost or misplaced some items. In at least 50 percent of the appraisals I make, I am told, "I used to have a dozen ice tea spoons, but now I can only find eleven" or "I'll just have to send you a picture of my cut glass bowl when I find it."

Even more serious discoveries are made when owners begin unpacking treasures from hiding or storage places. In one instance, I remember, a trunk filled with wonderful nineteenth-century quilts had been severely water-damaged—unbeknownst to the owners—and the quilts had literally rotted to pieces. In another, an entire set of sterling silver had been packed in the same box with a dozen small salt and pepper shakers. The salt had spilled all over the silver. By the time the box was opened, five years later, the silver had been eaten away by the salt, and many pieces were pitted beyond saving.

In some cases even furniture that owners thought they had stored in the attic or basement after a move has not shown up when we began to look for it. If you can't find something, or if you discover broken or damaged pieces, don't let this divert you. Let it emphasize the reason you need to finish the job at hand. Make a separate list of pieces you can't find as you go along, and if they show up later, mark them off. If they don't show up, begin a concerted search for them *after* you finish the appraisal.

The "It's Not Worth It" Pitfall

"It's going to be too much trouble," you sigh.

"I don't want to mess with all that stuff," your husband complains.

"We don't have anything *worth* listing," you contend.

"I don't know enough to make my own inventory," you say in one last attempt to avoid the job.

You may not know enough to begin making your list right this minute. But this book shows you how. In the following chapters I have divided personal property into four major categories. Within each category I guide you step by step to learn about what you have and how to evaluate it. I identify makers' marks on silver and china, bric-a-brac, and accessories. I tell you what details to look for on furniture to help determine the age and quality of your pieces. And I warn you about fakes and copies in the marketplace today. I provide value charts to help you establish the worth of your property. And I help you know when you need to call in an expert.

Familiarity Breeds Neglect—Another Type of Pitfall

Many of my clients undervalue the pieces they live with. Often this starts when a friend, interior decorator, or relative criticizes a piece. "I never have liked Victorian chairs," your decorator says, and that charming carved side chair instantly becomes a giveaway. Sometimes undervaluing is the result of the previous origin of a piece.

My neighbor was debating about which of her things she should take to an art museum's appraisal day. Christie's had sent five experts to our museum to identify and appraise antiques, and she was going to be one of the first in line.

"Why don't you take this picture frame?" I asked. (I had not appraised her pieces, but the beautiful malachite Art Deco frame was undoubtedly valuable.)

"Oh, not that," she exclaimed. "Aunt Martha kept that in her back room, and I only have it in the living room because it's the right size and color. It's no good."

"But have you ever really examined it? Is it marked? May I look at it?" I asked.

(You have to be very diplomatic when you're an appraiser and you're in a friend's home. If you say a piece is wonderful, you're buttering her up—trying to get a job. If a piece is not good, and you say so, you're running the risk of losing a friend. This time I felt I was safe. Christie's, not Emyl, was going to put a final value on the frame.)

Turning the piece over, I saw exactly what I had anticipated: "Tiffany Studios/New York." It was indeed very valuable.

The lesson to be learned from this experience is, never overlook anything. In making your inventory, pick up every item. Look for every mark. You may

Do you know the value of the pieces still stored away in your grandmother's attic? Unless you are following the marketplace, you may not realize that even mass-produced decorations like Maxfield Parrish prints have substantial value. This "Garden of Allah" print sold for $165 in a recent New York State auction. Photograph courtesy Savoia and Fromm

be surprised at what you find. Later you will learn what to look for and where, but now, as you formulate *how* you're going to work, plan to give every item some consideration.

The Price Pitfall

Don't undervalue the property around you by thinking it is worth only what you paid for it. I remember one woman who kept telling me how much everything was worth. Her value was the exact penny she had paid for everything, whether she'd bought it last year or thirty years ago. Resist the temptation to dismiss a chair as "no good" because you only paid $25 for it twenty-five years ago. Use the value charts I provide, and you will see how rapidly your values mount up.

Undervaluing your possessions is cheating yourself.

The Other End of the Price Pitfall—When You Overvalue

Sometimes you can overvalue. I've found those who do this usually err by not identifying an object properly, thereby thinking it something other than what it is, or by listening to others toss values around rather than finding out what things are really worth—both pitfalls I'll show you how to avoid. And most common of all is the error of believing family legends that inflate true value. Keep your wits about you and remember *you're* the detective now.

11

How to Make a Photographic Inventory

I am often asked, "Can't I just take some snapshots of my property?" Or, "Should I call in professional photographers and have them photograph my pieces?"

Certainly photographs and videotapes are much better than no record at all, and if this is what you wish to do, I encourage you. In fact, this chapter is designed to help you make a photographic inventory so complete and thorough that it will be accepted by your insurance company and may even be admissible in court should you ever have to document the quality and condition of your personal property! I assure you that, if you follow the instructions I provide on how to photograph your treasures—either with a conventional camera or a camcorder video camera—you may have a more accurate documentation of your property than many professional photographers will make. You see, they know about their photographic equipment, but they don't know about the objects they are photographing!

But the ultimate drawback of having only a pictorial record of your property is that you will not have a concept of the monetary worth of your possessions.

Photographs alone will not help you know how much insurance coverage you need. It is important to realize this, especially if you consider the fact that most states now impose a $1,000 limitation on silver that has not been listed and evaluated for your insurance. However, with good pictorial records you will have documentation that the property existed in case it is damaged or destroyed, and such proof is important in itself.

To understand the handicap of working from a photograph without any other written information, compare a photograph of an eight-inch sterling silver Revere bowl that retails for $1,200 with a silver-plated one that costs $45. Compare a photograph of a good reproduction sideboard valued at $5,000 with an almost identical eighteenth-century American piece worth $25,000. In photographs they may seem identical. In fact, you probably cannot determine from looking at the first set of photographs whether the bowls are sterling silver, silver-plated, stainless steel, or pewter.

An appraisal or even inventory that is carefully or professionally prepared tells you which is sterling, which plated, which antique, which a reproduction, and what the value of each is. Often a written professional appraisal costs no

Sterling silver? Silver plate? Neither. This candy dish or compote is stainless steel. But you'd never be able to tell it from a photograph.
Photograph courtesy Reed and Barton

more than a professional photographer's inventory. A quick check shows that the average price of a photographic inventory of a seven-room house could be between $300 and $600. This same collection could be professionally appraised for $600 to $1,200. (Appraisers' fees are discussed in chapter 28.) In fact, many businesses that were begun specifically to make professional photographic or video inventories have been unsuccessful.

But if you have the necessary equipment, *you* can and should make your own photographic inventory. To help you do so, here is a list of procedures to follow. These suggestions are meant for a still camera, but they apply to videotaping as well (though additional suggestions for video cameras follow).

1. Begin by making four corner shots in each room. Stand in one corner and photograph the corner diagonally opposite. Proceed until all four parts of the room are photographed.
2. Open all closets and cabinets and take interior photographs.
3. Include individual interior shots of cupboards and cabinets where silver, china, crystal, and so on are stored.
4. Photograph collections such as coins, dolls, and the like, both as a group and individually.
5. Photograph all items of antique value individually.

Using the "four corner" technique will help you get clear photographs of the entire room. Photograph courtesy Kindel

6. Take a close-up picture of your silver, china, and crystal patterns, featuring one of each type of item—for example, one dinner plate, one salad plate, one bread and butter plate, and one cup and saucer could be photographed together in a single frame. Then take a picture of the entire pattern assembled together.

7. Do not forget chandeliers and rugs. Make sure these show up in your four corner pictures.

8. When photographing individual pieces—a vase or figurine, for example—place a ruler in the front left corner to give dimensional proportion.

9. Include pictures of attics, basements, storage rooms, and lawn, porch, and patio furniture, as well as tools, appliances, and home entertainment equipment.

Most people have adequate photographic equipment to be able to take good, if not truly professional quality, photographs of their most valued personal property. Note how the owner used a ruler to establish relative size and then took the time to get the important identifying mark on the bottom of this Arts and Crafts covered serving dish. Because this is a fairly rare piece when found in sterling silver, wouldn't you think it was copper, brass, or stainless steel without evidence otherwise? Photograph courtesy Tom Norris

Basic Equipment

A simple Instamatic-type camera with flashbulb attachment can furnish you with adequate pictures for a household inventory to supplement a written appraisal or as a simple accounting of what you own, and of course it is best to use color film. However, this type of simple camera can only close-focus at about 3½ to 4 feet, so you may not get the desired detail on individual pieces.

If you have a Polaroid SX-70–type camera, you can get up to a ten-inch focus, which will give much clearer detail. The best pictures (without spending hundreds of dollars on lenses and equipment) are taken with a normal SLR (single lens reflex) 35-mm camera using slide film. These cameras can generally focus up to eighteen inches, and once you have the slide you can enlarge it on a screen for closer detail if necessary.

Ultimately, the best record of your personal property is one that supplements a written evaluation with photographs or tapes. Although pictures alone may not be sufficient, they are better than nothing. Just be sure to have two sets or extra tapes made and refer back to chapter 6 about where to keep your photographic record.

The New Technology—Camcorders

Many hand-held camcorder video cameras have a macro lens that enables you to get extreme close-ups. And there is the added advantage of being able to "talk" a family history (although you may want to emphasize that these stories are family legend after reading chapter 3). But with accurate information, you can *make* family history for future generations by relating how and when you purchased pieces while making the video. Michael Rulison, who has made videos of households and objects for me, offers the following suggestions:

1. Make video shots in a standard sequence in each room. Start a general shot at a doorway and go in one direction around the room. Stop at a corner and reposition the camera as needed. Continue until you reach the starting doorway and overlap the starting shot a little. (This proves completeness.) Circumstances may require both a low and a high pan along some walls to encompass the furniture as well as decorations on the wall.

2. Then begin again at the starting point and video individual pieces—tables, chairs, desks, and so on—in appropriate detail: the greater the presumed value, age, whatever, the more detail, including leg turnings, stretchers, upholstery fabric, makers' marks or labels, and repairs, restorations, and blemishes (use macro setting if need be).

3. Then video china, silver, and decorative items that are on the wall, on tables, chests, and mantels, or displayed in corner cupboards, vitrines, and the like. Do these one by one. Fill the video screen fairly fully with each item. Stop the camera and reposition items to show makers' names or marks on the bottoms. Make close-ups; you will be pleased with the detail your camera can capture, not only of marks, but of wood grains and other textures.

4. For sets of china, silver, or glassware, arrange a place setting or display showing one of each item, then video that display and show the maker's mark for one item. Narrate onto the tape the number of complete sets in the collection and the number of extras included in the group.

5. A few hints on lighting. Though extra light may help, even when your camera tells you the light is insufficient you may still get an acceptable picture. However, it is better to have plenty of light. Beware sunlight from windows. It can be so bright that anything close by, but not in the sun, may be underlighted. And avoid backlighting from windows or large bulbs. The side of the object facing the camera may be severely underlighted even though the camera does not register low light.

With the good-quality photographic equipment almost everyone owns or has access to today, there really isn't any excuse for not having photographs of your personal property. Believe me when I say that the time it takes now will be some of the most valuable you've ever spent if you *should* need those photographs in the future.

12

Beginning the Inventory, or the Emyl Method

The Right Tools

To make your inventory you will need (1) paper and pen (tape recorder or cassette), (2) tape measure or yardstick (a ruler will be too short in many instances), (3) magnifying glass, (4) flashlight—as strong as possible, and (5) optional equipment—scales, a black light, and calipers.

The most obvious way to make your inventory is to list and describe each piece in a notebook. However, if you own or have access to a tape recorder, you may wish to consider taping your account of your property. Certainly this is the quickest way to make your inventory, and once you have the tapes you can either put them away for safekeeping or have them transcribed. You learned in chapter 6 where to keep your records (inventory, appraisal, photos) and why.

For years I have used a tape recorder in my appraisal work and find that it saves me hours on each job. Not only can you talk faster than you can write, but your descriptions will tend to be better when you do not suffer from writer's cramp and can avoid your own poor spelling. After I finish each job, my secretary transcribes the tapes into permanent typed form for my clients. I suggest that you, too, may want to have a written list to refer to at some time. Thus it may be worth the time (if you do it yourself) or expense (if you hire someone) to transcribe the tapes.

In my work I use a microcassette recorder, which is small, lightweight, and reliable. Since I move around so much and like to have my hands free to handle the objects I am appraising, I simply attach a lariat to the hook at the side of the machine and slip the recorder around my neck, much like a microphone, thus giving me maximum freedom of movement.

In order to make distinctions between pieces, especially those that are similar to one another, you will need a tape measure or yardstick for making measurements.

Because marks can be hard to see if they are rubbed, faint, or small, you will also need a strong flashlight and a magnifying glass. (Incidentally, if your silver hasn't been polished for years and you need to see the marks on it, you might invest in some silver polish, but remember—don't get carried away and polish the whole piece now. Save that for later.) You will also need the flashlight and magnifying glass when looking under pieces of furniture you do not wish to move.

Optional Equipment

Scales

If you plan to do a thorough job of analyzing your silver, you will need an accurate scale. Postal scales, baby scales, bathroom scales, even fish scales have been used to weigh silver. The professional appraiser uses troy ounce scales, the official measurement for silver when it is warranted. Troy ounce scales are available from chemical and jewelry supply houses. But if you wish to make a conversion yourself, multiply each regular ounce by .9114583 on your hand-held calculator.

Black Light

Another tool the professional appraiser often uses in his work is an ultraviolet or black light. Several models of portable black lights are available, but you may not wish to invest in this equipment for a one-time use. However, if you are interested in porcelain or paintings as investments, you will find a black light essential. You can make your own black light for the cost of a black light bulb, available at hardware stores and novelty shops. Just screw the bulb temporarily into any lamp fixture that it will fit. But be warned that black light can be dangerous to your eyes. Read directions carefully, and as with all lights, don't look directly at the bulb itself.

Black lights are used to find damage and identify fakes: to analyze glass, find damage in porcelain, discern repairs to furniture and sculpture, and reveal overpainting of pictures. To use a black light properly, the room must be thoroughly darkened. A closet is best. The black light, which is actually violet or purple, then "sees" through the surface, revealing cracks, changes in texture, glue, blotches of paint, and other irregularities that the naked eye would miss. When there is an irregularity, the change or composition shows up "black" or "purple."

The black light is most useful for your purposes in examining china. Mended sections, cracks, and, even more important, erasures or additions of factory marks show up under this light. If you examine the bottom of any porcelain piece with a black light and see an area that fluoresces a different color, you can be sure that either a mark has been removed and the bottom glazed over to hide the erasure or that the mark has been added to the surface.

Just such a bogus piece of china surfaced in 1981. A call came from a local TV reporter.

"I understand you're an expert on china," he began.

"I specialize in silver and furniture," I explained, "but I know a lot about china. What's the problem?"

"An antiques dealer just getting started in the business has bought several antiques from another dealer. There's some R. S. Prussia in the group that may be fake. Will you look at it? We need someone to help the dealer get her money back if it is fake."

Since I am familiar with R. S. Prussia china, I told the reporter to come by. When he and his camera crew arrived, we unwrapped the "antiques"—some dented nineteenth-century silver plate, a couple of recent prints, and a pair of left- and right-handed mustache cups.

Somewhere in the back of my mind I remembered reading about fake mustache cups and saucers—but where?

Meanwhile, even a quick glance at the cups and saucers convinced me these were not R. S. Prussia. I didn't even need to look at the mark. (But where had I read about them? I wondered.)

"These definitely are *not* R. S. Prussia pieces," I stated.

The usual question followed. "How do you know?"

At this point I turned over one cup and saucer. R. S. Prussia was plainly visible.

"Let's compare this mark with another R. S. Prussia mark. There's *no* question this is the real R. S. Prussia mark," I insisted, taking a celery dish out of the corner cupboard.

"My husband inherited this celery dish from his grandmother's home, a South Carolina plantation," I explained. (Did I say grandmother? If a client had told me this story, I would have been *very* dubious!)

I turned over the celery dish.

"See!" I proclaimed.

"See what? It looks like the same to me," said the reporter.

I had to agree. They did look about the same.

"Let's use the black light," I suggested.

We took my light and the china and ducked into the coat closet. (There wasn't room for the camera crew.)

The light showed a distinctly different color surrounding the R. S. Prussia mark on the cup and saucer bottoms. There was no such distinction around the R. S. Prussia mark on the celery dish. (My husband's grandmother's, you recall.)

Next I began scraping at the center of the cup bottom around the spurious mark. A thin, flaky white substance began peeling off. We looked at the surface under the black light again.

My scraping revealed two changes—the same color surface as the outer part of the cup bottom showed up, and there was a faint impressed mark that appeared to be J . . .OO.

I wanted to scrape off the entire mark, but the reporter was hesitant. After all, the cups belonged to someone else, and a lot of money was invested in them—$600, in fact.

"Six hundred dollars?" I gasped. "Let's make a phone call."

I called Terry Kovel, the antiques pricing expert, and began explaining.

"Terry, there's a TV reporter here, and we're looking at a couple of R. S. Prussia mustache cups and saucers."

"With violets on them?" she asked.

"Yes."

"I'm looking at the same cups," she laughed. "Got a pair right here in front of me. We just taped a TV segment on fake R. S. Prussia."

"What is that mark showing up underneath the R. S. Prussia 'seal'—J . . . ?"

"JP 1200. We scraped the mark off to read it."

The mystery was solved. As I hung up I remembered what I had been struggling to recall.

I hurried to my library and returned with Dorothy Hammond's *Confusing Collectibles*. There was the story of the R. S. Prussia "seals," and the identical "left"- and "right"-handed mustache cups were illustrated. Interestingly, those cups had been marked "Brandenburg" and with a blue anchor, not with the bogus R. S. Prussia mark.

Eventually I probably would have remembered where I had read about the R. S. Prussia "seals," but it was the black light that provided the real evidence.

And yes, the antiques dealer got her money back.

But there's more! Almost seven years later, Janella Smyth, one of my associates, walked in, placed a newspaper in front of me, and asked, "Look familiar?"

"Mustache cups for right- and left-handers" read the caption beneath the photographs of two violet-decorated mustache cups.

Sure enough, the same dealer was *still* trying to pass off his pair of mustache cups and saucers and had them included along with other "rarities" in a feature article about his collection in a local newspaper.

Calipers

Finally, if you wish to examine furniture carefully in order to identify its age, a pair of calipers will come in handy. With the current rage for ladder-back and Windsor chairs, there are many deceptive pieces in the marketplace.

Because early furniture was most often made from green or unseasoned wood, the parts of the furniture later dried out and shrank. It is this shrinking that causes the side boards of a secretary or chest to split, drawer bottoms to split or separate, and the round turnings on chair members or bedposts to change shape slightly. The expert hopes and expects to find irregular shapes of finials, legs, and spindles.

A trained eye or sensitive hand can usually detect these irregularities once it is known what to look for. But the beginner will find calipers helpful. Take calipers bought at any hardware store and place them around the round part of the piece of furniture you wish to check. Tighten the calipers until they barely touch the wood and rotate them around the wood. (If you tighten them firmly, you can mar the wood when you turn them.) If the calipers become tight and drag, or if you see a space appearing between the instrument and the wood, then you have an irregular shape. In other words, the once round part has now shrunk and become elliptical or oval.

If, on the other hand, the calipers measure a perfectly round turning, *beware*. Modern kiln-dried wood shows very little shrinkage and remains perfectly round.

> If the piece is genuinely old, the round parts will not be perfectly round.

The Right Format

Before making your inventory, decide what form you want the list to be in. The purpose is to have a document that can:

1. Help you adequately insure your personal property by knowing what you own.
2. Serve as a record of what you owned if your personal property is stolen, damaged, or destroyed.
3. Provide sufficient descriptions to aid in the recovery of your property in the event it is stolen and later found.
4. Provide sufficient descriptions and value guides of your property so you can receive adequate compensation for your property if the need arises.

Whether you use a tape recorder or write out the descriptions of your pieces, the format will be the same. The following is a simple form I use in making appraisals.

Name, Describe, Value

First, you *name* the item you are appraising. Next, you *describe* the item. Finally, you decide whether or not you wish to declare a monetary *value* on the item.

Some of you will use this book as a guide to make a simple list or inventory of your personal property but will omit any values for the pieces. Others will go a step beyond the inventory and assign actual monetary values to the pieces. These values will be based on (1) prices already known and (2) price guides provided in the value charts.

To see how this simple format actually works, study the two examples that follow. The paper is divided into three columns. The first column is for two entries—what the object is and where it is located. You will decide how specific you wish to be about the location of each piece. The easiest way to make your inventory is to proceed in a logical, room-by-room sequence. If you follow this plan, make a room heading at the beginning of each new room or area, as I do in the first example. Often this is the only location identification needed.

You will also notice in this first example that only furniture is listed. This is because I recommend arranging your personal property in categories—furniture, silver, china, and crystal. This type of organization makes it easier for you to do the inventory in the first place and then to locate a specific item on your inventory after it is completed.

When you begin some of the other categories, such as silver or accessories, you may wish to be more specific in stating a location. Then the left-hand column may look more like the second example.

Example One

Article	Description	Appraised Value (*optional*)
FOYER Chest of drawers	Chippendale style. Four drawers. Made by the Baker Furniture Company.	$1,200
Side chair	Antique. Carved rose at the top. Needle-point seat. Victorian. Inherited from the Rogers family.	$395
Fern stand	Reproduction. Round top, long pedestal, Queen Anne feet. Mahogany.	$250
LIVING ROOM Camel-back sofa	Hickory Chair Co. Gold upholstery.	$2,000
Lounge chair	Round back, loose cushion. Green-and-gold upholstery—legs hidden by skirt.	$500
Drop-leaf table	English antique. Mahogany with inlay. One drawer with brass pull. Straight legs.	$650 in 1975 ? 1995

Example Two

Article	Description	Appraised Value (*optional*)
SILVER STORED IN DINING ROOM 12 goblets (*Mother's. Kept in corner cupboard.*)	Sterling silver. Gorham 272. Plain, with round base. No monogram.	$240 each
Silver service (*stored in sideboard*)	Sterling silver. Reed and Barton, No. 630. On raised feet with wooden handles and finials. Two pots, sugar and creamer. Tallest pot approximately 8 in. tall.	Not currently made $5,000
Silver service (*on top of sideboard*)	Silver-plated. Derby Silver Co. Monogrammed "AMB." On round base. Plain. Coffeepot, sugar, and creamer. Grandparents' wedding present. Dates from 1890s or 1900. Very good condition.	$750

This format is simple to follow. In each chapter that deals with a specific category, you will learn what information to include in the "description" column.

An alternate appraisal method is to use index cards rather than typing paper or a spiral notebook. In this case your cards will look something like this:

Sample Form

(Current date)

(Name of item)

Room here for
mark, if
present

(Description)

(Origin)

(Date of item)   (Current value)

Examples of Completed Index Cards

3-30-95

Tester Bed

Mahogany, straight canopy, with round, tapering posts. Shaped headboard
and blanket rail.

Custom-made. Cost $125 originally.

1962 $1,600

3-30-95

Girandoles (pair)

Marble square base. Brass girl and boy figures. 3 lights. Crystal prisms
with star design. Pair like this in Historical Society.

Inherited from Aunt Martha Brown in 1952.

1850s $900

Yet another alternative is to buy an inventory book. But whether you use a notebook, index cards, or tape recorder, the basic format remains the same.

Name, Describe, Value—First, name the item you are appraising. Next, describe the item. Finally, value the item if you wish.

To make the task go more quickly, make a general survey of your personal property before you begin your list. I call this taking an overview of your items. Separate your property into two categories.

1. The items you *know* about.

2. The items you *do not* know about.

If this seems oversimplified, it is not. Often people don't get their lists made because they make it hard for themselves. They begin in the middle, so to speak, starting with one piece they know nothing about. They put down something like "Big mirror hanging in the hall." Then they put down a large question mark. Next they move to an item they purchased recently. At this point they stop, sort through old bills looking for *that receipt alone*, and then go back into the room where they began making the list and move on to the next piece.

Approach the job in a systematic way. First, look over your house or apartment. Then quickly jot down each piece you have bought or for which you know the specific value. This list will include new pieces and antiques alike.

Now look over this list and determine which items can be verified by canceled checks or bills of sale. Place an asterisk beside these items so that, if you are planning to enter values on your list, you will know which bills or canceled checks you wish to look for—*all at one time.*

Now look over this list again. Next to the pieces for which you remember the purchase price or *know* the current value, write down that figure. Most people eventually throw away bills, but you may well remember almost exactly how much you paid for an item that you bought last year, ten, thirty, or even fifty years ago.

My clients constantly tell me, "I remember that we couldn't afford these dining room chairs when we bought them, but we made the sacrifice. They cost eighteen dollars each, and that was more than I was making a week teaching at that time!"

Obviously that $18 is going to be irrelevant in relationship to the present value of each chair. But to an appraiser, this original price may be a clue to quality. Further, it will be interesting to see the contrast between yesterday's and today's values. And, if the item is a recent purchase but the bill of sale is discarded, the price you paid for the piece may still be relevant.

Even if you do not plan to list specific values on your inventory, make a note of those prices you know anyway. If you ever do need to establish a *current* value for the pieces, a knowledgeable appraiser can more easily provide an *updated* comparable value if she or he knows how much the piece cost originally.

Thus, your first list may look like this:

Living room sofa	1975 purchase[*]
Pair of side tables	$500 in 1978
Mirror over mantel	$450 in 1977
Corner cupboard	Antique purchase[*]
Dining room chairs	Drexel 1965? $600?
Dining room rug	$850 1972
Flower prints	1978 purchase[*]

[*]An asterisk means to look up the bill of sale or canceled check, assuming you keep good records.

If you discover that you have included some items on the list that you really do not know about, underline them in red or cross through them: these pieces will fall into the second category.

This second category, the items you *do not* know about, will give you the most trouble. But if you think it is difficult to make the list with the pieces in front of you, just think what it would be like if they had been stolen or destroyed.

These are the items you inherited, the bric-a-brac you picked up at yard sales or were given as gifts. To inventory these "unknowns," you should do one of the following:

1. Make a basic list to establish proof of ownership of what you possess, but omit or estimate values.

2. Call a professional appraiser to determine values.

Most people fall somewhere between the two extremes of those who know everything about what they own and those who know nothing about anything. Making an inventory can be endlessly frustrating or very rewarding. Just remember to gather the right tools, take an overview of your property before you begin, and plan to consistently follow the simple formats I have shown you.

In today's computer-oriented world, you may want to transfer your inventory onto a diskette—the same way some people keep their recipes or Christmas card lists. There are commerical programs designed for inventory purposes, or you can utilize a database or spreadsheet that you already own. Just remember to store a backup copy outside your home.

13

The Language:
Knowing What to Call What You're Looking At

Just what is an antique? This elementary question is the one most debated in the antiques world today. It seems ironic that, although everyone talks eagerly about antiques, few people can agree on what an antique is. In fact, there are almost as many answers to this question as there are people giving answers.

The dictionary defines an antique as something old, not modern. But this oversimplistic definition does not tell us where "modern" stops and "old" begins. Basically, the question is, When, in numerical years, does an item become an antique? The two most widely accepted answers to this question are the legal definition and the connoisseur's definition.

An antique must have been made "prior to one hundred years before the date of entry," according to the U.S. Customs. Since antiques are of diverse national origin, this legal definition is generally accepted by the public at large. The definition is a "sliding" rule, which implies that an item made in 1889 became an antique in 1989 and that an item made in 1898 must wait until 1998 to become an antique. No consideration is given to quality, style, craftsmanship, or any intrinsic characteristic the piece might have that would make it an exception to this one-hundred-year rule.

Quality plus age are considerations to the connoisseur. Museum curators, elite dealers, students, writers, and scholars on the subject generally agree that an antique is a piece made prior to 1820, or possibly 1830 at the latest. The first part of the nineteenth century, they reason, saw the end of fine handcrafted workmanship, which is synonymous with antiques.

By the 1820s and 1830s, America and other industrially developed countries of the world had power-driven tools, which meant consumer goods could be mass-produced. In addition, the steamboat, which had been invented by Robert Fulton in 1807, became the means to transport factory-made products along America's inland waterways. The Baltimore and Ohio opened its first railroad route in 1830, and the transcontinental railroad was completed in 1869. Now factory-made products—Hitchcock chairs, silver flatware, and Sandwich pattern glass could be sent from New England via train or boat to Kentucky, Florida, Canada, or California.

Eventually the local craftsman began to fade from the scene. Once the individually crafted piece was replaced by the manufactured or mass-produced piece, the craftsman's art—hand-carved furniture, hand-beaten silver, hand-etched and blown glass—also faded away.

Now this is not to say that all craftsmanship died on March 4, 1820, April 19, 1830, or any time in between. Machine production is known to have existed in the metropolitan areas—New York and Boston, for example—in the early 1800s, and many fine craftsmen continued to create wonderful handmade pieces in the 1880s just as they still do today. However, by 1830 manufactured goods were plentiful and widely distributed.

Once the railroad was laid, commerce became profitable. Retail stores cropped up on main streets and crossroads alike. The people who could afford the new and fashionable demanded and bought the latest up-to-date *mass-produced* articles—furniture and household decorations, as well as hats, boots, and dresses. Handcrafted was often associated with "homemade."

To the connoisseur, an antique is distinguished by its handcrafted uniqueness and fine quality, made before 1820 or 1830. Thus, at least forty or fifty years separate an antique as defined by the connoisseur from an antique as defined by the law. Which definition you accept and use is your choice.

Unfortunately, however, the confusion over antiques does not stop here. To further complicate matters, there are other subheadings that must be understood if you are to know what you already own and become a more knowledgeable buyer or investor in antiques.

To see what this confusion is and how it arose, let's look at one of the most popular of all antiques, the elegant and graceful Queen Anne chair.

Queen Anne chairs became the fashion in England roughly between 1700 and 1730 and were named after the reigning monarch of the time. The Queen Anne chair is characterized by its slender vase-shaped back splat, gracefully curved cabriole leg, and dainty slipper foot. The style quickly crossed the ocean to America, where by 1720 it was taken up by American craftsmen and remained popular until the 1750s, when the Chippendale style became fashionable. (It is appropriate here to note that during the eighteenth and early nineteenth centuries styles that originated in England eventually came to America, but there was generally about a twenty-year lapse between the first appearance of the styles in the two countries.)

Between 1700 and 1750, or roughly fifty years, Queen Anne chairs were handmade by eighteenth-century craftsmen in England and America. The Queen Anne chairs made at this time are known as period Queen Anne chairs. The word "period," when used in speaking of antiques, means "made at the original time of the fashion." These chairs made between 1700 and 1750 are the true, undebatable Queen Anne chairs, which by any definition are antiques.

Now, furniture fashions have cycles, just as the length of hemlines, the width of men's ties, and the height of women's heels have cycles. It is said that clothing styles go in seven-year cycles. Fashions in furniture styles are said to go in one-hundred-year cycles. So, turn the calendar from 1750 to 1850, and you find Queen Anne chairs being made again. (Actually they were made this time in reaction to the elaborate and fussy Victorian style.) But this time there are certain changes.

To begin with, the chairs are now mass-produced with the help of power-driven tools in factories. Handmade nails are replaced by machine-cut nails. Hand-planed boards are replaced by circular-sawn boards. Nineteenth-century liberties are taken with the original eighteenth-century designs. In other words, one hundred years after the original Queen Anne chairs were made, other chairs are made in Queen Anne style, but with differences that had evolved during the one-hundred-year time lapse.

But wait—1850? If you agree with the legal definition of antique (an item over one hundred years old), these 1850 adaptations of the 1750 period Queen Anne chairs are also antiques. So are the Queen Anne–style chairs made in 1860, 1870, and 1880. To make the distinction between antique period chairs and antique adaptations, the word "style" is used. Thus Queen Anne chairs made one hundred or more years after the Queen Anne period are properly called Queen Anne–style chairs, as opposed to period Queen Anne chairs.

Now jump yet another one hundred years ahead to 1950. Queen Anne chairs are still being made. Only this time they cannot possibly be called antique. The correct term for currently manufactured pieces that are copied from older period antiques is "reproduction." Generally, a distinction between a current or recent reproduction, one made in the 1950s up to the present, and an earlier reproduction—say, one made in 1900 or even 1930—is indicated by the use of "old" before the word "reproduction."

These are the same "old reproductions" that I discussed in chapter 1, the Wallace Nutting, Margolis, and Charack pieces, to name just a few, which are also showing up in antiques shops and auction houses and are commanding very respectable prices today.

Up to this point I have not used the word "fake." Actually a fake is a piece made intentionally to deceive the public. The perfect example of a fake is the famous Brewster chair that was carefully and painstakingly created with the intent to deceive the public. This chair, which was typical of Pilgrim furniture, was proclaimed as a Massachusetts chair dating from Pilgrim times and bought by the Henry Ford Museum for $9,000. Later investigation revealed that, in reality, the chair was a fake made in 1969. There are not as many true fakes on the antiques market today (with the exception of art) as there are old reproductions and antique-style pieces (not period pieces, remember), which dealers or auctioneers misinterpret or misname "period pieces." You will learn about periods, reproductions, and fakes in the chapters that deal with the specific categories of personal property. But for now, get your vocabulary down.

Period—the term used to denote that a piece was made during the original time frame of the design.

Style—the term used to denote that a piece is in the fashion or nature of an earlier period but made at a later time.

Reproduction—the term used to denote that a piece was made in recent years but copied from an earlier design.

Fake—an item intentionally made to deceive the public into thinking it was made at an earlier time.

Collectibles

But what about pieces made in the 1890s or even 1930s that are not copies of any earlier style and are selling for thousands of dollars today? We have all read about the Tiffany magnolia floor lamp that sold for $100,000 in 1976 and $528,000 in 1984, art glass from the 1920s that is bringing thousands of dollars at auction, and the Arts and Crafts furniture from the 1905–1915 era that is breaking auction records every month. These fine works of art, which meet the connoisseur's requirement of excellent craftsmanship, still fall short of even the legal definition of an antique.

There is a catchall word that covers items made later than 1889 that are actively being bought and collected: "collectibles." Literally everything with any historical or investment interest these days is classified as a "collectible." Tiffany glass is a collectible. So is barbed wire. Mickey Mouse watches are collectibles, as are Cartier gems. All collectibles have two characteristics in common: (1) there are no more being made (except for the new fakes, and there's plenty to say about that later) and (2) people are collecting them.

But just as there are distinctions between period antiques and just antiques, so is there great distinction between the various classifications of collectibles. Usually the distinctions are based on two major factors—the quality of a piece and whether it is handcrafted or mass-produced (a Gustav Stickley chair or a Larkin oak chair).

Why, many people ask, are collectors buying objects only twenty to seventy years old, regardless of quality, when they could be buying older antique pieces? The major reasons are design and nostalgia.

Design

Design is the distinguishing characteristic of those "collectible" items from the 1890s through the 1930s. Tiffany glass, Art Deco furniture, Louis Icart prints, and Art Nouveau jewelry were all products of a distinct time in our civilization and culture. The tastes of this era were reflected in the designs of its "material culture"—from architecture to household furnishings.

It is impossible to mistake the characteristics of this time. When you see a piece of Art Nouveau jewelry—a brooch depicting a fully opened iris or lily with graceful curved petals—you know immediately that the pin was made in the 1880s to 1900s. At no other time in history was a design like that created.

Likewise, when you see an Art Deco chest of drawers you know it dates from the 1920s or 1930s. Nothing that looked like that was made in the 1860s or 1790s.

By the time the vogue for these collectibles erupted, the pieces were becoming respectably old and actually fairly hard to find. Thus, the unique design of these pieces, plus their new, respectable age, led to their appearance in the auction houses and antiques shops alongside other earlier pieces.

Nostalgia

But what about the Mickey Mouse watches and Fiesta ware, the early Barbie dolls and 1950 movie posters? These too are collectibles, and although they may not bring thousands of dollars, collectors are certainly willing to pay dearly for them. Why have they caught on?

I believe the major reason is nostalgia. In a world where permanence is becoming an obsolete word and a computer model is outdated a month after it is introduced, we yearn to hold on to the past.

The result? People are buying these collectibles. Buyers create a market. Once the market is established and a fad becomes popular, prices go up.

So whether you choose to keep, sell, or discard your collectibles or those that belonged to your mother or even your grandmother, you should know that the public's demand for these items has established a market, and these items have value.

In your home you probably have many such collectibles that you may once have overlooked but should now include in your inventory; just don't call them antiques—at least not quite yet. As a client once told me, "If the toys I played with as a child are now *antiques,* what does that make me?"

"Priceless," I replied.

14

When Age Isn't Enough

Now that you know and understand some of the terminology of personal property, let's look at one last myth that needs some clearing up.

Antique = Quality = Value

To many people, anything old—whether a period piece or collectible—simply because it is old is considered to be "quality," and quality equals value. Period pieces, old reproductions, collectibles, even this year's Christmas gifts all have value. And I can assure you that value mounts up rapidly if you lose your personal property and have to replace those items. The trouble is, there is so much talk about antiques being valuable today that people assume antiques are more costly than new items. This is not necessarily true.

Age alone does not determine either quality or the value of any piece, whether antique or new.

"Quality" is a difficult word to define because it has so many connotations. To some people, quality means "expensive." In reality quality means, quite simply, a particular characteristic. Quality can be good or bad. We speak of good qualities and bad qualities. But of course, when we speak of antiques of quality, we are speaking only of the good.

When you first look at an item you see the total object—a chair, a picture, a highboy, a fork, a spoon. Then you begin to break down the piece into its component parts—the design, the proportions, the materials used to make the piece, the finish on the piece, and so on. Actually, each individual aspect of the piece has its own quality.

Take a simple one-drawer nightstand, for example. It can be of fine design but made of poor materials. Or the finish can be excellent, but the piece can be squatty and poorly proportioned.

There are also degrees of quality within each classification of our personal property. Take, for example, a chest of drawers and a drop-leaf table. The two pieces of furniture immediately produce different mental images. Most people think of a drop-leaf table as a simple affair with four legs and two drop leaves. On the other hand, a chest of drawers suggests a much larger piece, one that is more expensive.

In reality, a fine mahogany drop-leaf table can be of superior quality to a Golden Oak chest of drawers with applied machine-cut decoration. Quality in personal property is determined primarily by materials used, artistic design, and craftsmanship. Immense variations in quality exist in each category of

Good-quality reproductions are a viable alternative when there is a scarcity of an item in great demand. Many more people want English knife boxes than were ever made in England during the eighteenth and nineteenth centuries. **Photograph courtesy Southern Heritage Reproductions**

personal property—furniture, silver, paintings, china, rugs, and so on.

There are silver-plated pieces that are more valuable than the same item made of sterling silver. A fine crafted piece of pottery can be better in quality than an inferior piece of bone china. A good machine-made rug can be of superior quality to a crude handmade Oriental rug.

You can learn to identify variations in quality by studying the two extremes, the best and the worst. You must remember that the best is the ideal and often unobtainable. The best may already be in the museum. Or it may bring hundreds of thousands of dollars at auction. In fact, the best may simply not be to your liking. Yet by studying the best, you will learn what to look for in pieces that you can afford so you can make the best purchase possible.

The classic book *Fine Points of Furniture: Early American* by Albert Sack, first published in 1950, is known as the "good, better, best" book. It remains the best source for understanding quality in American furniture. The lessons taught by Sack on distinguishing quality among American furniture pieces can be transferred to every area of the decorative arts. It is easy to find pictures of the best. Most antiques books are full of museum-quality pieces. It is not so easy to actually study the finest pieces because museums do not want their pieces handled. In fact, such items are in museums to preserve them from everyday wear and tear.

The best places to seriously study the varying quality of antiques are antiques shops and auction houses. Both places allow you to wander freely and closely examine the pieces you are interested in. But even more important, antiques shops and auction houses are learning grounds where you can ask questions. Do not be afraid to ask, "Why is this piece better than that one?" "Can you show me how this piece is constructed?" "Are there any replaced or repaired parts?" Or, the most general question of all, "Please tell me about this piece."

Don't be surprised if sometimes you receive an "I don't know" for an answer. Remember, no one can be an expert in all fields. It is not uncommon to hear antiques dealers discussing points that they have learned from their collector-customers. In fact, you should beware the glib expert who has an answer for everything.

Not long ago I was in an antiques shop where I overheard another customer ask the sales clerk about an English writing desk with a leather top and drawers that flanked the kneehole opening (the type you see in executive offices).

The desk was in perfect condition, the leather gleaming, the brasses polished, and the mahogany shining.

"About how old is this desk?" the customer asked.

"1820," was the specific reply.

"This leather certainly is in fine condition for a 160-year-old piece," the customer observed.

"Oh, that has been added recently. But it is hand-tooled English leather and appropriate to the piece," the clerk explained.

"And the wood is so beautiful. You don't expect to see a 160-year-old piece in this perfect condition."

"Oh, but you take care of pieces like this. There's no reason for it to be in other than perfect condition." (In my mind's eye I saw the weekly cleaning service in the executive's office banging the vacuum cleaner into the corners of the desk.)

The customer noted, "These look like new brasses," and started to open the drawers to further inspect the piece.

"Yes, most antiques have had their original brasses replaced. Brasses break and wear out over the years from constant use. No one considers a set of new brasses to be important as long as they are in the appropriate style." Just then the clerk was called away by another customer.

The customer looked further, then glanced up at his wife. "I wonder what his answer is going to be when I ask about the plywood drawer bottoms?"

Ask questions, but use your own common sense. And remember, the ultimate value of a piece will show a relationship to its quality. Granted, the world's finest nineteenth-century pine cottage chest will never compare with the medium-quality eighteenth-century mahogany Chippendale chest of drawers when it comes to cost. But the value of a *mediocre* cottage chest is certainly less than the value of a *fine* cottage chest. This is why potential antiques investors are always told, "Buy the finest-quality piece that you can afford." If you can't afford the eighteenth-century mahogany chest but can afford the nineteenth-century pine one, then buy the very best nineteenth-century pine chest you can find.

To learn about currently manufactured products, visit retail stores that carry a range of lines. Pick out an item like a bedroom set that is available in two price ranges—say, medium and high. Then ask the salesperson a simple but demanding question: "Why is this bedroom set more expensive than that one?"

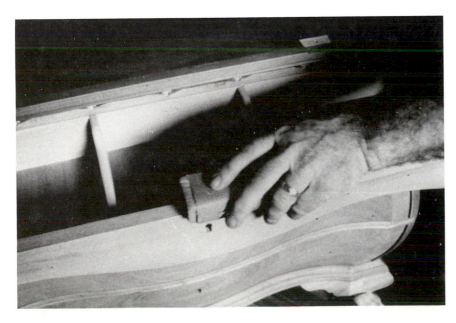

Sanding is more often done by machine than by tools these days, but where quality is a priority, attention to such details is essential. Photograph courtesy Kindel

You should then learn about the material used in its construction, the important but unseen parts (see chapter 1), and the finish the company uses. From the explanation you should learn what quality you can expect to find in currently manufactured items.

The same principles that apply to furniture apply to all decorative personal property. A knowledgeable salesperson can show you the difference in the quality of china, diamonds, rugs, lamps, and so on.

You Can Learn to Judge Quality

Judging quality is difficult for the novice who has never paid close attention to his or her personal property. But once you begin to examine a piece closely and make comparisons, you will find that you, too, can develop a sixth sense for distinguishing quality. You may begin looking without even knowing what you are looking for, but once you see the difference for the first time, an impression will be made, one you will remember. This is how experts learn.

Let me assure you that museum curators are not born knowing why Rembrandt paintings are superior to other Dutch paintings of the seventeenth century. Curators study, ask questions, and observe.

Nor did the eighteenth-century furniture maker create a superior Chippendale chair the first time he tried. He had to learn about his materials and his tools and discover how he could adapt the idea in his mind to his medium.

So you, too, by reading, asking questions, observing, touching, comparing, and making judgments both good and bad, can grow to learn the differences between poor quality and superior quality.

Condition—The Hard Facts

"This has to be valuable," I am told as I am handed a broken plate. "It's an antique, you know."

The only value a broken plate has, no matter how old it is, is its value as a study piece. If the plate was excavated at a historical site and has archaeological importance, then yes, the plate is valuable—but as an artifact, not as an antique.

The same is true of the eighteenth-century silver porringer that has been extensively mended or altered. And what good is a country rocking chair, no matter who sat on it, if the splats are broken and split, one rocker is gone, and the other is splintered? Condition is of primary importance in determining value. The more damage there is, the lower the value.

First, remember that the chances are, somewhere, there are other items just like the plate, the porringer, or the rocker, which are *not* broken, mended, or splintered. They have value.

Second, an object in bad condition is going to cost a lot to be put into repaired condition. Labor is expensive and hard to find these days. Once the broken piece is repaired, you are still going to have a repaired piece.

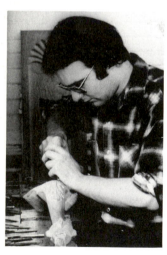

Quality is as important in the twentieth century as it was in the eighteenth and nineteenth centuries. Here master carver Carl Olson produces the acanthus decoration for the Kindel Winterthur reproduction line.

There are times, though, when you can buy a piece in "as is" condition, have it repaired at minimum cost, and end up with something worth more than your total investment. This is particularly true if you have a craft yourself and can avoid the expense of paying someone else to repair a piece. But in order to come out with a repaired or refinished piece worth more than your total investment of cash and time, you need to know (1) how much the repair is going to cost (money and time) and (2) how much it would cost to buy a comparable piece in good condition. Only if there is considerable difference between these two totals is the item in poor condition a worthwhile purchase.

If you can restore or repair the piece inexpensively for your own use, then do it. But do not think that you can restore or repair a piece and come out with an investment-quality antique.

Replacements

One question asked repeatedly is, "How much do changes affect the value of antique furniture?" To know this you must know what kind of change occurred.

Some major changes in furniture that always decrease value are:

Replacement of original headboard and/or footboard of a bed (this has often been done to enlarge the bed to double or king size or to make two beds out of one).

Replacement of chair legs (sometimes just the feet will have been replaced—either replacement is major).

Replacement of drawer fronts on chests, desks, and secretaries.

New doors hung on corner cupboards, secretaries, or linen presses (sometimes glass will have been replaced with wooden panels or vice versa).

Replacement of the original painted-glass section (eglomise) in Federal mirrors and shelf clocks.

Replacement of leaves or the entire top on tables.

Alterations

In addition to replacement parts, there are also major alterations that can greatly devalue a piece. The excessive refinishing of any piece is always damaging, as is the removal of hand-planed or handcrafted marks. It seems hard to believe that anyone would make these changes, but I have seen pieces that have been made to look "like new" by owners who did not want their friends to think they had to live with "old things."

Other alterations to beware of are the "improvements" made on pieces of furniture in an attempt to make them appear to be "better," "fancier," or "more expensive." It takes a sophisticated eye to detect many of these so-called improvements, so if you suspect a piece has been altered, you may wish to consult an expert. However, you should know that common alterations found on antiques today include:

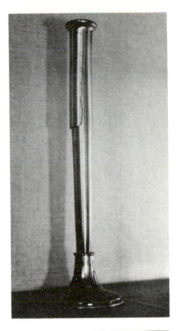

Even the highly desirable marks identifying this vase as a piece of Favrile from the Louis C. Tiffany furnaces do not make up for the fact that the piece is broken. There are many other pieces comparable to it that are not broken. Those are valuable.

During the later nineteenth and first part of the twentieth centuries, many fine eighteenth-century pieces were "enhanced" by adding a more elaborate base. This acanthus carved ogee bracket foot was added in place of a perfectly fine molded plinth base in an attempt to "dress up" a fine English breakfront. Yes, the feet do make the piece dressier and more elaborate, but they also decrease the value by several thousands of dollars. Let this serve as a warning to you before you begin "enhancing" fine-quality twentieth-century pieces you, your parents, or your grandparents purchased.

Later carving of chair backs, legs, and arms.

Adding of inlay to any case piece—desks, secretaries, chests, breakfronts, sideboards, Pembroke and dining room tables, and so on.

Reshaping of tops of tables, aprons of highboys and lowboys, cornices of secretaries, corner cupboards, pewter cupboards, and so on.

Embellishment of desk and secretary interiors.

Just remember, most legs and arms can be carved, inlay can be added to most large pieces, and top surfaces often can be reshaped.

Of course, you may find a genuinely rare antique in poor condition or one that has had old repairs that you may still wish to purchase. Perhaps in the case of the rare piece in poor condition you may simply wish to preserve it as an artifact from the past.

But more often you will come upon a good-quality item that has respectable "old" repairs. Some such pieces are still very expensive. At this point you will want to find out (1) how much the repair depreciates the value of the piece and (2) once again, what a comparable piece in pristine condition would cost.

For example, you may find a lowboy that is basically in its original condition—with the exception of having a new top. However, since the top was added seventy-five or one hundred years ago, it may now almost be an antique. What you will learn from consulting an expert or from your own research is:

1. The replaced top is considered a major repair.
2. The value of the piece with new top is $5,000–$6,000.
3. The value of a pristine piece of comparable quality, design, and age is $12,000–$18,000.

With this information, you can make a sensible judgment about your choices.

There is one final factor you should be aware of that will affect the value of your personal property—fashion. This fickle factor changes as regularly as the seasons.

We are familiar with the effect fashion has on our wardrobes as we discard last season's "fashionable" mistakes. We are even aware of the effect of fashion on our decorating habits as we change our ivory walls to magenta and replace our beige wall-to-wall carpeting with colorful geometric Oriental rugs. We realize when we discard the Spanish Provincial bedroom set for an Early American–type pencil-post bed and Windsor-style chair that fashion is expensive. But how many of us realize that antiques have distinct fashions that affect their value in the marketplace?

Years ago when I was working in an antiques shop, the single most requested item was an English sideboard. Everyone, it seemed, wanted a sideboard on which to place a silver service or Oriental bowl, flanked by silver candelabra or brass candlesticks. Naturally, when a sideboard sold, it was replaced with another sideboard, which always was more expensive than its predecessor. I watched the price of sideboards creep up slowly from

$1,500 to $2,500 to $3,500. Meanwhile, only occasionally would a lone customer come in looking for a mahogany corner cupboard. At the time they were selling for around $900 to $1,000.

Today, you can still buy an English sideboard comparable to the commonly found types that were selling between $3,000 and $3,500 for $3,500 to $4,000. But corner cupboards have become the "hot" item, and even plain ones are now selling for $3,000 to $6,000. Exceptional ones are much more expensive. Why has one remained basically the same and the other taken such a jump? Fashion. Supply and demand.

In my grandparents' and parents' active collecting days (1920s–60s), milk glass was a favorite. Yet today it is often more frequently found packed away than on display. Why? When you read the following passage by the well-known columnist Gladys Taber, you'll run straight to your attic to find your grandmother's milk glass or begin looking in antiques shops for a piece or two.

> The old corner cupboard with the H hinges was in the house when we came. The milk-glass collection began with the blackberry spooners and just kept growing. There is a memory attached to every piece, from the swan compote found under a pile of old rugs in a junk shop to the covered dish with the hand on top and a green jewel on one finger, which came from a country auction.

She goes on to write more specifically about these pieces:

> With milk glass it is hard to choose a favorite pattern. It is usually the one you are looking at. The hand-and-dove dish is one I love. This is an oblong dish with lacy edge and on the cover is a delicate hand holding a dove (I have no idea why). A jeweled ring is on one finger. On some the jewel is missing, but the green glass emerald is on mine. The blackberry spooners are the result of much hunting, as is the blackberry cream pitcher. The swan pattern is one of the most graceful, and the swan compote is especially dear to me because it slants on the base, showing some glassmaker was dreamy the day he turned the base. The swan salts are lovely with spring wildflowers in them.
>
> I believe in using a collection, and we do use the milk glass, but I am careful to wash it in warm, not hot, gentle soapsuds and dry it with a soft towel. The lacy-edged vegetable dishes are used for fruit or flowers, but not for very hot vegetables.

But wait—because Gladys Taber also tells us, though she may not realize she is doing so, *why* milk glass moved out of fashion.

> The early milk-glass makers, I am told, used a type of sand in the process which modern glass makers do not have. In any case, once you collect a few pieces, you would never confuse the authentic pieces with the modern copies, although the patterns are copied. The modern

piece is opaque with a glassy surface. The old piece has an opalescent glow and a soft sheen. Finally, if there is any doubt in my mind, I pick the piece up and feel it carefully, especially along the design and edges. I cannot analyze the difference in feeling exactly except to say that in the old there is a softness, almost a fragility. The best way for anyone who wants to collect this loveliest of glass is to take a fully authenticated piece in one hand and a modern copy in the other, and look at them and feel them.

Unfortuniately not everyone possesses the feel or eye needed to distinguish the copy from the authentic, the fake from the real, and too many copies, fakes, and reproductions confuse the unsophisticated collector. Brass beds, wicker chairs, Tiffany-style leaded-glass lamps, and pressed glass—to mention a few obvious areas—have plummeted in popularity when collectors have gotten burned. Usually the appearance of "new" copies starts a new popularity of the old, and the market for the antique begins to go up. But once the public buys a couple of fakes in an antiques shop or flea market, the market for the antiques goes soft and starts down.

And such stories as the one I related about R. S. Prussia mustache cups in chapter 12 reinforce the public's wariness of entire categories of antiques and collectibles.

When you can identify a particular item or type or period that is currently out of vogue, buy authentic pieces at low or stable prices, and hold them until they become fashionable once again, you have identified the true investment antique.

Fashions do come and go, especially as the life-style magazines present appealing looks we want to emulate. Presently turn-of-the-century romantic paintings are rising. Victorian furniture and accessories, especially linens, are finding a strong market. At the same time, in contrast with the Victorian look, the stark Arts and Crafts products of the 1905–1920 era have found an avid following.

On the other hand, luster ware is nowhere near as widely collected as it was in the first part of the twentieth century, and a number of people consider tapestries and medieval pieces to be some of the best buys around. Eighteenth-century American silver has taken a backseat to late-nineteenth- and early-twentieth-century silver, and American pewter has not moved in the last couple of years.

And some fashions that were temporarily out of vogue have made impressive, sometimes even spectacular, comebacks. Among these are fine English furniture, decorative Oriental accessories from the nineteenth century, and American folk art.

Sometimes the same objects are revived under new names. Whatever happened to "kitsch"? I was asked not too long ago. You remember "'kitsch," don't you? In the early 1980s every magazine had colorful photo-features about dimestore glass, Fiesta ware, filling station memorabilia, Mickey Mouse and other Disneyana. The articles were sprinkled with such words as "sock-'em," "fad," "camp," and even "tacky."

What's in fashion? Believe it or not, these Art Deco chairs sold in the $1,500 range at Skinner's Auction Galleries in 1985. Many collectors are now searching through tag sales and secondhand stores for the better-quality 1950s furniture.

Dimestore glass, Fiesta ware, filling station memorabilia, Disneyana, and all the other "kitsch" are still with us—but have taken on a new respectability. Entire antiques shows are devoted to "modernism," and twentieth-century culture has come into its own.

Geographic fashions also affect the value of antiques. Generally, the population of an area wants what its earliest settlers had. The older a geographic area's history, the earlier the region's taste in antiques.

For example, New England antiques lovers want eighteenth-century American pieces; Midwesterners prefer nineteenth-century or Victorian antiques.

When the buying public of an area wants early pieces (eighteenth-century Queen Anne, Chippendale, and Federal antiques), the later pieces (nineteenth-century Empire and Victorian antiques) go underpriced and unpurchased. Yet these "rejects" are highly desirable in other sections of the country.

The opposite is also true. A Texas dealer who now lives in Connecticut told

Though the quality of this Victorian table would be recognized everywhere, there is a stronger demand for Victoriana in California than there is in, say, New Hampshire. Regional tastes and preferences affect the cost and value of antiques. Photograph courtesy Weschler's Auction Gallery

me she buys her "early" antiques in Texas, where they are less expensive than in the Northeast. But, she added, she takes nineteenth-century porcelain pieces that she buys inexpensively in Connecticut to Texas.

Smart dealers capitalize on these regional fashions. Southern and midwestern dealers buy Victorian pieces in New England at low prices and transport them to Alabama, Texas, Ohio, and Wisconsin, where they sell at high prices.

At the same time, regional antiques and collectibles have their highest value in that specific region. The coin silver spoon made in Charleston, South Carolina, may be worth $300 there but will sell in Boston for $20 or $30, the price of any coin silver spoon. A log cabin quilt made and signed by a Wisconsin pioneer has much more value if sold and kept in Wisconsin than it ever would have in New York. Even a Philadelphia Chippendale chair that can find a home in Stuttgart, Tokyo, or Rio will bring a higher price when sold in the Philadelphia region.

Fashions and fads in the antiques world are usually created by a series of coinciding events. First, there is a large show or exhibit of a particular collection or category of art objects at a major museum or restoration. For example, there might be a showing of silver snuffboxes or an exhibit of Neoclassical furniture. Articles and books on the subject suddenly begin appearing. Next, magazines start running features about these objects.

As a result, the public begins to go into shops asking, "Have you any silver snuffboxes?" or "I'm looking for a Reclaimer." By now, someone who just happened to have a collection of silver snuffboxes or a house full of Neoclassical furniture decides to sell these items at auction. Record prices and headlines follow, naturally, and by now a bull market has been created.

Until the marketplace suddenly becomes saturated with either the real things (dragged out of storage) or reproductions, imitations, and sometimes fakes. At this point the fashion fades away or goes back into storage.

Until fifty or one hundred years later, when another generation rediscovers silver snuffboxes and Neoclassical furniture.

Learn to identify quality in your personal property. When you can make distinctions of quality, you will also be a wiser shopper and better investor in personal property.

Next, always observe the condition of items, either before making a purchase or before listing your property on your inventory. Mint condition in an antique raises its value. You must also know the condition of your property in order to submit a fair insurance claim if the need ever arises.

Remembering that all old things are not equally "in fashion" will serve as a clue to why some items are more valuable at times than others and why the value of antiques can fluctuate.

And age—whether a piece is truly an eighteenth-century period piece or a later, late-nineteenth-century adaptation in the earlier style of the century—is of paramount importance.

Value can be thought of as the sum total of *quality, condition, fashion,* and *age.*

15

Saving Time Begins with Getting Organized

If you follow my advice in chapter 12 and make a preliminary survey of your property, dividing it into the pieces you know about and those you do not know about, you will have taken the first big step in avoiding unnecessary frustrations and wasted time.

Next, divide your property into the following four major categories, which cover the vast majority of personal property:

- Silver
- China and crystal
- Furniture
- Accessories and bric-a-brac

You may begin your inventory with any one category and do the rest in any order. But keep to the categories.

I have chosen to begin with silver, since it is so frequently stolen today and has such a high cumulative value. If you have a lot of silver, it may also take you the longest time to inventory it.

The china and crystal category covers sets and groups of china and crystal, including serving pieces, plus pressed and cut glass. Individual decorative items fit in the accessories and bric-a-brac category.

Furniture is a large and important category, but you can cover it quickly because, unlike crystal or silver, you will not have lots of pieces to count.

Accessories and bric-a-brac are saved until the end. These pieces generally are less valuable when viewed one at a time, but the final replacement figure for these accent pieces can be staggering.

"But why can't I just start in one room and list everything in that room in all categories and then move on to the next?" I am often asked.

You can. But do you always leave everything in exactly the same spot? Even museums change the pictures around. A good inventory is best made when it divides property into major categories. If you list your property with your insurance agent, you may learn that some insurance companies have one rate for silver and another rate for furniture. If you want to insure crystal and porcelain against breakage, there is yet another rate. By organizing the categories ahead of time you will better know what kind of insurance you need.

Also, by using categories you learn how much of a particular item you have. For example, if you have your silver scattered throughout the house, from the dining room and kitchen to the bedrooms and living room, with some stored in the attic, you probably have a great deal more silver than you thought.

Movers and packers who specialize in shipping antiques always place items in categories. Crystal is packed together. Pictures are crated together. Figurines are wrapped individually and sealed in one box. This allows for better accounting at the end and for safer passage en route.

A category listing is also easier to work with when listing values. It is simpler to "stay in gear" and work in one category than to shift from the cost of a silver-plated round tray to a set of crystal liqueur glasses, to a den sofa, to your fireplace tools, back to a single German beer mug, and then on to the coffee table.

Accompanying each of the category chapters that follow are value charts to assist you. The value charts located at the end of each category are intended to be used as a gauge by which you can approximate the value of your personal property. We know that, if a manufacturer makes twenty-five lines, each line will have a different price. Once the line is in the retail store, the store owner or manager makes the final decision as to what price each piece should be sold for. If all prices were the same, there would be no reason to shop around for the good buy.

But because you have neither the time nor the resources to search out all the current prices for your personal property, I have compiled value guides to assist you in determining the estimated worth of your household furnishings. These value charts should be used with the understanding that the prices are compiled by combining several price lists of comparable quality. In no instance are the prices from one company's line used alone. The values given are replacement prices for products currently in production. In some instances additional charts are provided that are relevant to some antique and collectible items. However, because antiques values fluctuate so widely, depending on condition, alterations, quality, location, and the knowledge and whims of each individual dealer, antiques values usually are omitted. But a close reading will give you clues to the value ranges of several antiques.

If you begin amassing total values that far exceed your expectations or current insurance, you may wish to call in a professional appraiser. (Information on appraisers is found in chapter 28.) Remember that these prices are average values for general types of personal property and are not to be considered the specific value, down to the last dollar, of a particular chair, china pattern, or sterling silver water pitcher.

I have not written another antiques price guide to add to the ever-growing list, but I have included a short chapter (chapter 32) on price guides.

Part Four

WHAT IS IT
AND WHAT IS IT
WORTH?

16

Silver:
Sterling and Silver Plate—All That Glitters Is Not Gold

Because retail silver prices fluctuate with the cost of silver bullion, prices quoted today may change tomorrow. But because silver is a precious metal, it will always hold its relative value, even though its cash value will vary, depending on world economic conditions. However, bullion value bears no relation to the value of true antique silver. There is no relationship between the value of an eighteenth-century cake basket worth $50,000 and the value of one troy ounce of silver mined yesterday.

When Cartier Was Upstaged by a Little Teapot

Two basic types of silver are found in most homes, sterling and silver plate. Both are valuable, and a few silver objects can easily mount into thousands of dollars if it becomes necessary to replace them. If you don't know about your silver, you may let a wonderful treasure slip through your fingers or even out the door and never know the difference. This almost happened to a client of mine a few years ago.

I was busily at work in her dining room, examining the silver, while she gathered up other silver pieces from around the house and brought them to me.

Suddenly she appeared at the dining room door and in a trembling voice exclaimed, "The cigarette box and teapot are gone!"

This has happened to me so often that my reaction is always the same. "No, you just don't remember where you've put them."

"Not this time," she insisted. "They were right there two days ago because I polished them. I didn't want you to see what a terrible housekeeper I am!"

None of my assurances convinced her that her pieces might be around. It seemed she was also having some remodeling done.

"Any one of the workmen could have picked them up," she insisted.

"Well, if they're gone, let's get a good description of them so you can call the insurance company," I said.

"The little teapot didn't amount to much. Oh, it had sentimental value. My grandmother gave it to me, but I know you can't put a price on sentiment. It's just silver plate, probably—all I can do is tell you what it looked like.

"But," she continued, "the cigarette box is quite valuable. It came from Cartier and had all our groomsmen's signatures on it. My husband is going to die!"

"Go ahead and call your insurance company. Tell them what's missing. But tell them you want to wait a couple of weeks before turning in a value, just to give the silver time to show up," I advised.

Sure enough, only a few days later they appeared—in her two-year-old's toy box, of all places—both filled with Lego blocks and coated with Play-Doh.

The cigarette box was exactly what she had said—a current Cartier piece costing, at that time, about $250.

And the little teapot—that little silver-plated gift from Grandmother— was a sterling Queen Anne pot, made in 1697 in London and the earliest piece of hollowware I have ever seen in a private home, with a value exceeding $5,000 at that time.

What You Need to Know About Silver

The following sections explain the marks found on silver so you can correctly identify your silver on your inventory.

American Sterling

"Sterling" is the most frequently found mark on American sterling silver, but you may also find the notations "925," "925/1000," and "Sterling. Weighted" on pure silver pieces.

Sterling silver pieces are made of 925/1000 parts pure silver combined with 75/1000 parts of other metal, usually copper, added to make the silver durable and pliable. "Sterling. Weighted" means that the piece itself is sterling silver and that a dark, powdery, leadlike substance has been inserted into the base to provide additional balance and weight to the piece. Almost any piece that is only marked "sterling" will be more valuable than a comparable one marked "Sterling. Weighted." By about 1860 sterling silver became the American standard used in "solid" silver (as opposed to silver-plated) items, and the marks "Sterling," "Sterling. Weighted," and the numbers "925" or "925/1000" make this silver easily detectable.

Rule of thumb: American silver marked "Sterling" will not predate 1850 and usually dates after 1860.

American Coin Silver

Before 1850–1860, "solid" silver pieces only contained 900/1000 parts of pure silver, with 100/1000 parts of other metals. This silver was known as coin silver and was often marked "coin," "pure coin," "standard," "premium," or "dollar." Sometimes the letters "C" or "D" were used. Just as often, coin silver was marked with only the maker's name, and sometimes there was no mark at all.

American coin silver often dates from early Colonial days. Seventeenth- and eighteenth-century coin silver was usually marked in one of the following ways:

Initials

Last name

Initial/initials and last name

Later in the nineteenth century, American coin silver was usually marked in one of the above manners or with a complete company name and sometimes even a location.

Another common practice was to mark coin silver with "pseudohallmarks." These marks implied that American silver was as fine as English silver, which was clearly hallmarked. These pseudohallmarks—usually a profile, animal, or star—should not be confused with English hallmarks (English marks are discussed later in this chapter). Pseudohallmarks might look something like the following:

Because coin silver is not always clearly marked so but may be
- unmarked
- marked C, D, standard, premium, or dollar
- marked only with initials or with a name
- marked with pseudohallmarks

it is often overlooked and even discarded as plated silver.

On the other hand, if a piece of silver is not marked, rather than concluding it is coin silver, look at the place on the surface where the greatest wear occurs. For example, on the back of a spoon, the curve of the bowl will receive wear both from dining use and where the spoon rests on the table. If you see a different color showing through the silver surface—usually golden or brass looking— you will know the piece is silver plate, not pure coin silver.

I have picked coin silver spoons out of discarded shoeboxes filled with kitchen throwaways. In fact, there are times when I almost have to force my clients to show me a piece I *know* is coin silver but which they think is silver-plated.

This is a typical example of how coin silver makers marked their pieces in the first half of the nineteenth century. By looking up the last name, Stedman, in Kovels' American Silver Marks, you can quickly identify J. C. Stedman's location and date.

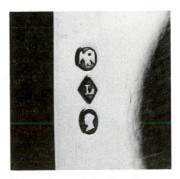

Typical pseudohallmarks found on American coin silver.

The style of the maker's name—his initials and last name punched horizontally—helps you identify the other marks as pseudohallmarks rather than true English hallmarks.
Photographs courtesy North Carolina Division of Archives and History

Every day nineteenth-century coin silver teaspoons comparable to this one are discarded because they are not marked "Sterling." Though the spoon may not be terribly valuable (usually around $15–$30), it does represent a small piece of American history, and its value will undoubtedly increase in future years.

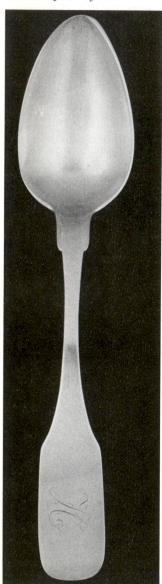

One day I was working through the stacks of sterling silver on my client's dining room table when I spied a coin silver baby cup at the end of the table. The temptation was to jump ahead and look at the cup then, but I decided to save the best until last.

Just as I was coming to the cup, the owner walked into the room.

"Don't bother with that," she said, "it's only plated. I didn't even mean for it to be out here."

I insisted that I had to see the cup. Only when I told her I thought it was very valuable would she let me examine it.

And indeed it was. The cup was silver, made by an important regional silversmith in the 1840s, and is now housed in a museum for others to see and learn from and insured for over $3,000. But because the cup was not marked "Sterling," the owner thought it was nothing. The truth is, if the cup *had* been marked "Sterling," it would have had only one-tenth the value.

Marks and Where to Find Them

Most American silver, both sterling and coin, will be marked on the reverse side, underneath, or bottom.

On *flatware* (knives, forks, and so on) the marks are most frequently found where the handle begins on forks, spoons, and serving pieces. On knives the marks may be very small and can appear either lengthwise along the beginning of the handle (near the blade) or horizontally around the beginning of the handle.

On *hollowware* (bowls, trays, goblets, and the like) the marks most frequently appear in the middle or along the rim or border of the piece. The marks can be very small, so look carefully. If you do not see any marks on the bottom, look around the base of the piece, particularly on candlesticks, or rims of coasters, ashtrays, or any piece that is a combination of silver and glass or china.

Distinguishing Quality in Sterling Silver

Remember my statement that there is no relationship between the value of an eighteenth-century cake basket worth $50,000 and the value of one troy ounce of silver mined today? Even though a piece of sterling or coin silver can be melted down for the pure silver, the value *above and beyond* the bullion content of any piece of sterling silver is based on its *quality,* whether the piece is English, American, Continental, or South American.

Craftsmanship and design are the two most obvious traits of quality, though of course the present condition of a piece also influences value. Do not confuse your own personal taste with design. If your preference is for elaborate silver, chased and repoussé, for example, you will want to distinguish between the well-executed and the poorly or not-so-expertly executed, repoussé piece.

Crudely produced handcrafted silver will have an "unfinished" appearance, whereas carefully crafted pieces will be distinguished by crisp lines and

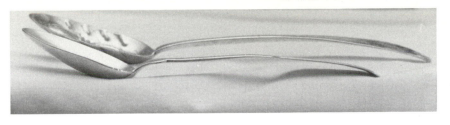

Notice the difference between the thickness or width at the top (near the bowls) and middle of the handles of these two spoons. This is referred to as "gauge" and is often a mark of quality. Better pieces are generally though not always made from a thicker piece of silver.

angles, well-balanced designs, and fine detail. Poor design is usually obvious when you look at a piece and observe that the motif is too large or fussy for the size of the object or that the piece is unbalanced or out of proportion. Learning the telltale signs of craftsmanship is part of connoisseurship and results from many years' study and firsthand examination. But its rewards are substantial, as you are able to make distinctions the usual layperson cannot.

Even manufactured pieces vary in craftsmanship and design. Look for clear, precise designs and good detail, even on new pieces. Designs are often stamped onto the silver, and if this technique is not well executed, you will notice obvious differences in the depth and clarity of the design.

The most common error in assessing silver is judging a piece by its weight. How often have you heard someone say, "This must be a fine piece. Feel how heavy it is!" In reality, the weight of a piece of silver is determined by its gauge or thickness—not, as I commonly hear, by how much silver is in the piece. If you take a thick piece of silver, one-half inch, and a thin piece of silver, one-sixteenth inch, both have 925/1000 parts silver in them. But the thicker piece, just like a thicker board of lumber, will be bigger and therefore heavier than the smaller piece. Exquisite chasing or a lovely design can be executed on a thin piece of silver as well as on a thick piece, so do not let the weight of a piece be your only basis of judgment. True, it is unusual to find superior craftsmanship in a flimsy piece of silver, but be aware that weight alone is not the criterion of craftsmanship or quality.

English Sterling

English sterling silver is collected by antiques connoisseurs. Fine English silver epitomizes the silversmith's art. It is displayed in museums and is the topic of one-hundred-dollar scholarly books and the subject of full-page color advertisements in expensive magazines. Sotheby's, Christie's, and other auction houses devote entire auctions to English silver—sometimes issuing hardbound catalogs for the sales. But beware. Unless you can correctly read English hallmarks, you can let a wonderful piece of silver slip by unknowingly. Or you can be taken when you buy a piece that you are told is English silver, only to find it is not.

Once a young wife whose in-laws had sent her boxes of silver, china, and linen asked me to go through her attic and tell her "what was what."

Silver, china, and linen were *not* what this couple wanted. They were a young family with a toddler and another baby on the way. If anything, they wanted fewer possessions.

"I think I'll just give most of this to the Medical Wives' Bargain Box," she explained. "But if they're going to throw it all away, I don't want to waste their time messing with it."

When I opened the first box I was literally dumbstruck. Here were beautiful Georgian silver pieces that she was going to *give away*.

"Have you ever heard of Hester Bateman?" I asked as I lovingly fondled a 1783 Hester Bateman cake basket.

She hadn't, of course.

Right there in the middle of a dusty, drafty attic I embarked on one of my silver lectures, until I realized she really didn't want to know who Hester Bateman was.

"Look," I explained, "the girls at the Bargain Box are just as likely not to know who Hester Bateman was as you. But these are wonderful pieces that a collector would cherish forever. Let me find these pieces a home where they will be loved for what they are—not resented because they have to be polished and stored and insured."

The young wife agreed, and within a few days I had found buyers for these pieces, and the couple was considerably better off financially. This is an example of almost losing money because of not knowing how to read English silver marks.

But just as often—perhaps even more often—silver-plated pieces are passed off as English silver because they have "hallmarks" on them. This happens so frequently that later I have a section that shows some of these often misinterpreted marks. But for now, let's see what English hallmarks really do look like.

Identifying English silver is simple once you know how and have a reference book close at hand. But if you've never been told how to read these hallmarks, you'll be fooled every time.

English silver is marked with four and sometimes five important symbols.

1. Lion. Look for a full lion, facing left. The lion denotes the piece is sterling.

2. A letter. A letter contained in a shield or cartouche can be matched to the key provided in English silver marks books. Because the same letters are used over and over, the type of print used and the enclosing shield change with each alphabet cycle. Since different cities use different letters in different shapes, it is important to identify the city first so that you can learn the year by matching the letter. The illustration at left shows how one letter changes to distinguish various years.

3. The maker's mark, usually his initials. The value of English silver is greatly affected by who made it. The best known of the English silversmiths are Hester Bateman, Paul Storr, Paul de Lamerie, and Matthew Boulton. As you might expect, these makers' marks have been forged many times, and spurious pieces of their silver exist in the marketplace.

1721　　F

1741　　f

1761　　f

1781　　f

1801　　F

1821　　f

4. One of several marks known as "guild" marks. These tell the town where the silver was made. Those most frequently seen are

a. leopard's head / London (crowned or uncrowned)   **c.** crown / Sheffield

d. castle / Edinburgh

b. anchor / Birmingham   **e.** harp / Dublin

For other towns' hallmarks, see the English silver books listed in Chapter 35.

5. A sovereign or monarch's head may or may not appear.

Thus a full complement of hallmarks for a piece made in London in 1820–1821 by Paul Storr would look like the photograph at right.

A full complement of English hallmarks, including the lion, crowned leopard's head, monarch's head, date year, and maker's mark. By matching these with the table for English hallmarks, you can identify the year, origin, and maker's name. Photograph by Jon Zachary

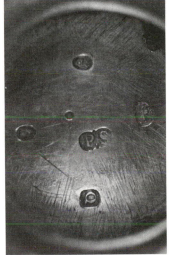

Warning! English hallmarks have been faked and forged over the years. Silver thought to be English sterling may be a cheap imitation silver plate.

English silver hallmarks, unlike American manufacturers' marks, which appear on the bottom or underneath surface of the silver piece, can appear anyplace on the silver. Look on the body, around the rims and edges and handles, as well as on the bottom. Pieces that have separate parts—for example, a basket and handle or teapot and lid—should have corresponding marks on all the different parts.

Each individual part of this fine Regency tea urn by Paul Storr—the body, cover, center warming iron (where hot coals were placed), and its small cover—are clearly hallmarked. If any one piece were a later replacement, the value of the piece would be decreased. Photograph by Jon Zachary

Those familiar with American marks will immediately recognize the lion, "G," and anchor as early Gorham marks. Also, the presence of the word "coin" confirms the American nineteenth-century origin of this piece. Yet it was listed on an inventory as "English sterling." To tell the difference, compare these marks with the English hallmarks also shown here. Photograph courtesy North Carolina Division of Archives and History

Confusing Marks

Just as American coin silver pseudomarks sometimes mislead the public, so some American marks used on silver-plated pieces that closely copy English hallmarks are equally confusing. Even some American *sterling* marks are confused with English marks.

One American sterling company whose marks are often mistaken for English marks is Gorham. The Gorham sterling mark consists of a lion (remember, the lion in English silver means sterling), a G (the letter is used to denote a year), and an anchor (Birmingham's mark). Though none of these marks as used by Gorham closely resembles the English marks, I have seen many Gorham pieces listed as "English silver, fully hallmarked."

American Manufacturer Marks
Commonly Misinterpreted As English Hallmarks

Barbour Silver Company

Sheffield Silver Company

Crescent Silverware
Manufacturing Company

Watson Company

Gorham Corporation

The Watson & Briggs Company

Reed & Barton

E. G. Webster & Son

A final word: English silver remains of high quality in the 1980s. New York's most famous silver store, Tiffany, carries English silver today, as it has since the nineteenth century.

English hallmarks are not at all difficult once you have seen good, clear examples and especially if you have the opportunity to see the real next to marks imitating the English hallmarks. Most likely you will not be able to remember exactly what letter in what outline represents which year. But books, especially the small, pocket-size hallmark paperback booklets, are designed to be carried "in the field" by collectors and dealers. These are often available in museum bookshops, specialty bookstores, and even in some antiques shops and jewelry stores. If all else fails, Bradbury's *Book of Hallmarks* is available through Seven Hills Books, 519 West Third Street, Cincinnati, Ohio 45202.

The following short story illustrates how people mistakenly believe knowing English hallmarks is an "elitist" ability. A few years ago my then fifteen-year-old daughter, Joslin, and I were antiquing in the English flea markets. She was still grumbling about being half-asleep (it was about six A.M.) when she saw a pair of small silver tongs among mostly junk (yes, they have junk in England, too). Reaching down and picking them up, she asked the owner how much.

"They're a pound, love, they're not very old," he replied.

"No, but they're well marked. I'll take them," she answered, giving him the pound note.

The dealer turned to his companion and said in mild disbelief, "She knew they were hallmarked, and she's an American!"

Believe me, she is *not* an antiques fanatic. If she can learn to read hallmarks and get the good buys, so can you.

European or Continental Silver

Yet another type of "solid" (not silver-plated) silver is the kind made in Europe known as Continental silver. Just as each guild in England had its own distinct mark, so did all the silver centers of Europe, from Russia to Italy, from Spain to Switzerland. As you can imagine, there are thousands of Continental hallmarks.

Volumes have been written on Continental silver, and much of this silver has journeyed across the ocean to America. However, identifying the individual country of European silver is often difficult, and even experts sometimes do not know.

For your general information, the marks I most commonly find on Continental silver in homes in my daily appraisal work are as follows:

1. An ornate capital letter with a crown or fleur-de-lis at the top / France

2. A half-moon or crescent and a crown, accompanied by the number 800 / Germany

3. A castle or shaped center design encircled by numbers Eastern European countries

4. A Roman or classical profile accompanied by other hallmarks / Italy

Continental silver can almost always be identified by its distinctive style. Look for the same motifs associated with European furniture— garlands or swags, wreaths, bow knots, and so on. However, identifying the specific maker, guild, or even country of Continental silver is much more difficult than it is for English silver. Photograph courtesy Weschler's Auction Gallery

Continental silver is also often marked with numbers. For example, "12" or "13" are German marks denoting the silver content.

Generally speaking, the silver content in European silver is 800/1000, or slightly lower than the 925/1000 content of English and American sterling. However, the value of Continental silver lies in its age, quality, and design, and it is not considered inferior because of its lower silver content. Only when silver is melted down does the raw silver content affect its value.

Like English silver, Continental silver can be marked almost anywhere. In very ornate pieces with figures, you may find the marks more easily by looking on the reverse side, where the outline of the mark may be more obvious. Sometimes the marks are hard to distinguish from the decoration on the ornate front side.

South American Silver

Finally, much Mexican and South American sterling is found in American homes today. This silver is usually immediately distinguishable because of its hand-hammered finish and distinct Latin American design. The silver is commonly marked "925," often accompanied by the word "sterling," with the maker's name and country of origin.

At one time, Latin and South American silver was considered vastly inferior to American silver, and indeed there is a great variety in the quality. Some is crude, poorly designed, and badly finished. Other pieces are refined and have a rich patina. Almost all of the silver is heavy in weight, as silver in these countries is plentiful and at one time was even cheap. Before sterling silver became so expensive, South American silver was valued only at its scrap, or meltdown, value. Today, with so much silver having been melted down in the early 1980s when the price for raw bullion skyrocketed to fifty dollars an ounce, and with the drastic cutback in sterling silver production by American manufacturers, South American silver is being reappraised. Most appraisers are now using comparable American prices for South American silver when insuring it for their clients.

South American and Mexican silver, once casually dismissed by many collectors, is finding a new market as the craft and design attract more attention. Photograph courtesy Richard A. Bourne Company

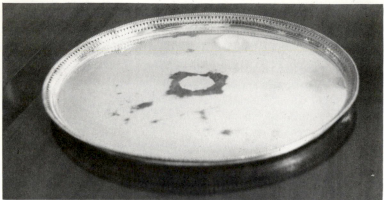
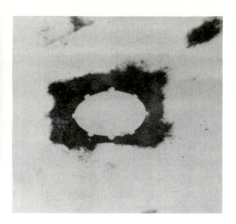

During the eighteenth century and first part of the nineteenth century, a piece of sterling silver would be "inlaid" into fine silver or copper pieces that were intended to be engraved with a monogram or coat of arms. Thus when the engraving was cut into the sterling silver, there would be no copper to show through. The layer of pure silver around the sterling silver inlay has worn away on this tray to clearly show how the sterling silver plaque was inlaid into the copper. These sterling silver plaques are most frequently found on trays and turkey or meat domes. Even if no copper shows through, the inlay can be detected by blowing onto the monogram or coat of arms. A faint outline will appear through the vapor left by your warm breath if a sterling silver plaque is present.

Silver Plate

Silver plating is the process whereby a thin layer of pure silver is placed over a base of another metal—sometimes copper, but more often a white metal. The oldest silver plate is known as Sheffield, named, of course, for the city in England where it originated in the eighteenth century. Sheffield silver was produced by a process in which a layer of silver was hand-rolled onto a base metal and the edges sealed. This process was generally replaced by electroplating in the nineteenth century. Unfortunately the name Sheffield has turned into a generic term and is commonly given to any and all silver-plated items, particularly those with a copper base. The term has even been adopted by the Sheffield Silver Company, a Brooklyn firm established in the 1920s. Your chances of having true eighteenth-century Sheffield silver are slim, *and you can be guaranteed that if the piece is marked "Sheffield," it is not true eighteenth-century Sheffield silver.*

The most common method for distinguishing early Sheffield plated silver is the fingernail test: run your finger across the bottom of the piece, and if you feel a rolled-over edge and your nail catches on this irregular groove, you *may* have a piece of Sheffield silver. Unfortunately imitations of eighteenth-century Sheffield have been made by copying the technique. True Sheffield silver can be as costly as sterling silver; a silver expert can advise you about specific prices.

> If your piece is genuine Sheffield, do not have it replated.

Victorian and Modern Silver Plate

The majority of "antique" silver plate seen today was made either in England or America in the nineteenth century. It is distinguished both by its marks and its design. Just as South American silver was once scoffed at, so this nineteenth-century silver plate was once overlooked by collectors.

However, because silver from the 1870s, 1880s, and 1890s is now respectably old and fits into Victorian and Art Nouveau restorations and decor, it is once again in fashion. Many wonderful pieces that were common in Victorian times are no longer made—lemonade or water pitchers, epergnes and baskets, condiment sets and pickle castors. These are now being reevaluated for their design and historic context. And oh, yes—naturally, prices are rising.

Another reason for the increase in the value of antique silver plate is the cost of sterling silver today. Furthermore, dealers tell me that customers who *used* to buy sterling pieces are now asking for fine-quality silver plate. "They don't want to worry about sterling being stolen, but they are not willing to give up the appearance of fine silver," one dealer explained.

Even new silver plate is more expensive than ever before because of the combined cost of the metal (both the silver and the base metal) and ever-increasing labor and manufacturing costs. A new silver-plated goblet can retail for $50–$125, which is comparable to the cost of purchasing a used sterling silver goblet in an antiques shop.

Distinguishing Quality in Silver Plate

As prices and demand rise, you want to 1) select the best quality silver plate you can afford to assure that it will hold its value if you are buying and 2) correctly identify the quality of the pieces you already own. Review the passage on distinguishing quality in the section on sterling silver, as the same principles apply to silver plate.

But also pay attention to the base metal. Pieces with a copper base, identifiable either by the marking or when you see the copper showing through, are usually the best-quality silver plate. Few companies use a copper base today.

Remember my warning about judging a piece of silver on weight alone. In reality, some of the white metal base used today literally is "heavy as lead" and is of poor quality. Look for finished surfaces, crisp design, the depth of any raised work. If there is a cut-out (reticulated) border, are the angles clear and clean? Are there flaws where handles are attached to the body? And remember to look at the total piece for a well-balanced design and general aesthetics. If the piece isn't pleasing to your eye, it probably is not well designed.

Identifying Silver Plate

To identify your silver plate, look for the following marks on the back:

Triple plate	A1
Quadruple	Silver plate
Plate	Sheffield Reproduction

Advertisements from the **Illustrated Price and Premium List** *of the Great London Tea Co., 801 Washington Street, Boston, Massachusetts, 1884.*

These symbols all denote silver plate:

NS	Nickel silver
EPC	Electroplate on copper
Silver on copper	Silver on a copper base
EPNS	Electroplate silver on nickel base
EPWM	Electroplate on nickel with white metal mounts (usually feet, finials, handles)
EPBM	Electroplate on Britannia metal

Other confusing terms . . . all names for silver plate:

German silver	Argentine silver
Nevada silver	Craig silver
Alaska silver	Inlaid silver

The most confusing term associated with silver plate is "Britannia." The confusion exists because some pieces were actually made (and sold) entirely of Britannia metal, a pewter-type alloy, but Britannia metal was also used as the base for silver plating. Then, to further confuse matters, "Britannia" appears in the name of the Meriden Britannia Company, which made silver plate and sterling silver. For your purposes, you may consider any "Britannia" pieces you own to have a value of silver-plated or pewter pieces. All sterling silver made by the Meriden Britannia Company is clearly marked "Sterling."

Silver-plated items made today range in value from pieces that cost as much as some sterling silver to very inexpensive items. Many manufacturers have two lines of silver plate, one more costly than the other.

> Warning: Most of the silver plate coming out of the East—India primarily— is not fine quality. It may be marked to look like English sterling silver. While an expert can tell the difference, much of this silver is sold at flea markets as sterling. Look carefully at the marks.

Inventorying Your Silver

A few snapshots of your silver are not going to do you much good if you lose it. You need to know what you had. In most states, unless you have insured your silver separately for its replacement value you are limited to $1,000 cash recovery or replacement.

You may use the value chart to find an approximate value for much of your silver. This chart is not exact to the penny. I would have to come into each of your homes to make a truly accurate appraisal of your personal property. But I have taken the time to make these guides to assist you in learning whether or not you have adequate insurance coverage and whether you need the help of a professional appraiser.

The Format

Remember—name, describe, value.

Set up your routine before you start. Decide whether you are going to use index cards or lined paper (two or three columns).

First, enter the name of the piece, and if it is in multiples (twelve forks, two candlesticks, and so on), include the number.

Describe the object. Refer to the picture-description guide for help. Begin at the top or bottom of the piece, not in the middle. Always find out if your silver is sterling or plated by referring to the marks, and record this information. If you do not know, put the marks that appear on the piece (being careful to clearly represent the shapes of the letters, since some manufacturers have marks similar to those of another company) on your page. A silver appraiser can read these marks and know what the piece is.

Be sure to list any peculiarities about your silver in your description. Just one unique characteristic may help you reclaim your silver if it is stolen and

SILVER DECORATIVE MOTIFS

Acanthus		Guilloche	
Adamesque		Lobed	
Beading		Reeding	
Egg & Dart		Reticulated	
Etching		Scalloping	
Foliage		Scroll	
Floral		Spiral	
Gadroon		Interloped	
Greek Key			

recovered. Remember the story of the bent tine in chapter 12. These peculiarities are especially important to note on silver because so much of it is exactly alike.

While I was viewing the thousands of pieces of flat silver on display at the police station at Fairfax, Virginia, after the infamous Halberstam murder in Georgetown and the subsequent arrest of master thief Bernard Welch, the one comment I heard most frequently was, "You know, that could be my silver—it's my pattern. But I don't really have any way of proving it's mine."

Whether or not you choose to include the price, a careful listing of your silver is of utmost importance. Please do it.

Hints on How to Proceed

List your flatware (knives, forks, vegetable spoons . . .) separately from your hollowware (pitchers, trays, and so on). Arrange your pieces according to patterns before you begin. Put all of each pattern together. If you know the pattern name, list it. If not, describe the pattern. Then match your pattern to the closest class in the value charts for approximate current value.

Try to identify the manufacturer by comparing the mark with those in the chart of pieces most commonly found. Try to specifically identify the flatware pieces that you have, paying particular attention to the following:

1. Do your butter knives have hollow or flat handles?
2. What kind of salad servers do you have?
  a. All sterling
  b. Sterling handle with plated tines and bowl
  c. Sterling handle with stainless-steel tines and bowl
  d. Sterling handle with plastic or wooden tines and bowl
3. What kind of ladles do you have?
  a. Mustard (5¼ in.)
  b. Cream/sauce or mayonnaise (6⅜ in.)
  c. Gravy (7 in.)
  d. Soup (11 in.)
  e. Punch (12 in. or longer)
4. What kind(s) of soup spoons do you have?
  a. Bouillon, round bowls (5⅜ in.)
  b. Cream/soup, round or oval bowls (6⅛ in.)
  c. Large soup, round or oval bowls (7⅜ in.)
5. What kind(s) of carving sets do you have?
  a. Steak carving set (9–10 in.)
  b. Roast carving set (11–13 in.)
  c. Sharpening steel

Be sure to note monograms and inscriptions since these can help with recovery and identification if the silver is lost.

Sterling silver flatware. If you are looking for a fair market value (what you can sell the items for) for estate, donation, sale, or divorce purposes, the most common American sterling flatware pieces (knives, forks, spoons, and the like) average $20 to $40 each, and usual serving pieces (tablespoons, flat servers, and so on) range between $50 and $150. Punch ladles and large berry spoons, large cold meat forks, solid silver salad servers, and asparagus servers range from $150 to $500, depending on size and pattern as well as condition.

Silver-plated flatware. Figure an average of $12 per piece for replacement with *new* silver plate. If your silver-plated flatware is badly worn, figure it on replacement "in kind"—used silver-plated flatware that would be purchased at a flea market or house sale—at $1–$3 each.

Coin silver flatware. List the mark (initials, notation—coin, D, premium, and so on—or pseudohallmark). Research these in a coin silver book (see chapter 35). For coin silver made in the nineteenth century in the northern states, use the coin silver value chart. All others—seventeenth- or eighteenth-century silver and that made in other states—can have historical and regional value, and an expert should be consulted. Also, coin silver with a sheaf of wheat or flower basket motif is generally more valuable, as is that with coffin-ended handles.

Coin silver hollowware. Prices are rapidly increasing in this underpriced area. Consult an expert.

English silver. English silver varies more in value than does most American silver because its value is based on its age and who made it. Consult the hallmark section to identify the origin and age of your pieces.

For nineteenth- and twentieth-century English flatware, you may use the value charts provided for Class III as a *very general* gauge. English hollowware and eighteenth-century flatware should be valued by a silver appraiser.

Hints on Fakes

Because silver is generally marked, once you know how to read the marks, you are not as apt to be fooled into buying fake silver pieces as you are glass or furniture fakes.

The faking of English silver is punishable by law, but of course this does not stop everyone. Before you pay a great deal of money for English silver, I would advise you to buy it from a reputable source or have the silver checked by an expert if it is offered to you as a "once-in-a-lifetime chance."

Marks have been forged, especially those of the most famous smiths. And marks have been cut out of old pieces and added to new ones. For example, it is relatively simple to cut the marks from the round bottom of a badly damaged eighteenth-century mug and place this bottom in a nineteenth- or even twentieth-century mug in pristine condition. Sometimes recent letter dates are rubbed so they become illegible, and the silver is sold as eighteenth century.

You should also be aware of altered English silver. Fine Georgian silver was on occasion reworked into another piece that could be offered at a higher price. The meat platter that was given handles and turned into a tray or the mug given a lid it was never intended to have are two such obvious "transformations."

But mostly you need to watch out for silver-plated pieces sold as sterling—just because they "have some hallmarks"—and silver-plated ware with a little copper showing through marked "Sheffield."

Yes, Paul Revere Silver Is Faked

Each year we prepare many appraisals of donations going to museums and historical societies across the country. As you will see when you read the chapter on donations, this is serious business for appraisers, as we are held responsible by the IRS for the values we assign these pieces.

This year one piece we were asked to appraise was a small open standing salt with a pedestal base, oval body, and handles at the sides. The piece was clearly marked "PR" in the same-style letters, shape, and so forth as the authentic Paul Revere mark. However, when we looked carefully at the piece, we noticed that the oval body was the exact shape as a large eighteenth-century soup or serving spoon. There were even very light traces of a design on the back of the bowl, a design often found on fine period spoons. And when we examined the handles, we found they were crudely attached to the sides of the body, whereas Paul Revere silver is admired for its fine craftsmanship. Clearly the piece had been "made up" with the distinct purpose to deceive. And it had—at least once.

There are fakes and frauds in American silver, but once again these examples usually involve pieces and marks that bring a great deal of money. Silver is too expensive to waste the time making fake 1820 spoons that would only sell for $20 to $30 each. But it would be worth someone's time to create a Paul Revere porringer.

Value Guides and How to Use Them

To effectively figure the approximate retail or replacement value of your American sterling silver flatware for your inventory, choose the pattern illustrated on charts I, II, or III that most closely matches yours. Find the cost of each piece and enter that price on your inventory. Remember that the values stated in this book are average composite sale prices at the time of publication. Further, many manufacturers and retailers often feature additional promotional discount sales on silver. If you wish to use one price for all your sterling patterns, turn to chart IV, which gives an average value for estate or used silver found in antiques and silver specialty shops, and enter those values on your inventory.

The replacement cost of most sterling silver and silver-plated hollowware can be figured by referring to the values in charts VI and VII.

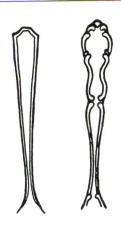

CHART I
Plain Patterns, Patterns with Small Scallop or Scroll Motifs
Examples: Rondo, Hepplewhite, Faneuil

Teaspoon	$50.00
Place fork	$60.00
Place knife	$50.00
Dinner fork	$70.00
Dinner knife	$55.00
Place, dessert, soup, ice tea, or grapefruit spoon	$50.00
Salad, ice-cream, or fish fork	$50.00
Cocktail, pickle, or lemon fork	$50.00
Demitasse spoon	$30.00
Baby feeding spoon	$40.00
Baby fork or spoon	$35.00
Child's fork	$50.00
Child's knife	$35.00
Child's spoon	$40.00
Bonbon spoon	$60.00
Butter serving or cheese knife	$50.00
Cake, pie, or pastry server	$50.00
Cold meat fork	$115.00
Cream/sauce ladle	$65.00
Flat server	$125.00
Gravy ladle	$115.00
Jelly server or sugar spoon	$70.00
Sugar tongs	$60.00
Salad fork, salad spoon, berry spoon, large vegetable spoon (all silver)	$185.00
Salad serving set (silver and wood)	$115.00
Tablespoon (solid or slotted)	$115.00
Steak carving set (two-piece)	$165.00
Roast carving set (three-piece)	$275.00
Punch ladle	$375.00

CHART II
More Elaborately Ornamented Patterns
Examples: Stieff Rose, Repoussé, Strasbourg, Chantilly, Pointed Antique, Prelude

Teaspoon	$65.00
Place fork	$65.00
Place knife	$65.00
Dinner fork	$100.00
Dinner knife	$70.00
Place, dessert, soup, ice tea, or grapefruit spoon	$65.00
Salad, ice-cream, or fish fork	$65.00
Cocktail, pickle, or lemon fork	$65.00
Demitasse spoon	$38.00
Baby feeding spoon	$55.00
Baby fork or spoon	$42.00
Child's fork	$65.00
Child's knife	$45.00
Child's spoon	$55.00
Bonbon spoon	$75.00
Butter serving or cheese knife	$65.00
Cake, pie, or pastry server	$85.00
Cold meat fork	$140.00
Cream/sauce ladle	$80.00
Flat server	$150.00
Gravy ladle	$140.00
Jelly server or sugar spoon	$75.00
Sugar tongs	$75.00
Salad fork, salad spoon, berry spoon, large vegetable spoon (all silver)	$200.00
Salad serving set (silver and wood)	$140.00
Tablespoon (solid or slotted)	$140.00
Steak carving set (two-piece)	$200.00
Roast carving set (three-piece)	$325.00
Punch ladle	$500.00

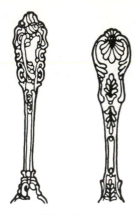

CHART III
Ornately Decorated, Elaborate, and Heavy Silver Patterns
(For Jensen patterns, double these prices.)
Examples: Malvern, Grand Baroque, Melrose, English King

Teaspoon	$70.00
Place fork	$70.00
Place knife	$70.00
Dinner fork	$115.00
Dinner knife	$75.00
Place, dessert, soup, ice tea, or grapefruit spoon	$70.00
Salad, ice-cream, or fish fork	$70.00
Cocktail, pickle, or lemon fork	$70.00
Demitasse spoon	$45.00
Baby feeding spoon	$60.00
Baby fork or spoon	$48.00
Child's fork	$78.00
Child's knife	$60.00
Child's spoon	$65.00
Bonbon spoon	$85.00
Butter serving or cheese knife	$70.00
Cake, pie, or pastry server	$100.00
Cold meat fork	$165.00
Cream/sauce ladle	$95.00
Flat server	$200.00
Gravy ladle	$165.00
Jelly server or sugar spoon	$100.00
Sugar tongs	$100.00
Salad fork, salad spoon, berry spoon, large vegetable spoon (all silver)	$275.00
Salad serving set (silver and wood)	$165.00
Tablespoon (solid or slotted)	$165.00
Steak carving set (two-piece)	$165.00
Roast carving set (three-piece)	$250.00
Punch ladle	$625.00

CHART IV
Average Cost of Used Silver Patterns Found at Antique and Specialty Shops
(Do not use these values for highly collectible silver patterns, especially Art Nouveau patterns.)

Teaspoon	$28.00
Place fork	$32.00
Place knife	$25.00
Dinner fork	$36.00
Dinner knife	$28.00
Place, dessert, soup, ice tea, or grapefruit spoon	$32.00
Salad, ice-cream, or fish fork	$32.00
Cocktail, pickle, or lemon fork	$25.00
Demitasse spoon	$15.00
Baby feeding spoon	$22.00
Baby fork or spoon	$22.00
Child's fork	$30.00
Child's knife	$22.00
Child's spoon	$25.00
Bonbon spoon	$35.00
Butter serving or cheese knife	$28.00
Cake, pie, or pastry server	$35.00
Cold meat fork	$60.00
Cream/sauce ladle	$35.00
Flat server	$60.00
Gravy ladle	$60.00
Jelly server or sugar spoon	$35.00
Sugar tongs	$40.00
Salad fork, salad spoon, berry spoon, large vegetable spoon (all silver)	$115.00
Salad serving set (silver and wood)	$50.00
Tablespoon (solid or slotted)	$55.00
Steak carving set (two-piece)	$75.00
Roast carving set (three-piece)	$115.00
Punch ladle	$300.00

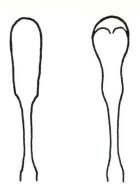

CHART V
COIN SILVER FLATWARE
Plain Pattern from 1820 to 1850

(Highly sought after individual makers' pieces, especially makers working from Washington, D.C., south, as well as pieces in the sheaf of wheat or basket of flowers designs will be 50 percent and more above these prices.)

Teaspoon	$20.00
Dessert- or soup-size spoon	$35.00
Luncheon fork	$35.00
Dinner fork	$45.00
Butter or breakfast knife	$25.00
Sugar spoon	$30.00
Mustard ladle	$30.00
Salt spoon	$18.00
Tablespoon	$50.00
Unusual serving pieces (cake knife, fish knife . . .)	$100.00

CHART VI
SILVER-PLATED HOLLOWWARE
Replacement Value Chart Guide

	LOW	HIGH
Bonbon dish	$12.00	$75.00
Open serving bowl	$40.00	$135.00
Covered butter dish	$20.00	$150.00
Bread tray	$22.00	$165.00
Bread and butter plate	$10.00	$50.00
Chafing dish	$115.00	$675.00
Covered entrée dish	$50.00	$350.00
Compote	$20.00	$435.00
Well and tree	$75.00	$375.00
Water pitcher	$35.00	$400.00
Sandwich plate	$20.00	$160.00
Silver service, four-piece	$100.00	$2,125.00
Tray or waiter	$100.00	$1,250.00
Water goblet	$10.00	$165.00
Baby cup	$10.00	$45.00
Trivet	$10.00	$50.00

Sterling—Francis I Compote   *Sterling—Candlestick*   *Sterling—Paul Revere Pitcher*

CHART VII
STERLING SILVER HOLLOWWARE
Replacement Value Chart Guide

(Prices will vary according to weight, design, manufacturer, age, and quality. These prices are to be used as a guide to currently manufactured sterling silver items.)

	LOW	HIGH
Baby brush and comb	$35.00	$80.00
Juice cup	$60.00	$150.00
Milk cup	$85.00	$325.00
Rattle	$50.00	$125.00
Porringer	$110.00	$300.00
Water goblet	$225.00	$1250.00
Cordial glass	$24.00	$50.00
Bonbon dish	$75.00	$250.00
Low candlestick (pair)	$75.00	$600.00
Tall (plain) candlestick (pair)	$175.00	$425.00
Three-branch (plain) candelabra (pair)	$425.00	$1,200.00
Five-branch (ornate) candelabra (pair)	$1,300.00	$7,300.00
Cake or sandwich plate	$250.00	$600.00
Water pitcher (plain)	$1,350.00	$1,800.00
Bud vase (7 in.)	$50.00	$125.00
Julep cup	$175.00	$275.00
Bread and butter plate (plain)	$125.00	$200.00
Salt and pepper shakers, 4 in.	$75.00	$175.00
Sugar and creamer set	$275.00	$600.00
Cigarette box	$325.00	$650.00
Dresser set (mirror, brush, and comb)	$375.00	$625.00
Military set	$125.00	$175.00

Tea service:	LOW	HIGH
Plain design		
Teapot	$1,275.00	$1,750.00
Coffeepot	$1,450.00	$2,000.00
Covered sugar bowl	$775.00	$1,250.00
Creamer	$500.00	$900.00
Waste bowl	$550.00	$1,000.00
Scrolled motif		
Teapot	$1,650.00	$2,500.00
Coffeepot	$1,750.00	$2,500.00
Covered sugar bowl	$800.00	$1,150.00
Creamer	$650.00	$800.00
Waste bowl	$700.00	$850.00
Repoussé / hand-chased		
Teapot	$4,000.00	$8,000.00
Coffeepot	$4,500.00	$8,400.00
Covered sugar bowl	$2,750.00	$4,500.00
Creamer	$2,200.00	$4,500.00
Waste bowl	$2,500.00	$4,500.00
Revere bowls:		
14-in. diameter	$2,100.00	$2,900.00
10-in. diameter	$900.00	$1,350.00
7-in. diameter	$325.00	$750.00
5-in. diameter	$225.00	$450.00

Pieces not frequently found in sterling silver (*only the large trays are made by American silver companies today. The other items are found in antiques shops, auctions, and tag sales*):

Well and tree	$500.00	$3,500.00
Large tray or waiter	$5,000.00	$24,000.00
Covered entrée dish	$350.00	$3,200.00

LONDON (Silver Hallmarks)

Year	Letter	Year	Letter	Year	Letter	Year	Letter	Year	Letter	Year	Letter	Year	Letter	Year	Letter	Year	Letter
1678	a	1712	i	1744	i	1780	e	1815	U	1850	P	1888	N	1923	h	1958	C
1679	b	1713	k	1745	k	1781	f	1816	a	1851	Q	1889	O	1924	i	1959	d
1680	c	1714	l	1746	l	1782	g	1817	b	1852	R	1890	P	1925	k	1960	e
1681	d	1715	m	1747	m	1783	h	1818	C	1853	S	1891	Q	1926	l	1961	f
1682	e	1716	A	1748	n	1784	i	1819	d	1854	T	1892	R	1927	m	1962	g
1683	f	1717	B	1749	o	1785	k	1820	e	1855	U	1893	S	1928	n	1963	h
1684	g	1718	C	1750	p	1786	l	1821	f	1856	a	1894	T	1929	o	1964	i
1685	h	1719	D	1751	q	1787	m	1822	g	1857	b	1895	U	1930	p	1965	k
1686	i	1720	E	1752	r	1788	n	1823	h	1858	c	1896	a	1931	q	1966	l
1687	k	1721	F	1753	s	1789	o	1824	i	1859	d	1897	b	1932	r	1967	m
1688	l	1722	G	1754	t	1790	p	1825	k	1860	e	1898	c	1933	s	1968	n
1689	m	1723	H	1755	u	1791	q	1826	l	1861	f	1899	d	1934	t	1969	o
1690	n	1724	I	1756	A	1792	r	1827	m	1862	g	1900	e	1935	u	1970	P
1691	o	1725	K	1757	B	1793	s	1828	n	1863	h	1901	f	1936	A	1971	q
1692	p	1726	L	1758	C	1794	t	1829	o	1864	i	1902	g	1937	B	1972	r
1693	q	1727	M	1759	D	1795	u	1830	p	1865	k	1903	h	1938	C	1973	s
1694	r	1728	N	1760	E	1796	A	1831	q	1866	l	1904	i	1939	D	1974	t
1695	s	1729	O	1761	F	1797	B	1832	r	1867	m	1905	k	1940	E	1975	A
1696	t	1730	P	1762	G	1798	C	1833	s	1868	n	1906	l	1941	F	1976	B
1697		1731	Q	1763	H	1799	D	1834	t	1869	o	1907	m	1942	G	1977	C
1698		1732	R	1764	J	1800	E	1835	u	1870	p	1908	n	1943	H	1978	D
1699		1733	S	1765	K	1801	F	1836	A	1871	q	1909	O	1944	I	1979	E
1700		1734	T	1766	L	1802	G	1837	B	1872	r	1910	P	1945	K	1980	F
1701		1735	V	1767	m	1803	H	1838	C	1873	s	1911	q	1946	L	1981	G
1702		1736	a	1768	n	1804	I	1839	D	1874	t	1912	r	1947	M	1982	H
1703		1737	b	1769	o	1805	K	1840	E	1875	u	1913	s	1948	N	1983	I
1704		1738	C	1770	p	1806	L	1841	f	1876	A	1914	t	1949	O	1984	K
1705		1739	d	1771	Q	1807	M	1842	G	1877	B	1915	u	1950	P	1985	L
1706		1739	d	1772	R	1808	N	1843	H	1878	C	1916	a	1951	Q	1986	M
1707		1740	e	1773	S	1809	O	1844	J	1879	D	1917	b	1952	R	1987	N
1708		1741	f	1774	T	1810	P	1845	k	1880	E	1918	c	1953	S	1988	O
1709		1742	g	1775	a	1811	Q	1846	l	1881	F	1919	d	1954	T		
1710		1743	h	1776	a	1812	R	1847	M	1882	G	1920	e	1955	U		
1711				1777	b	1813	S	1848	A	1883	H	1921	f	1956	a		
				1778	C	1814	T	1849	O	1884	I	1922	g	1957	b		
				1779	d					1885	K						
										1886	L						
										1887	M						

BIRMINGHAM (Silver Hallmarks)

Year	Mark	Year	Mark	Year	Mark	Year	Mark	Year	Mark	Year	Mark	Year	Mark
[lion][anchor]		1801	d	1837	O	1873	Y	1908	i	1946	W	1979	E
1773	A	1802	e	[lion][anchor][mark]		1874	Z	1909	k	1947	X	1980	F
1774	B	1803	f	1838	P	[lion][anchor][mark]		1910	l	1948	Y	1981	G
1775	C	1804	g	1839	Q	1875	a	1911	m	1949	Z	1982	H
1776	D	1805	h	1840	R	1876	b	1912	n	[anchor][lion]		1983	J
1777	E	1806	i	1841	S	1877	c	1913	o	1950	A	1984	K
1778	F	1807	j	1842	T	1878	d	1914	p	1951	B	1985	L
1779	G	1808	k	1843	U	1879	e	1915	q	1952	C	1986	M
1780	H	1809	l	1844	V	1880	f	1916	r	1953	D	1987	N
1781	I	1810	m	1845	W	1881	g	1917	s	1954	E	1988	O
1782	K	1811	n	1846	X	1882	h	1918	t	1955	F		
1783	L	1812	o	1847	Y	1883	i	1919	u	1956	G		
[lion][anchor][mark]		1813	p	1848	Z	1884	k	1920	v	1957	H		
1784	M	1814	q	[lion][anchor][mark]		1885	l	1921	w	1958	J		
1785	N	1815	r	1849	A	1886	m	1922	x	1959	K		
[lion][anchor][mark]		1816	s	1850	B	1887	n	1923	y	1960	L		
1786	O	1817	t	1851	C	1888	o	1924	z	1961	M		
1787	P	1818	u	1852	D	1889	p	1925	A	1962	N		
1788	Q	1819	v	1853	E	1890	q	1926	B	1963	O		
1789	R	1820	w	1854	F	[lion][anchor]		1927	C	1964	P		
1790	S	1821	x	1855	G	1891	r	1928	D	1965	Q		
1791	T	1822	y	1856	H	1892	s	1929	E	1966	R		
1792	U	1823	z	1857	I	1893	t	1930	F	1967	S		
1793	V	1824	a	1858	J	1894	u	1931	G	1968	T		
1794	W	1825	B	1859	K	1895	b	1932	H	1969	U		
1795	X	1826	C	1860	L	1896	w	1933	J	1970	V		
1796	Y	1827	D	1861	M	1897	x	1934	K	1971	W		
1797	Z	1828	E	1862	N	1898	y	1935	L	1972	X		
1798	a	1829	f	1863	O	1899	z	1936	M	[anchor][lion]			
1799	b	1830	G	1864	P	[anchor][lion]		1937	N	1973	Y		
1800	c	1831	H	1865	Q	1900	a	1938	O	[anchor][lion]			
		1832	J	1866	R	1901	b	1939	P	1974	Z		
		1833	K	1867	S	1902	c	1940	Q	[anchor][lion]			
		[lion][anchor][mark]		1868	T	1903	d	1941	R	1975	A		
		1834	L	1869	U	1904	e	1942	S	1976	B		
		1835	M	1870	V	1905	f	1943	T	1977	C		
		1836	N	1871	W	1906	g	1944	U	1978	D		
				1872	X	1907	h	1945	V				

SHEFFIELD (Silver Hallmarks)

Year	Mark	Year	Mark	Year	Mark	Year	Mark	Year	Mark	Year	Mark	Year	Mark
	[lion passant · crown]	1805	B	1838	S	1871	D	1904	m	1937	u	1972	E
1773	E	1806	A	1839	t	1872	E	1905	n	1938	V	1973	F
1774	F	1807	S		[lion · rose · head]	1873	F	1906	o	1939	W	1974	G
1775	H	1808	P	1840	u	1874	G	1907	p	1940	X		[rose · lion marks]
1776	R	1809	K	1841	v	1875	H	1908	q	1941	y	1975	A
1777	h	1810	L	1842	x	1876	J	1909	r	1942	Z	1976	B
1778	S	1811	C	1843	z	1877	K	1910	s	1943	A	1977	C
1779	A	1812	D	1844	A	1878	L	1911	t	1944	B	1978	D
1780	C	1813	R	1845	B	1879	M	1912	u	1945	C	1979	E
1781	D	1814	W	1846	C	1880	N	1913	v	1946	D	1980	F
1782	G	1815	O	1847	D	1881	O		[crown · lion]	1947	E	1981	G
1783	B	1816	T	1848	E	1882	P	1914	w	1948	F	1982	H
	[lion · crown · head]		[lion · crown · head]	1849	F	1883	Q	1915	x	1949	G	1983	J
1784	I	1817	X	1850	G	1884	R	1916	y	1950	H	1984	K
1785	V	1818	I	1851	H	1885	S	1917	z	1951	I	1985	L
	[lion · crown · head]	1819	V	1852	I	1886	T		[crown · lion]	1952	K	1986	M
1786	k		[lion · crown · head]	1853	K	1887	U	1918	a	1953	L	1987	N
1787	T	1820	Q	1854	L	1888	V	1919	b	1954	M	1988	O
1788	m	1821	Y	1855	M	1889	W	1920	c	1955	N		
1789	X	1822	Z	1856	N	1890	X	1921	d	1956	O		
1790	L	1823	U	1857	O		[crown · lion]	1922	e	1957	P		
1791	P	1824	a	1858	P	1891	Y	1923	f	1958	Q		
1792	U	1825	b	1859	R	1892	Z	1924	g	1959	R		
1793	O	1826	C	1860	S	1893	a	1925	h	1960	S		
1794	m	1827	d	1861	T	1894	b	1926	i	1961	T		
1795	q	1828	e	1862	U	1895	c	1927	k	1962	U		
1796	Z	1829	f	1863	V	1896	d	1928	l	1963	V		
1797	X	1830	g	1864	W	1897	e	1929	m	1964	W		
1798	V	1831	h	1865	X	1898	f	1930	n	1965	X		
1799	E	1832	k	1866	Y	1899	g	1931	o	1966	Y		
1800	N	1833	l	1867	Z	1900	h	1932	p	1967	Z		
1801	H		[lion · mark · head]		[lion · mark · head]	1901	i	1933	q	1968	A		
1802	M	1834	m	1868	A	1902	k	1934	r	1969	B		
1803	F	1835	p	1869	B	1903	l	1935	s	1970	C		
1804	G	1836	q	1870	C			1936	t	1971	D		
		1837	r										

Between 1780/1853, the Crown and Date letter are usually enclosed in the same shield on small articles.

EDINBURGH (Silver Hallmarks)

Year		Year		Year		Year		Year		Year		Year		Year		Year	
		1737		1769		1800		1832		1864		1895		1927		1960	
1705		1738		1770		1801		1833		1865		1896		1928		1961	
1706		1739		1771		1802		1834		1866		1897		1929		1962	
1707		1740		1772		1803		1835		1867		1898		1930		1963	
1708		1741		1773		1804		1836		1868		1899		1931		1964	
1709		1742		1774		1805		1837		1869		1900		1932		1965	
1710		1743		1775		1806		1838		1870		1901		1933		1966	
1711		1744		1776		1807		1839		1871		1902		1934		1967	
1712		1745		1777		1808		1840		1872		1903		1935		1968	
1713		1746		1778		1809		1841		1873		1904		1936		1969	
1714		1747		1779		1810		1842		1874		1905		1937		1970	
1715		1748		1780		1811		1843		1875		1906		1938		1971	
1716		1749		1781		1812		1844		1876		1907		1939		1972	
1717		1750		1782		1813		1845		1877		1908		1940		1973-4	
1718		1751		1783		1814		1846		1878		1909		1941			
1719		1752		1784		1815		1847		1879		1910		1942			
1720		1753		1785		1816		1848		1880		1911		1943		1975	
1721		1754		1786		1817		1849		1881		1912		1944		1976	
1722		1755		1787		1818		1850		1882		1913		1945		1977	
1723		1756		1788		1819		1851		1883		1914		1946		1978	
1724		1757		1789		1820		1852		1884		1915		1947		1979	
1725		1758		1790		1821		1853		1885		1916		1948		1980	
1726		1759		1791		1822		1854		1886		1917		1949		1981	
1727		1760		1792		1823		1855		1887		1918		1950		1982	
1728		1761		1793		1824		1856		1888		1919		1951		1983	
1729		1762		1794		1825		1857		1889		1920		1952		1984	
1730		1763		1795		1826		1858		1890		1921		1953		1985	
1731		1764		1796		1827		1859		1891		1922		1954		1986	
1732		1765		1797		1828		1860		1892		1923		1955		1987	
1733		1766		1798		1829		1861		1893		1924		1956		1988	
1734		1767		1799		1830		1862		1894		1925		1957			
1735		1768				1831		1863				1926		1958			
1736														1959			

The English hallmarks for the major silver guilds—London, Birmingham, Sheffield, and Edinburgh—as supplied by the Assay Offices of Great Britain.

17

China:
Replacing the Broken Plates
Can Break You

For years you could go to a jewelry store or china department in a department store and buy a plate to match your set and pay the same price for the new one that you had paid the year before or the year before that—no longer. China prices are increasing as steadily as furniture prices and only slightly less erratically than silver.

A major cause for this increase can be traced to the cost of energy today. The ovens in which china is glazed must be kept at constant temperatures twenty-four hours a day. Since you know how expensive it is to heat your home, you can imagine how expensive it is to maintain a consistent high temperature in a china factory.

A few years ago I overheard a conversation in New York's Royal Copenhagen shop on Madison Avenue. A salesperson was explaining that, if the oven furnaces were ever shut down, it would require a great deal of time and money to bring them back to the temperature necessary to achieve the unique glaze on the beautiful Royal Copenhagen figurines and china.

This consistent increase in overhead costs has brought about many changes in the porcelain market. And a look at how the porcelain market has changed in the past decade can provide an interesting study of the ever-changing antiques and collecting scenes. About twelve years ago a bank had hired me to act as the agent for a large collection of pre–World War II Meissen china that had been purchased in Germany in the 1930s. The bank needed to get the most money possible to settle the estate but had had little success in locating a local buyer.

I contacted both Sotheby's and Christie's and requested a preauction estimate on this large Meissen "Onion" pattern service. At that time neither auction house appeared interested in selling the china. In fact, one house suggested that I could figure out a preauction value myself by multiplying the total number of pieces by $3.

"Even the large tureens?" I asked, knowing full well that these brought several hundred dollars in antiques shops.

"Even the large tureens," was the reply.

Multiply a 225-piece set of Meissen "Onion" china, including rimmed soup bowls, nut dishes, covered vegetable dishes, egg cups, knife rests, a mustard pot, hors d'oeuvres serving dish, lozenge-shaped serving dishes, a water jug, and wine funnel by $3 and you come up with $675!

Three years later, in 1980, just such a set of "Onion" Meissen—227 pieces, in fact—sold at auction for $10,000. In 1981 yet another "Onion" service consisting of 226 pieces also sold for $10,000. A far cry from $675.

Obviously, as the price for new china has gone up, the desire for fine antique and even semiantique china sets among dealers and collectors has increased. What this means to you and me is that the cost of replacing a china service, whether it be Meissen, Lenox, Haviland, or even Bavarian china, has now reached astronomical proportions.

The overnight success of porcelain and pottery mail-order replacement services is yet another testament to our desire to purchase, at premium prices, china no longer being made. Discontinued or no longer manufactured china used to be very inexpensive. However, the desire to complete "Grandmother's set" or to replace broken pieces has driven up the cost of secondhand china. Replacement china companies have become major businesses. This means that when you wish to replace broken or destroyed china, it may be possible and it may be expensive.

Among the many china replacement services are the following:

Replacements, Ltd.: PO Box 26029, Greensboro, NC 27420.
Pattern Finders: PO Box 206, Port Jefferson Station, NY 11776.
The Matchmakers: 1718 Airport Court, Placerville, CA 95667.

Types of China and How to Distinguish Them

For the purposes of your inventory, you need to know that there are two major categories of china commonly found in the dining room and kitchen— porcelain (china) and semiporcelain or ironstone (pottery).

One distinction always made between porcelain and semiporcelain is that porcelain is translucent, meaning light can pass through it. The usual way to test your china is to put your hand at the back of a plate, then hold the plate in front of a strong light. If you can see the outline of your hand, it is porcelain.

On the other hand, pottery is opaque; you cannot see through it. Semiporcelain is actually pottery based but with a porcelain-type glaze that makes it more durable than pottery, which is easily broken.

Porcelain

"Porcelain" is often used interchangeably with the term "china" to mean high-quality and expensive dinnerware. Porcelain collectors know that there are two classifications—hard paste, the porcelain made with kaolin as its main ingredient, and soft paste, which is largely bone ash. For more specific details about hard and soft paste porcelain, consult the books listed in chapter 35.

Relatively little porcelain is of American origin. Until the mid-nineteenth

The majority of china found in American grandmothers' china cabinets will be European, as are these platters from Bavaria and Austria. **Photograph courtesy Richard A. Bourne Company**

century almost all china in America was imported. William Ellis Tucker is considered the first American china maker, but Tucker china is extremely rare and seldom found in private homes. In fact, the majority of porcelain called "Tucker" is actually French nineteenth-century china generally termed "Old Paris."

But even after American china companies were established, French, English, and German china remained so popular in America that we did not develop many large and important porcelain manufacturing companies. Lenox and Pickard are two exceptions. Even today, when you walk into a china department and look around, you will see that the majority of the fine porcelain displayed is still imported from England, Germany, and Denmark and bears the names Minton, Wedgwood, Rosenthal, Royal Copenhagen, and so on.

Proof of Americans' preference for European china is established the moment you mention Grandmother's china. I have never heard of a grandmother yet who did not have at least one set of Haviland china. There is so much Haviland china around that it requires several volumes to catalog the hundreds of patterns.

The Haviland factories in Limoges, France, manufactured china that was decorated in the French style for the American market. Everyone is familiar with the usual Haviland dinner sets decorated in pastel floral motifs. But not everyone knows that the Haviland factories also produced such diverse pieces as terra-cotta vases and sculptured busts.

Haviland china is highly treasured and widely collected today. Those fortunate enough to have inherited a set are always seeking to replace broken or damaged pieces. On the other hand, serious Haviland collectors are always looking for the rare items to enhance their collections. The wise investor in Haviland china knows it is often possible to buy an entire set for less money per piece than it costs to buy the individual pieces to assemble a set.

It is important to know the age of your porcelain, and much of the mystery surrounding this can be cleared up by knowing two dates, 1891 and 1914. If the name of the country, such as England, China, Japan, or France, appears on

Have you ever seen a grandmother who didn't have at least one piece of Haviland china? I haven't. **Photograph courtesy Richard A. Bourne Company**

Remove the paper label as I have done on this reproduction of a nineteenth-century porcelain bowl and the unknowing person can be fooled by the presence of the gold number into thinking it is a genuinely old piece. Every time you go into a gift shop, look around at "new" lines of reproduction pieces to avoid making this mistake yourself.

the bottom of your china, it dates after 1891, in accordance with the McKinley Tariff Act, passed in 1890, which required that the name of the country of origin appear on porcelain imported into the United States. If the additional words *Made in* appear, the china is even more recent and postdates 1914.

The majority of the china you will find in sets, whether your grandmother's or even great-grandmother's, will date from the end of the nineteenth century or into the twentieth century.

Before 1891, porcelain might be
> unmarked
> marked with the pattern name
> marked with the pattern number
> marked with the company's name
> marked with the company's symbol
> marked with the company's name and symbol
> marked with the painter's symbol or number
> marked with a registry mark, if English

Warning! Paper labels with the name of the country can be attached to china to get it past Customs. Once inside the country, these labels can be removed and the new piece sold as "antique." Do not assume that because a piece has no marking on it it is "antique" or "valuable."

Just as sterling silver has become expensive and many items are no longer made, so some porcelain has become rare and certainly out of the reach of the average buying public. Notable among such porcelain are the patterns decorated with rich cobalt-blue and bold gold borders. Cobalt, a pigment made principally of cobalt oxide and alumina, has become so expensive to extract that it is prohibitive to use in manufacturing china. Rich gold borders are also becoming decorations of the past. When a china pattern is made in the 1980s with gold and cobalt, resembling the patterns of twenty, forty, or sixty years ago, the price can range as high as $150, $200, even $250 for a single dinner plate!

Warning! An exception to gold being a mark of expensive china is when semiporcelain items have the notation "18," "22," or "24"-karat gold. This notation was used on inexpensive, souvenir-type china to entice buyers.

Modern, or twentieth-century, porcelain can range in value from very inexpensive to the high hundreds of dollars. The value can often be determined by knowing the manufacturer. Following is a basic guide:

Fine Quality	Good Quality	Medium Quality
Minton	Lenox	Mikasa
Herend	Gorham	Noritake
Rosenthal	Spode	
Royal Copenhagen	Noritake	
Royal Doulton	Hutschenreuther	
Royal Worcester	Schumann	

The Second Best—Semiporcelain

As for your second-best china or kitchenware—what should it be called? Many choose "semiporcelain," while others prefer "ironstone." Ironstone ware was first made in England and became immediately popular because of its strong (or ironlike) properties combined with its colorful decoration on the porcelain-type glaze. Extremely fine English ironstone of the nineteenth century, especially Mason's, is widely collected—particularly large serving pieces such as soup tureens, covered vegetable dishes, and cake plates, and at times it is more expensive than porcelain.

The ironstone produced in America by the end of the nineteenth century was made in both an off-white glaze and decorated patterns. This "second-best" china is now also highly collectible. For example, pieces made by the Homer Laughlin China Company are now being snatched up by collectors. Some collectors concentrate on buying dinnerware made by one particular company; others collect specific patterns often made by many companies.

One of the most famous and most often collected ironstone patterns is "Willow," which has been made by companies from England to Japan and back again to the United States. It exemplifies the kind of semiporcelain china you may find in your home that now has "collectible" value.

Like porcelain manufacturers, pottery manufacturers have various qualities of wares. The following is a general guide:

The "Willow" pattern has been produced in England, America, and Japan as well as other countries since the nineteenth century. In the 1980s it is found in antiques shops, attics, dining rooms, and department stores alike.

Fine Quality	Good Quality	Medium Quality
Dansk	Fiesta	Homer Laughlin
Coalport	Franciscan	Hull Pottery
Mason's	Metlox	Johnson Brothers
Spode	Russel Wright	Pfaltzgraff
Villeroy & Boch	Vernon	Mikasa
Wedgwood		Sango

Among the currently collected popular American china is that made by such companies as Buffalo Pottery Company, Castleton China, Fulper Pottery, W. S. George Pottery, Hall China Company, Hull Pottery, Knowles, Taylor & Knowles, the Homer Laughlin Company, McCoy Companies, Pickard China, Roseville Pottery Company, Salem China Company, Sebring Pottery Company,

American semiporcelain varies greatly in quality, desirability, rarity, and value. This pair of signed Deldare platters had the quality and desirability and was sufficiently rare to command a sale price of $880 in an early 1988 sale at Savoia and Fromm Auction House.

Shawnee Pottery Company, Stangl Pottery Company, Steubenville Pottery Company, Syracuse China Company, Universal Potteries Incorporated, Weller Pottery, and Russel Wright. Check the bottom of your china to see if you own collectible kitchenware. But the value difference among American companies is vast. For example, Deldare pottery pieces made by the Buffalo Pottery Company easily sell in the $150 to $950 range, whereas Hall China Company pieces are usually in the $5 to $65 range. A quick check in two or three price guides will give you an idea of just how valuable your pieces may be.

Confusing Names and Marks

Just as the nineteenth-century American silversmiths imitated English hallmarks, so American china companies freely drew upon English and European names and hallmarks. For example, you find Chelsea, the name of one of the most famous eighteenth-century English porcelain companies, used by the Chelsea Pottery Company of West Virginia. The American companies also liberally copied English ironstone marks and used such typically English symbols as the unicorn, lion, crown, horse, and Hibernia in their American marks.

One company that adapted a foreign name and symbol was the French China Company, an Ohio firm, which used a fleur-de-lis and the term "La Française" on its products at the turn of the century. They later became the French Saxon China Company and used as a hallmark an armored head, coat of arms, suit of armor, and crossed swords in a cartouche. Under this they placed the term "French Saxon China." I cannot tell you how many times this particular china has been brought to me to be appraised as Sevres or Limoges china.

In fact, even Sevres, the French china literally fit for a king, was imitated in East Liverpool, Ohio, when a company called itself the Sevre China Company and marked its wares with a fleur-de-lis. No matter how fine their line of hotelware dinner sets, bowls, plates, and toilet seats, only the person unfamiliar with the true French Sevres mark and china could think that this American semiporcelain was the real thing.

The China Syndrome—Fakes and Frauds and Just Stupid Mistakes

Although the misnomers just described are examples of copying and imitating, they are not truly fakes. The majority of fakes come out of Japan and the other Oriental countries.

One of the most blatantly copied and falsely sold chinas is the type known as Jasperware, made after the famous English Wedgwood Jasperware. This china, easily identifiable by its pottery body in blue, green, yellow, lavender, and so on and decorated with classical scenes executed in white, originated in eighteenth-century England; however, both the type and name have been copied numerous times. The correct spelling is Wedgwood. Counterfeit Wedgwood is often spelled "Wedgewood." Twentieth-century factories in

Read this advertisement very carefully. "Inexpensive Reproductions" from England of fine English porcelain and semiporcelain companies including Spode, Copeland, Wedgwood. (Even correctly spelled, so how can you distinguish the reproduction from the original?) What is alarming is that this ad appeared in the March 1907 Connoisseur.

both Germany and Japan freely copied Jasperware-type glaze and style, and these copies are often passed off as nineteenth-century English Wedgwood.

Unfortunately, china marks can be removed from the bottoms of plates and saucers with the help of a grinding wheel or hydrochloric acid. These methods are often used on nineteenth- and twentieth-century china made originally in Japan or China and sold in the United States either as being older than it really is or as an example of English, French, or German china. (And, as I mentioned earlier, marks can also be added.)

Frequently china is sold for something it is not—due just to plain stupidity. You have to be very careful when buying china in antiques shops and flea markets because it so often is wrongly marked. (The seller may not know what the china is but always seems to know what price to put on it.)

I will never forget the experience I once had when I wandered into an antiques shop located in a large shopping mall. The majority of furniture in the shop was from the 1900s and 1920s, and I was beginning to wonder whether or not the shop could rightfully claim the name "antiques" shop when one item caught my attention. Perched on top of a pie safe (once again of questionable age) was a blue-and-white plate with a historical scene at the center. The plate was badly cracked, but on the sticker I read the following:

> Antique blue-and-white plate.
> "As is" condition. $16

I was shocked. Only two or three years before I had bought that identical plate in the A&P for forty-nine cents. In fact, I had a stack of those plates in my kitchen cabinet. I used them every single day, none of them was cracked, and none was worth $16. I wondered if the crack made the plate worth $16.

Ever since the nineteenth century, historical scenes, such as this one of Lafayette at Benjamin Franklin's tomb, have been popular motifs for earthenware. Do not be misled into thinking a current reproduction is a true antique. Begin by looking for a mark and then comparing it to the information in this book. **Photograph courtesy David and Linda Arman**

Perhaps I was mistaken. Was this really the same plate? Knowing full well it was, I nonetheless took it from the rack, turned it over, and read:

Original copper engraving of Historical Colonial Scenes printed of Staffordshire Ironstone. Detergent and Dishwasher safe.

Dishwasher safe? It would seem to me that anyone would know that an *antique* plate would not have the words "Dishwasher safe" on it. (I know time is flying, but I don't think it is passing *that* rapidly.)

Common Confusions

While speaking of fakes and frauds, I would like to clear up some of the confusion surrounding two china companies.

Very often a piece of china that has two marks, "Pickard" and "Haviland," will be brought to me. The Pickard China Company, founded in Chicago in 1894, had its beginnings as a company that decorated china imported from France. Thus the china was imported bearing the Haviland mark (remember the 1890 law), and once it was decorated, the Pickard mark was added. Much of the china was exceptionally well painted, and early pieces of hand-decorated Pickard china are now collected. Particularly sought after are pieces bearing the signatures of any of the following artists: E. S. Challinor, Leonard Kohn, Podlaha, Hessler, Vokral, and Klippon.

Then there is the matter of the most misunderstood of the generic china terms—Dresden. Dresden is actually a town in Germany where the Meissen factory was located (just as Limoges is a town in France where Haviland china was manufactured). But the term "Dresden" is commonly used by the layman when speaking of the floral spray motif that often appears on Meissen china. This general term is then interpreted to mean that any china with this floral decoration is Meissen china. In reality, this floral spray motif was, and is still, used by many china manufacturers, and Meissen made many patterns of china aside from this one. The floral-patterned china was particularly popular in the 1930s, and many Eastern European china companies made patterns imitating the original eighteenth-century Meissen floral design. ("Louise" is one particular pattern made in the 1930s, and another current popular adaptation is the "Empress" pattern.) Yet I am often handed a plate clearly marked "Bavaria" or "Czechoslovakia" and told, "This is Meissen china."

Hints on China

Accurate Dating

Look carefully at the backs of dinnerware china. China made in popular patterns and sold in sets in the late nineteenth and twentieth centuries will be clearly marked. Fine, early English china by such companies as Rockingham, Minton, Coalport, and Worcester can be identified by studying scholarly

 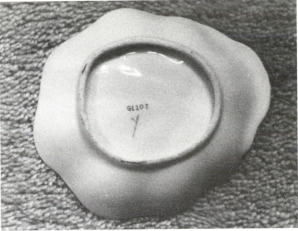

From across the room this appears to be a fine-quality English porcelain piece by Crown Derby. Turn it over and the stylized number and marking tell you it is not what it appears to be but is a Japanese "imitation."

books on porcelain and by learning the appropriate markings. This fine china, like Sevres and Meissen, has been frequently imitated. Unless you know how to distinguish the real from the fake, do not invest in this china unless you buy it from a reputable firm that will guarantee to refund your money should the china turn out to be other than what it is stated to be. To further research specific markings, refer to *Kovels' New Dictionary of Marks* (Crown, 1986) and other books listed in chapter 35.

Even when buying fairly inexpensive china in flea markets and antiques shops, take the time to inspect the back for marks. Before spending your money, look for the words "Made in," or the country where the china was made, and compare what you now know—that this would be nineteenth- or twentieth-century china—with what the tag or the shop owner tells you about the china.

Detecting Condition

Only buy china in the best condition. Sometimes repairs, even major ones, will not show up under normal light. If possible, use a black light for a quick check of both condition and authenticity of the mark. If that is not possible, use your fingers. A small hairline crack, which may be invisible to the naked eye, can be detected by "thumping" or ringing porcelain with your finger. Porcelain has a distinct clear ring, and if you notice a dull thud, there is damage somewhere.

As a quick reference, at the end of this chapter there is a list of china companies most frequently encountered. Further research is always recommended to learn all you need to know about a specific company, but this synopsis may help you decide whether or not you wish to go further.

Inventorying Your China—How to Proceed

Organize your china before entering it on your inventory. Group together all the pieces of the same pattern, just as you did with your silver. In the left-hand column note a general description, such as "large dinner set of English bone china" or "group of dessert plates."

Next, in the center or description column, enter the pattern name and company, if you know it (for example, "Kutani Crane by Wedgwood"). If the specific name of the pattern is not given, but the manufacturer's name or mark is present, enter this. (Remember to draw the mark if the name is not stated.) Even if you know the pattern name, make some descriptive comment so you or a future generation can distinguish one pattern from another.

To describe the pattern, start at the outside rim and move toward the center. An example of a simple description might read like this: "Having a gold band and floral border; the center is decorated with one large floral design." (You may want to refer back to the silver chapter for additional descriptions of motifs.) Also note the colors of the china, such as "blue, green, pink, and yellow predominating" or "the china is decorated in an all-over pastel floral motif."

Now list how many of each item there are in the china set—twelve dinner plates, eight cups and saucers with two additional saucers, one teapot, two round open serving dishes, and so on.

If you wish to enter prices based on the value charts that follow, state both the cost of the individual item and the total unit cost. For example, twelve plates at $25 each, total $300. Finally, add up the entire value of the set and list it. You will be amazed at how rapidly your china mounts in value.

Notes on Using Value Charts

There are as many china patterns as silver patterns, and the china patterns go out of production even more rapidly than do silver patterns. The charts I have provided will help you *estimate* the replacement value of your china. Three classes are provided.

The first class is for the usual "inexpensive" kitchenware you use every day. This category will help you determine the value of both collectible dinnerware from the 1920s and 1930s and today's current semiporcelain dinnerware. Needless to say, patterns vary in price, but this chart will give you an approximate value.

The second class relates to good-quality bone china, or porcelain, usually found at the lower end of the English and American company lines and sold in jewelry stores and good china departments. In this category will fall some familiar china patterns made by King Albert Bone China, Lenox, Noritake, and Wedgwood. *This category may be used to figure an approximate or rough value of the usual Haviland patterns.*

The third class relates to elaborately decorated fine china with gold borders. In this category will fit such manufacturers as Lenox, Minton, Crown Derby, and so on. Match your pattern to the closest class by comparing the illustrations.

CLASS I

Pottery, semiporcelain, and ironstone (including that available in department stores and some collectible 1930s dinnerware patterns such as Harlequin)

	LOW	HIGH
Dinner plate	$5.00	$20.00
Salad plate	$4.00	$15.00
Bread and butter plate	$3.00	$10.00
Cup and saucer	$5.00	$20.00
Rimmed soup bowl	$5.00	$20.00
Cereal bowl	$4.00	$15.00
Fruit or dessert bowl	$3.00	$10.00
Platters		
Oval, small	$15.00	$35.00
Oval, medium	$20.00	$45.00
Oval, large	$25.00	$65.00
Round, medium	$20.00	$45.00
Round, large	$25.00	$65.00
Vegetable bowls		
Open, round	$10.00	$35.00
Open, oval	$10.00	$35.00
Covered, round	$30.00	$75.00
Covered, oval	$35.00	$85.00
Tureen, covered	$40.00	$100.00
Tureen, covered with stand	$60.00	$135.00
Teapot	$25.00	$55.00
Coffeepot	$25.00	$55.00
Sugar, covered	$20.00	$35.00
Creamer	$12.00	$25.00
Gravy boat	$18.00	$40.00
Gravy boat with stand	$25.00	$50.00
Celery, butter, or pickle dish	$18.00	$25.00

CLASS II

Simply decorated English bone china, American porcelain by Syracuse, Lenox, Pickard, Noritake, "Queen's Ware," and commonly found Haviland patterns

	LOW	HIGH
Dinner plate	$10.00	$40.00
Salad plate	$8.00	$28.00
Bread and butter plate	$5.00	$20.00
Cup and saucer	$10.00	$60.00
Rimmed soup bowl	$12.00	$35.00
Cereal bowl	$7.00	$30.00
Fruit or dessert bowl	$5.00	$28.00
Platters		
Oval, small	$35.00	$135.00
Oval, medium	$50.00	$175.00
Oval, large	$75.00	$200.00
Round, medium	$40.00	$150.00
Round, large	$50.00	$210.00
Vegetable bowls		
Open, round	$30.00	$125.00
Open, oval	$30.00	$125.00
Covered, round	$40.00	$150.00
Covered, oval	$40.00	$150.00
Tureen, covered	$95.00	$165.00
Tureen, covered with stand	$125.00	$210.00
Teapot	$50.00	$160.00
Coffeepot	$60.00	$185.00
Sugar, covered	$25.00	$65.00
Creamer	$20.00	$55.00
Gravy boat	$40.00	$115.00
Gravy boat with stand	$65.00	$145.00
Celery, butter, or pickle dish	$35.00	$75.00

CLASS III

Fine English and American porcelain, gold-decorated patterns. (It should be noted that the prices for exceptional imported English, French, and Hungarian patterns may actually exceed the "high" values by hundreds of dollars.)

	LOW (Simple, gold rims, floral motif)	MEDIUM (More richly decorated patterns)	HIGH (Elaborate, extremely fine china)
Dinner plate	$50.00	$100.00	$200.00
Salad plate	$35.00	$60.00	$75.00
Bread and butter plate	$25.00	$50.00	$90.00
Cup and saucer	$55.00	$115.00	$195.00
Rimmed soup bowl	$50.00	$75.00	$150.00
Cereal bowl	$45.00	$75.00	$150.00
Fruit or dessert bowl	$20.00	$35.00	$75.00
Platters			
Oval, small	$95.00	$200.00	$285.00
Oval, medium	$120.00	$225.00	$350.00
Oval, large	$150.00	$250.00	$400.00
Round, medium	$120.00	$225.00	$350.00
Round, large	$150.00	$250.00	$400.00
Vegetable bowls			
Open, round	$110.00	$200.00	$250.00
Open, oval	$110.00	$200.00	$250.00
Covered, round	$275.00	$400.00	$600.00
Covered, oval	$275.00	$400.00	$600.00
Tureen, covered	$375.00	$575.00	$650.00
Tureen, covered with stand	$525.00	$725.00	$1,050.00
Teapot	$225.00	$375.00	$550.00
Coffeepot	$185.00	$300.00	$500.00
Sugar, covered	$110.00	$200.00	$350.00
Creamer	$90.00	$165.00	$285.00
Gravy boat	$125.00	$200.00	$350.00
Gravy boat with stand	$175.00	$250.00	$400.00
Celery, butter, or pickle dish	$50.00	$100.00	$200.00

Quick China Reference

Ahrenfeldt. France. See Limoges.

Antique Trader Plates. America. An inexpensive line of commemorative plates.

Bareuther. Germany. An inexpensive line of commemorative plates and bells.

Bavarian china. Many companies were working in Bavaria prior to World War II, producing good, but not exceptional, china for the American market. There are great quantities of Bavarian china around. Many pieces can be replaced through china replacement services.

Belleek. Ireland. Begun in the 1850s, Irish Belleek is fragile, popular, and valuable. Prices can range from a few dollars for currently made, smaller pieces to thousands of dollars for antique pieces. See Belleek, Willets.

Belleek, Willets. America. Both the pieces and the marks will be similar to the Irish Belleek, but the name "Willets" will always be present. Though collectible, not generally as valuable as Irish Belleek.

Bing & Gröndahl. Denmark. Though established in the 1850s, B & G, as it is called, is best known for its line of porcelain figurines, Christmas plates, and other commemorative items.

Boehm. America. Established in 1950, Boehm Studios produce both commercial (and affordable) porcelain plates, flowers, figurines, and the like and rare works of art worth thousands of dollars.

Capo-di-Monte. Italy. Very popular in the nineteenth and early twentieth century, Capo-di-Monte pieces usually have Italian or Mediterranean-type naturalistic decoration, raised or in high relief. Still being produced today.

Carlsbad. Germany and Austria. Both tableware and accessories dating from the 1890s through the 1940s are frequently encountered.

Coalport. England. One of the fine English factories; pieces marked "Coalport" are greatly treasured.

Copeland Spode. England. See Spode.

C. T. Germany. The word "Germany" may or may not appear. Generally a midrange-priced porcelain, but because the pieces belonged to Grandmother, they may be considered "very valuable."

Cybis. America. Cybis porcelain figures date from the 1940s to the present and are expensive.

Davenport. England. Fine-quality semiporcelain made between 1793 and 1887.

Delft. England and Holland. Eighteenth-century pieces will be unmarked or marked in symbols. Pieces with the word "Delft" are of modern vintage. The eighteenth-century pieces are extremely valuable, even in imperfect condition. The modern pieces are generally moderately priced.

Dresden. Germany. Dresden is a town in Germany, just as Limoges is a town in France and Staffordshire is a region in England. Thus "Dresden" has become a term used for any china made in Dresden, Germany. To make things more confusing, the Meissen factory is near Dresden, so many people mistakenly believe that when the term "Dresden" is used, the china is made by the Meissen factory. Actually the chances are slim that the piece your mother calls "Dresden" was made by Meissen. Pieces made by *most* of the Dresden, Germany, factories will be in the midrange of values. See Dresden figurines.

Dresden figurines. Germany, Italy, France, Japan, America. Many people refer to porcelain figures or groups decorated in eighteenth-century clothing as "Dresden." In reality these types of figurines as well as copies were made in almost every country and in every quality. Condition is also very important, as fingers and details (especially on those that have the meshlike crinoline lace skirts) are delicate and fragile.

Elite. France. See Limoges.

Guerin. France. See Limoges.

Haviland. France and America. Without a doubt, Haviland china is thought to be valuable more than any other table china because of its great popularity in the nineteenth and early twentieth centuries. Yet much Haviland is modestly priced in antiques shops. Haviland is still being made today. See Limoges.

Herend. Hungary. An old factory whose new products are extremely popular and expensive.

Hochst. Germany. Dating from the eighteenth century, Hochst is considered one of the greatest factories.

Hummel. Germany. Almost every home has at least one Hummel figure. Value is based on age and subject as well as condition. The secret to knowing the age lies in the mark. Values generally range from $75 through the mid-hundreds. See the listings for Goebel and Schmid in chapter 25, "Limited Editions."

Hutschenreuther. Germany. A midline-quality factory. The "1814" mark is often misinterpreted as the year. The company still exists.

Kaiser Porcelain. Germany. Though established in the nineteenth century, the Kaiser items you might acquire will most likely be limited edition plates and sculptures.

KPM. Germany. KPM is one of the most confusing porcelain marks because it was used by many factories. Fine-quality eighteenth- and nineteenth-century porcelain can be identified as "KPM," but midrange-quality twentieth-century porcelain can also be marked "KPM."

Limoges. France. Limoges is actually a location in France where there were many factories, including Haviland. The fuller names are Haviland Limoges, Elite Limoges, Ahrenfeldt Limoges, and so on. Generally a midpriced china.

Lladro. Spain. Lladro figurines are among today's most popular accessories and are often purchased in Europe and in finer department and jewelry stores in America. Prices will vary greatly.

Longport. England. Fine-quality semiporcelain made between 1793 and 1887.

Mason. England. Highly collectible semiporcelain made in the nineteenth century.

Meissen. Germany. The Meissen factory is one of the greatest porcelain factories and dates from the early 1700s. Many people mistakenly think all

Meissen china is very valuable. Though it is of fine quality, its value depends upon what it is—the pattern, quality, design, and so on. Exceptionally valuable pieces will almost always need to be appraised and insured.

Mettlach. Germany. Mettlach is the town where the greatest German steins were produced by the Villeroy & Boch factories. Steins marked "Mettlach" almost always range from the low hundreds to the thousands of dollars. There are also Mettlach pitchers, plaques, vases, and the like.

Minton. England. Anytime the "Minton" name appears, you are dealing with fine-quality china. Pieces date from the eighteenth century to the present.

Nippon. Japan. The word "Nippon" means Japan. Much china marked "Nippon" was made by the Noritake company. Most pieces range from a few dollars through the low hundreds for exceptional items.

Noritake. Japan. Once very inexpensive, older (pre–World War II) Noritake pieces are now increasing in value and are collectible. The currently manufactured pieces are less expensive than Lenox and fine English company lines.

Occupied Japan. Any china marked "Occupied Japan" was made between 1945 and 1952. Though highly collected, this is inferior-quality china, usually worth only a few dollars, and great quantities of it are still available.

Pouyat. France. See Limoges.

Quimper. France. Quimper, a tin-glazed and hand-painted pottery, is more popular today than ever. Though first made in the seventeenth century, the pieces most frequently seen will date from the twentieth century. Values generally range from a low of $25 to hundreds of dollars.

Royal Copenhagen. Denmark. Best known for Christmas plates and figures. A wide range of values.

Royal Crown Derby. England. Dating from the 1750s, Royal Crown Derby items are of superior quality and are generally expensive.

Royal Doulton. England. Dating from 1815, the twentieth-century figurines are some of the most rapidly advancing collectibles in today's market and can range into the thousands of dollars.

Royal Worcester. England. Begun as the Worcester factory in the eighteenth century, the names "Worcester" and "Royal Worcester" are synonymous with quality and value. Currently Royal Worcester produces several "limited edition" series of porcelain sculptures. Their Doughty birds are considered works of art.

R. S. Prussia. Germany. R. S. Prussia was produced from the 1870s through the 1950s. It is now so highly collected that fake R. S. Prussia decals have been mass-marketed to be attached to poorer-quality porcelain! Most R. S. Prussia pieces are valued in the midhundred range, but with so many fakes around you should get all the information possible and probably consult an appraiser.

Rudolstadt. Germany. Most pieces will be marked R. W. or Royal Rudolstadt. Generally midrange value.

Sarreguemines. France. Though the factory dates from the eighteenth century, most pieces will be later nineteenth and earlier twentieth centuries and be modest in value.

Schumann. Germany. A midline-quality factory.

Selb. Germany. Selb is a town in Germany, just as Limoges is a town in France and Staffordshire is a region in England. Pieces marked Selb are midrange quality.

Sevres. France. Sevres is a town in France, just as Dresden is a town in Germany and Staffordshire is a region in England. Thus "Sevres" has become an abused term. In addition to the misuse of the Sevres name, there are many fakes around. You want to get all the information possible and probably consult an appraiser.

Spode. England. In existence since the eighteenth century, the factory has gone through several name changes and variations. Whenever the name "Spode" appears, the items are of significance.

Staffordshire. England. Staffordshire is actually a location in England where many factories developed, particularly in the mid-nineteenth century. However, many figures and sculptures made in the mid-nineteenth century in Staffordshire were not marked. Prices can vary, from thousands of dollars for some Staffordshire pieces to only modest values for others. Remember, any piece marked "England" or "Made in England" will be more recent.

Villeroy & Boch. See Mettlach.

Wedgwood. England. Produced by one of the earliest English factories, Wedgwood china has always been desirable and expensive. Jasperware pieces are particularly collectible.

18

Crystal and Glassware

For many years crystal was considered an item brides selected and used only on special occasions. For years crystal prices seldom changed. When you went to the store to buy new crystal, you found that, like china, the price for your water goblet was the same or within $.50 to $1 of what it had cost a year or so before.

And when you went to an auction of household property and bid on a complete set of fine lead crystal, you could easily buy it for $.50 to $2 per stem, sometimes less. Crystal sets, like china sets, just were not considered valuable. But they are today. The rise has been radical.

Once again, the change has been precipitated by the increased cost of buying the new. When Irish cut-crystal goblets cost between $40 and $80 per stem, buyers rush to buy older crystal—not yet antique, but of equal and sometimes superior quality to that being sold in stores today. So before you throw out the crystal because you don't have any place to store it, you should realize that this onetime "giveaway" can now stand on its own and demand its own price.

Fine cut crystal is more popular than ever, and sets from estates are now being featured and sold through fashionable auction houses. As many patterns are discontinued and prices for the newly purchased pieces soar, a competitive market for crystal that is only a few years old is emerging. Photograph courtesy Weschler's Auction Gallery

Highly stylized Art Deco glassware, especially martini sets and other cocktail accessories, are becoming quite fashionable once again. Photograph courtesy Richard A. Bourne Company

Types of Household Glass and Crystal

There are three basic categories of glass or crystal in most homes. First is the everyday drinking glass, which may even have come from Hardee's or McDonald's with the purchase of a fast-food order. Believe it or not, these are fast becoming collector's items. In fact, if you really want to start investing in collectibles for the next generation (or the one after that), you should carefully pack these glasses away and never allow them to be touched by human lips again.

Investment aside, most homes have a variety-store-quality collection of glasses, from jelly jars to inexpensive parfait glasses, which only need to be photographed or briefly noted.

Next there is usually a group of glasses comparable to semiporcelain or ironstone dinnerware. This is machine-made glassware produced in modern factories and considerably less expensive than fine lead or hand-blown crystal. Machine-made stemware is usually referred to in crystal departments as casual stemware. But before you throw out this glassware or neglect to list it on your inventory, you should realize that even this can easily run as much as $15 and more per stem.

In the same category you can list your mother's or grandmother's stemware, which she bought for only a few pennies in the 1920s, 1930s, and 1940s. This glassware, which is often pastel-colored (green, pink, blue, or yellow), is the popular collectible of today commonly called "Depression glass." Depression glass, which was sold in large sets, is the equivalent of much of today's machine-made glass.

Once the fashion for this colorful and decorated glass died, the goblets, sherbets, and lemonade pitchers were packed away in attics, given to charities, or simply thrown away. But during the 1960s so much interest in Depression glass was rekindled that articles written on the subject appeared

The soft pastel colors of the Depression glass of the 1920s and 1930s has led to an increasing audience over the past decade.

in magazines, price guides were published, and suddenly Depression glass became a hot collector's item—usually bought or traded at flea markets or through collectors' clubs.

Depression glass generally is still not an expensive item in terms of antiques values. But once again, if you take twelve water goblets that can be sold for $6 each, you end up with $72. And if you have the twelve sherbets, twelve juice glasses, and twelve ice tea goblets to go along with the twelve water goblets, multiply $72 by four and you quickly total $288 for a group of glasses you might be ready to toss in the junk pile. On the other hand, the cost of some rare patterns or pieces in certain colors can rival that of true eighteenth-century glassware. For example, a footed, pink pitcher in the "Doric" pattern by Jeanette is valued in the $600–$800 range.

Collectors of Depression glass buy both specific patterns, such as "Open Rose" and "American Sweetheart," and glassware made by specific companies. Among the most familiar of the glass companies were the Cambridge Glass Company, the Imperial Glass Company (known for its famous Nuart and Nucut lines), the Jeanette Glass Company, and of course the Fostoria Glass Company, which is still operating in Moundsville, West Virginia.

The third category is the finest glassware—hand-blown or hand-cut lead crystal. Fine crystal is called lead crystal because it contains lead oxide, the ingredient that makes the glass clearer in color and gives it the bell-like ring when the rim of the glass is tapped or "pinched," a sound not found in other stemware.

To understand why crystal is so expensive to produce today, you should know that each portion of a goblet—the bowl, stem, and base, or foot—is made separately. Each part is either hand-blown or hand-molded, and then the goblet is assembled and the pieces fused together by a craftsman. The goblet is then given to another craftsman, who cuts or etches the design by hand. If the crystal has a gold or platinum rim, this is hand-painted by yet another craftsman. With the cost of labor and manufacturing what it is today, it is little wonder that a goblet finely cut or richly decorated in gold can equal and sometimes exceed in cost a sterling silver spoon or fork.

Over the years I have found that the questions audiences ask are one of the best barometers of new areas of interest. In the past months I have had one or more questions about Steuben crystal of the 1950s to 1970s—how to identify it and what it's worth. This is a clear signal that people are soon going to be more knowledgeable about Steuben pieces and pay premium prices for those that can no longer be purchased from the Fifth Avenue gallery.

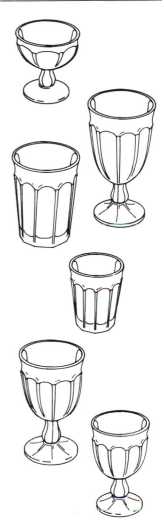

Even if your machine-made, second-best stemware can be bought on sale for $6 or $7 each, by the time you add all the pieces up, the total can be substantial. Line drawing courtesy Noritake

Quality and Condition of Glass and Crystal

As with china and silver, there are grades of quality in crystal. In the value charts you find two listings for crystal stemware. The first is for good-quality crystal, such as that sold today by Noritake, Astral, and Lenox. You can also use this chart to estimate the value of the Heisey glass that you or your mother bought for $2 or $3 per stem in the 1930s and 1940s. However, do remember to take condition into consideration when listing and valuing your crystal. A

The fine craftsmanship of Steuben pieces, combined with their timeless, classical design, makes these not-so-old pieces a new collecting field. Photograph courtesy Weschler's Auction Gallery

crystal goblet that is nicked in several places around the rim can be ground down to a smooth lip, but this can be expensive and the piece will not be in its original perfect condition.

The second chart provides value guides for the finest crystal—that which is hand-cut or richly decorated with deep gold borders. This is the crystal often associated with such companies as Baccarat, Waterford, and Stuart.

A Problem Inherent in Glassware

One of the most frustrating aspects the layperson learning about glassware encounters is that simple question, "Who made it?" There is literally no place to mark stemware except on the bottom; thus, much stemware was never marked even with the manufacturer's name. Many designs were given pattern numbers rather than names. Needless to say, the number and name of a specific pattern were seldom remembered or passed on to the next generation.

Many reprints of glass maufacturers' catalogs are now available, and you can also occasionally identify your mother or grandmother's pattern when looking through old copies of women's magazines. Both articles and advertisements will provide a lot of information for the genuinely curious who are willing to spend some research time.

Pressed Glass

Although most homes do not have a complete set of nineteenth-century pressed glass, this is such a broadly collected favorite that it seems appropriate to discuss it here.

I mentioned earlier that pressed glass values are in a holding pattern at present. The values go up a little each year, and it is certainly getting harder to find the pieces you want. But prices have not suddenly escalated the way they have in the area of Art Nouveau bronzes, for example.

American pressed glass presents a capsule study of fashions and values that is relevant to all antiques—glass, furniture, and art alike.

When pressed glass was first made in the mid-nineteenth century, the public could not get enough of it. Hundreds of pressed glass patterns were made with pieces in each pattern, ranging from egg cups to covered compotes. To be fashionable, a complete set of pressed glass for the dining room was essential.

The popularity of pressed glass reached its height at the end of the nineteenth century when suites and sets were "in." Just as you wanted a suite of matching furniture in your bedroom, so you wanted a set of matching pressed glass, a set of Gorham sterling silver flatware, and a set of French Haviland china adorning your dining table.

Pressed glass was also so inexpensive that it could literally be bought by the barrel. It was purchased from dry goods stores, five-and-dimes, and that wonderful new phenomenon, the catalog store. Eventually, however, the passion for pressed glass died out, and the covered compote, cake stand, and forty-eight goblets were relegated to storage.

But by the late 1920s the public once again became enamored of the nineteenth century's pressed glass, and by the 1930s *research* on Early American pressed glass patterns was begun, notably by Ruth Webb Lee, whose numerous books and articles on the subject (which led to the collecting boom of that time) are still read today. In her *Handbook of Early American Pressed Glass Patterns,* Mrs. Lee wrote: "It is not so many years ago that collectors of American blown glass and writers on the subject attached little importance to later commercial glassware which flooded our markets during the decades immediately preceding and following the Civil War. Collectors of rarities found no pleasure in acquiring anything so plentiful as

Pressed glass from the nineteenth century, once the most popular item for American collectors, is still around but not half as sought after as it once was. Too many reproductions of the old patterns, even sold in museum gift shops, undoubtedly confused the novice. Photograph courtesy Garth's Auctions

Can you guess the auction sale price of these cut and colored nineteenth-century glass accessories? Together, the total is around $2,000. Photograph courtesy Richard A. Bourne Company

glass made in America from 1840 to 1890, but the urge to buy essentially American antiques grew stronger.... Today discriminating collectors are as keenly interested in matching sets of this popular glass, both crystal and colored, as they used to be in acquiring the rare forms of blown glass."

The moral is, just wait long enough and everything comes back into fashion. Now it is almost time for pressed glass to be rediscovered—once again.

Cut Glass

Almost every house has one or more pieces of cut glass, ranging from a simple bonbon or nappy to an elaborate punch set or even a cut glass lamp. The most frequently found American cut glass comes from the Brilliant period of the 1880s to the 1900s, when cut glass was the rage of the day, the way pressed glass had been a few years earlier. But unlike pressed glass, very fine, heavy, large cut glass items, such as lemonade pitchers, decanters, and punch bowls, were very expensive when first made and are equally expensive now. Many factories produced cut glass, and the patterns of cut glass were almost as numerous as sterling silver patterns. Each pattern has a name, and there are many pattern books that list these for you. The decorations most frequently used in cut glass are the hobstar, quarter fan, ribbed, diamond, and caned motifs. These appear separately and in various combinations on every type of cut glass item made. By the late nineteenth century, cut glass was made on an assembly line rather than by an individual craftsman.

Cut glass is always a collector's item, and the combination of cut glass and sterling silver in powder jars, occasionally on pitchers, and even on bonbons, where a silver frame and handle make a basket motif, is highly sought after.

156

Cut glass was often decorated in a combination of deep cutting with pictorial cutting, frequently referred to as intaglio cutting. The combination usually included the quarter fan or diamond deep cuts with an intaglio floral motif. The floral design appeared to be engraved and was more shallow than the deeply cut fans or diamonds.

One of the big confusions in cut glass is distinguishing it from the pressed glass that was copied after cut glass patterns. Pressed glass is made by pressing the pattern into a mold, while cut glass involves the mechanical cutting of the glass by a wheel. Molded edges are rounded and irregular. Cut edges are sharp and angular. Your fingers can quickly learn the difference once you have handled enough of each type of glass. However, to confuse matters further, there are Nucut and Near-cut and Press-cut glass, which more closely resemble cut glass than the usual pressed glass. Just the use of the word "cut" in the name is confusing.

A great deal of cut glass is currently being produced in the European countries, primarily Czechoslovakia, and, once again, marked by a simple, removable label. However, the new cut glass is made in more contemporary shapes, and the motifs of the cuttings are interpreted differently. I haven't found much confusion between old and new cut glass.

If you have difficulty deciding whether a piece is cut or pressed glass, compare it with another piece that you know to be cut glass or pressed glass. Here are some differences to note:

Feel. Pressed glass is made by pressing the pattern into a mold. Cut glass involves the mechanical cutting of the glass by a wheel. Molded edges are round and irregular. Cut edges are sharp and angular. Your fingers can quickly learn the difference once you have *felt* the difference.

Mark. If you see the marks "Nucut," "Near-cut," or "Press-cut," the glass is pressed, *not* cut.

Color. Cut glass has a much clearer, crystallike color because of the high lead content.

Sound. Cut glass has a higher ringing tone than pressed glass.

Weight. Cut glass is considerably heavier than pressed glass.

It is quite fashionable to speak of signed cut glass, although it has been said that perhaps only 10 percent of cut glass made during the Brilliant period was signed. Looking for the signature on cut glass is like knowing the hallmarks on English silver. Once you know what you are looking for, it's easy. Signatures on cut glass are usually in oval or circular forms and are very faint. They were applied by dipping a precut die of the trademark or emblem into acid. This die was then pressed into the glass at a smooth point. To find a signature on cut glass, be sure to look on the *uncut* surface, usually the interior. Shift the piece around in different light until the very faint impression is caught. However, so little cut glass was signed that most often you are wasting your time.

The value of cut glass is dependent upon the condition of the piece, the brilliance of the cutting, the rarity of the piece itself—usually even a simply cut pitcher will be more expensive than most finely cut tumblers, simply because more tumblers were made than pitchers. Also look for unusual

Floral intaglio motifs are used alone or in combination with cut designs. Line drawing courtesy Hudson-Belk

Run your fingers over glass to determine if it is cut or molded.

"Is my cut glass bowl a signed piece?" If so, its value will generally be greater than if it is unsigned. But as you can see, there is no place to sign an elaborately cut piece on the outside. Look on the smooth, interior surface for a signature. Photograph courtesy Richard A. Bourne Company

shapes. A fine heart or cloverleaf-shaped bonbon dish will be more valuable than a simple round bonbon dish.

Hints on Glass Fakes and Copies

Glass is one of the most commonly copied and faked of all antiques. I believe this is because there are so many glass collectors. Tourists, antiques shop browsers—everyone wants to buy a small memento or have a collection that can be added to bit by bit. Not only can a piece of glass easily be carried home, it can be set out on display after a quick rinsing off. Furthermore, since glass is fairly inexpensive to make, it is worth the time and trouble to copy or fake antique glass that can be sold for a large profit. You might refer to the admonitions included in chapters 14 and 34 to remind you that this is a very precarious area.

Pressed glass patterns have been copied for years. Many companies claim that these newer pieces are made "from the original molds," but glass experts tell us there is a difference in the weight and color between the old and the new.

Now even Depression glass is being reproduced. However, most sets of crystal found in homes today are just what they appear to be—wedding presents from the twentieth century—and they should be included on your inventory.

> The more spectacular pieces of cut glass are now showing up at some of the larger auction houses, thus indicating the viable interest in cut glass in the marketplace.

Describing and Inventorying Your Crystal

Follow the same procedure in listing your crystal that you followed when you entered your china. Categorize each pattern and list the number of individual pieces you have, such as goblets, sherbets, juice glasses, and so on.

Because so little glassware is marked and most pattern names are forgotten, describe the design as best you can. If you find yourself stuck for words even after referring to the glass decorative motifs on page 162, sketch the basic style of your goblet beside the listing or attach a photograph to your inventory.

To verbally describe crystal stemware, note the shape of the bowl (globe-shaped, flared at the top, and so on) and any pattern or design on the bowl (floral band, swirled motif, gold rim . . .). Next state whether the stem is short, long, notched, round, whatever. Almost all stemware has a round base if it is in goblet form.

Finally, total up the number of pieces in each pattern, the same way you did with the china, and estimate an approximate replacement cost by using the accompanying value charts.

Casual Stemware

(Use for current machine-made glass and the usual Depression glass patterns. It should be noted that some rare Depression glass serving pieces are now selling for hundreds of dollars.)

	LOW	HIGH		LOW	HIGH
Goblet	$10	$25	Bud vase	$8	$25
Ice tea	$10	$25	Salt and pepper shakers	$6	$20
Sherbet	$10	$25	Pitcher	$15	$50
Wine	$10	$25	Vinegar cruet	$8	$35
Tumbler	$10	$25	Cake plate	$12	$35
Salad/dessert plate	$10	$20	Open bowl	$15	$50
Candlesticks, 4-in. pair	$15	$60	Relish dish	$8	$25
Sugar bowl	$10	$30	Decanter	$38	$65
Creamer	$8	$25			

Crystal Stemware I

(Use for good-quality lead crystal, including much Heisey glass.)

	LOW	HIGH		LOW	HIGH
Goblet	$20	$40	Bud vase	$16	$42
Ice tea	$20	$40	Salt and pepper shakers	$18	$40
Sherbet	$20	$40	Pitcher	$50	$115
Wine	$20	$40	Vinegar cruet	$35	$50
Tumbler	$20	$40	Cake plate	$35	$55
Salad/dessert plate	$20	$40	Open bowl	$32	$115
Candlesticks, 4-in. pair	$60	$135	Relish dish	$25	$50
Sugar bowl	$22	$45	Decanter	$75	$200
Creamer	$20	$40			

Crystal Stemware II

(This is for excellent-quality crystal—hand-cut—usually imported, including some crystal by Stuart, Orrefors, Baccarat, Waterford, and crystal with a rich gold band. Some patterns can far exceed the "High Values.")

	LOW	HIGH		LOW	HIGH
Goblet	$50	$100	Bud vase	$60	$125
Ice tea	$50	$100	Salt and pepper shakers	$75	$175
Sherbet	$50	$100	Pitcher	$110	$350
Wine	$50	$100	Vinegar cruet	$60	$150
Tumbler	$50	$100	Cake plate	$95	$250
Salad/dessert plate	$55	$100	Open bowl	$110	$350
Candlesticks, 4-in. pair	$90	$175	Relish dish	$60	$125
Sugar bowl	$50	$80	Decanter	$165	$500
Creamer	$50	$80			

Well-Known Glass Manufacturers

Anchor Hocking		Imperial Glass Co.	
Cambridge		Indiana Glass Co.	
C. Dorflinger		Jeanette Glass Co.	
Duncan Miller		Libbey	
Federal Glass		McKee Glass Co.	
Fenton Art Glass		Millersburg Glass Co.	
Fostoria		New Martinsville Glass Co.	
Fry		Northwood Glass Co.	
T. G. Hawkes		Pairpoint	
A. H. Heisey		Steuben	
J. Hoare		United States Glass Co.	

Glass Glossary

Amberina. The color will shade from light amber to rich ruby.

Aurene. Has a lustrous, iridescent appearance, was made by Steuben, and is similar to Favrile made by Tiffany.

Bohemian. By fusing two layers of glass, one clear, the other red, blue, amber, or green, figures and designs can be cut away.

Burmese. Opaque glass shading from a pastel yellowish color to light red or rose.

Cameo. Glass made of layers of different colors, of which part is cut or carved away to create a design.

Cranberry glass. Obviously the color of cranberry juice. Inexpensive cranberry glass was made by applying a thin layer of color over clear glass (flashed). Lighter than ruby glass.

Favrile. One of many types of glass made by L. C. Tiffany and recognizable by its iridescent surface and metallic design. Signed in either initials (L.C.T.) or the name "Tiffany."

Gallé. A French glassmaker noted primarily for extremely fine cameo glass.

Handel. A maker of glass-shade lamps (and some other glass objects). Handel items are highly prized and extremely valuable.

Lalique. Most noted as a maker of fine glass and exquisite jewelry working in France in the early twentieth century. The factory continues today producing the frosted designs he originated. Of substantial and increasing value.

Loetz. A Bohemian factory mostly associated with sterling silver overlay art pieces of high quality and value.

Mary Gregory. A term for glass having white-enameled figures painted on it, usually blue or red. Made around the world and greatly reproduced.

Milk glass. Opaque white glass called that because it looks like milk. Also available in colors—blue, green, amethyst, and black. Available in great quantities and greatly reproduced.

Moser. A Bohemian factory begun in the mid-nineteenth century and still operating as Ludwig Moser & Son (Sohne). Many new Moser collectors are emerging, and prices are climbing.

Murano. Actually a location in Italy, but glass with swirling colors is often referred to generically as "Murano."

Pairpoint. A maker of glass, silver, and glass-shade lamps of high collectible and monetary value.

Ruby glass. A deep red or ruby color. Greatly copied and reproduced since its nineteenth-century origin.

Satin. Called that because of its smooth, satin-type finish. Will often have a white lining and can be decorated over the smooth finish.

Slag. Thick-bodied glass with a swirl of color, usually purple, blue, pink, red, or tan. Often said to look like a marble cake. Greatly reproduced since its nineteenth-century origin.

Steuben. The Steuben Glass Works is considered the greatest continual maker of American glass and is still in existence today. All Steuben pieces are expensive and of the highest quality.

Tiffany. Louis Comfort Tiffany and the Tiffany Studio are known for different types of art glass as well as stained-glass windows and lamp shades. See Favrile.

Venetian glass. Venice has been the seat of fine glassmaking since the fifth century. Venetian glass has become a generic term for many types of glass that originated in Venice—some valuable, others of souvenir quality.

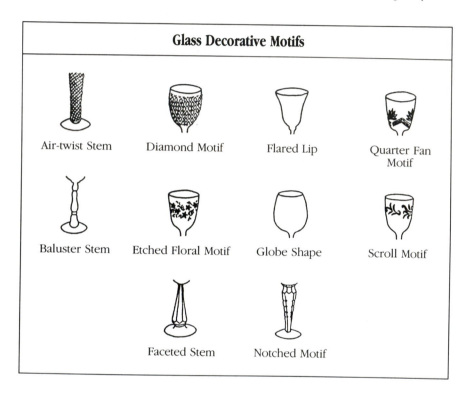

Glass Decorative Motifs

Air-twist Stem   Diamond Motif   Flared Lip   Quarter Fan Motif

Baluster Stem   Etched Floral Motif   Globe Shape   Scroll Motif

Faceted Stem   Notched Motif

19

Furniture:
Chip off the Old Block or Chipboard?

Unless you have an exceptionally fine collection of silver or jewelry, or a specialized collection such as coins or guns, the single largest investment in your household personal property is probably your furniture. Whether antique, old reproductions, or new doesn't really matter. Furniture is expensive to buy these days.

Entire series of books have been written on furniture, and I would be foolish to think I could educate you completely in all facets of styles, construction, and values in one chapter. (No one person knows everything anyway.) So, based on observations made in my clients' homes and the questions I am most frequently asked, I am sharing the information I think will be of greatest help to you. This chapter concentrates on the styles and types of furniture I see most often in your homes and in antiques shops, furniture stores, and at auctions.

I will not deal with early-sixteenth- or seventeenth-century furniture. Chances are you do not have pieces from this period. But I will deal with these furniture *styles* made in the twentieth century, which you may well have. I will not delve into rare Newport blockfront secretaries or Philadelphia highboys. But I will tell you about the reproductions and copies of these rare and extraordinarily valuable antiques. After you have read my comments, if you examine your highboy or secretary and believe it to be a period piece, call in an expert.

Remember the terms in chapter 13 distinguishing between period pieces and later pieces made in the same style? Knowing the difference in terminology is essential to understanding furniture. To further clarify the difference between "period" and "style," date ranges of the original period are given for each style heading.

Also, a quick reread of chapter 14 will reinforce the points you need to recall when checking pieces for repairs and alterations.

It is important to realize that these styles are not unique to America. Traditionally styles originated in England or Europe and were then adapted in America, usually after a short time lapse. The earlier the period—Queen

Anne, for example—the greater the time lapse. By the end of the nineteenth century the many world expositions (Columbian Exposition of 1893 in Chicago, World Exhibition of 1900 in Paris), combined with greater technology meant various styles developed almost simultaneously throughout the world. The dates given in the text generally cover both the English and American original periods, but because of the English use of reigns to define styles, use the following chart as a reference.

Monarch	Dates of Reign	Furniture Period Names
James I	1603–1625	Jacobean
Charles I	1625–1649	Carolean
Commonwealth	1649–1660	Cromwellian or Commonwealth
Charles II	1660–1685	Restoration
James II	1685–1689	Restoration
William and Mary	1689–1694	William and Mary
William III	1694–1702	William III or William and Mary
Anne	1702–1714	Queen Anne
George I	1714–1727	George I—early Georgian
George II	1727–1760	Early Georgian
George III	1760–1811	Later Georgian
George III	1811–1820	Regency
George IV	1820–1830	Regency
William IV	1830–1837	Late Regency or William IV
Victoria	1837–1901	Early Victorian up to 1860
		Later Victorian 1860–1901
Edward VII	1901–1910	Edwardian

Let's begin then with the *styles* and *types* of furniture most commonly found in homes and shops today, so you can correctly identify the pieces on your inventory.

Pilgrim Furniture—There Isn't Much Around

STYLE: Jacobean or William and Mary
           Also referred to as Tudor, Renaissance, Carolean, Early American, and Baroque
AGE: 1600–1700, seventeenth century
ORIGIN: England and America, primarily; also Spain, France, Italy, Germany

During the 1920s Wallace Nutting brought the public's attention back to what he termed "Pilgrim" or "Colonial" furniture, the furniture of the seventeenth century, including Brewster and Carver chairs, trestle tables, joint or joined stools, butterfly and gateleg tables, and Hadley chests. Few pieces actually survived from the 1650s, so the majority of joint stools and

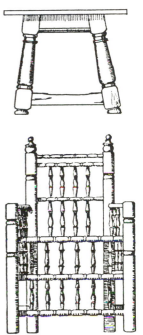

This imposing Jacobean piece may even legally be termed an "antique." But it does not date from the 1600s or 1700s. It is a nineteenth-century interpretation of the Jacobean style. Photograph courtesy Weschler's Auction Gallery

In adapting the seventeenth-century styles to the twentieth-century home, many liberties were taken with the original style and form. Recognizing furniture forms that did not exist in the original period is one way of identifying reproductions. In 1915, when these reproductions were at the height of popularity, Charles D. Thomson voiced his disapproval of these "adaptations" in the April issue of Good Furniture.

The familiar curving lines of Queen Anne furniture are often embellished by the addition of a shell motif. In fact, adding a shell in the late nineteenth and early twentieth centuries to a plain eighteenth-century Queen Anne piece was one way of "enhancing" it.

butterfly tables found today are indeed nineteenth-century or even Nutting's 1920 reproductions or, as in the case of the infamous Brewster chair discussed in chapter 14, a modern fake.

Not only was there relatively little furniture made to begin with (there were fewer people living then), but period seventeenth-century furniture tended to be big, cumbersome, squarish, heavy in appearance, and uncomfortable. Large panels and turned parts are major identifying points. Little period furniture survived. However, the seventeenth-century *style* of tables—butterfly, trestle, and gateleg—have frequently been copied and are often found in homes today. The quality of reproduction pieces ranges from custom-made to the cheapest veneered "bargain basement" variety.

Queen Anne—A Graceful Lady

STYLE: Queen Anne
AGE: 1702–1760
ORIGIN: England and America

By the eighteenth century one of the most popular of all styles, Queen Anne, emerged with its lovely curves and graceful lines replacing the large,

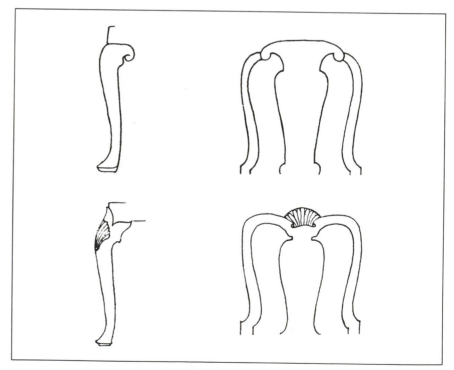

One of the most frequently copied styles, Queen Anne furniture comes in a variety of qualities. The pieces do not have to be very old to demand high prices when fine quality is present. This Biggs Furniture Company reproduction sold for $800 at Weschler's Auction Gallery in early 1987.

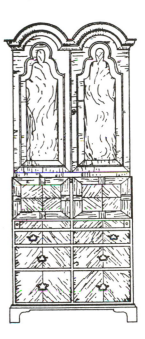

bulbous furniture of the seventeenth century. Queen Anne–style furniture can be identified by looking first at the legs and then at the top of the piece in question. The cabriole leg curves outward at the knee and then tapers at the ankle. The foot may be slippered, padded, trifid, or, once the Chippendale influence begins, ball-and-claw.

The top of Queen Anne furniture usually repeats the graceful curve. A Queen Anne secretary is identified by its domed, curved top, and Queen Anne chairbacks repeat the graceful curved line at both the crest rail and the back splat.

Queen Anne furniture may be totally plain or embellished with carving—the shell motif is most frequently used. While period Queen Anne furniture is scarce and expensive, it is not rare. The style of Queen Anne furniture was frequently copied in the nineteenth century and continues to be manufactured today.

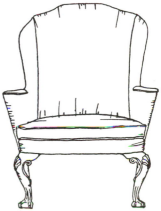

Chippendale—The Gentleman Cabinetmaker

STYLE: Chippendale
            Also referred to as English Georgian
AGE: 1750–1790
ORIGIN: England and America

Chippendale furniture became stylish in the second quarter of the eighteenth century and lasted in America until almost the end of the century, or around 1785 or 1790. There are many variations of the basic Chippendale style, with Chinese Chippendale, characterized by its fretwork, being the most familiar.

Chippendale furniture retains some of the characteristics of the Queen Anne period, but it is generally distinguished by its straighter lines and heavier feeling. These characteristics are most easily seen by comparing a basic side chair, a table, and a secretary from the two periods.

Three chests, three ages, three prices. Each can be described as a Chippendale mahogany chest of drawers with molded top above four graduated drawers, flanked by fluted quarter columns, with ogee bracket feet, but only one can use the term "period." The first piece is the eighteenth-century Philadelphia chest (photograph courtesy Craig and Tarlton), *the middle is a currently manufactured chest in the Kindel Winterthur Collection* (photograph courtesy Kindel), *and the last is an old Biggs reproduction* (photograph courtesy Weschler's).

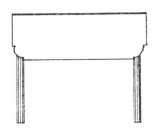

Yes, you will find curved lines in the Chippendale chair back splat, but they are framed by a boxier and straighter outline. The ball-and-claw foot becomes a major characteristic, and the curved leg of the Queen Anne is replaced by the straight leg characteristic of the Chippendale period. The top of a Chippendale secretary will be straight across or have a broken swan-neck pediment, which is characterized by its triangular or scroll outline.

Fine Chippendale furniture is considered by many to be the epitome of grand elegance. It is more imposing than Queen Anne furniture, and its strong lines and boldness are largely responsible for its popularity. English Chippendale furniture is often classified as "Georgian," and later Edwardian renderings of the Chippendale style are also often found in America. Because of the great popularity of Chippendale furniture, as well as its size, which requires large boards of wood and greater labor costs, even reproduction Chippendale furniture can be expensive, as Kindel's Winterthur line and Century's National Trust of England, Wales, and Northern Ireland collections testify.

Adams Furniture—An American Hiccup

Following the Chippendale period, at the end of the eighteenth century or around 1780, America jumped right into the Hepplewhite period. But in England, which is the predominating influence on American furniture styles, the mid-eighteenth century saw a new development, the Adams style, named after brothers who were also designers, Robert and James Adam.

During this time, the ideal fine English home was one in which the architecture, furniture, wallpaper, fabrics, silver, even furniture arrangements were perfectly coordinated. The Adams period is characterized by circles, ovals, urns, and garlands, and the furniture begins to be lighter in feeling.

However, during this time—the 1760s and 1770s—Americans were more involved in political unrest and pioneering than they were in developing new high fashions. Thus, relatively little of the Adams influence is found in American furniture.

Hepplewhite—A Chance to Express Ourselves

STYLE: Federal
            Also referred to as Hepplewhite and Sheraton
AGE: 1780–1815
ORIGIN: America and England

As the 1780s arrived, Americans were looking for new styles to show off their newfound independence, both political and economic. The Hepplewhite period dominates American taste from the 1780s until the turn of the nineteenth century.

The motifs of the Hepplewhite period—inlaid shields and urns—and the lighter, more delicate feeling of the furniture had actually evolved from the Adams style, which of course had evolved from the Chippendale style. Thus, when you compare the evolution of English furniture from Chippendale to Adams to Hepplewhite, the change seems more gradual than when you go from the American Chippendale period straight into the American Hepplewhite period.

American Hepplewhite furniture can often be distinguished from English Hepplewhite furniture by the ornamentation added to the basic style. By the 1780s Americans were proud of their country's accomplishments, and typical

American symbols were used in furniture ornamentation. Eagles, crossed arrows, the American shield, even stars appear on tables, chair backs, clock cases, and secretaries. (Of course to incorporate these designs in the furniture, inlaying and carving were refined and perfected.)

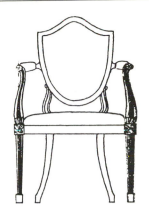

Because of the American motifs found during this time, many scholars call the era from 1780 to 1810 in America the Federal period. You will hear Hepplewhite, Sheraton, and Federal used interchangeably. But obviously Federal is not a term used in discussing English furniture of this era.

Hepplewhite furniture has experienced a resurgence of popularity in recent years. The smaller, daintier proportions of the style, in combination with lighter wood colors, make it more suitable for many smaller homes, apartments, and town houses than the larger and darker Chippendale (or later Empire or Victorian) furniture. Many reproductions of Hepplewhite furniture were made in the twentieth century, and the older, finer custom-made pieces are commanding high prices today.

Sheraton—Moving into the Nineteenth Century

By the end of the eighteenth century, the Industrial Revolution was picking up steam and styles were changing more rapidly than they had at any previous time in history. Developing simultaneously at the end of the Hepplewhite era was the Sheraton style, which began around 1790 and extended into the first decade of the nineteenth century.

Remember that the Sheraton period is often included in the broad term "American Federal period." In fact, Sheraton is a much maligned word in the antiques world. Many people simply consider the Sheraton period an extension of Hepplewhite and refer to all Sheraton furniture as "Hepplewhite." Still others insist upon calling Sheraton furniture "Duncan Phyfe." In reality, Sheraton furniture has its own special style, which I illustrate here, but don't be surprised if you hear it called Federal, Hepplewhite, or Duncan Phyfe.

The easiest way to distinguish Sheraton furniture from Hepplewhite is by comparing the legs and the wood. The characteristic Sheraton leg, whether on a chair, table, or chest of drawers, is rounded and may be turned or fluted. (The Hepplewhite leg is square and tapering.) The characteristic use of inlay in the Hepplewhite period is replaced with plain drawer fronts and tabletops of either solid wood or veneer during the Sheraton period.

Sheraton chairs are distinguished by their backs, of which there are two major types. One has an angular or squared-off back (when contrasted with the Hepplewhite shield back), with either an open carved center splat design (this may be similar to the Hepplewhite style) or vertical splats, which sometimes resemble chair legs or columns.

The other type of chair is the one often called Duncan Phyfe, which is recognizable by the wider, horizontal crest rail. The rest of the chair back may be totally open with only another horizontal slat, or there may be a carved, often lyre motif, back splat.

(Reading along, you have already learned a lot of furniture terminology that can be used in writing your descriptions. For example, you now know that a splat is the vertical back, which runs up and down from the crest rail to the seat. A slat is the horizontal back, which runs across from one side—or stile—to the other.)

The Sheraton chest of drawers is easily distinguishable from the Hepplewhite chest because of the shape of the legs and the higher, or raised, aspect of the piece. Also, the inlay found on sophisticated Hepplewhite sideboards or Pembroke tables is replaced by fluting, reeding, or turning on fine Sheraton pieces.

Sheraton furniture is not as popular as Hepplewhite, Chippendale, or Queen Anne. It is therefore often less expensive than other, more favored styles. Many fine Sheraton period pieces are available in the marketplace. But be careful: the style was copied and reproduced at the turn of the century, as it continues to be today.

Poor Duncan Phyfe

Duncan Phyfe's name has become associated with a style of furniture, when in fact Phyfe, who worked in New York from 1780 to 1840, made furniture in *several* styles. It is not at all uncommon to hear a Sheraton, Empire, or Victorian chair called a Duncan Phyfe chair. This would have been fine (Chippendale, Hepplewhite, and Sheraton had styles named after them) except that Duncan Phyfe's style *changed* following the changing tastes of his time. Thus, while other cabinetmakers followed only Hepplewhite's designs, for example, Duncan Phyfe's designs also followed the tastes of the Sheraton and Empire styles. It is best not to refer to Phyfe as a style but to go by Sheraton, Empire, and Victorian instead. However, remember the name if someone tries to sell you a "true" Duncan Phyfe piece. The "Duncan Phyfe style" was mass-produced in the 1930s through the 1950s.

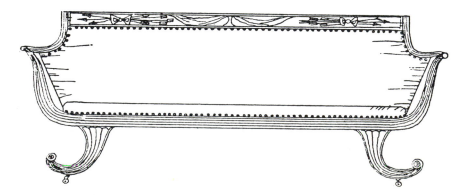

Empire

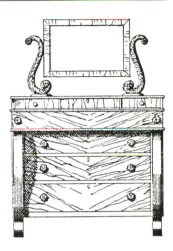

STYLE: Empire
Also called Duncan Phyfe and Regency
AGE: 1815–1850
ORIGIN: America and England

You leave one area of confusion only to step into another. The designation "Empire furniture" can be just as bewildering in its way as the term "Duncan Phyfe." But all this can easily be cleared up.

American Empire furniture was actually made from about 1810 until the beginning of the Victorian period, or 1850. Very high fashion Empire furniture is carved, gilded, and quite unlike any other style. The decorative motifs derive from architecture (the Greek key and palmette), nature (cornucopias and serpents), and classical mythology (dolphins, griffins, and caryatids). On the other hand, the common man's Empire furniture tends to be heavy, bold, and either richly ornamented or starkly plain.

There is as wide a difference in the quality of Empire furniture as exists in any style. The high-style furniture of the 1815–1830 era is usually spoken of as Neoclassical, whereas the more commonly found, much less stylish pieces are simply called Empire.

The typical American Empire furniture found in today's homes is often mistakenly called Victorian because both styles are large, heavy, and dark. As a result, Empire pieces are generally lumped in with the rest of the nineteenth-century furniture, and the varying styles of almost one hundred years are termed "Victorian."

The usual Empire household furniture is characterized by its straight lines, mahogany veneer, and basic plainness. You have seen hundreds of Empire chests and tables, but perhaps you called them Duncan Phyfe or Victorian.

Because Empire period furniture was being manufactured and shipped throughout the country, much of it looks alike. Also, this was the era of mass-manufactured Hitchcock chairs and mantel clocks.

The typical Empire piece is the most underpriced furniture around these days. Because it is veneered and was often heavily varnished (as was popular in the late nineteenth and early twentieth centuries), much of the furniture has missing veneer and a grungy, crackled finish. Empire furniture is also

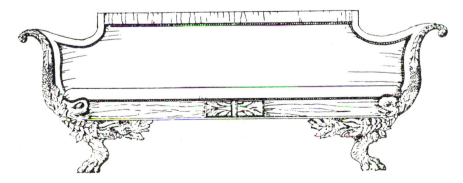

oversized for many of today's homes. But just wait! Prices are already beginning to creep up as the cost and quality of modern furniture astound the public. Empire is on the verge of being rediscovered.

You need to know that reproductions of Empire furniture were made in the twentieth century. Look for modern tool marks and screws and the absence of wear to tell the difference. But also remember, 1830 is the benchmark date given for modern-type tools and the introduction of *manufactured* furniture. The majority of later Empire pieces were manufactured, *not* handcrafted. Further, an abundance of period Empire furniture is still available today, which accounts for the lower prices even of true period pieces. Generally speaking there is little difference in value between the ordinary *period* Empire piece and the later reproduction pieces, even though there can be one hundred years' difference in age. Quality and condition are of utmost importance in establishing values for Empire pieces.

Queen Victoria—A Much Abused Lady

STYLE: Victorian
Also referred to as Gothic (1840–1860), Rococo (1845–1875), Renaissance (1850–1880), Eastlake (1870–1900), and Cottage (1840–1900)
AGE: 1840–1900
ORIGIN: America and England

Queen Victoria ascended the English throne in 1837 and remained there until her death in 1901. Every dominant style of furniture made during those sixty-four years bears her name. The era began quietly with a gradual change from the plain but large Empire furniture to a more decorated style with the embellishment of Empire pieces. A rose was carved on the back of a sofa, the horizontal splat of a chair was made to resemble a Gothic arch, and soon the Victorian era was in full swing.

There are five major substyles of Victorian furniture with a great deal of overlapping of their years of popularity. But once you learn what motifs characterize each, the substyles can be easily identified.

Victorian Gothic

The first substyle is the Gothic (1840–1860). Victorian Gothic furniture is characterized by the architectural motifs found on the great European cathedrals built during the fourteenth century. There are arches, trefoils, quatrefoils, and rosettes all intertwined and conjoined. Gothic Victorian furniture is not as popular or as frequently found as the next substyle.

Victorian Rococo

The Victorian Rococo style is the most familiar of the Victorian substyles and uses the same decorations as the original Rococo period (eighteenth century) but interprets them differently. The word "rococo" comes from the French word *rocaille* and means "rock" or "shell." So Victorian Rococo furniture is an intermingling of flowers, shells, grapes, foliage, all brought together in curved, flowing, even "rocky" lines. Some of the pieces are more elaborately decorated than others, but the flowing, curved line is consistently present. Included in this large substyle are characteristics of Louis XV furniture, also exemplified by the cabriole line, scroll, and floral motifs. Rococo is the most popular of all the Victorian substyles and has been expensively priced for quite a while.

As you now know, by the time Victorian Rococo became fashionable furniture was largely manufactured rather than handcrafted. For this reason it can be very difficult to distinguish between period nineteenth-century pieces and those reproduced in the 1930–1950 era. Today, Victorian Rococo pieces are being reproduced both in America and in inferior quality in the Orient.

Victorian Renaissance

The Victorian Renaissance came into fashion around 1850 and lasted through the 1870s. By this time, furniture manufacturers in New York and Michigan could easily meet the public's demand for the latest fashions, and these new pieces were quickly bought to replace old, out-of-style furniture.

The public got what it wanted—large, heavily decorated furniture with strong European overtones. Scrolls and flowers were still used, but in a more geometric fashion. Bulls'-eyes and shields appear frequently, but the most distinguishing motif of the Renaissance style is a cartouche used as the center decoration on chairs, beds, mirrors, and sideboards or buffets. The entire shape of this style departs from the Rococo rounded shape and the Gothic pointed or turreted shape. Renaissance pieces are more rectangular or squared and geometric in total perspective. The large size of this style has limited its popularity. Victorian Renaissance furniture can still be found and is usually priced in the middle line of the Victorian styles.

Victorian Eastlake

Following the Renaissance, and incorporating some of its characteristics, is the fourth substyle, Victorian Eastlake furniture (1870–1900). Inspired by the English architect Charles Locke Eastlake, this substyle is identifiable by two main characteristics.

1. Burl wood or veneered panels appear on drawer fronts, cupboard doors, and chair backs. If this decoration is not present, you can almost bet that
2. An incised motif (carved into the wood) will be in its place. Pilasters on chests and table legs were reeded during the Eastlake period.

The Eastlake style has been passed over in favor of the other Victorian substyles. Eastlake furniture has yet to become fashionable and thus is plentiful and affordable. Because the furniture is generally less imposing than

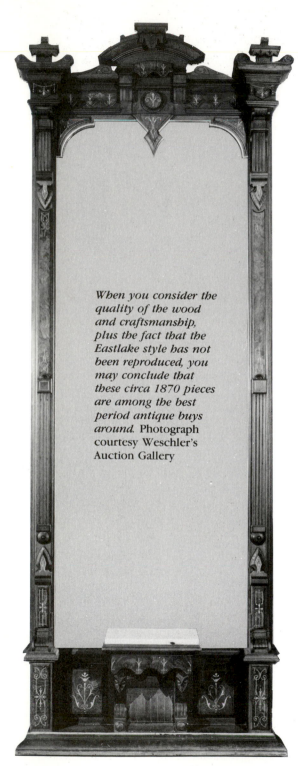

When you consider the quality of the wood and craftsmanship, plus the fact that the Eastlake style has not been reproduced, you may conclude that these circa 1870 pieces are among the best period antique buys around. Photograph courtesy Weschler's Auction Gallery

other Victorian substyles, is usually made of walnut (instead of the later golden oak), has some style (the burl panels in particular), and is still available at a reasonable price, it is a good buy if you like the style. To my knowledge, unlike the other "sleeper"—Empire furniture—Eastlake furniture has not been mass-reproduced.

Victorian Cottage

The fifth substyle is known as Victorian Cottage (sometimes called Spool style). This fashion lasted from around 1840 until the end of the nineteenth century and has never really gone out of style. The furniture is everywhere, from Cape Cod cottages to crossroads stores in the Midwest, and is characterized by its simple style and spool (or Jenny Lind) turnings. The furniture was mass-produced and was inexpensive when it was made. In fact, it is probably more expensive now in relation to its value than it was when it was first made. The furniture was often sold in suites and painted or stenciled. Much of what you find today has had the paint removed.

Because the "country look" is popular today, cottage furniture, though neither terribly old nor of fine quality, is in great demand, and prices are creeping up.

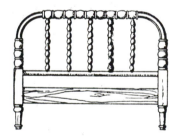

Belter—A Star Is Born

Before concluding with Victorian styles and moving on to Golden Oak and Mission furniture, a comment should be made about Belter furniture.

Fifteen years ago if you wanted information on John Belter, you would have searched to find a scant bibliographical entry or a sentence or two about his work under "Victorian furniture." Today Belter furniture is pictured on the covers of slick magazines, in auction house catalogs, and in expensive full-page magazine ads. At least one new article about Belter appears every month.

During the 1850s John Belter developed revolutionary techniques that allowed wood to be curved, shaped, and carved. His laminated furniture, mostly of rosewood, exemplifies the Victorian Rococo style. Although Belter's name is not yet as familiar as Chippendale's, the prices paid for his furniture now equal those of fine eighteenth-century furniture—and a few years ago you couldn't give it away.

The Overlooked International Style—Art Nouveau

One furniture style that was never as popular in America as it was in Europe is Art Nouveau. The curves and flowing lines associated with the Art Nouveau style appeared in every decoration in Europe in the 1890s, from staircases to statues. American artisans produced wonderful accessories in this sensuous style, but no major American Art Nouveau furniture was ever *mass-produced*. A few advertisements can be found for music cabinets and side-by-sides that hint at the flowing Art Nouveau lines, but the imposing cabinets, dining room tables, beds, and seating furniture so popular in France and Belgium never caught hold on this side of the Atlantic. One Chicago company, Karpen, did produce an Art Nouveau line, but this furniture simply does not show up often and, as a result, has no serious market. The brass beds, with their scrolled and interlooped head and foot posts, approach Art Nouveau, but this style has been so reproduced that its market has softened.

Perhaps the lines of the Art Nouveau style were too free, just too much for the rather proper and restrained American public. Or maybe there was a quiet, unspoken resistance to ideas coming out of Europe in the days preceding World War I.

Oak—Gold Is Right

STYLE: Golden Oak
AGE: 1890–1920s
ORIGIN: America and now many Oriental reproduction imports

How many times have you heard the rather elitist comment, "There was no good furniture made after 1840" . . . or 1850, or whenever? Yet one of the most popular styles of vintage furniture is the Golden Oak style. It was popular in its day, and it remains popular these many decades later.

At the end of the nineteenth century and during the first quarter of the twentieth century, oak was the favorite of the great American middle class. Golden Oak furniture was mass-produced and generally inexpensive, was sold in showrooms, from catalogs, and even given away as premiums by the Larkin Soap Company. My own father has told me many times of the day in his childhood, in 1918 or 1919, when the Golden Oak secretary arrived at his home. He helped move the new secretary in and hauled the 1800 cherry Chippendale secretary up to the attic for storage. (Thank goodness they kept it in storage until my mother rescued it in 1938! Unfortunately, however, the Golden Oak secretary was given away in the 1950s.)

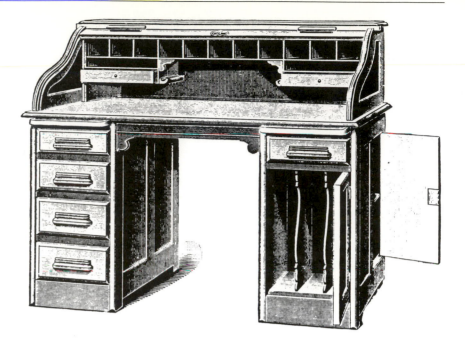

"I really couldn't figure out, even in my child's mind, why they wanted to replace the beautiful, heavy cherry secretary with that ugly light oak piece," he recalls today.

Today's generation looks at oak differently—they consider it to be "antique," although it was retailed new as late as the 1930s. There is much speculation as to what brought this inexpensive furniture back into fashion—but probably the respectability of its increasing age, combined with its durability when compared with some of today's chipboard furniture, are as good reasons as there need to be.

Golden Oak furniture is easily recognizable by its wood grain alone. The major styles concentrate on large, oversize pieces reminiscent of Empire furniture (which, you see, was just about one hundred years before Golden Oak furniture—remember it is said that styles go in one-hundred-year cycles) and the angular, straight, almost barren furniture associated with the Mission style.

> Warning: Golden Oak furniture became highly popular again so quickly that entrepreneurs both here and in the Orient are making copies and reproductions. It is not uncommon to see an 1880 Golden Oak table with 1988 Golden Oak chairs sold as a group in antiques shops.

Arts and Crafts and Mission Furniture

STYLE:　Arts and Crafts
　　　　Also referred to as Mission
AGE:　1905–1920
ORIGIN:　America and England

Once the furniture manufacturers had thriving businesses, they learned they had to keep the public buying. If fashions never changed, there would be no reason to buy new furniture once a house was furnished.

The end of the Victorian era, the 1880s and 1890s, saw a reaction to the ornate furniture of the mid-nineteenth century, beginning first in England and then moving to America. In resistance to the trefoils, flowers, cartouches, incised grape leaves, burl woods, oyster veneers, and turned spools of the previous fifty years, a new, austere fashion developed. The Arts and Crafts style, as it was called, was extremely linear and mostly devoid of superfluous decoration. In America the movement was interpreted by such fine craftsmen as Elbert Hubbard and Gustav Stickley. But the style was quickly picked up by the furniture manufacturers, and the less expensive mass-produced versions of this furniture made by the Grand Rapids, Michigan, companies became known as Mission furniture, after the austere Spanish style associated with New Mexico and Texas. Since this section of the country held much fascination for the faraway East Coast, it caught on, both as a name and a style.

And it has caught on again. Some seventy years after the Stickley companies published their catalogs, *Craftsman Furniture Made by Gustav Stickley* and *The Work of L. and G. Stickley,* they have been reprinted, and their names are once again famous.

The current vogue is in higher swing in New York and California than in other sections of the country. But interior decorators are looking for this furniture to combine with Tiffany Studio lamps and Rookwood pottery to create a total look. However, as is true with all furniture styles, the value of Arts and Crafts furniture is directly related to the *quality* of the furniture. Whenever a style has a revival, until articles and books have covered the area unknowing buyers may incorrectly assume one piece is as good as another and make unwise purchases.

Because a great deal of this furniture does exist and will be "discovered" in the next few years, now is the time to learn clues to distinguish the inexpensive, "generic" furniture from the craftsman's pieces of finer quality.

Bruce Johnson, who has written widely in this area, has the following advice:

1. Look for a maker's label. Metal labels, paper labels, and decals, as well as stamped and branded names, often occur on well-preserved pieces. But partial labels or evidence of a label, perhaps removed when a piece was refinished, is often found. By learning the design, size, and kinds of labels different makers used, you will be more attuned to discovering

There are two reasons why this Arts and Crafts chair that might have been cast out a few years ago recently sold for $800. First, the maker, David Kendall, was identified. Second, it is similar to an armchair featured at the Boston Museum of Fine Arts exhibit, "The Art That Is Life." Photograph courtesy Savoia and Fromm Auction Services

an attributable piece even though the complete original label is no longer present.

2. If a number is found on a Mission piece, do not assume this refers to the year it was made. For example, "12" has nothing to do with 1912. These numerals may refer to a catalog number. Research may lead to the correct attribution of such a piece.

3. When an unlabeled piece is found, begin by looking for the details that will distinguish the high quality from the mediocre.

Johnson cites the following as details to look for:

- In finest-quality Mission furniture, one piece of wood is extended through the joining piece, leaving the securing tenon visible. Some companies made false tenons, which they glued onto the exterior surface, thereby giving the impression that the joining wood was tenoned through. To determine whether a tenon is a true extension of the joining limb or is a cosmetic tenon, look for tiny nail holes where the fake tenon would have been nailed on. Another clue is unmatched wood grain on the tenon.

- Similar to the extended tenon is the exposed peg that joined one piece of wood to the next. Once the peg was secured in the receiving piece of wood, it was cut off flush with the level surface. Evidence of these pegs often occurs on chair arms. But manufacturers of mediocre Mission furniture often used a screw to join the two pieces rather than an elongated peg. The screw was then covered by gluing on a mushroom-like or rounded button.

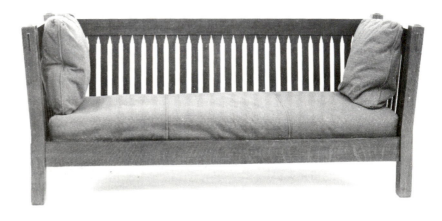

- Another sign of fine-quality Mission furniture is the corbel, which adds strength at pressure points where two pieces of wood are joined. Corbels represented added cost and production time in Mission furniture.
- Interior construction was also of great importance to the best makers of Mission furniture, and good-quality pieces will have dovetailing in the back as well as the front.
- Quarter-sawn oak is considered desirable because, when oak is cut on the angle producing the beautiful figured or "tiger"-figured graining, the result is a stronger board that is less apt to warp or split. Though fewer boards can be produced from one log, this method combines strength and beauty, a mark of superior quality.
- The finest-quality pieces of Mission furniture usually also have hand-hammered hardware, often copper. However, because hardware was made by several different specialty companies and sold to many furniture makers, it is not possible to attribute a piece of furniture to one maker on the basis of hardware alone. Just as there is varying quality in construction and wood, so is there varying quality in the style and material of hardware.

  Further, Gustav Stickley, whose furniture epitomized fine quality, often used a Shaker-influenced, round wooden knob on his pieces rather than hand-hammered metal pulls. Another style of wooden knob often found on better-quality Mission furniture is the chamfered, pyramid, or peaked-style knob.
- Upholstered Mission pieces with the original green, red, or brown leather are always sought after by discerning collectors. Though the covering may be worn, connoisseurs of fine-quality Mission furniture seek these leather-covered pieces, especially if the original pyramid-type tacks are also present.

> If you find any labeled Stickley furniture and don't buy it, you'll regret it later. Exceptional pieces are already being sold for thousands of dollars, and record prices are being made and broken.

The maker, the quality, the rarity—it makes no difference whether you are judging an eighteenth-century piece or a twentieth-century Arts and Crafts piece. The settle on the far left sold for $3,300 at Skinner's. The settle on the left sold in the same sale for $33,000. Why? Maker, quality, rarity. Photographs courtesy Skinner's

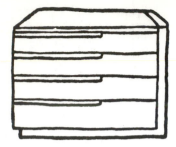

Art Deco—Fred and Ginger, Enter Right

STYLE: Art Deco
AGE: 1925–1945
ORIGIN: International

Coming in on the coattails of the understated, austere Arts and Crafts movement but with the new worldly sophistication sired by World War I, the 1920s and 1930s gave birth to a new style—Art Deco. The straight lines and geometric design of the Arts and Crafts movement were elaborated upon by using bleached and burl wood combined with chrome hardware and legs. Furniture of this period is still hovering in limbo. The accessories of the period—everything from Lalique perfume bottles and Chiparus figurines, which sell at the international auction houses, to Depression glass and Fiesta ware, which sell at flea markets—are now hot. The exceptionally fine furniture by Louis Majorelle and Josef Hoffmann is being sold at auction for thousands of dollars. The mass-market boom is just beginning, especially for pieces anticipating the "space age," those with sleek designs and upholstered in their original covering.

What's Next—We've Only Just Begun. . . .

Just when you thought it was safe to clean out your attic! Now even upholstered chairs of recent decades are being grabbed up. Unique styling, design, and original upholstery are major selling points.

Danish modern, Eames chairs, plastic chair frames with Naugahyde-covered cushions, Parsons tables, modular units, even redwood-and-mesh-style wrought-iron patio and porch furniture and floor-model radio and television cabinets are all finding buyers in the various marketplaces from used-furniture stores to publicized auctions. You don't need a crystal ball to see a bright future for 1930s and 1950s (the war years of the 1940s eliminate most of that decade) decorative arts. What you do need is the knowledge to distinguish the fine-quality pieces from the inferior- or lesser-quality ones. One clue will be the manufacturer's label on these mass-produced pieces. But other clues will include use of high-grade materials, good proportions and design, durability, and condition—those same characteristics you seek in eighteenth- and nineteenth-century pieces.

The Alsos: Windsor and Wicker

Windsor chairs became Americanized around 1740 and have been made continuously since then. Two major kinds of Windsors I see frequently are the New England versions with either turned legs or bamboo-type legs. The third type of Windsor, the distinctive Philadelphia version with ball or bulb feet, is less common. The biggest problem with Windsor chairs is that they were made for such a long time—through the eighteenth and nineteenth centuries—in the same style and same method that even experts can be fooled into thinking an 1830 chair that has had excessive wear dates from 1790. Windsor chairs are riding the high tide right now, and even chairs labeled "Wallace Nutting" and sold correctly as twentieth-century reproductions can be expected to bring over $500. An exceptional eighteenth-century museum-quality Windsor chair with elaborate turnings and the maker's stamp can sell for more than $10,000.

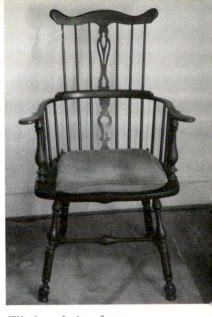

Windsor chairs of every age are found everywhere. Distinguishing manufactured "adaptations" like this one is fairly easy. But be warned. Fine custom-made Windsors that copied the measurements, style, and woods of the earlier chairs can be deceptive. And when these better-quality, though reproduction, Windsors are sold today, especially those by Nutting, the prices can rival some period Windsor chairs.

It really is not that difficult to tell a twentieth-century reproduction from an eighteenth- or nineteenth-century chair, even though they may appear alike—on the outside. A closer look at the feet and the stretcher (if present) as well as the arms (if present) will show the signs of a century or more of constant wear on period Windsor chairs. These were utilitarian pieces and more than almost any other furniture form will show the toll of usage. Also, look closely for subtle differences in the turnings—both for expected wood shrinkage and for replacements. Most reproduction Windsor chairs, even the custom variety, have a crisp, clean precision when compared with true period chairs.

Wicker furniture, as we know it in our homes today, was first made in the mid-nineteenth century. Because of its combined properties of strength and pliability, wicker can be and has been made into every style conceived by the human imagination. The most popular wicker style embodies the Victorian Rococo, and the more elaborate the piece, the greater its price tag. Like Windsor chairs, wicker pieces are being made today, and it is difficult to distinguish some reproductions from some antique (the word is used loosely) wicker. I have been told that old wicker is much heavier than reproduction wicker, which, by comparison, is lightweight. Obviously condition must always be considered in valuing wicker, as broken parts weaken the entire piece and repairing broken wicker furniture can be both costly and time-consuming.

Our Total Look

The two other major furniture styles not covered already are French and American country.

America's divergent background has always been evident in our home furnishings. French Provincial is mixed with American gingham and highlighted with a touch of Oriental cloisonné and porcelain. This mélange makes our interior design international to some, eclectic to others.

Our preference for styles goes in cycles as dictated by current events (when President Nixon went to China, our interest in Oriental styles was rekindled), museum exhibits (the reopening of the American Wing at the Metropolitan Museum of Art created new reproduction lines), major auction sales (the Christie's sale of Mrs. Prescott's English collection was followed by many articles on the increasing interest in English furniture), and advertising (as orchestrated by the furniture manufacturers and Madison Avenue).

Fashion Abroad

The two major French styles most often reproduced are Louis XV and French Provincial. Louis XV pieces are characterized by curved legs, delicate proportions, and typical French embellishments (especially brass or bronze doré galleries and foliage mounts). Much Louis XV furniture features elaborate inlay in one of two designs—parquetry (geometric designs) and marquetry (floral and classical designs). These were the sophisticated motifs appropriate to the court of Louis XV.

French Provincial is just what it says—the French style but with a provincial, country, or less sophisticated flair. The same lines and many of the same motifs as the Louis XV style are used—particularly the floral designs— but the interpretation is simpler and less elaborate than when found in Louis XV furniture. Also, these motifs are part of the French Provincial furniture

The charm of the faded gros- and petit-point needlework upholstery on these Louis XVI–style chairs, combined with the fine quality of the frames and their "antique" appearance, make these chairs and others like them even more attractive than exorbitantly expensive and fragile period chairs to many collectors. Furthermore, French furniture blends with almost every style, making it attractive to a wide range of buyers. Photograph courtesy Weschler's Auction Gallery

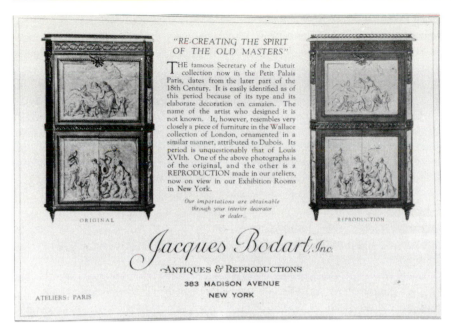

"RE-CREATING THE SPIRIT
OF THE OLD MASTERS"

THE famous Secretary of the Dutuit collection now in the Petit Palais Paris, dates from the later part of the 18th Century. It is easily identified as of this period because of its type and its elaborate decoration en camaïen. The name of the artist who designed it is not known. It, however, resembles very closely a piece of furniture in the Wallace collection of London, ornamented in a similar manner, attributed to Dubois. Its period is unquestionably that of Louis XVIth. One of the above photographs is of the original, and the other is a REPRODUCTION made in our ateliers, now on view in our Exhibition Rooms in New York.

Our importations are obtainable through your interior decorator or dealer.

Jacques Bodart, Inc.

ANTIQUES & REPRODUCTIONS

383 MADISON AVENUE
NEW YORK

ATELIERS: PARIS

ORIGINAL   REPRODUCTION

itself, carved in the wood rather than added to the piece. The sabots and chutes on Louis XV furniture were separate parts and made of different materials.

Most French furniture found in homes and the usual antiques shop is not period but a later reproduction—sometimes imported, sometimes American-made. Worldwide, Louis XV is probably the most popular style of all time. Many European reproductions are mistakenly thought to be period pieces, so even if you are told that the French-style pieces came from Europe, remember: Europe has had furniture companies that produced *reproduction* furniture as long as America. And many of these European reproductions are more faithful to the original style than our American adaptations.

In 1885 the New York firm of Sypher and Company advertised "fine cabinetwork constantly received from all the best makers of Europe, as well as from our own factory." The French pieces they were selling—and remember this was 1885—included chairs "in gold or white-and-gold, and too gorgeously mounted for a quiet taste, in damasked satins or flowered velvets" and sofas, lounges, and ottomans, all in the "French taste."

The conclusion is obvious. Never purchase a reputed Louis XV period piece (or any other period French piece, for that matter) unless you are extremely knowledgeable, have an expert examine the piece, or are purchasing the piece from a well-known dealer who specializes in *period* French furniture.

Fashion at Home

American country furniture is easily identifiable but difficult to date. The actual furniture pieces are mostly utilitarian—chairs, storage pieces (corner

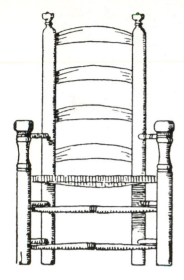

cupboards, pie safes, and the like), and tables. The lines are angular and the decoration simple. The wood is that of the region—pine, ash, maple, oak, poplar, and, for the better pieces, cherry and walnut. Country craftsmen made the same pieces—tables, beds, desks—in the same styles, with the same tools, and out of the same materials for years.

In contrast, the city craftsmen were always seeking the newest styles, latest inventions, and imported materials (mahogany being the favorite wood, of course). Thus, you may find a simple Chippendale secretary made of walnut, with panel doors, a molded straight top, and shaped bracket feet, which you would normally date 1780, then discover in a family inventory or history that the piece actually was made in 1830, when you would have expected the family to be buying Empire fashions. This is why most country pieces are broadly dated—a pine corner cupboard may be listed circa 1800–1850, or a ladder-back chair may simply be called "nineteenth century." I remember one museum exhibit of country furniture that labeled some of the chairs circa 1800–1900!

Country furniture is highly sought after, and our renewed interest in ecology and the natural life has heightened its popularity. Country styles also evoke dreams of the bucolic life with warm apple pies, a cheery kitchen, and a blazing fire as we commute to the city for another day's work in the skyscraper.

City Chest and Country Cupboard—A Few Specifics

The big investors, dealers, and collectors have always sought the finest authentic antiques. Money is not an object for them. Fine and rare pieces always bring top dollar, now $1–$2 million and more. But there are other thoughts on the relative value of antiques.

Some investors are noting that the highly formal antique pieces, while terribly expensive, do not show the percentage increase of some of the less expensive items. For a $100,000 table to show a 50 percent increase in its auction price, it would have to sell for $150,000, and a $360,000 chest of drawers would have to bring $540,000. But the pine corner cupboard you bought last year for $1,400 in a country antiques show will see a 50 percent increase when it reaches $2,100, and the simple walnut drop-leaf table that sold for $325 two years ago already has a replacement value of $500, or a 54 percent increase. Furthermore, the corner cupboard and drop-leaf table are within reach of many buyers, while very few people can seriously compete for a $250,000 chest.

Reproductions, Frauds, and Fakes

There are plenty of fakes around. But you really don't need to be too concerned with furniture fakes, at least not the rare, expensive ones. For the faker to earn enough money to make faking worth his time, he has got to sell the piece either to a museum or to an "uptown" dealer. If the piece is good enough to get by the museum curator or this class of dealer, chances are it

may go undetected until it indeed *is* an antique. And anyway, if the fake is of such superior quality, it is probably worth what you paid for it. Before worrying about fake antique furniture, the general public must learn to beware buying furniture that is not as old as it is purported to be.

At least two or three times a week I go into a private home and am told, "This is a Chippendale desk," as I stand in front of an 1890 lady's writing desk with machine-cut dovetails, mahogany veneer drawer fronts, and machine-cut screws attaching the sliding brass hinges to the writing surface.

"Chippendale style," I suggest.

"No, real Chippendale. . . . The dealer told me this could have been made by Chippendale himself!"

If it has been an unusually rough week, I am often tempted to say something like "How many women had their own writing desks in 1760, especially ones with brass hinges screwed into the sides that are marked 'Pat. Applied for, June '95'?"

But the appraiser who puts it that way isn't going to stay in business for long, and anyway, if the desk gets burned up, I want the owner to receive a justified $600 for the desk—neither get ripped off for $75 nor paid $5,000.

Only when you become knowledgeable about antiques can you keep from falling for such dealer sales pitches—especially if you like the piece anyway.

A few pages over I am going to give you specific signs to look for—both good and bad—when you are examining the furniture in your own home for your inventory list and when you are antiques shopping. But here I want to share some extra hints and facts that will make you more astute. These clues along with the other points made throughout this book provide information it has taken me (and other professionals) years to learn.

> First, always remember that thousands of reproductions are made for every antique.

The fine reproductions of one hundred, seventy-five, and even fifty years ago are being sold as "period" pieces by unknowing dealers. If you keep this fact in the back of your mind, you will be less gullible.

Individual taste will dictate which of these two American chests you would choose to buy. The chest above left is obviously more "country" in its simplicity and styling, while the chest above has a serpentine front and ball-and-claw feet—obvious characteristics associated with a more sophisticated "city" look. But personal taste aside, the choice of woods as well as the greater skill required to produce the Chippendale chest above are reasons it is more expensive than the Sheraton chest. Photograph courtesy Craig and Tarlton

PAT. APP. FOR JUNE '95

YALE LOCK

Second, almost every local area had a craftsman (back in the 1920s, 1930s, and 1940s) who used to sell antiques and make reproductions.

These people would comb the countryside and backwoods buying antiques—many of which had been discarded for "finer" new pieces. They would bring these antiques into their shops and make copies to sell to customers who wanted "old-looking" new pieces.

Sometimes such a vendor would sell the antique itself—once it was copied—but usually not before he had "improved" it a little. If the craftsman liked inlay, he would add a little inlay to the walnut chest of drawers. Or if he thought an eagle would look nice on the card table apron, he would add an eagle.

And about those feet. Our craftsman tried sitting at the secretary, but it was just too high, so before he sold the eighteenth-century Chippendale secretary, he removed the bold ogee feet and added shorter bracket feet.

Every antiques dealer or appraiser who is truly knowledgeable about furniture has seen hundreds of these pieces—often the very same desks, secretaries, and chests that end up being cataloged and classified in New York auction sales as "restored." These are also the same desks, secretaries, and chests that may turn up in antiques shops labeled "period" pieces.

Third, if you are going to buy and invest in antique furniture, learn not only how to identify the periods and styles, but also what pieces of furniture were made in what time frame.

By now you can correctly identify this lady's writing desk. Though the basic form is Queen Anne, the feet are a cross between the Chippendale ball-and-claw and the Empire "hairy paw," the carving on the lid might be thought by some to be Jacobean and by others to be Art Nouveau, and the busts are very "French"—so you know that the combination of all these styles means the desk can only be a turn-of-the-century adaptation for the "modern woman." Photograph courtesy Richard A. Bourne Company

Take the "Chippendale lady's writing desk." Not only was this obviously not a period piece, but the form, a small desk on raised cabriole legs, in these proportions did not exist in eighteenth-century England.

The same can be said for the wicker rocking chair that came over on the *Mayflower*. A wicker chair with rockers had not been conceived in 1620.

And there is no such thing as a period Queen Anne sideboard. Sideboards were not designed and made until the 1760s—some forty years after the Queen Anne period.

> Fourth—and this is particularly important if you are going to invest in antiques—learn what prices should be paid for what pieces.

This will take study and an investment on your part of both time and money, but it will save you thousands of dollars in the long run and keep you from buying antique items that are something other than what they are purported to be.

Let me illustrate how important it is to know how much to pay.

A few years ago I found I had some time between appointments in another city, and as I drove down the road I saw a tempting antiques sign. The automatic pilot took over, and suddenly I found myself inside an antiques shop.

The owner was nowhere around, but I thoroughly enjoyed browsing undisturbed through a collection of English brasses, German porcelain, and a mixture of English and American furniture—mostly old reproductions and Victorian pieces. Then a pair of chairs caught my eye. English, twentieth-century makeups, I thought matter-of-factly. (Appraisers never take holidays, I've decided.)

I started past the chairs, and then I wondered, How much does the shop owner get for this type of chair? I wandered over and began reading the ticket, which was attached to one chair by a daintily tied ribbon.

"Pair of rare maple Chippendale armchairs, Philadelphia, 1780."

I thought I was dreaming. The wrong ticket got on the chair, I reasoned. I looked at the ticket on the other chair. Identical.

To begin with, the chairs were not maple. They were a combination of oak and burl walnut. Second, Philadelphia chairs are usually walnut or mahogany—rarely maple, to say nothing of English oak and veneer. The chairs were not Chippendale—they were Queen Anne—but some people do call those style chairs Chippendale, no matter. Third, the chairs no more dated from 1780 than I did. Everything was wrong—the proportion, the tool marks, the wood combination.

Then I looked at the price—$1,500 for the pair. The last time a pair of 1780 Philadelphia armchairs went for $1,500 would have been three or four years earlier. I didn't doubt that these chairs might sell for $1,500, but Philadelphia 1780 armchairs were then bringing $1,600, $1,800, and $2,000 apiece at Sotheby's and were retailed at $3,500 to $5,000 a pair in many shops at that time.

Just about this time the shop owner appeared.

Despite the dealer's belief that this chair is an eighteenth-century American Chippendale, the object itself tells us otherwise. In reality it is an old reproduction, mass-manufactured adaptation of the Queen Anne style.

"Aren't they lovely chairs," he began. "And so rare. I was extremely lucky to get them. Do you know how much they would cost in New York?"

"How much?" I asked.

"Oh, at least $2,000 or $3,000 apiece."

"But that would be $4,000 or $6,000 for the pair! Why are you selling them for $1,500?" I couldn't resist asking.

"I don't really have that much equity in them," he said a little apologetically. "You see, they belonged to an old family friend, and she asked me to sell them for her."

Where was the logic? Why not tell the friend to send them to New York and make a couple of extra thousand dollars? Because, of course, they were not rare Philadelphia Chippendale chairs dating from 1780; they were English 1920s chairs, and if they had been auctioned off in New York that year, the pair would have brought $300 to $400 top dollar!

If you know prices, you will keep from being "taken" many times, particularly if the dealer has mistaken and often grandiose ideas about his merchandise. My advice: If you're serious, pay the $50 or $100 a year to subscribe to or purchase auction catalogs for sales that feature pieces similar to those you wish to purchase. Study the pictures, the descriptions, the estimates, and, when the sale price lists arrive, the selling prices. You will soon see a pattern emerging. Philadelphia Chippendale armchairs of similar quality sell within a specific price range. The exceptional piece—better carved, label present, unusual ironclad provenance, and so on—will sell for more. But you'll soon be able to discern such differences from the catalog description and your own better-educated and trained eye.

When you walk into an antiques shop and see a stylish Hepplewhite chest of drawers beautifully inlaid and in pristine condition with a tag reading "New England, 1790, $800," be ready to find machine-made dovetails or plywood drawer bottoms. But if you examine the chest and are convinced that it is a 1790 piece and you can afford it and you like it, buy it. After all, a reproduction chest of drawers bought today from a retail furniture store would have a price tag 50–500 percent higher than the one you're looking at, depending on its quality.

> Fifth, and finally, never buy antique furniture without asking yourself the most basic of all questions, "Does it *look* old?" Follow this up with, "Does it *feel* old?" and, finally, "Does it *smell* old?"

It is amazing what you sometimes find if you let your mind and senses rule your eagerness to get a "steal."

The Truth About Old Furniture

Before reviewing the signs that distinguish old furniture from new, let me repeat what Michael Gordon wrote about fakes in *Antiques Monthly* in the 1970s:

Being a world center for fine arts and antiques, London is also a world center for conservators and reproducers. I have been shown examples of restoration that were simply flabbergasting, especially when I was told how little it cost to have the work done. Therefore, don't assume because the piece you are buying seems "so cheap" it has not been worked on; also, don't assume that because the shop you are buying it in is reputable it could not be a reproduction. The person selling you the piece may just not know what has been done to it or just when it was made.

We are alert to new fakes, but are we ready to accept nineteenth-century fakes? Hopefully, after reading this book you are.

I will never forget one such, a highboy. It was an imposing piece with a closed bonnet, large cabriole legs, and whorl feet. It was carved, crossbanded, and had a large cartouche at the top center. The highboy was obviously a reworked period highboy, Victorianized in a variety of many styles and fashions, including a mixture of Queen Anne and Louis XV. I asked the owner what she knew about the piece.

She opened a drawer and handed me a fragile letter dating from the 1890s. The highboy, the letter stated, dated from the 1680s, descended through several notable families, and was brought into Baltimore by a finely titled gentleman who sold it—to the present owner's ancestors.

I had been prepared for the owner to say she thought the piece was eighteenth century. This happens frequently, and actually when I had asked my question I was stalling for time while figuring out how to tell her that the highboy was not as antique as she perhaps thought. But the written statement threw me.

I carefully explained that the piece, though it began life in the seventeenth century, had been "modernized," and that cabriole legs and whorl feet had not even been conceived of in 1680 for starters.

The owner now cheerfully shows off the bogus letter when asked about the highboy. But the truth is, there have always been gullible antiques lovers who have bought with their emotions, helped along by a glib seller's "documentation."

How can you avoid being such a victim? You can't always. But there are some precautions you can take.

Examining Furniture—Some Specifics

First, approach each piece of furniture with great suspicion. Expect something to be wrong.

Look for the following signs:

- *Circular saw marks.* These are a sure giveaway that a piece was made after 1830 or 1840. Look along the piece of wood where it would have been sawn—the end of a board—for example, at the back of a drawer in a chest of drawers, along the bottom of a chair frame, or the flat edge

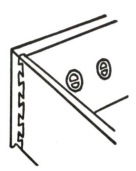

Machine cut dovetails. New, round screws.

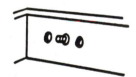

Interior view of drawer. Old post holes, new replacement screw.

Good: evidence on front of drawer of first set of post holes.

Warning! No evidence of post holes—newly veneered drawer front.

of a tabletop. Once you see and can identify circular saw marks, you will always recognize them.

- *Plane marks.* These are a good sign that a piece is earlier than 1840 or 1860. Plane marks can be seen, but they can also be felt. Because they are usually on interior surfaces, you will want to learn how to *feel* them as well as know what they look like. I always ask my audiences to rub their fingers over the insides of their hands, both the fingers and palms. The rolling indentations that you feel are similar to the feeling of irregular plane marks. It is these irregular ripplings that experts feel for when they run their fingers under the top of a chest or along a drawer bottom. You want to find these plane marks on drawer bottoms and the underneath surface of top boards of chests made before 1850. Always check the top—replaced tops are frequently found.

- *Round circles and clean feet.* Old wood that was cut "green" shrinks. Also, if regularly rubbed against another surface, all wood is eventually going to wear down. Look for obvious signs of wear on the bottoms of all feet, and on country-style chairs, which might have been sat in and tilted back (and even rested against a wall or porch railing), see if the back legs are worn at the back and look for signs of wear across the back. Look at chair stretchers to find possible wear from constant rubbing. Examine drawer side bottoms for signs of wear from opening and closing the drawers—they should be *smooth* from wear. If all circles are round and all interior surfaces are sharp, ask yourself, Where are the signs of normal wear?

- *Handles and screws.* "I bought this piece because it has the original brasses," one owner told me. Yes, she got new brasses and a new chest! There is much to-do about replaced brasses. But ask anyone who owns an old chest with the original brasses or hardware, and he will tell you—they break! The constant pulling on a drawer or door year in and year out weakens the handle, and often it breaks—it's that simple. If a piece has "its original brasses," and they are secured by a rounded head screw with wide grooves, be suspicious—the whole piece may be new, or else you've got some old parts combined with new drawers or doors, or some such combination.

Do not worry if you find that the antique chest or desk has had more than one pair of brasses. This is the norm, not the exception. But do check all the drawers to make sure that the postholes (the holes where the earlier brasses had been) match in all drawers and that the interior holes match with the drawer fronts. Often new drawer fronts have been added to an old backing, particularly in English pieces and any veneered piece.

While examining the handles and screws, remember to check the locks. This is one place where even the expert craftsman, who made a very fine reproduction using hand-cut dovetails, wooden pegs, and the proper dimensions in copying an antique, may have become careless. First look at the lock itself. Many eighteenth-century locks had two or more bolts and were held in place by handmade screws or hand-forged nails. Very often these locks were large and took up almost the entire depth of the drawer ledge. By the nineteenth century, smaller locks predominated, but once again look for old nails and screws used to attach the locks to the drawers in early-nineteenth-century pieces. Many locks of the later nineteenth century will have the manufacturer's name or a patent designation imprinted on them. When you find a "period" Chippendale desk with a perfectly fitted lock labeled "Yale," look the entire piece over again.

- *Dovetails.* Early hand-cut dovetails have slight irregularities to them. If you compare a perfect machine-cut dovetail with an irregular hand-cut one, you can see the difference immediately. Remember, though, that by the mid-nineteenth century furniture was manufactured, and thus you can have an "antique" Victorian piece with machine-cut dovetails. What you do not want to see are machine-cut dovetails in a "1780 Chippendale chest of drawers."

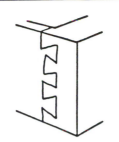
Irregular, hand cut dovetails.

Machine cut dovetails.

- *Patina and color.* Some experts claim that they can tell by the patina or finish of a piece whether it is old or not. I have seen many eighteenth-century pieces with twentieth-century finishes that I had written off as "old reproductions" until I looked inside. Don't stop with the outside color—look inside. The unfinished backs of corner cupboards, chests, sideboards, grandfather clocks, and the like turn dark from constant exposure to air. Contrast this darkness with the unfinished drawer interiors inside a slant-front desk where little air ever reaches. These drawers look like new—light and often almost shiny. Now look at the drawers in the bottom of the desk (or any chest of drawers). The sides should be "cleaner" or lighter than the dark back board of the desk, but the back board of the drawer will be darker where air has circulated between the protective desk back and the drawer backs than at the sides—but not as dark as the board at the back of the desk.

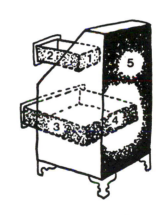

- *Marriages—for better or for worse.* While you have the drawers open, check the interior sides of all the drawers for similar dovetailing and coloration. Chests and desks are often made up of composite "old pieces," and if there are distinctly different dovetails or colors between the drawers, think twice. This test should *always* be given to chest-on-chests and highboys. The two separate pieces may have been put together at different times or, in antiques terminology, "married." If there are distinct differences, you can be fairly sure the pieces were not originally intended to be together. Even if the color and dovetails match up, check the depth of the two pieces and make sure they align correctly at the back. A distinct difference in depth is a warning sign. And, of course, this is the test to give a secretary or breakfront or any case piece that has two parts but where the top may have doors and the bottom drawers.

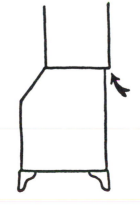

- *Feet, legs, and aprons.* Just as constant wear on handles and knobs leads to breakage, feet and legs take the brunt of wear on any piece of furniture. In days of heavy spring and fall cleaning, secretaries, chests, corner cupboards, and the like were tugged and dragged out of their niches, often causing damage to their feet and legs, especially delicate, thin legs. Even today I often see considerable damage to the feet and legs of furniture caused by our modern invention—the vacuum cleaner. To tell whether or not feet have been replaced or changed on chests and desks, you need two tools—your hands and your eyes. Just as you *feel* drawer bottoms for hand-planed marks, feel for this same undulated unevenness on shaped aprons that connect the legs and feet on Hepplewhite and Sheraton pieces. An absolutely sharp, rough-edged apron is a warning sign. Always check for the same signs, which may indicate a new molding or frame, on a Chippendale chest or secretary. Next, learn to recognize with your eyes the correct perspective that a period case piece should have. Furniture made during the eighteenth-century Chippendale and Hepplewhite periods had taller feet, whether they were ogee or bracket, than later copies of this style. Once you can sight the correct perspective of a period case piece, the copies will immediately be identifiable because of their "cut-down" proportions, which begin with the feet. By learning that a Chippendale foot should be approximately five to seven inches tall on a period desk, for example, when you see a short or truncated three- to four-inch foot, you will be suspicious and either look for cut-down or replaced feet or question the age of the entire piece. Just as feet and legs can reveal the age of a person, they can also indicate the age of a piece of furniture. Straight stretchers, when present in eighteenth-century chairs, are joined to the legs at the outside. Inset straight stretchers always create suspicion.

I have made my share of mistakes, but one of the most frustrating involved another expert (which at least gives me comfort).

I was called in to help an elderly client price some objects for sale. Most

Sharp, unworn surfaces are always warning signs. To tell whether or not feet have been replaced, you need two tools—your hands and your eyes. Photograph by Jon Zachary

Not only do you detect the expected signs of wear on the legs and stretcher of this period American chair, far left, but you also see that the stretcher is connected to the outside of the leg. Photograph courtesy Craig and Tarlton

The expert can immediately tell that this chair base, left, is typical of a reproduction. Can you? Note the absence of wear on the foot. The stretcher is slightly inset where attached to the leg. Legs and feet can give you an instant answer to the age of upholstered pieces that can appear older than they are.

of the pieces were ordinary household furnishings. There were a few Victorian pieces, an oak table, and a couple of interesting beds. But in one corner was the piece you hope to find but seldom do—a fine Hepplewhite (or Federal) side chair, crisply carved and wonderfully proportioned. Next to it was a matching armchair that was just as "right."

When I asked the owner about the chair, everything she told me was what I wanted to hear. She had found the chairs in an 1830s house in her small hometown. One was in bad condition—the stretcher broken, the back loose—but she bought them and took them both to a cabinetmaker. The year was 1938. He fixed and tightened them but did not refinish the chairs or alter them in any way.

I told her that I thought the chairs were worth a good deal of money—if sold to the right dealer. If she wanted, she could sell them herself, but that would take time. She needed the money. Since she was going to the hospital, she asked me to take the chairs home and ask the dealer to come see them.

I took the chairs home, put them in my living room, and went to my library. There they were, illustrated in all of the right books—Nutting, Miller, Sack!

I called a dealer I knew would be interested, and he agreed to drive several hundred miles to see them. Meanwhile my husband came in, took one look at the chairs, and said, "Those old chairs look good for reproductions. Where are you going to put them?"

Blasphemy! And worse—blasphemy from a layman. "Just wait until you see them advertised in *Antiques* magazine!" I retorted.

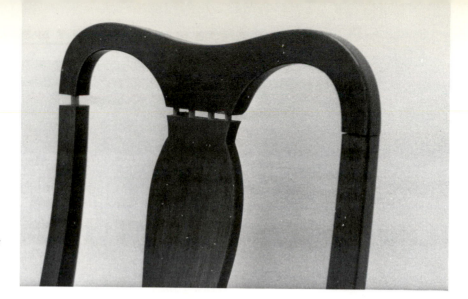

The round dowels used to join the crest rail to the stiles of this Queen Anne–style chair positively identify it as a reproduction.

The dealer arrived the next day and when he saw the chairs became as excited as I. We examined them carefully. No saw marks, good signs of wear, wonderful carving, perfect proportions. You couldn't ask for much more. We'd done our homework. We were satisfied. We settled on a price above the one tentatively quoted to my client. The dealer drove away.

Late that night the phone rang. While unloading his truck, the dealer had pulled one chair out by its top rail. The old glue was loose, and the crest rail slipped out. There, for the expert to see, was a perfect, round, machine-cut dowel connecting the crest rail and stile—the sign to the knowing eye of a fine old reproduction made around 1920. "And I was deciding which of my customers to call first," he sighed.

Of course the chairs were returned. As handsome reproductions they sold for $500.

The moral of this story is that anyone can—and most people do, sometimes, at least—make a mistake. If you think you have a genuinely rare piece, ask a true expert. Do not take the word of a neighbor or antiques hobbyist. If the expert believes you do have an exceptionally valuable piece, a rare find, don't believe him or her. Ask another expert. If they both give the same verdict, independently of one another, then you may begin to raise your hopes.

One snowy night I drove a distance to look at a ball-and-claw sofa that the owners described to me as an "eighteenth-century Chippendale piece." They had been told by a knowledgeable expert—but knowledgeable in another area of antiques—that their sofa was worth $50,000.

"Mrs. Jenkins, he told me he didn't know if it was English or American, but he said that didn't matter. That sofa is worth $50,000," the husband eagerly exclaimed over the phone.

I genuinely wanted to see an American ball-and-claw Chippendale sofa in a private home. I had only seen them at Winterthur and the Metropolitan Museum of Art's American Wing.

But the moment I saw the sofa I knew I would have to be the bearer of sad tidings. The sofa, if indeed it were eighteenth century, was English, I explained, thus making the $50,000 price unrealistic. To support my explanation, I carefully showed the owners pictures of English and American pieces and cited the differences in perspective, styling, and proportions.

Then I asked a very basic question: "Have you looked for a label or tag under the seat?"

They hadn't. We pulled out the sofa, tilted it over, and there was the answer. "Kittinger Company, Buffalo, New York." Even so, the owners were doubtful (and more than a little embarrassed that they had never seen the label).

"Kittinger? Don't they make Williamsburg reproductions? This sofa was inherited. It's not a new piece," they protested.

They did not know that the Kittinger Company has been making very fine furniture for over one hundred years. In fact, some of their old reproductions are, by definition, antiques—but not worth $50,000.

The husband shook his head sadly. "You don't know how many times I've spent that $50,000."

Furniture Glossary

Armoire. Large cupboard usually having doors above drawers and of French origin. See *Linen press.*

Bergère. An armchair of French origin having the space between the armrest and seat closed or upholstered. See *Fauteuil.*

Canapé. The French term for a sofa.

Cassone. The Italian term for a chest.

Cellaret. A box, either freestanding on legs or to be placed on another piece of furniture, to hold wine and spirits bottles.

Coromandel screen. An Oriental folding screen with carved Oriental motifs, usually people, birds, and so on.

Fauteuil. An armchair of French origin having the space between the armrest and the seat open. See *Bergère.*

Linen press. The English or American version of the French armoire.

Marquetry. Inlay in a floral, scroll, or other nongeometric design. See *Parquetry.*

Parquetry. Inlay in a geometric design (as in parquetry floors). See *Marquetry.*

Provincial. Reference to pieces from the countryside, as in French Provincial.

Trestle table. A table with crossed base. Associated with medieval times.

Vitrine. A cabinet with glass used to display porcelain, silver, and the like. Can either be vertical with glass door at front or horizontal with lift-up glass top.

Wellington chest. A tall chest having a hinged wooden flap at one side that overhangs the drawers and locks. The drawers cannot open when this is locked.

Welsh dresser. A display or storage piece with open shelves at the top and drawer or cupboard below. Associated with English taverns.

Describing and Inventorying Furniture

To list your furniture, proceed in a logical room-by-room progression. Inspect each piece and classify it as period, antique, or reproduction as best you can. Use the pictorial guide for descriptive terms. This, combined with the illustrations in this chapter, should make your descriptions accurate and informative. For estimates of replacement prices for reproductions, refer to the value charts. Some museum reproduction lines far exceed the exceptional chart.

Value Charts for Currently Manufactured Furniture Styles
(These prices are not *for antique or period pieces.)*

	GOOD QUALITY	EXCEPTIONAL QUALITY *(hand-rubbed finish, hand-carved motifs, often custom-made)*
QUEEN ANNE STYLE		
Side chair	$425	$1,500
Armchair	$475	$1,800
Lowboy	$1,200	$4,400
Highboy	$2,000	$7,000
Tea table	$525	$1,450
Drop-leaf table (Sofa arm size)	$395	$1,700
Candle stand	$250	$575
Secretary	$1,800	$9,000
CHIPPENDALE STYLE		
Sofa	$1,850	$4,050
Side chair	$500	$1,500
Armchair	$550	$2,000
Wingback armchair	$695	$2,575
Breakfront	$4,500	$14,000
Chest of drawers	$825	$2,800
Serpentine or blockfront chest	$1,500	$4,200
Desk, slant front	$2,400	$6,500
Secretary	$3,200	$13,000
Pembroke table	$600	$1,500
HEPPLEWHITE STYLE		
Pembroke table	$550	$895
Shield-back side chair	$400	$1,100
Shield-back armchair	$450	$1,500
Martha Washington chair	$625	$1,850
Sideboard	$2,200	$7,200
Dining table	$1,600	$3,200
Secretary	$1,800	$9,200
SHERATON STYLE		
Card table	$675	$1,400
Pedestal dining room table	$1,875	$3,000
Beds:		
Four-poster	$900	$2,150
Four-poster, carved with canopy	$1,800	$3,500

	GOOD QUALITY	*(These styles are not frequently found in exceptional quality)*

EMPIRE STYLE
Side chair	$235
Armchair	$300
Sofa	$1,050
Carved sofa	$1,700
Sewing table	$400
Rocking chair	$320

VICTORIAN STYLE
  (floral carving)
Armchair	$500
Sofa	$1,000
Side chair	$200
Rocker	$425
Chest	$1,300

GOLDEN OAK STYLE
Side chair	$95
Armchair	$125
Round table	$375

FRENCH STYLES
Louis XV side chair	$350
Louis XV armchair	$400
French Provincial side chair	$325
French Provincial armchair	$375
Dresser	$600
Armoire	$2,000

COUNTRY STYLE
Ladder-back side chair	$125
Ladder-back armchair	$150
Windsor side chair	$110
Windsor armchair	$160
Hitchcock side chair	$125
Hutch or cupboard	$1,400
Corner cupboard	$1,000
Bedside table	$225
Occasional table	$425

Furniture Decorative Motifs

Acanthus		Conch Shell		Escutcheon		Quarter Fan Inlay	
Bellflower		Crest Rail		Finial		Shell or Fan	
C-Scroll		Cross Banding		Fret		Slat	
Cartouche		Dentil Molding		Garland or Swag		Splat	
Chamfered or Canted Corner		Egg and Dart		Paterae			

Furniture Feet and Legs

(These can be clues to identifying styles.)

Ball and Claw		Fluted		Raised Ball		Square Tapering, inlaid (or cuffed)	
Block or Marlborough		Ogee		Reeded		Stretcher Base	
Bracket (straight)		Padded Queen Anne Foot		Slipper or Snake Foot (padded)		Whorl Foot	
Cabriole				Splayed Foot			

20

Bric-a-Brac and Accessories: Little Things Mean a Lot

It's the little things in life that get you," my mother always told me.

When it comes down to remembering all of your possessions, the little things are certainly hardest to recall, yet the value of the accessories you have sitting around on bookcases, coffee tables, shelves, and stuck away in corner cupboards and hall closets can truly be astounding.

"But they didn't cost very much to begin with," I am often told.

Maybe. But have you noticed the price tags on "little things" in antiques and gift shops lately? A simple ashtray is now $12 or $18 instead of $1 or $2. The Beatrix Potter figurines you used to buy for nieces' and nephews' birthday presents are now over $30 each.

We all have spent hundreds, often thousands, of dollars on "little touches" to make our homes attractive. These accessories often express our personal tastes more than our furnishings do. You walk into a crafts shop and choose a basket you would like to use in the kitchen. You stroll through an antiques shop, intending only to browse, until you fall in love with a vase you can't live without. You save all your Christmas checks until you can afford a pair of Williamsburg reproduction candlesticks and hurricane globes. Just a few dollars here and there, yet these purchases mount up. But you know how much they cost. You bought them.

What about the Staffordshire figurine that you loved as a child and now treasure as an adult? Or the pair of vases willed to you by your husband's aunt? These are now antiques, and their value may surprise you.

Even appraisers can have their own share of surprises. Among my own treasures is a miniature Staffordshire poodle, only one inch tall. When I was a child it was always kept on a shelf in the corner cupboard, and now I keep it on a shelf in my corner cupboard. I knew it was valuable, but its value to me was much more sentimental than monetary. Had I been forced to state a value, I probably would have said $100, followed by a big question mark. Well, I saw one for sale, and I was tempted to take it home as a companion for mine until I inquired, "How much?" It was $400! Today it would cost a few hundred dollars more.

You definitely need to include your accessories in your inventory, and once you discover more about them and their value, you may wish to ask your insurance agent about breakage coverage.

The values of bric-a-brac and accessories vary radically according to where they are sold. In fact, one reason people so often purchase small accessories in antiques shops and flea markets and at auction is because "they're too cheap to pass up." If you've seen a set of Haviland china plates priced at $30 each, then walk into a store and find the same design selling for $12 per plate, you are often tempted to buy the plates just because they are $18 cheaper than the ones you saw first.

Prices for antique accessories are greatly affected by both the tastes of each geographic region and the rarity of the item. Nineteenth-century European china—R. S. Prussia, Royal Bayreuth, and Beehive, for instance—are avidly collected in the Midwest but often politely overlooked on the East Coast. Fiesta Ware is highly popular in Texas and often discarded in Maine. A Satsuma cup and saucer may sell for $35, but a Satsuma vase can easily bring $700. A Depression glass plate in a common pattern may sell for $5, but a Depression glass plate in a rare pattern can cost $25. Thus, it is almost impossible to assign accurate values to all the variations in all the classifications of accessories and bric-a-brac you have in your home.

Here is a list of accessories and bric-a-brac that I have compiled from the thousands of items I see in private homes. Use this list to identify and approximately date your pieces. Before buying new accessories—especially antiques—learn what the "current activity" is in the marketplace. Are the particular pieces you wish to buy now in vogue? If so, you may end up paying top dollar. Are they being reproduced? If so, you may be taken.

Among the numerous accessories used as accents, I often find English ironstone and porcelain pieces.

First, take a good look at your porcelain accessories. Some of them may have a diamond-shaped marking with letters, numbers, and Roman numerals. These are known as registration marks. You can discover the exact date of many English pottery pieces if you know how to read an English registration mark. Two designs were used in the nineteenth century, and if you find one of these marks, compare it with those on the accompanying chart. (Incidentally, this marking was also used on some metal items in England.)

The following marks identify the day, month, and year of many English products, especially porcelain goods.

> Knowing what is currently fashionable can help you know when to buy, when to sell, and what to avoid as a possible fake, fraud, or reproduction if you are not an expert in the field.

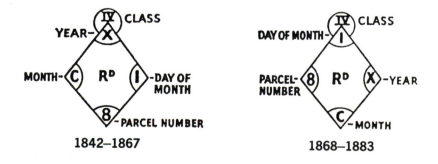

1842–1867   1868–1883

The following lettering system was used between 1842 and 1867. Match the year letter at the top to the following chart.

1842–1867
Year letter at top

A = 1845	N = 1864
B = 1858	O = 1862
C = 1844	P = 1851
D = 1852	Q = 1866
E = 1855	R = 1861
F = 1847	S = 1849
G = 1863	T = 1867
H = 1843	U = 1848
I = 1846	V = 1850
J = 1854	W = 1865
K = 1857	X = 1842
L = 1856	Y = 1853
M = 1859	Z = 1860

The lettering system below was used from 1868 to 1883. Match the year letter to the following chart.

1868–1883
Year letter at right

A = 1871	L = 1882
C = 1870	P = 1877
D = 1878	S = 1875
E = 1881	U = 1874
F = 1873	V = 1876
H = 1869	W = (March 1–6)
I = 1872	1878
J = 1880	X = 1868
K = 1883	Y = 1879

Months for both series.

A = December
B = October
C or O = January
D = September
E = May
G = February
H = April
I = July
K = November (and December 1860)
M = June
R = August (and September 1–19, 1857)
W = March

After 1883 the mark changed to a simpler form that used the abbreviation "R^D" and accompanying number.

R^D No. 1 registered on 1 January 1884.	R^D No. 291241 registered on 1 January 1897.
R^D No. 19754 registered on 1 January 1885.	R^D No. 311658 registered on 1 January 1898.
R^D No. 40480 registered on 1 January 1886.	R^D No. 331707 registered on 2 January 1899.
R^D No. 64520 registered on 1 January 1887.	R^D No. 351202 registered on 1 January 1900.
R^D No. 90483 registered on 2 January 1888.	R^D No. 368154 registered on 1 January 1901.
R^D No. 116648 registered on 1 January 1889.	R^D No. 385088 registered on 1 January 1902.
R^D No. 141273 registered on 1 January 1890.	R^D No. 402913 registered on 1 January 1903.
R^D No. 163767 registered on 1 January 1891.	R^D No. 425017 registered on 1 January 1904.
R^D No. 185713 registered on 1 January 1892.	R^D No. 447548 registered on 2 January 1905.
R^D No. 205240 registered on 2 January 1893.	R^D No. 471486 registered on 1 January 1906.
R^D No. 224720 registered on 1 January 1894.	R^D No. 493487 registered on 1 January 1907.
R^D No. 246975 registered on 1 January 1895.	R^D No. 518415 registered on 1 January 1908.
R^D No. 268392 registered on 1 January 1896.	R^D No. 534963 registered on 1 January 1909.

English Semiporcelain

English semiporcelain or ironstone has always been very popular for accessories. Unfortunately, breakage and division by families have broken up most of the large dinner sets originally crafted. Today the individual pieces, particularly teapots, pitchers, cream pitchers, decorative plates, and serving pieces, are highly prized items. Further, today's taste prefers the "earth" colors—greens, Chinese reds, and so on—but the blue-and-white patterns also have a renewed market. The majority of these pieces date from the nineteenth century, though many of the factories or potters began in the eighteenth century. Following is an account of some of the most frequently found English porcelain and pottery makers and information on specific types of popular accessories.

Staffordshire

English ironstone pieces are often generically called Staffordshire. Staffordshire refers to the district in England where pottery factories flourished during the eighteenth and nineteenth centuries. (Remember, Dresden and Limoges are both names of towns rather than the names of specific companies.) Originally, Staffordshire was used when referring to the eighteenth-century work of Ralph and Aaron Wood. But now Staffordshire refers to literally any English figurine or decorative semiporcelain that has a "nineteenth-century" appearance, particularly the popular historical-view dinner sets in the 1810–1850 period. Among the popular Staffordshire factories are Ridgway, Clews, Adams, and Mason.

Staffordshire Animals

During the nineteenth century, Staffordshire figurines, both of living personages, such as Queen Victoria and Prince Albert, and historical figures from life and fiction, such as Macbeth and Uncle Tom, George Washington and Benjamin Franklin, were popular mantelpiece or chimney decorations. Staffordshire potters also made figure groupings of dramatic scenes, such as "Romeo and Juliet" or "St. George Slaying the Dragon." But most popular of

all were the Staffordshire animals, particularly the spaniels, whippets, and poodles. Many more Staffordshire animals were made than is commonly known, including zebras, gazelles, foxhounds, and Dalmations.) The extreme popularity of these figures led to the inevitable copies, and these have been faked as frequently as any single item in the antiques world. Staffordshire animals were reproduced in Germany and the Orient, and even current manufacturers are still turning out Staffordshire animals, which are often sold as nineteenth-century originals.

Notable Potters and Factories

William Adams. This Staffordshire, England, firm dates from the eighteenth century and is still in existence. The company is particularly noted for the Adams Rose design and Dr. Syntax plates. Early Adams Rose pieces are not marked, but the later pieces are; the very late ones will be labeled "England." Prices for Adams Rose plates begin at around $50, and prices for the fine early and larger Adams Rose pieces can range into the hundreds of dollars. Most Adams ware is moderately priced semiporcelain. Be particularly wary of the Dr. Syntax plates, as these were forged in the later nineteenth and early twentieth centuries.

Mason-Ashworth ironstone. One of the most popular of the Staffordshire pottery companies was that founded by Charles James Mason. The most popular of the Mason china is brightly colored in blue, orange, green, and rust, often copying Oriental floral motifs. In the mid-nineteenth century the company became associated with Ashworth and Brothers. Like Adams ware, both Mason and Ashworth pieces are highly desirable, but the bright coloration characteristic of the Mason designs adds to their current popularity and value.

Ridgway. Note that, just like Wedgwood, Ridgway does not have an *e* in it. Much of the Ridgway of the 1830–1850 period is not marked and can be confused with other English companies. A typical Ridgway decoration is in the same Oriental style and coloration as that of the Mason Company. However, the factory is perhaps even better known for the flow blue–style decoration.

Flow Blue

This is a generic term that refers to the ironstone china manufactured from the 1830s to 1890s. The term came about when the cobalt color flowed out of its lines and covered large areas of the decoration. However, "flow blue" can also refer to green, sepia, and purple wares, which also flowed in the kiln. Much flow blue is decorated with a historic scene, such as "Lafayette's Landing," or landscape scenes of famous buildings, "Mount Vernon," "Independence Hall," and so forth. Be warned that fakes and reproductions abound!

Blue Chelsea

One of the popular patterns at the turn of the century made by the ironstone or semiporcelain companies was "Blue Chelsea," also called "Chelsea" and sometimes "Grandmother's Chelsea." Once again, the name has become a generic term that refers to any of the ironstone ware that is white and decorated with a raised blue sprig. Presently "Blue Chelsea" has fallen into relative obscurity when compared with the much more popularly collected Haviland or Nippon china, but you may find these pieces and wonder about them. If you like them, display and enjoy them.

Lusterware

Lusterware had its origins in the ancient East, and there is evidence that Italians and Spaniards used lusterware in the fourteenth and fifteenth centuries. However, today we are most familiar with the English lusterware of the nineteenth century. Luster is created when a very thin layer of gold is applied to a pottery base. The resulting color, or "luster," varies from a copper to pink. When a thin layer of platinum is placed on pottery, the resulting luster is silver. This luster provided the middle class with "silver" tableware by imitating the fine English sterling and Sheffield wares found on more affluent tables. Unfortunately lusterware has been reproduced as frequently as the Staffordshire animals. Tremendous amounts of copper luster were made in the first part of the twentieth century when lusterware was highly regarded as a collector's item. First look at the bottom to see if the piece is marked "England" or "Made in England." Generally I have found that the newer luster has a much thicker and heavier feeling than the almost translucent glow of nineteenth-century luster. Lusterware is not as popular now as it was in the earlier part of the twentieth century, probably the result of the preponderance of fakes. However, I seem to have seen more inherited lusterware being displayed in the past two or three years than, say, five or ten years ago.

Later English Nineteenth-Century Art Pottery

The whole decorative world of the late-nineteenth-century and twentieth-century designs has been rediscovered. Art pottery is handmade, individually decorated pottery produced both in America and England at the end of the nineteenth century when interest in "crafts" became popular, just as it did again a few years ago. But just because a piece is handcrafted rather than mass-produced does not mean it will be of outstanding quality. Further, some of the workshops became successful cottage industries and turned out the same design or line on a large scale. Always remember that for each fine-quality period design there were literally thousands of inferior-quality copies, many of the type that were sold in dimestores or by catalog. Thus rarity, as well as quality, design, and individual maker (plus, of course, condition), affect the value of art pottery.

Therefore, always get full information on any marks on pottery pieces.

Makers often changed their marks, and thus the slightest difference in marks or age can help date a piece and mean a substantial difference in its value.

Among the most frequently found English art pottery makers in American homes are the following:

Lambethware. England. A line of art pottery made by the English Doulton Company, expensive when made and valuable today.

Moorcroft. England. William Moorcroft was highly acclaimed during his lifetime and was even appointed potter to **Queen Mary** in 1928.

Pilkington. England. The tiles and luster-finished earthenware made at the turn of the century in Manchester and highly prized by specialist collectors.

Twentieth-Century English Figurines, Including Tobies

Very popular during the twentieth century were figurines, particularly those depicting beautiful women. The figurines were developed in two major styles. One embodied the romantic image of ladies in long flowing skirts and large hats depicted in a pastoral or countryside setting. These are still made today by Royal Worcester and Royal Doulton. The extreme opposite of the romantic embodiment of innocent womanhood was the sophisticated and alluring Art Nouveau female figure, often depicted as scantily dressed or even partially nude (in the "September Morn" tradition) or in a sophisticated

Toby jugs have been popular since the eighteenth century. This grouping that spans two centuries clearly shows distinctions between the style and models of this ever-popular form. But remember, tobies have also been imitated and faked. Photograph courtesy Richard A. Bourne Company

masquerade motif. These Art Nouveau female figures were not only ignored, but even thrown away during the middle part of the twentieth century. Now, of course, these figurines are collector's items. In addition to porcelain, the figurines were executed in metals (bronze, often in combination with ivory, and spelter).

Other popular English figurines include Toby jugs, which were first made in the eighteenth century. Not only are Toby jugs still in current production (even these are more expensive than they used to be, with a medium-size Toby jug costing about $50), but they were greatly copied in the Orient in the early and mid-twentieth century. I remember being quite surprised when I discovered that a Toby jug that had been in my grandfather's room, which I had always assumed was a Royal Doulton piece, was clearly marked "Japan" on the bottom. Remember, this mark could be removed by the use of hydrochloric acid or a grinding wheel and the piece sold to the unknowing person as an "unmarked English nineteenth-century character jug."

Fine English Porcelain

Many of the English companies that made earthenware or ironstone also produced magnificent fine porcelain. Among these are Spode, Ridgway, and Wedgwood. Collectors of fine English porcelain seek wares by Derby, Worcester, Rockingham, Swansea, and Minton. Each of these companies used specific marks to denote their wares of different times. Numerous books have been published that include a full complement of porcelain hallmarks. However, great confusion exists among these companies because some of the decorators moved from one firm to another, and some of the companies themselves imitated European marks. For example, the famous Meissen crossed swords appear on some Minton porcelain. (Incidentally, Minton china from the late nineteenth century is highly collectible.)

Complete sets of English porcelain now command a king's ransom. Recently a set of Worcester china, consisting of several hundred pieces, was offered wholesale to a dealer for $9,800.

European Porcelain

European porcelains are found so frequently in American homes because they were brought into the country by the immigrants who could bring a treasured pot or favorite cup and saucer but could not bring large furniture. What better testimony to how greatly we value the little antique pieces we have sitting around. How often my clients say, "I could stand to lose everything except my great-grandfather's mug" or "I cherish the blue vase brought from Austria by my grandparents more than any piece I have ever bought."

Another reason for the predominance of European porcelain in America is the absence of any American porcelain manufacturers until late in the nineteenth century.

Most of the European porcelain found in homes today is from the

Volkstadt, Rudolstadt vase, c. 1890. **Photograph courtesy Richard A. Bourne Company**

nineteenth rather than the eighteenth century, but all fine porcelain should be appreciated. To see why it is of increasing value, let's look at some European porcelain companies.

Herend

Founded in 1839, the Herend factory has produced fine porcelain for almost a century and a half. Located near Budapest, Hungary, the factory is surrounded by the Bakory woods. Until 1970 the porcelain was fired in wood-burning kilns heated by timber from the surrounding forests. The first firing took thirty to thirty-two hours to complete. Inside the kiln the wood fire was built up to 1,740 degrees Fahrenheit and was then allowed to subside slowly. During these long hours, any draft from a crack in the kiln door or from the factory chimneys could crack or warp the entire firing. Only in 1970 were these kilns replaced by more efficient and better controlled gas-burning ovens.

Actually, little nineteenth-century Herend is found in this country, but modern Herend china is very desirable and is carried by fine jewelry stores everywhere. Herend is noted not only for its dinnerware with fine large serving pieces, but also for its charming figurines. Just as your grandmother wanted to set her table with Heisey glass and Bavarian china, so today many people want Waterford crystal and Herend china.

Delft

Delft ware is commonly defined as tin-glazed pottery. The most familiar Delft was made in Holland, but it was also made in England during the seventeenth and eighteenth centuries. Unlike many of the other porcelain or pottery factories that you have read about, several Delft factories actually died out in the first part of the nineteenth century, and Delft ware was not revived until the 1870s, when the factories once again began making the blue-and-white Delft that is generally recognized today. Earlier Delft was frequently polychromatic as well as blue and white. The difference in value between the eighteenth- and the nineteenth- or twentieth-century Delft is astounding. A modern Delft fifteen-inch plate may cost around $200, but an eighteenth-century fifteen-inch Delft plate easily sells for $1,200 and more.

> There is very little eighteenth-century Delft around, and you can be sure that if "Delft" or "Holland" appears on the bottom, the piece is post-1891.

Quimper

Another pottery that is currently popular is Quimper, but like Delft, the pieces we are familiar with are primarily those made in the nineteenth and even twentieth century. Records show that Quimper potters were in existence as early as the fifteenth century; Quimper, like Limoges, is the name of a place

in France. Quimper ware is characterized by its bright polychromatic paintings of French peasants and farm animals. The Quimper factory was purchased in 1983 by an American couple, Paul and Sarah Jansen. Quimper is being manufactured and imported today, but it is much more expensive than the usual pottery available in gift shops and department stores. For example, a dinner plate costs over $20, and tureens are over $200. Furthermore, there is a "reproduction" line of Quimper imitating the peasant motif. This is marked *"K G Criation, Armor, France, Fait main"* and is less expensive than the new, imported Quimper. An average price range for your new Quimper could be determined by using the low end of the Class III good-quality porcelain items. The older Quimper is highly sought and commands premium prices, depending on age, condition, design, and the specific piece.

R. S. Prussia

After reading about the bogus R. S. Prussia mustache cups in chapter 12, I'm sure that every time you see an R. S. Prussia piece you're going to put it down and run away. Don't. Just keep your wits about you. But you also need to know that R. S. Prussia–type china has been heavily reproduced by Oriental companies, including some rather attractive pieces made by Noritake. This, combined with the availability of the fake R. S. Prussia seals, should make you extremely cautious. But true R. S. Prussia is highly collectible, so if you like it, take the time to learn about it, and if you own true R. S. Prussia pieces, you can sell them for a lot of money.

The original porcelain was made by two brothers, Erdman and Reinhold Schlegelmilch, who each operated factories in an obscure little German town. R. S. Prussia reached its height of popularity at the end of the nineteenth century, at which time the wares were imported into the United States. In 1911 a chocolate pot could be bought for $.69, and a seven-piece celery set, consisting of the tray and individual relish dishes, cost $1.25. A dozen bread and butter plates were $2.10, and a 10¾-inch urn-shaped vase cost $1.35. Today the celery dish by itself would easily sell for $125 to $150. Sugar and creamer sets can range from $100 to $800, and vases usually start at $250 and go as high as $5,000. Anyone want to say anything about investing in personal property?

It should be noted that Schlegelmilch china marked R. S. Prussia is considered to be of better quality than other products from the same factory. R. S. Germany, for example, can be bought for only a quarter of the price of R. S. Prussia pieces.

Royal Dux

Another china that has taken astronomical jumps in value is Royal Dux porcelain, made in Bohemia and imported at the beginning of the twentieth century. The figurines were not terribly expensive at that time, but today Royal Dux figurines often bring $200, $500, and even $800 each, as do some of the vases and bowls.

Royal Bayreuth

If you have an unusually shaped ashtray or sugar or creamer around the house that you know isn't too old but is unlike anything you have ever seen—let's say that the ashtray is in the shape of a crab, the covered sugar looks like a tomato, and the creamer is in the shape of a shell—these may well be products from the Royal Bayreuth factory of Bavaria. These novelty pieces date from the very end of the nineteenth century up to approximately the time of World War I. To some, these are inexpensive novelty pieces; to others, they are the basis for an entire collection. Under no circumstances should they be casually thrown away. Another interesting product from the Royal Bayreuth factory is known as Tapestry ware, made by stretching a piece of fabric over the china body, which was then decorated and glazed, resulting in the slightly irregular or granulated surface that characterizes the floral and scenic pieces of Royal Bayreuth. Tapestry-type pieces are even more valuable than the novelties. Ironically, the Bayreuth Company is known in Europe as the manufacturer of extraordinarily fine-quality porcelain of the eighteenth century, which can be compared with the products of the Meissen factories.

Royal Austria

A commonly found mark on late-nineteenth-century china is that of a beehive, associated with Royal Vienna or Beehive, Austria, china. As was true of so many European factories, this mark and china had its origin in the eighteenth century, but most that we see today consists of nineteenth-century porcelain portrait plates, vases, or cups and saucers, many copied after the eighteenth-century designs of Angela Kauffman. Royal Austria is sometimes mistaken as Sevres because many of the shapes and even types of designs that were used by the finer Sevres factory in France were also used by the Austrian factory. The china remains desirable but moderately priced when compared with the much more expensive Sevres pieces.

Sevres

Sevres is perhaps the most famous of all porcelain. Yet Sevres is little different from any other product of the European factories that we have discussed. During the eighteenth century, Sevres produced the finest of porcelain wares, but in the nineteenth century the wares became less expensive, mass-produced, and extremely popular. Needless to say, the fakes, frauds, and reproductions of Sevres porcelain are too numerous to count. The marks have been copied, the style has been copied, the shapes have been copied, the decorations have been copied—all to such an extent that now you often see a listing in an auction catalog of "Sevres-type" porcelain. This description is the same used by the auction houses to differentiate period furniture from furniture in the *style* of a period. Thus, if you see a piece labeled "Sevres-type," know that it was made by another company but is of good quality and was copied after the Sevres designs. The difference in price between a Sevres-type urn and a real Sevres urn will be the same that exists between the value of a Georgian-*style* chest of drawers and an eighteenth-century *period* Georgian chest of drawers.

To distinguish between the real and the copy, you must study the fine Sevres pieces in museums carefully and look at the quality of the painting. Once, while handling an estate appraisal, I came upon a basically good three-piece mantel set known as a garniture. "Could they really be Sevres?" I wondered. I decided not; the painting was not sufficiently good. I concluded that they were of the Sevres-type. I explained to the heirs of the estate the difference between Sevres and Sevres-type and predicted that a reasonable sale price for the three pieces would be in the $1,000 to $1,500 range. The group eventually was sent to an auction house, where it was catalogued as a "highly important three-piece Sevres cobalt-blue mantel garniture" and given a preauction estimate of $3,000 to $4,000. However, when auction time came around, the group had been correctly identified as "Sevres-type" and sold for $1,500. But if sold in a fancy shop specializing in nineteenth-century French decor, this group could easily have brought $3,000 to $4,000.

Scandinavian Porcelain

Mention should be made of two Scandinavian factories, Bing & Gröndahl and Royal Copenhagen. Both Danish factories originated in the nineteenth century and still operate today. Both factories produce very fine quality figurines characterized by a clear, bright glaze. Both companies primarily use blue-and-white coloration and are well known for their dinnerware as well as for Christmas and other commemorative plates. The figurines of both factories are valuable and will eventually, I believe, be more highly treasured and valued than they are today. Meanwhile, the famous Christmas plates are widely collected. As you would expect, the glaze and type of this fine porcelain have been widely imitated, especially in the Orient.

Hummel

Almost every house has at least one Hummel figurine—perhaps bought in Europe as a souvenir item or from an American store as a christening or birthday gift. Little matter where it was purchased. The truth of the matter is, Hummel figurines are expensive, even those currently made and available in gift shops and department stores. There are collectors clubs devoted exclusively to Hummel figurines, and numerous books have been published for the Hummel collector. As you would expect, because of this great popularity, fakes abound. Most of the imitations have come from Japan, marked with a simple paper label when imported to the United States (the label is later removed). There is a difference in the glaze and material used in the imitation figurines, but to make the distinction you should know both the genuine Hummel markings and the specific designs and characteristics of the figurines.

When valuing Hummel figurines, the rarity of the individual piece and its particular size are always a consideration, as is the age of the piece. Since some of the figurines have been in production for forty years or more, the earlier ones obviously bring more money. Many people do not realize that Hummel figurines were also made into ashtrays, candlesticks, and lamps—and even Nativity scenes. It is important to note that not all figurines made by the Goebel factory are based on M. I. Hummel designs. To be sure that your Goebel is indeed a Hummel, check for the impressed "M. I. Hummel" marking on the base. Hummels are much more collectible and valuable than Goebels that are not Hummels. You should also know that not all Hummels are colored. Some of the figurines, especially the religious ones, such as angels and Nativity figures, are white.

Oriental Porcelain

A particularly hot subject in antiques today is the fine Oriental porcelain of various dynasties. These pieces are bringing thousands of dollars in the international marketplaces and attracting headlines. It has been my experience that the majority of the truly valuable Oriental porcelain from the later centuries B.C. and earlier centuries A.D. are in European rather than in American collections. The pieces that do exist in America generally have been bought through one of the international auction houses or elite shops specializing in Oriental porcelain or came from famous collections when they were dismantled. Thus the owners know what they have. Most Oriental porcelain found in American homes as accent pieces can be broken down into two large groups: 1) export china and 2) nineteenth- and twentieth-century Japanese china.

Export China

Export china was made primarily in China in the second half of the eighteenth century and throughout the nineteenth century for import into

America. Of course porcelain made prior to the McKinley Act of 1891 is seldom marked, and thus there can be a question about its age—is it eighteenth or nineteenth century? A careful study of the style of painting characteristic of the two different centuries, plus an understanding of the shapes that are typical of the different times, helps the student of export porcelain to date these pieces.

The oldest of this china, once called Lowestoft and now generally referred to as Chinese export, is distinguished by the light gray or blue cast to the glaze and the distinctive floral motif. Much of the china is simply decorated, but the most highly prized is the Armorial Chinese export china, which was made specifically for families and exported from China. Armorial china was shipped to the European countries as well as America, and these pieces are always valuable.

Two popular patterns of export china are often found in today's homes. The first, "Canton," is recognizable by the center decoration of a pagoda-type house with mountains and trees in the background and painted blue on white. There are variations in the border that surrounds the center motif, but most common is the raincloud band. Condition is always important in valuing china, and Chinese export china is no exception. Remember, a broken dish has only archaeological value. However, because collectors today are so anxious to assemble whole sets of "Canton," there is more of a market for a chipped plate or nicked serving dish than ever before. Value also depends on the rarity of a piece. Fewer large covered serving dishes were made than dinner plates and even fewer candlesticks or inkwells than table china.

The market for "Canton" is large and thriving, but this particular pattern is most popular in the New England areas, where it was originally imported.

The other extremely popular export china is "Rose Medallion." This china is distinguished both by its rose motif and the rose coloring. Usually the china has a group of four panels that alternate flowers, birds, and butterflies with groups of people, often depicted in a house. When only flowers, birds, and butterflies appear, the china is referred to as "Rose Canton." On the other hand, when only the people are displayed, as they sometimes are at the center of a plate, the china is referred to as "Rose Mandarin."

Everything said about the blue-and-white "Canton" applies to "Rose Medallion." Probably more unusual pieces and a wider variety of shapes were made in "Rose Medallion," and pieces of all kinds, even those marked "Made in China," can be found for sale in fine antiques shops. Both patterns are currently being reproduced. In fact, the "Canton" pattern is reproduced by Mottahedeh as part of its Historic Charleston line.

Other Chinese export patterns of the nineteenth century include "Tobacco Leaf," "Fitzhugh," and "Nanking." Export china is valuable both because it is old and because it is appropriate to period restorations and museums. Chinese export was the favorite of American presidents and is once again in great favor. Although this means you can quickly find a buyer for any you wish to sell, you must also beware cheap imitations, all of which are rather garishly painted when compared with authentic pieces.

Tobacco Leaf. **Photograph courtesy Weschler's Auction Gallery**

Japanese Porcelain—Imari

Imari china originated in Japan in the seventeenth century, but that which we most often see today is nineteenth- and of course twentieth-century Imari. Characteristic Imari china is distinguished by the unmistakable deep orange red color, cobalt blue, and gilt highlights, often combined with turquoise and yellow. Imari patterns often depict floral decorations, birds, and symbols of the Japanese culture. As in the "Rose Medallion" pattern, panels often are used that alternate one decoration or motif with another. Imari bowls are widely collected, as are plates and chargers. The more unusual, and therefore more valuable, items are candlesticks, tall vases, and pieces with unusual shapings. Imari continues to be reproduced today, but once again the paintings seem a little too bright and too clean when compared with nineteenth-century Imari.

The charming, colorful floral motif of Imari china was adapted by English potters and used in both porcelain and ironstone, notably in the extremely expensive Royal Crown Derby Imari pattern and the ever-popular Mason ironstone Imari patterns. A very liberal translation of the Imari floral motif and coloring is found on some Gaudy Welsh china.

The price for Imari seems to have no limits. Only a few years ago you could buy a simple scallop-bordered Imari plate in perfect condition for $20 to $25. Today, if you can find that plate for under $150, you consider it a steal, and I have seen prices soar as high as $250 and up.

Satsuma

Satsuma was manufactured in Japan in the seventeenth, eighteenth, and nineteenth centuries, but the majority seen today dates from the later nineteenth century. Satsuma can be difficult to describe, yet once you see a piece you never forget its characteristics. The china often depicts brightly dressed Japanese figures in red, blue, green, orange, and gold, and the china itself has an almost brocadelike appearance. There is so much movement in the design and so much contrast between the gold and other colors that

Satsuma takes on a three-dimensional aspect. The gold is often raised or even beaded. Not long ago Satsuma went unappreciated. Many people once considered the overall decoration gaudy—the bold, rich colors and crowded details were just too much. Today others love these very same details, and Satsuma ware is now very sought after and widely collected.

Kutani

Kutani ware is a stepchild. It originated in Japan in the seventeenth century and lasted for only a short time. But during the nineteenth century, when Japanese porcelain became popular in the Western countries, Kutani was once again produced. Connoisseurs refer to the nineteenth-century ware, which is found in so many homes, as "revived" Kutani. If you look for the term "Kutani" in many scholarly encyclopedias of antiques, you will find only a mention of the seventeenth-century factory. Yet if you go into homes on a daily basis, as I do, you know that nineteenth-century Kutani abounds.

Kutani is perhaps more like Satsuma than any other of the Japanese designs. It is characteristically decorated in deep red orange with much gold highlighting; usually it depicts a landscape scene with birds in the air and generally has a floral border. Kutani china was extremely popular in the 1880s and 1890s, and sets, demitasse cups and saucers, chocolate sets, and dessert sets were frequently given as wedding presents.

I have a Kutani chocolate set that was a wedding present to my great-grandparents in the 1880s. I discovered this china packed away in the basement one day and asked my father if I might have it, since he wasn't using it.

"Yes, you may have it," he replied, "on one condition—that when I come to your house I don't have to look at it. I never did like the stuff, which is why it's packed away in the basement!"

This only points up once again the adage that our parents have questionable taste, our grandparents acceptable taste, but our great-grandparents superlative taste. My father never did particularly like his grandparents' things, but a generation later I find them extremely attractive.

The simpler Kutani is moderately priced and can be compared in value with the more common Haviland patterns. Of course, the more richly decorated and highly gilded pieces are more expensive.

Nippon

The Nippon ware of the later nineteenth and early twentieth century can be compared with Depression glass in the new surge of its popularity. If you have a piece of porcelain marked Nippon, it was made between 1890 and 1921. With the passage of the McKinley Tariff Act of 1890, imports from Japan to the United States were marked with the word "Nippon," which is Japanese for Japan. They continued to mark their export wares in that way until 1921, when the Treasury Department of the United States decreed that imports to the United States should be marked "Made in ____," with the English word inserted for the country of origin. Thus Japan's exports to the United States began to be marked "Made in Japan." It should be noted that many Nippon pieces, when viewed from a distance, can be mistaken for English or European china. I remember being quite taken aback when I discovered that a dish I had positively identified, from across the room, as very fine quality Royal Crown Derby in the Imari pattern turned out to be Nippon. Nippon successfully imitated Belleck, R. S. Prussia, Wedgwood, and Limoges, among others.

Unusual and well-executed pieces of Nippon china now bring hundreds of dollars. It is not uncommon to find a biscuit barrel or cracker jar with a price tag of $250 or more, and humidors range from $200 to $300. But the average plate, colorfully decorated in the Oriental styling with perhaps a touch of the Victorian floral motif, is still reasonably priced at from $25 to $50.

Noritake

The best known of the Nippon, or Japanese, companies is Noritake. This company, founded in 1904 by the Morimura family in Japan, began exporting their first real dinner services to the United States around the time of World War I. Noritake products are growing in popularity and value.

Noritake ware is best known by the red or green letter "M" encircled in a wreath. Above the wreath is often the word "Noritake" and below it "handpainted." The designs are generally simple, mostly depicting landscape scenes, and Noritake is found both in the usual dinnerware pieces—cups and saucers, plates, and so on—and in sets such as nut bowls and tea sets. The Noritake Company is still in existence today (after a period during World War II of ceasing their exports to the United States) and makes a combination of kitchenware, glassware, and dinnerware, as well as the more expensive lead-crystal and porcelain dinner sets. The "Azalea" pattern, which was designed by Noritake exclusively for the Larkin company, is so popular that you often find it listed in separate categories in mass-produced price guides.

Occupied Japan

Last are those frequently found ten-cent store items marked "Occupied Japan." These were the porcelain wares made in Japan during the years of Allied occupation immediately following Japan's surrender at the end of World War II. These pieces, which cost $.15–$.25 in the 1940s, are now collectibles and are bringing anywhere from $5 to $35, in an inexpensive flea market, to $15, $30, and $50 among collectors.

Other Oriental Accessories

Cloisonné

Many books that were published in the 1950s and 1960s omitted cloisonné—it was just not in fashion.

You could find it in antiques shops, and you would even see pieces in people's homes. But American buyers were not actively going out and seeking cloisonné until the mid-1970s.

Basically, cloisonné is made by soldering small strips or wires of metal, sometimes true gold and silver, onto a copper or brass base. Enamel paste in a variety of colors is then applied within these wires to create often beautiful and colorful designs. Cloisonné is commonly used in combination with bronze in vases, many of which have been converted into lamps.

> Always examine cloisonné carefully, as it may have been dropped and dented. The dents can be hard to see from the outside. The best way to check is to feel around the interior of the piece for these defects.

As with porcelain, damage to cloisonné depreciates the value. However, since many cloisonné pieces are purchased primarily for decorative purposes, if you don't mind a dent, you can get a damaged piece for less money. The different quality of cloisonné also affects its value. And I'm sure you know that much new cloisonné comes into the country with the infamous "paper label" that is quickly removed, and the new piece is erroneously sold as "antique"— usually at an inflated price.

Cinnabar

Oriental accessories often are made of cinnabar, the red lacquer or "vermilion" ware made by applying hundreds of coats of vermilion one on top of the other. Once hard, a design is carved into the lacquer. The cinnabar process has been around for centuries, but the majority of what you see today is either from the nineteenth century or may even be very recently made. There is usually a difference both in the color of new cinnabar and in the quality of its design. Even the new cinnabar can be costly, however. Pieces most frequently found are covered boxes, small snuff bottles, and vases. However, be aware that some of the new pieces are not true cinnabar at all but cheap imitations made from molded composition material, much like chipboard imitations of plywood. If you don't know—don't buy.

American Art Pottery

American art pottery runs the gamut from the magnificent pieces of Adelaide Alsop Robineau to inexpensive mass-manufactured items in the "style" of individually crafted pottery. It is worth your time to have at least a nodding acquaintance with American art pottery today because it is so often written about and so much is packed away in attics and basements or sold at flea markets. Like so many "hot" items, much art pottery that truly is quite valuable today was originally purchased for only a few dollars. But museum exhibitions, scholarly articles, and feature stories in glossy magazines have contributed to the public's awareness of their value.

You can review the section on English art pottery, and the following list is provided as a quick reference to the better-known potters and a broad, beginning reference to value ranges. Be aware that many potters and workshops have greater regional than national value and importance. Do not dismiss as insignificant a maker who is not listed here.

Frequently Encountered
American Art Pottery Makers

Buffalo Pottery. New York State. One of the large factories, Buffalo produced several different lines, and thus the pieces are not necessarily rare, but many are very valuable. A "hot" collectible today. See *Deldare*.

Brush. See *McCoy*.

Cowan Pottery. Ohio. Primarily the manufacturer of "florist" quality ware, the pieces today usually range below $100. Some limited-edition and "art pieces" are more valuable.

Dedham Pottery. Massachusetts. One of the most sought-after lines, the crackleware glaze pieces with blue figures bring many hundreds of dollars according to the design and mark.

Deldare Ware. New York State. A highly sought after line made by Buffalo Pottery.

Fulper Pottery. New Jersey. Makers of a variety of items including lamps, vases, smoking accessories, and so on, in simple but very Art Nouveau shapes. A wide range of values.

Grueby. Massachusetts. Best known for matte glaze vases, the company also made architectural tiles. Vases usually cost several hundred dollars.

Hull. Ohio. Still in existence today, Hull made both art pottery and commercial wares. The commercial wares are generally inexpensive and very plentiful, but the art pottery pieces are more expensive and can be distinguished by the marking.

Knowles, Taylor and Knowles. Ohio. Makers of inexpensive commercial ware, Knowles made one line of art pottery known as Lotus Ware, which has received a lot of attention. This means some people will mistakenly think all Knowles pieces are valuable, but they are not.

McCoy. Ohio. Primarily mass producers of commercial wares that sell in the $15–$45 range unless highly unusual. The Brush Ware line is more expensive, usually in the $40–$100 range.

Newcomb. New Orleans. Unquestionably one of the most sought after and most valuable art pottery lines. Pieces can easily fall into the high-hundred- and low-thousand-dollar range.

Niloak. Arkansas. The marblelike, satin glaze of Niloak is unmistakable even when the paper label is no longer present. Prices generally fall in the $20–$60 range.

Red Wing. Minnesota. Because there are mass-manufactured commercial wares as well as art pottery, Red Wing pieces range from only a few dollars to the low hundreds.

Rockingham. England and America. This is a trade name that describes a reddish or almost chocolate-brown glaze. Pitchers and tea- and coffeepots are most common. The most sought after pieces have an embossed or relief scene. The ware originated in England in the mid-nineteenth century and was copied in America. Values vary greatly according to the piece and its motif.

Rookwood. Ohio. Perhaps the best-known art pottery, the value for Rookwood pieces runs the gamut from a few dollars to thousands, depending upon the piece, maker, age, glaze, motif, condition, and so on.

Roseville. Ohio. A prolific maker of both machine-made commercial and handmade art pottery lines, meaning the values can range from a few dollars into the midhundreds for finer pieces.

Shawnee. Ohio. Commercial maker of inexpensive items that might be classified as the "everyman's" art pottery. Values generally in the $15–$60 range.

Van Briggle. Colorado. Pottery from the early 1900s widely sought after and valuable. The Art Deco designs of the 1930s were very popular at the time. The company is still working. The marks, date, and design can mean the difference between a $30 and a $300 item.

Weller. Ohio. One of the largest producers of both art and commercial lines. Collectors seek one line of Weller, and thus some designs are much more valuable than others. Values continue to increase and now average around $100–$200 for better pieces.

Art Nouveau and Art Deco Accessories

At the end of the nineteenth century a new art, or Art Nouveau, style of design emerged, characterized by a freely curving, flowing line. The graceful curve was adaptable to natural forms—flowers, swaying trees, the female figure—and artists used these lines and forms in every medium of the decorative arts, from furniture to jewelry to lighting fixtures to stained glass.

The most famous American artist who worked in the Art Nouveau style is, of course, Louis Comfort Tiffany.

However, the Art Nouveau movement was internationally popular, and the finest work was created in Europe, particularly France. We are all familiar with the famous French bronze statues that epitomize the Art Nouveau period.

Actually, the popularity of sculpture and statuary was a boon for the nineteenth-century artist who could at last support himself financially through sculpture. An artist could create a piece of sculpture, have his design cast in molds, and then "pour" as many figures into the molds as he wished and as the public would buy.

These decorative sculptures soon appeared in turn-of-the-century foyers, parlors, and music rooms as the expanding middle class demanded the latest in accessories. As a result spelter, an inexpensive white metal, was used to make the figures, which were then given a bronze-type finish. They were now affordable for the masses.

Art Nouveau bronzes are immensely popular at the moment and are selling for thousands of dollars at the international auction houses. However, even the less expensive spelter figurines and statuary carry price tags ranging from a few hundred dollars to the low thousands.

Remember that all of the products of the Art Nouveau era were mass-produced in factories, foundries, workshops, and galleries. Because the entire Art Nouveau and later Art Deco styles were so unpopular during the 1950s and 1960s, it is easy to forget how plentiful pieces in these styles are.

Less expensive and poorer-quality interpretations of these styles were also made and sold through mail-order catalogs and in dimestores to the masses in the early 1900s.

However, every time a style becomes fashionable, usually starting with the rediscovery by a museum of the finest-quality pieces, the vogue creeps slowly but surely into our lives, and even once inexpensive pieces become collectible. Just as an investor may pay $100,000 for a signed Tiffany lamp, so a collector with more modest means will buy a Tiffany-type lamp—made originally for a modest 1900s home—for $500.

Everything said about Art Nouveau accessories applied to Art Deco accessories of the 1930s, although the style is different, with the Art Nouveau's flowing lines replaced by straight angles, and natural forms—flowers and the human body—discarded in favor of geometric and orderly motifs. But the media remained the same, and the Art Deco style appears in furniture, jewelry, lamps, and glass.

Caution—A Word About Bronzes

Because so many of the Art Nouveau and Art Deco accessories are bronze, this is an appropriate place to send a clear, loud warning to everyone that bronzes are a specialized and rarefied area: fakes abound. Recastings, similar designs, fake signatures, inferior quality—you name it—the pretenders come in every conceivable form. If you like a bronze advertised in a newspaper,

This bronze equestrian group of "The Outlaw," above is after the model by Frederic Remington and is typical of the bronzes sold at the well-known auction galleries. Photograph courtesy Weschler's Auction Gallery

The second grouping, above right, also from a Remington model, is currently being cast by Sun Foundry in Burbank, California, and can be purchased by a simple telephone call. Photograph courtesy Sun Foundry

magazine, or even *The Wall Street Journal,* buy it—but not as an investment. For further reading on the fake and fraudulent bronze trade, check with your research librarian. Sam Pennington's advice on folk art fakes in chapter 34 applies to bronzes as well and should be closely heeded.

Art Nouveau and Art Deco Metal and Leather Accessories

The most familiar of the Art Nouveau accessories, and the ones I most frequently see in private homes, are the American and English manufacturing companies' silver dresser sets adorned with blossoming flowers and romanticized ladies. Mirrors, brushes, pin trays, covered powder jars, and hair receivers, along with perfume vials and picture frames, are commonly found in both sterling silver and silver plate. Sterling silver brushes, which must have their bristles replaced, are often no more valuable than the weight of the silver, but large sets and richly decorated picture frames bring hundreds of dollars. Of course, silver-plated accessories are less valuable.

In reaction to the Art Nouveau style, and in keeping with the stark furniture exemplified by Stickley and seen in many Mission pieces, several fine workshops and factories turned out other metal (mostly copper and brass) and leather accessories. All Art Deco accessories have value today as the style becomes increasingly popular. However, among the most prized items are those bearing the Roycroft name. The Roycroft shop existed between 1895 and 1938 and produced many of the accessories found in homes during this time, including candlesticks, sconces, desk sets, lamps, bowls, and the like. Their leather goods included pocketbooks, match cases, and even book bindings. Although all Roycroft pieces are collectible, those made between 1895 and 1915 are most desirable.

Lamps aren't the only metal objects that attract Art Nouveau and Art Deco collectors. This Bradley and Hubbard cast-iron spittoon sold for $160 at Savoia and Fromm.

Art Glass

During the mid-nineteenth century and later, corresponding with the Art Nouveau movement, art glass became immensely popular. Art glass was made in every European country and America and was copied the world over. Art glass designers vied to produce new types of glass, and once the newest technique and style gained popularity, all the other designers and factories immediately copied it.

For these reasons, art glass and glass accessories are the most dangerous areas for the nonexpert in the antiques field. No other medium has been imitated more times and in greater degrees of varying quality than glassware, including copies of art glass made for the mass market. Because art glass is a

Beautiful early-twentieth-century art glass by Lalique is collected for its age even though some of the same designs are still being manufactured and sold by retailers today. Photograph courtesy Henry J. Young Jewelers

For the knowledgeable buyer, art glass presents an endless array of makers, designs, and quality. But it has been so often copied that this is not a field for the novice. Photograph courtesy Richard A Bourne Company

rapidly growing investment area, many fake examples of glass have been signed with the name of a prestigious company to facilitate a sale. Often when the fake piece is compared with the authentic one, the absence of a signature is noted on the *real* piece!

Most fake and reproduction glass is imported from either central Europe or Mexico. One reason glass is so easily faked is that so much of it was made originally, no one is immediately suspicious when more pieces appear on the market. However, a proliferation of *one design* that begins to show up at each auction and every antiques shop should make you suspicious.

The other point to remember about glass is that, while the finest art glass was made originally for the wealthy connoisseur, once the rest of the population demanded the new fashion, imitations appeared in mass production. Inexpensive vases, glasses, pitchers, and the like were purchased through dimestores. In fact, it was the public's demand for art glass that gave birth to Carnival glass, known as the "poor man's Tiffany." But wouldn't you know! Even the poor man's cheap Carnival glass has now been cheapened further by the current reproductions.

Carnival glass. **Photograph courtesy Richard A. Bourne Company**

The difference in period glass and reproduced glass is often similar to the differences in china—the weight and color of the newer pieces are giveaways.

Glass copies are frequently sold today through museum and restoration gift shops. Even though they are sold as reproductions, once you mix the reproductions in with the old collections, just a piece or two at a time, it is easy for the new to become confused with the old and eventually be passed off as antique.

If the art glass in your home is genuine, of the period, in perfect condition, and of superior quality, you do indeed have something of value. However, if you are looking for an area of antiques to invest in and are just beginning, my advice would be to stay away from art glass. (For a list of many art glass terms, see the glass glossary in chapter 18.)

Lamps and Candlesticks

Entire books have been written on individual lighting devices from Betty lamps and candlesticks to night lamps to Tiffany lamps. Lamps exist in profusion, and why not? Without proper lighting our night hours are wasted. Therefore from the earliest times a lamp was a necessity, even in the most primitive of homes.

Candlesticks and lamps have been made out of every conceivable material—from metal to glass to porcelain. Though candlesticks were far more common, as we in America know them, the crude oil- or fat-burning lamps used by the pioneers and commonly called Betty lamps were the earliest.

For years I wondered why the lamps were called Betty lamps, asked many knowledgeable people, but received no answer. However, the word "betynges" refers to the crude fat used as fuel in early torches or lanterns. Thus the small metal lamp with an extended handle, which could be hooked over and hung from a mantelpiece, was referred to as a betynges, or Betty, lamp.

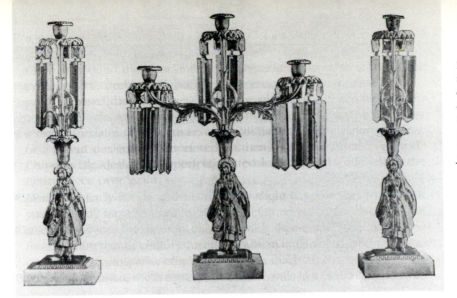

Though there are many true nineteenth-century girandoles available in the market, a glance at this set of reproduction girandoles advertised by H. C. Valentine in the mid-1930s should alert you to proceed cautiously.

Originally there were countless numbers of these lamps in existence, used by the pioneers in their humble cabins and homes through the nineteenth century.

Among the most popular nineteenth-century lamps were those made by the famous New England glass companies. Both oil-burning and then, later, gas lamps are available in all varieties of glass and in every conceivable shape. And, of course, these have all been reproduced. To identify nineteenth-century lamps correctly, you must first be able to identify the product they are made of—end-of-day glass, milk glass, and so on.

Later, the lamps of the nineteenth century and early twentieth century were carried to new heights by the famous Tiffany Studio products. These leaded-glass shaded lamps were so rapidly copied and reproduced that now all lamps of this type (unless marked by Tiffany, Handel, or Bradley and Hubbard, to name a few of the lampmakers of the time) are referred to as "Tiffany style." Although most "Tiffany" lamps turn out to be reproductions and copies, occasionally you will find the real thing—and what a find it is!

As I completed an appraisal one day, my client called me back.

"There's one other thing I'd like you to look at. It's a Tiffany lamp," she said in a matter-of-fact way.

Of course I did not expect to see a Tiffany lamp (I had been disappointed so many times), but I followed her into her basement. There she unpacked a lamp—with two broken glass panels, but labeled "Tiffany."

"About eight years ago I bought this lamp at a white elephant sale for one dollar," she told me. "We needed another lamp, and we had spent all our money on moving here. I put it up in my son's bedroom with the two broken panels turned toward the wall, and he used it for five years. When I finally got around to buying a new lamp and was packing this one away, I saw the Tiffany mark. I had never seen it before. Do you think I can sell it? Are people really buying Tiffany lamps?"

The lamp sold six months later at Christie's for $2,800—broken panels and all.

Though not by Tiffany or Handel, this unsigned American leaded art glass shaded lamp on a metal lily pad base is glamorous and more affordable. Photograph courtesy Weschler's Auction Gallery

Now granted, this was not a $58,000 or $250,000 Tiffany lamp, but it was a pretty good return on a one-dollar investment. If you think you have a Tiffany lamp, examine it closely on the base and on the shade for the Tiffany signature. If you find nothing, assume that the lamp is *not* by Tiffany. However, an expert in this area can positively identify your lamp, and, I repeat, even Tiffany-type lamps are selling for hundreds of dollars today.

When making your inventory, be sure to include lamps. Even mass-produced, store-bought lamps are expensive today because of manufacturing costs. Yet these accessories are often overlooked in household inventories.

Looking Glasses

The earliest mirrors or looking glasses in America were imported. Historically the first mirrors were only highly polished sheets of metal. Later, during the eighteenth century, cutting an even layer of hand-blown glass that would not break in the cutting or would not be terribly irregular once it was cut was extremely difficult. Mirrors remained very expensive until the nineteenth century, and for this reason early period mirrors are extraordinarily expensive.

In addition to the cost of the mirror itself, there is the frame to be considered. Because mirrors were so expensive, they were found in only the wealthiest homes and then in the finest rooms as a status symbol. As a result, the frames of early mirrors are often outstanding examples of craftsmanship.

The most familiar style of mirror from the eighteenth century is the highly carved wooden Chippendale frame with a bird motif—either a bird perched at the center of a broken-neck pediment or else a carved phoenix at the center of the fretwork crest. These eighteenth-century mirrors were reproduced in the nineteenth century, particularly during the Centennial period. Many of the modern European copies of both these and the Chippendale Rococo gilded mirrors are often mistakenly sold as period American mirrors.

It wasn't until the Hepplewhite period that many mirrors were actually made in America. By the Sheraton period, mirrors were found in more modest homes, and the typical Sheraton mirror having a gilt frame and an eglomise panel (a decorative glass section usually depicting a landscape scene or a flower motif) became both common and popular.

> For a mirror to have an investment value, all the parts must be original.

Unfortunately I find many mirrors and clocks in which the eglomise panel is replaced by a Currier and Ives–type nineteenth-century print, often cut out of a book or magazine. The picture usually replaces an eglomise panel that had been cracked or in which the paint was wearing off. Even a worn or cracked panel is considered acceptable as long as it is the same age as the rest of the mirror and frame.

Highly ornate Sheraton or Federal mirrors with gilded eagles and elaborate Corinthian columns flanking the mirror are expensive. However, simple mirrors with a molded cornice and rounded columns at the sides (often called tabernacle mirrors) can still be purchased for as little as $100. A manufacturer's label generally doubles the value of a nineteenth-century mirror.

Be sure to include your reproduction and new mirrors on your inventory. Today a good-quality mirror with a simple frame generally ranges from $150 to $250, but fine mirrors bought from interior decorators' shops have now escalated in price and are often in the $1,000-plus range.

Clocks

I find the age of clocks to be greatly misunderstood. Quite regularly I am shown a 1920s mantel or shelf clock and told, "This clock is very old and very valuable. It probably dates from the eighteenth century."

Striking clocks, as we know them, date from thirteenth-century Europe. Of course, Galileo is given credit for the stimulus for making pendulum clocks. But by the first part of the nineteenth century, case clocks, either tall,

Probably the most copied style of mirror in the 1920s and 1930s was the convex mirror, often called a Philadelphia busybody. True period convex mirrors are expensive and hard to find. Photograph courtesy Craig and Tarlton

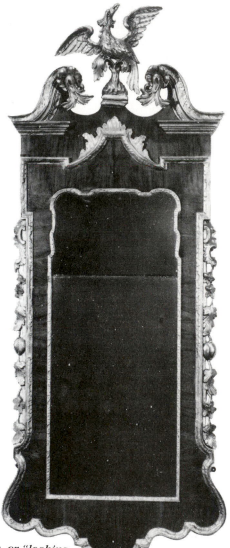

Period mirrors, or "looking glasses," as they were called, were expensive when they were made and remain so today. Mirrors of this quality sell for *five figures,* and any offered for less are reproductions. Photograph courtesy Craig and Tarlton

Even if the eglomise panel is cracked or the paint is wearing off, Federal mirrors should be left intact to retain their greatest value to the collector. Photograph courtesy Craig and Tarlton

228

imposing grandfather clocks or smaller mantel or shelf clocks, were frequently found in wealthier American homes. By the end of the nineteenth
century, clocks were mass-produced, and these abound. A walk through any
flea market reveals numerous oak case clocks, some reproductions, some
fake, and some authentic. Even on television there are advertisements for
clocks that "look as good as antiques" and can be purchased for only $29.95.

> Because there are so many clocks from the nineteenth century and
> particularly the early part of the twentieth century, only those clocks that
> are unusual because of their fine cases or uniqueness (such as calendar or
> regulator clocks) command a great deal of money.

*This unusual Ansonia
"swinging doll" clock
attracted much attention
at Savoia and Fromm
Auction Services.*

But what money clocks can demand! Some regulator and calendar
clocks have been valued at thousands
of dollars, and the prices on even the
most common shelf clocks at flea
markets are always a little staggering
to me.

Before investing in a clock, be
sure that you are truly buying what
you are told you are getting. The
clock should be in working condition, with all parts original, even the
glass or eglomise panel (if a
nineteenth-century shelf clock) and
all the parts of the case, including the
finials and the feet. Of course, if you
want to buy a chipped veneer mantel
clock for the works to place inside a
perfectly conditioned mantel clock
that is missing its parts, you have a
different situation.

Beware banjo clocks in particular.
These have been reproduced for
years and are sometimes sold as
early-nineteenth-century clocks when
in reality they are seventy-five years
younger than that.

You can look for an increase in
the value of Art Deco shelf clocks,
particularly those with the statuary
motifs characteristic of Art Deco, and
clocks from the 1930s made in combination with lamps.

*Warning! Banjo clocks have
been reproduced for years.
Period banjo clocks, like the
one pictured at left, are not
terribly rare, but they are
very expensive.* **Photograph
courtesy Craig and Tarlton**

21

Art:
Old Master or Just Old?

What better way to remember a foreign trip than to pick up a little souvenir painting? Why do all the beaches have art galleries? Who doesn't love a beautiful mountain landscape hanging on his wall? Pictures and prints abound. But there is a tremendous difference in quality between a mass-produced etching or print, an anonymous oil, and a masterpiece.

No other aspect of the antiques world is as glamorous as the art market. Art sales are where the really big money changes hands. Is there anyone who doesn't know the worth of a Van Gogh today?

Though the reality of finding such a painting in a home is slim, it can be done. A friend of mine found an original portrait of an American president hanging in an antiques shop, identified simply as "Portrait of an English Gentleman." Somewhere along the way, as the painting went from one owner to another, to an auction house, to a purchaser, was passed on to an heir, back for sale again, the identity of the president was lost. But it wasn't by luck that the painting was identified. The distinguished southern collector who discovered the lost painting was a student of American history, and he recognized the subject of the painting as President James Monroe. The portrait currently hangs, on loan, in the Department of State in Washington, D.C., and scholarly research has established that it was painted in 1829 by Chester Harding. The historical importance of this discovery cannot be measured in terms of money.

Great painters of every period have been imitated and faked, even during their lifetimes. Many artists were copied in their own time because they were so popular. While those paintings may have been sold as copies during the artist's lifetime, once the artist's work fades into obscurity it is forgotten which is the real painting and which is the copy. Then, once the artist and his work are rediscovered, it can be difficult to distinguish the original from the copy without an expert's examination.

A similar problem occurs when it is not known that an artist's works have been copied. The artist dies; later, when the artist's works come back into vogue, the public and experts do not know that copies had been made. Then many pictures that have the artist's signature—signed by the copier, of course—will be sold as the artist's work.

Will the next generation of art collectors know that this painting in the style of and signed Modigliani was really painted by Elmyr de Hory? The 1988 bidder knew this and still paid $24,750 when it sold in the sale of Governor John Connally's property. Photograph by Fritzi Harry, courtesy Maine Antique Digest

Other Confusing Situations

Pictures that are hand-painted—watercolors, acrylics, oils—comprise an endless list. There are etchings, engravings, woodcuts, lithographs, mezzotints—on and on. And they can easily fool even the expert as to quality.

One nationally known dealer attended an auction where he was attracted to a small picture.

"Is it a watercolor?" he inquired of a friend, who was working at the auction house.

"Oh, yes," the friend assured him.

The dealer knew that the auction assistant had trained under an expert who specialized in art, so he took his word and bought the picture.

Once he had the picture home and kept looking at it, the dealer became more and more concerned. Finally he took the picture out of the frame and underneath the mounting found clearly printed "New York Graphic Society." The watercolor was a print, of which hundreds had been struck.

It is little wonder, then, that many books on art begin with an apology explaining that the world of art is so complicated, problematic, and technical that there is no way to cover the various topics and explain all one needs to know. I will not tell you any differently. You already know that fakes sell for thousands of dollars and that art fraud is one of the IRS's favorite targets. This chapter will offer a few guidelines so you will know what information to

Romantic and sentimental mid-nineteenth-century art has been largely ignored in recent decades. But the mid-1980s saw a revival of interest in this period. When the oil painting "Arrival of St. Nicholas" by Edmund C. Coates sold at Skinner's for $52,250 in 1984, there was little doubt that St. Nicholas and new interest in this art genre had indeed "arrived."

gather before seeking a professional's advice. The usual art-related call that comes into our office begins:

"I have a picture I need to have appraised."

"Who is the artist?" we ask.

"I don't know."

"Do you know the medium? Oil, watercolor, drawing?"

"I don't know. Let me get it down."

And so the conversation—or lack of conversation—goes.

Answer each of the following questions as best you can *before* making such a call.

1. *Who is the artist?* Always seek this answer first. The value of art hinges on the specific artist more than on any other point.

2. *What is the medium?*

print	intaglio	watercolor
wood block	screen	gouache
lithograph	photo-etching	pastel
photolithograph	drawing	tempera
engraving	pencil	acrylic
mezzotint	ink	oil
aquatint	charcoal	mixed media

You may not be able to determine this specific information yourself. But knowing the medium can determine authenticity and affect value. Granted, a great pencil drawing will be more valuable than a poor oil, but a general rule of thumb is that oil works will be more valuable than other media works, such as watercolors, prints, or drawings, by the same artist.

3. *What is the subject?*
   still life
   landscape
   wildlife
   hunting or sporting scene
   marine or seascape
   genre (scenes of people in specific time or regional setting—for
      example, Dutchmen sitting around an open fire, French courtiers in
      outdoor scene)
   primitive or folk art
   figure study
   portrait
   illustration (created from or to accompany a story line)

Of course, individual artists are known for their work in specific subject matters—Toulouse-Lautrec's French circus scenes or Norman Rockwell's American home life illustrations. However, some subject matters are more popular and thus generally more expensive than others.

So many people are disappointed to learn that a family portrait may not be as valuable as they had thought. Unless painted by an acknowledged artist, portraits usually have sentimental or family value only and thus only replacement value rather than market value.

4. *What is the size?* You need to measure both the dimensions of the art itself and the larger frame dimensions. Note whether the picture is matted. The quality of the frame can be significant, as some are more valuable than the picture.

5. *What is the conditon?* Restoration and condition greatly affect value, so examine all artwork carefully. Tears in a canvas, foxing or staining of paper are obvious flaws you might encounter.

Sculpture, bronzes, photographs, and other art forms follow the same guidelines as paintings and pictures. Be sure to gather all possible details before submitting the information to the expert or appraiser.

Besides the preceding information, the art expert will also consider the following when appraising art:

1. Style
2. Quality
3. Historical importance
4. Provenance (prior ownership, showing or exhibitions, awards)
5. Known sale prices for comparable works

Another alternative is to gather the information and go to an art museum library, either a nearby private or state art museum or college or university that has a strong art history department. The research librarian should be able to assist you in finding both historical and market information relating to the particular artist.

Don't forget the frame around the picture. Fine-quality frames in excellent condition are often worth more than the artwork. Photograph courtesy Bobby Langston Auctions

Look for the obvious. If your picture is labeled a museum reproduction, its value is decorative, not that of a work of art.

You should also know that works by famous Old Master painters and household names such as Monet, Gainsborough, Picasso, Rembrandt, and the like are usually reproductions or lithographs of originals and of little or no value. But if you think you might have a true masterpiece, you might begin with a visit to an art museum. Tell the research librarian you wish to see an illustrated book on the particular artist whose work you have. If you find your picture there, you know you have a copy.

But, as I've said many times, any treasure can appear at any time and in almost any place. Thus, should you believe you have such a treasure, find an appraiser who

1. is knowledgeable in art
2. will take a look at the piece and determine whether or not it merits appraising—without charge or for a reasonable minimum fee

3. charges on a basis of time, not percentage of the appraised value of the piece, if it does merit further research to establish authentication and valuing.

Before paintings and prints can be valued, they must first be authenticated and then appraised. Art is a highly specialized area, and very few appraisers of artwork will be able to handle other personal property in your home. On the other hand, the general personal property appraiser is often unqualified to authenticate and appraise artwork. It is possible, however, that an appraiser who has had a lot of experience in antiques will suggest that you have your paintings appraised or tell you that, no, what you have is not of sufficient value to warrant an investment in an appraisal.

22

Magical, Mysterious Oriental Carpets

Oriental rugs are known to have been brought to America on merchant ships in the eighteenth and nineteenth centuries. Wealthy Americans who fancied the Eastern, or "Turkish," styles in the second half of the nineteenth century filled their grand houses with Oriental rugs. A few years later when American interior designers "discovered" Oriental rugs in the 1920s and 1930s, both the artisans of the East and the rug manufacturers in America worked overtime to meet the public's demand for Oriental design rugs. No longer did you have to be fabulously wealthy to have, well, if not a true Oriental rug, at least a rug of Oriental design, on your floor. These 1920s and 1930s rugs, both handmade and machine manufactured, are frequently found in our parents' and grandparents' homes today.

True, it is possible that you may find extremely fine and valuable rugs that were brought to America in the eighteenth and nineteenth centuries. But rugs are fragile, no matter how well made, and they are susceptible to wear, moths, water, and sun damage. If a rug has been used continually over the years, its valuable days may have passed, regardless of how fine it was originally, especially if there are large bald spots, faded areas, or pet stains.

Then again, some not-so-old rugs are found in poorer condition than older rugs. Wear is the product of usage, not necessarily age. One of the most common misbeliefs you will hear about Oriental rugs is that wear is an indication of great age. But regardless of the age, when a rug has great visible wear, its value is substantially reduced, no matter how old or rare it is.

A little hint! One dealer who knows the difference between the two-thousand- and the twenty-thousand-dollar rug told me that the best rugs he has ever found have been rolled up and stored in trunks in basements and attics. One reason for their higher value: they have not been walked on and so are in better condition.

Generally speaking, Oriental rugs are divided into three age categories:
1. Pre-1900 rugs are considered antique and, in good condition, command the highest prices.
2. Rugs from 1900 to 1930 are termed "semiantique" and are considered primarily decorative. Their values are strongly influenced by size (the largest are not compatible with our smaller rooms today) and color.
3. Post-1930 rugs are considered modern.

Ultimately the value of Oriental rugs, like most decorative items, is dependent on age, color, design, condition, and size. In addition, Oriental rugs are judged on their tribal origins. One tribe's work may be superior in craftsmanship to that of another tribe, or another's work may be recognized for its exceptional designs. It is the combination of these points that establishes the market value of Oriental rugs.

The "Right" Color May Be Wrong

Recognizing that rugs are used as a focal point when decorating a room, you quickly realize that the color of an Oriental rug is of prime concern. As our taste in colors changes, so does the value of specific rugs. For example, the burgundy rugs of the 1930s, no matter what the condition, size, or quality—or price—will be passed over if your color scheme calls for salmons and Chinese reds.

Choice of color was very important to the design of traditional tribal rugs, and master dyers were responsible for treating the wool with natural vegetable dyes to achieve exactly the right color. But when specific "decorator" colors became a consideration, traditional colors were sometimes replaced, and thus the rugs were no longer faithful to their original design concept. This might be compared to combining a Hepplewhite shield back with a Queen Anne cabriole leg: the chair may still serve its purpose, but the connoisseur will recognize that it is not "right." So the knowledgeable rug expert knows tribal designs and colors and looks for the best-quality rugs, "faithful" to the tribe's best work.

The predominating colors in this 1930-ish Turkish prayer rug are lavender, ivory, and gold, typical of the color schemes of the 1920s and 1930s that are not as popular in the 1980s. Photograph courtesy Weschler's Auction Gallery

It is essential for you to know that in the 1920s and 1930s, when decorators declared burgundy and mauve as choice colors, reds were actually over-painted to become shades of mauve and burgundy! Many dealers suggest rubbing a damp cloth over the surface of a carpet as a quick way to detect these painted-over or painted-in shades. The added color will rub off onto the damp cloth. Another way is to compare the color of the back of the rug with that of the top surface. Obviously the colors should be the same, or, if there is fading, the top surface should always be lighter, never darker, than the back. If you detect a reddish color on the back, but the wool appears purplish or deeper red on the front, be wary.

When judging an Oriental rug, it is essential to know whether yours is a genuine handmade Oriental or a later machine-made rug in "Oriental pattern," or for that matter a Russian or Belgian handmade reproduction of an older, more valuable rug. It usually takes an expert to make this latter distinction unless a label is still present.

The Other Side of the Rug

With a little practice, however, you can learn to distinguish between machine-made and handmade rugs. Machine-made rugs are easily detected by their even and symmetrical weave when viewed from the back. However, finely woven handmade rugs are frequently symmetrical on the back, and the novice may mistakenly believe a fine handmade rug is actually machine-made. Look carefully at the distance between the knots. As a rule, the fine handmade rug will have close, tight knots when compared with the wider-spaced, looser knot of the machine-made rug.

Further, the usual handmade rug will have a slight irregularity to the weave, an indication of hand production. Again, this may be compared with the slight irregularities you notice when comparing handmade dovetails with machine-cut dovetails. For this reason, the importance of looking at the reverse cannot be sufficiently stressed. Think of it as looking at the interior of a piece of furniture. Some of the modern rugs of Oriental design currently being produced are now so faithful to the original tribal rugs that they even copy the dye variations. Only if you look at the back can the subtle distinction be seen.

The top surface of a rug is what appeals to the eye—the design, the color, the size— but the reverse side can reveal the true quality and condition, whether it is handmade or manufactured, and even whether the colors on the surface are the original, true colors! **Photograph courtesy Weschler's Auction Gallery**

The salmons, blues, and ivories, as well as the geometric motifs, make Heriz rugs currently fashionable. The result? The cost of these rugs has increased many times over in the past fifteen years.
Photograph courtesy
Richard A. Bourne Company

While examining the back, look for further signs of wear. Obviously faded or bald spots, or even painted-in sections that have been added to cover up places where the wool has worn down to a nub (or to change the color, as mentioned earlier), can be seen from the top side of the rug. But a careful survey of the back will also reveal cracks, tears, and brittle places you may not detect from the top surface.

Slight misshaping of a good Oriental rug is not a major deterrent. There is often a two-to-four-inch variation between one end and the opposite end of handmade rugs. But a much larger variation may require the services of a specialist, which can be expensive and may not be totally successful.

Ultimately many fine Oriental rugs that may not suit the present taste will slip by unappreciated. If you are interested in rugs for their decorative appearance alone—and there is nothing wrong with that—your decisions on what to buy or what to keep will be dictated by personal preference. But if you wish to develop a connoisseur's knowledge of Oriental rugs, an exciting, lifelong adventure lies ahead.

One final note. The Oriental rug market is often spoken of as having investment possibilities, but you are now aware of the many pitfalls that await the nonexpert. Furthermore, as an Oriental rug expert explained, Oriental rugs of true investment quality are usually purchased by rug dealers from Europe and the East, who then take these rugs to Europe. Even the major auction galleries in America more often sell rugs that are primarily of decorative interest. However, these "decorative" rugs may be sold to American collector-investors who mistakenly think they are buying the finest investment-quality Oriental rugs. As you now know, those "investors" are most likely buying semiantique and good-quality rugs, but not investment-quality rugs. When a true Oriental rug expert speaks of investment-quality carpets, he is speaking in terms of $20,000 to $70,000, not $2,000 to $7,000.

23

Militaria:
The Most Often Thrown
Away Bag of Gold

I don't mean to sound sexist—after all, I'm a woman—but ask any man in the antiques business what the most overlooked item in a house is and you'll hear "The trunk of military souvenirs. You see, women just don't know about those things."

To give women their due, maybe the men toss out perfume bottles and Barbie dolls. But realistically, the chances may be quite high that you might come across a trunk with World War I, World War II, Korean, or even Vietnam items in it and have no idea of the values.

To keep you from either unwittingly selling these items far below their value or, worse yet, tossing them out, I went for information to the source—a fellow who managed to pay for two years of his college education from the profits he made selling the World War II items he found in a trunk he had bought from an estate. According to Steve Minor, returning veterans often packed away their uniforms in old trunks or footlockers and then tossed in a box of mothballs. When the trunks are opened some forty-plus years later, they are assumed to contain nothing but some "smelly old uniforms and mothballs" and are tossed out. Ironically, if anything is kept, it is most often the footlocker, which is probably worth about $25. But what may be underneath those uniforms is as good as greenbacks.

First off, always remember that, like toys, almost every military item is a form of money regardless of its age. Though you may dream of finding Revolutionary or Civil War artifacts, your chances are greatest of uncovering World War II items. But don't despair—these bring a lot of money these days, as do Vietnam items!

World War I. Despite the greater age of World War I items, market demand is not terribly high at present. Most frequently found are shoulder patches. These were often handmade and range from common to fairly scarce and rare. General price gauges: common, $15; average, $30–$60; scarce, $75–$125; and rarest, $500. The point about shoulder patches, Minor says, is that you may find a collection, as soldiers traded them among one another, so the value for several can mount up quickly.

World War II. World War II items fall into three categories: SS, Nazi German or American government issue, and Japanese. "For starters, almost everybody brought back a standard-issue German helmet, and they're worth $75–$125." Once again, shoulder patches are frequently found and are worth from $5 to $15 each. The first Iron Crosses, worth only $20 twenty years ago, are selling for around $75 today.

There is great demand for American and German aviator items, with the usual sterling silver wings in the $30–$40 range. But for rare wings you can add a zero, from $300 to $400 and up. And should you find a leather flight jacket with insignia among the mothballs, you're probably looking at $300 and up.

Not only were Nazi items brought back during the war, but they were collected by GIs stationed in Germany after 1945. As a result, there are many collections worth thousands of dollars on today's market yet to be discovered in attics, basements, and even garages. Minor suggests two most frequently found Nazi items and their value ranges:

Daggers: Army daggers ($150–$250 for common types)
SS daggers ($400–$800)
"Honor daggers" presented to high-ranking dignitaries and officers ($1,000–$10,000)
Helmets: Army helmets ($75–$200 and up)
Waffen SS helmets ($500–$1,000 and up)
Luftwaffe paratrooper helmets ($500–$1,000 and up)

Interestingly, not as much came back from the war in the Pacific as from Germany because Japanese soldiers seldom surrendered, and the humidity and heat in the Pacific Islands resulted in rusting and rotting. But if you do have a standard-issue samurai sword, for example, its value will generally range from $250 to $400. But because some Japanese officers carried family swords from the fourteenth and fifteenth centuries, the potential of finding a true antique Japanese sword with exceptional value does exist. And there is

reason to check Japanese swords with an expert. Some antique sword blades were replaced for war purposes with standard-issue army blades. Thus some swords have standard blades but old and valuable handles, many with fine craftsmanship and some even with jewels.

Vietnam. You may be astounded to learn that Vietnamese items are generally more pricy than those from World War I or World War II! The rarer Vietcong and North Vietnam relics are now bringing phenomenal prices considering their recent vintage. Even the more common American Vietnam items quickly mount up. For example, American soldiers often had Vietnamese craftsmen and tailors copy American patches—unofficially, of course. These handmade patches generally have a minimum value of $10, but the rarer ones are already bringing over $100 each. And Green Berets with the unit patch inside are selling in the $75–$200 range.

Tips for Capitalizing on Your Newfound Treasure

When you open the "million dollar" footlocker, you may toss out the mothballs, but, Minor recommends:

- Leave the collection together. Several items belonging to one individual (uniform, insignia, medals, documents, letters, scrapbook) are worth more as a group than as individual pieces—often double as much.
- Never clean anything. Leave that job to the experts. A rare insignia or medal often becomes less valuable when it is polished. Furthermore, minimize handling, as items stored since 1917 or 1945 will be dry, brittle, and fragile.
- To sell the items for the highest prices, an auction is usually best since collectors seek out auction houses that specialize in militaria. Perhaps best known is Manion's International Auction House, P.O. Box 12214, Kansas City, KS 66112.

24

Firearms

Firearms logically follow militaria. But while military items are often undervalued, firearms are often overvalued. There are wonderful eighteenth- and early-nineteenth-century firearms worth thousands of dollars, but these must be appraised by experts. Much more common are later-manufactured firearms dating from the end of the nineteenth and twentieth centuries. Furthermore, many people often assume that a nineteenth-century shotgun is worth a couple of thousand dollars just because it is so old, but its value is almost always closer to a couple of hundred dollars.

To learn the value of firearms, you must first gather specific information—type, make, and so on—relating to your firearms. To simplify getting this information, use the form given here, which incidentally is a perfect illustration of the old adage "Necessity is the mother of invention." Though I was unfamiliar with firearms, I found I was often asked about their values, and I needed to know what information was pertinent to pass on to someone more knowledgeable than I. Thus, with the help of a few men familiar with firearms, I devised a simple form for you to follow when listing nineteenth- and twentieth-century firearms on your inventory.

Once you have gathered the information, chances are you can find a reasonable value range in one of many firearms price guides published each year. You see, firearms, much like comic books, are so widely collected, bought, sold, and traded that standardized price guides as well as condition ratings are generally accepted as accurate. If you choose this route and consult one of the price guides, be sure to cite its name and publication date by the figures on your inventory. Or you may omit the value, content that you have listed the information you need should anything happen to the items at a later date.

Firearms

Manufacturer, Brand Name, or Importer's Name:_____

_____

Model and/or serial number:_____

If handgun, type of gun: **If shotgun,** type of action:

☐ Single shot   ☐ Single shot

☐ Revolver   ☐ Double barrel

☐ Clip   ☐ Over/under

☐ Semiautomatic   ☐ Side by side

Caliber:_____   ☐ Pump

If rifle, type of action: Gauge: _____

☐ Bolt

☐ Lever

☐ Pump

Number of shots:

☐ Single shot

☐ Semiautomatic

Caliber:_____

For all firearms:

Age:_____

Condition:_____

Ornamentation or style:_____

Comments:_____

_____

_____

25

Limited Editions

Warning! The entire topic of limited editions is murky water. Though few limited editions are either limited or "valuable," high-powered advertising has led the public to invest in these items.

Limited editions are found in almost every category of objects from porcelain to silver to art. Because commemorative porcelains, Christmas plates, and porcelain sculptures, along with prints, are probably the best-known "limited editions," the information on these items is presented here, but the same points can be applied to all categories of limited editions.

- Most commercially advertised limited editions are fairly inexpensive when first introduced on the market.
- The term "limited edition" has no specific limit. An edition can be limited to 2, 5, 25, 2,500, 25,000, or even 250,000 copies.
- The ultimate value of any object, whether mass-produced, one of a kind, or in a limited edition series lies in its quality. Thus it is possible that an object can be one of twenty thousand and be of better quality than one of a kind.
- Some companies make both "open" and "limited" editions of similar objects.
- When objects are in large limited editions, the mint or pristine condition as well as quality will affect the objects' ultimate value.
- Sterling silver and gold, or gold-inlaid limited edition plates, medals, ingots, bars, figures, and so on can have fluctuating value tied to the metals market.

Though it seems easy enough to learn the cost of any limited edition currently being sold—all you have to do is read the magazine or newspaper ad—it can be unbelievably difficult for a layperson to find information about limited edition items that are no longer being sold. Though most of the general guides cite some specific limited edition prices and provide a brief thumbnail sketch about the company, there have been so many limited editions issued in recent years that invariably the item you wish to know about is not in the books.

Today, probably the most comprehensive book for a layman on limited edition items is *Collectibles Market Guide & Price Index,* fifth edition

(Collectors' Information Bureau, edited by Susan Jones, 1988). Here you can find information on the various companies, individual artists, and sources for buying and selling, as well as information on collecting, displaying, and insuring your collection, trends, and even features on the manufacturing process used to create various items. Particularly useful for those wanting to begin a collection of limited edition issues is a checklist of criteria to use in evaluating the many different categories of collectibles. But what about prices?

A price index that cites thousands of the most widely traded limited editions in today's collectibles market is included in the back. It is interesting to observe that this list includes bells, dolls, figurines, graphics, plates, and steins—but cups and saucers and pitchers, two "must have" collectibles of an earlier generation's display cabinet, are not included in today's sought-after limited editions. This observation leads, of course, to the conclusion that all items do have their day, and the investment potential of any type of item will fluctuate as one generation's taste precludes another's.

The same company can produce limited editions in varying sizes. These small Boehm birds were sold originally in fine jewelry and gift shops, but other Boehm issues can be very exclusive and sell for thousands of dollars. **Photograph courtesy Weschler's Auction Gallery**

Early Danish limited edition commemorative plates are now being sold in competitive auctions, but more recent years' issues have yet to attract such a selective audience. **Photograph courtesy Weschler's Auction Gallery**

And, of course, this raises the question, "How do you accurately assess values on limited editions?" Needless to say, accurate values can be elusive. *Plate Collector, Collectors News,* and the Bradford Exchange are among the publications and services that provide pricing information, both through ads and through bringing buyers and sellers together. However, as in all areas of personal property, there can be a distinct difference between an asking price and a purchase price. (You might want to jump ahead and read Dick Jenrette's comments on the difference in the spread between the asking and selling prices of stocks and antiques in chapter 33.)

It is true that the value of some antiques and collectibles can escalate almost overnight. If we only had crystal balls, we would all invest in those items. But if the collector chooses pieces that he likes and wants to live with, that will enhance his life and provide pleasure and beauty to his home or office, then his investment cannot be measured in dollars alone.

So to those connoisseurs who turn up their noses at limited editions and tell me, "You *know* collector's plates will never go up in value," I reply honestly, "I don't *know* that." Whoever thought that pressed glass, which cost a few pennies and was bought from Woolworth's by the barrel, would be displayed in museums and be the subject of twenty-five-dollar books? Or who would have thought that the Battersea or enamel boxes sold as travel souvenirs in eighteenth-century England would bring hundreds, even thousands, of dollars some 175 to 200 years later?

I once made that very same statement to a well-known antiques authority. "You don't really believe that, do you?" he asked.

When you've been in as many homes and seen as many objects collected by as many people as I have, your perspective is tempered somewhat. You see, once after appraising the contents of a house filled with Tiffany sterling silver, six full dinner services of the finest (and most expensive) porcelain for twenty-four, sets of Baccarat *and* Steuben crystal—all items of the finest craftsmanship and quality being made today—the husband asked if I had a few minutes to see his collection. "Those are my wife's choices," he confided, "but these are my *investments*." Opening the wall safe, this wealthy client pulled out caches, ingots, medals, and sculptures, all in mint condition, all from the Franklin Mint. If this fabulously rich man with an almost fabled Midas touch is investing in Franklin Mint limited editions, who am I to dismiss them?

After all, he has bought what he liked, and he is keeping it in pristine condition for future generations. Furthermore, he is always guaranteed the base metal value as a bottom-line return on his money.

Just remember that investment is part of the sales pitch, and the hard sell exists in the antiques and collecting world just as in any other business.

Companies and objects well known for limited editions include

Anri. Carved wooden Italian pieces once in the less expensive category, now a more collectible series with values in a wide range often in the low to middle hundreds.

Baccarat. Fine-quality crystal items and paperweights. Generally in the midhundreds.

Bareuther. Holiday plates in the less expensive category.

Berlin. Holiday plates and mugs in the less expensive category.

Bing & Gröndahl. Commemorative porcelain items mostly in the $50–$150 range, but porcelain figurines in the hundreds.

Boehm. Porcelain sculptures. Values ranging from the low hundreds into the thousands of dollars. Also see *Lenox*.

Danbury Mint. Sterling silver, silver plate and other metals plates, bars, and ingots with values fluctuating with the silver and metals markets.

Dorothy Doughty. Porcelain sculptures for Royal Worcester. Often range into the thousands of dollars.

Flambro. An importer of the currently popular circus-related china collectibles generally in the $10–$100 range.

Fostoria. Glass plates in the inexpensive category.

Franklin Mint. Silver ingots, plates, sculptures, and the like. Usually modest values.

Goebel. Figurines, plates, bells, plaques. Values have a wide range, usually $50–$250.

Gorham. Once known for Christmas ornaments, now recognized for a line of limited edition china figures and dolls, some of which range in the high hundreds up to a thousand dollars.

Hamilton Mint. A variety of metal bars, ingots, and plates generally in the inexpensive category, though prices can fluctuate with the metals market.

Haviland. A wide range of china objects from Christmas ornaments to historical plates. Usually in the $30–$100 range.

Hummel. See *Goebel* and *Schmid*.

Hutschenreuther. Primarily plates, mass-advertised and widely ranging from inexpensive to hundreds of dollars.

International Silver. Metal, sterling, and silver-plate plates, bars, ingots, and ornaments in the medium price range.

Ispanky. Porcelain sculptures and other porcelain items, which range from the hundreds to the low thousands.

Kaiser. Porcelain sculptures and plates. Wide range, but generally in the midhundreds.

Kirk. Sterling, silver-plate, and pewter items. Of good quality, but for the mass market.

Edwin M. Knowles. Plates and other china pieces, mass-advertised and generally inexpensive.

Lenox. A variety of china objects from commemorative plates (including the Boehm plate series) to vases. Usually in the $50–$125 range.

Lladro. China sculptures and plates. The sculptures are in the hundred- to thousand-dollar range, while the plates are less valuable.

Mettlach. See *Villeroy & Boch*.

Pickard. Plates usually in the $50–$150 range.

Reed & Barton. Christmas ornaments, plates, and the like in various metals of good quality and in the middle price range.

Rosenthal. Christmas plates (less well known than B & G or Royal Copenhagen) in the $50–$75 range.

Royal Copenhagen. A variety of porcelain items with the different plates, mugs, and so on ranging from $30–$500. The porcelain figures are more valuable.

Royal Doulton. Porcelain figures can run into the high hundreds, low thousands.

Royal Worcester. Porcelain and pewter figures, of good, wide-range quality. See Dorothy Doughty.

St. Louis. Fine-quality paperweights, generally in the midhundreds.

Schmid. Bells, plates, and other china objects. Prices range from $12–$100.

Spode. A variety of china items including bells, cups, plates, and the like and generally around $50.

Swarovski. The creator of the cut-crystal figurines now so very popular. Ranging from a few dollars into the hundreds.

Villeroy & Boch. Also known as Mettlach. The antique steins and plaques run into the high hundreds and thousands of dollars. New ones are less expensive.

Wedgwood. Numerous vases, cups, plates, and other china items, both bone china and earthenwares, ranging into hundreds of dollars.

Wheaton. A variety of limited editions in the inexpensive range.

26

Basements and Attics:
Junk or Junque?

MY idea of complete and total happiness is when I am turned loose in a grungy basement or attic filled with cobwebs, dust, crawling things, and lots of boxes and told, "Look to your heart's content!"

So many of you feel the same way that I am repeatedly asked, "What about all the things in my attic and basement? Are they really valuable, or should I just throw them away or have the Salvation Army come take everything away for me?"

I have two answers.

First, *never* give or throw away a trunk or box without taking the time to go through it.

Several years ago, after our second child arrived, my father got tired of stumbling over toys scattered throughout my house.

One day, when I was visiting my parents' home, my father said, "I have a bunch of old trunks in my basement. I'm going to put them all out for trash, but if you can use one as a toy chest, you can have it."

Delighted at the offer, I went immediately to the basement.

Two hours later I reappeared. "Do I get to keep the junk in the trunk?" I asked, beaming.

In the trunk I had uncovered sterling silver button hooks, an envelope filled with hair jewelry dating from the 1860s, two charming 1830 silhouettes, an 1817 sampler, and an Art Deco inkwell—for starters.

Every day, treasures like these are thrown away because no one bothered to look. In the haste of cleaning up, anything can be carelessly discarded. In a few fortunate instances, Goodwill, the Salvation Army, or a secondhand shop will be the recipient of these throwaways. But in far too many instances it all ends up on the dump pile.

On the other hand, it greatly disturbs me when I see people chasing after rainbows in the dream of striking it rich . . . which leads to my second answer.

People waste far too much time chasing after the value of a torn-up comic book, while they ignore the $4,000 china cupboard filled with their crystal and best china.

I inadvertently got involved in just such an experience when a client brought in an "extremely rare" 1864 Lincoln and Johnson campaign banner. A museum in Kentucky had authenticated it several years before, I was told.

But the owner had not wanted to sell it, even though the museum offered to purchase it. Then someone in Kentucky told someone in Tennessee about it, and since Johnson had lived in Tennessee, a museum there wanted it.

The banner looked like an old faded piece of cloth to me, but who was I to dispute the judgment of two museums?

Since refusing those offers, the owner had come on hard times and now wanted to sell the banner. But since he now lived in North Carolina and since Johnson had been born in that fair state—a native son, no less—he wanted to sell it to the State Museum of History.

I knew nothing about political banners, but I called a friend at the museum, described the banner, and yes, the banner sounded most interesting to him. At that point I called the Smithsonian and spoke to an expert in political memorabilia. Once again, it sounded most interesting—even rare. Could I send photographs?

Even though the Smithsonian's interest was appealing, my client said he'd rather the banner stay in North Carolina, so I traipsed down to the museum with it. They were to examine it and get back to me.

A few days later I got a call from them.

"If you hadn't uncovered some great finds in the past," the curator began, "I'd tell you to throw your old dish towels in the hamper instead of bringing them to me!"

The rare, museum-quality 1864 political banner turned out to be a Civil War centennial souvenir dish towel, all of ten years old!

For every story that discounts basement junk, there is another to make you spend hours hunting for that discarded treasure that is "worth a bundle."

David Redden, a collectibles expert, recalled with great glee the story of a German toy that was found in an estate that eventually ended up at Sotheby's.

"It was a nice little tin boat, about thirty inches long, made by the German toy company Marklin. It was a mass-produced industrial toy, but it had a wind-up clockwork motor and was still in perfect condition. It sold at auction for $21,000!"

In reality the tin toy was the battleship *Weissenberg*, rigged with four lifeboats, anchor, bridge, cannons, gun turrets, and twin masts bearing banners, and the clockwork mechanism operated a four-bladed rear propeller.

A few points about its value are immediately obvious. First, the toy was in perfect condition. Second, its clockwork mechanism made it rare. Third, it was sold under the best-possible circumstances—through a prestigious international auction house after being correctly identified. It was featured and advertised before the auction so toy collectors from around the world could compete for it.

Before You Throw It Away . . .

The list of potentially valuable items stored away in attics and basements seems endless, even overwhelming. To help you decide whether to further investigate the potential salability and value of your discoveries, ask the following questions:

- What is the condition? (Remember all my admonitions about condition!)
- Have you seen others like it? (If so, you may already have an idea of its potential value.)
- Have you looked for the clues given throughout this book that tell you

  > **what** is it
  > **when** was it made
  > **where** was it made
  > **who** made it

  in order to know **what** it's worth?
- Have you checked a price guide? (Though price guides are just that—guides—you truly can get a reasonable gauge of the value *range* on most collectibles once you have correctly identified the object and its condition.)
- How much time are you willing to spend in searching out its value?

If you believe you have sufficient items of historical interest, you may be able to have someone from your local historical society or museum look over the contents to determine if any items would be of interest or value to them. Be aware, however, that these societies or museums will not automatically accept such gifts. Many museums and historical societies have limited storage facilities or already have duplicates of items and must be selective in the gifts they accept. They also often have rigid cut-off dates or specific types of collections and will only accept donations that meet their criteria. In such cases, usually an acquisitions committee will decide what gifts or donations to accept, and you may not know for months if your gifts are accepted. However, other museums and societies are actively seeking donations and would be overjoyed to receive appropriate gifts, either to place in their collection or perhaps to sell to raise funds.

Then again, even if the museum you contact first is not interested in your particular items, the curator or director may be able to put you in contact with another museum or restoration that will be interested in your pieces.

Comic Books. The simplest way to learn if your comic books have value is to check them out in Robert M. Overstreet's *The Comic Book Price Guide*. This guide is so respected that people buy and sell comic books according to Overstreet the way stock is traded according to the Dow Jones market report. Read the sections on collecting, condition, and the market, and remember that you can apply most of what Overstreet says about comics to other items of personal property.

Stoneware. One of the largest and most active markets in American decorative arts is that for the utilitarian nineteenth-century pottery known as stoneware. Ironically, your great-grandmother's best Limoges porcelain dinner plate may have a value of only fifteen dollars, but her stoneware crock

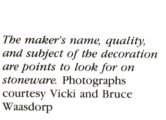

The maker's name, quality, and subject of the decoration are points to look for on stoneware. Photographs courtesy Vicki and Bruce Waasdorp

might be worth several hundred dollars. And where are you apt to find it? In the basement or attic. The value of stoneware is based on two factors—its decorative appeal and the rarity of the piece. For example, a simple crock with a common floral cobalt-blue decoration may only be worth $45, but one with a highly unusual motif like an Indian on horseback or landscape can be worth thousands. On the other hand, even a plain, undecorated stoneware crock, if signed by a little-known potter, may be worth several hundreds of dollars strictly on the rarity of the signature. Condition is also important, and a small chip or hairline crack can drastically reduce the monetary value of stoneware. But sometimes, if the object is sufficiently rare, the flaws will make little difference. For these reasons, you undoubtedly will want expert guidance should you find any signed or unusually decorated stoneware.

Tools. A hot collectible at the moment, tools from the 1920s and 1930s, as well as turn of the century, are finding buyers. Well-known names (Stanley is the best known, of course) can add value, and the more unusual the tool, the greater its potential for value. Two items that are highly sought after are brass-mounted rulers and wooden planes. Tools in excellent condition are preferred (used tools are seldom in mint condition), but don't assume that a worn or rusty tool is necessarily worthless.

Photograph Albums. Pictures that show historical landmarks can have value, as can those depicting occupations that no longer exist. Of course, pictures of famous people or of historical events—Civil War, strikes, interesting interiors, and so on—have value. There seems to be a current interest in photographs that are "quaint"—scenes of children, pets, and the like.

Books. Most books have minimal value, and family Bibles are valuable only to the family to whom the information is pertinent. However, some almanacs, children's books, cookbooks, gardening books, and first editions have value. In all categories, first editions have the greatest potential for value, but not all first editions are valuable. Most modern books are clearly marked "first edition," but to see if an older, unmarked book is a first edition, look at the title page and note the date. Then turn the page over and check the copyright date. If the two dates correspond, the book is a first edition. All A. L. Burt and Grosset and Dunlap books are reprints, and their only value lies in the story or, in a few instances, the illustrations (for decorative value.)

Kitchenware. Most old kitchen utensils and furnishings have value. Ice-boxes, wooden or metal, are being collected, as are old washboards and hand-operated washing machines. Although the values are limited, an entire collection or group of nineteenth- and twentieth-century goods can quickly add up to a few hundred dollars if you find the right buyer. The newest market for kitchen items is for 1920s, 1930s, and early 1940s Art Deco pieces. Streamlined irons, sleek, rounded toasters, and early Mixmasters of distinctive designs are being bought for their decorative as well as utilitarian appeal. Materials (plastic, chrome, hand-hammered aluminum), colors (the brighter the better), and motifs (stylized silhouettes and geometric designs) all appeal to the latest breed of collectors.

If you've followed the popularity of the "country look," below left, you know early kitchenwares are collected today. Photograph courtesy Garth's Auctions

But do you know that sleek, exceptional kitchenwares from the 1930s are now in the hundred-dollar-and-up range? Photographs courtesy Main St. USA, Venice, California

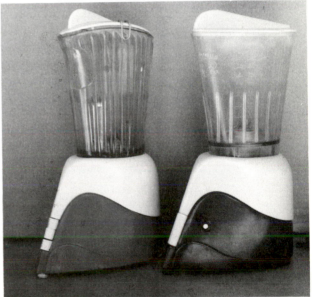

Maps, Charts, and Aeronautical, Bicycling, Nautical, and Automobile Collectibles. There are collectors for all of these items. The most valuable are those generally associated with a historic event—a Civil War map, a tail insignia from a World War I biplane, a souvenir from the *Normandy*. You may have read about the highly successful sale of articles from the S. S. *United States* only a few years ago. If you uncover items in these categories, you should contact a specialist dealer.

Cards. Old baseball or football cards, postcards, advertising cards, valentines, greeting cards—in fact, any kind of card can eventually find a collector. However, many of these paper items have been reproduced, and most have minimal value when compared to the cost of your sterling silver or crystal. But if you come upon an entire collection of nineteenth-century baseball cards and give them to your six-year-old neighbor, you are giving money away! Most modern trading cards, however, have a value of $.50–$1. If you want to keep them for another fifty years, the situation will be quite different, but you may not be around to cash in. If you plan to keep such items for their potential value, store them carefully, label them, and tell somebody! Every sports newscaster in the country delights in telling how his mother threw away his card collection when he went off to college!

Sporting Goods and Memorabilia. As sports-minded as we all are today, it goes without saying that sports souvenirs and sporting equipment are avidly sought after. Old tennis rackets, crewing oars, golfing items, ticket stubs to famous sporting events, World Series and Super Bowl programs—all are collected.

The gleaming beauty of silver, the relatively inexpensive cost when purchased new, and knowing these ornaments can be passed from generation to generation as a memento of Christmas sentiment make sterling and silver-plated Christmas ornaments highly collectible.

Architectural Accessories. Old doorknobs, locks and brasses, even ceramic tiles are collected and often used in modern and restored homes. In fact, as a result of the thriving restoration market, numerous architectural specialty shops have sprung up across the country. Furthermore, many architectural accessories—latches, hinges, bolts, and so on—are being mounted against dramatic stark backgrounds and being displayed as folk sculpture.

Christmas Ornaments. Nineteenth- and early-twentieth century glass, tin, and mirrored Christmas decorations are hot items. Steve Bemiller at Garth's Auctions in Ohio reports selling some of the German and Japanese ornaments I remember buying for $.05 and $.10 as a child for $12, $20, and $35! However, many are also being reproduced. Choose carefully if you are buying. Currently popular, though new, items among Christmas decoration collectors are the crystal, porcelain, brass, pewter, sterling, and silver-plate ornaments brought out in recent years by Waterford, Wedgwood, Gorham, Kirk, and so on. These are limited editions, and there now seem to be many thousands more collectors than there were ornaments made in the early years of production.

Smoking Items. Cigar molds, cutters, labels, tobacco figures, boxes—all have been collected for years. The resurgence of specialized smoking goods stores has led to more collectors and to more reproductions. If you come upon any of the dollhouse rugs given away by Fatima cigarettes or the pictures of athletes and actors from the cigarettes at the turn of the century, you have items worth a few dollars each. You should also know that some of the fine tobacco tins can reach into the hundred-dollar range—but remember, *condition*!

Campaign Collectibles. Banners (beware! I learned *my* lesson), buttons, ribbons, and medals (the older and more obscure the candidate, the better) are sellable. Several books have been written about campaign collectibles, but know that there are also many fakes and reproductions, especially ones used as advertising gimmicks.

Legal Documents, Land Deeds, Letters, and Diaries. Never discard a bunch of letters or deeds tied up in yellowing string without examining them closely. To begin with, if the envelopes are still present, the canceled stamps may be of value. But second, many letters relate to historic events—of either local or national interest. Guthman Americana once assembled a collection of diaries and journals that were eyewitness reports of the 1781 surrender of Yorktown as told by a young Pennsylvania lieutenant. They were worth thousands of dollars, but just as amazing is the fact that the collection had been divided and Guthman had purchased the papers from separate sources. But you should also be aware that many disappointments can occur when letters and documents that appear to be authentic turn out to be old, even period, copies. One such letter, found at the bottom of a trunk, had every

Tobacco items come in a variety of objects and materials. One thing they all have in common—a rising market. **Photographs courtesy Mid-Hudson Galleries**

outward appearance of having been written by Lincoln, and it was even appraised at $5,000–$8,000 . . . until a handwriting expert determined it was, in fact, a copy.

Pocket Knives, Fountain Pens, and Spectacles. Many small everyday items get packed away in old trunks. Often these were associated with family members and kept as reminders of Grandmother or a favorite uncle. Once a generation or so has passed, however, the sentimental value may be forgotten, and then items become just "old things." But there are collectors for old things, and the items in each of these categories have values ranging from a few dollars for the commonplace to hundreds of dollars for the rare. As the desire to re-create period settings (inspired by our life-style magazines) grows, these once neglected collectibles may become more popular. And remember, there is also a new generation of collectors emerging that knows only of ballpoint pens and computer keyboards and is going to be fascinated by fountain pens!

Sewing Box Goods. Knitting needles, sewing birds, thimbles, buttons, and darning eggs have long been high on the collectibles list. Though the collectors are specialized, they are worth seeking out if you discover you have such items, particularly those dating from the nineteenth century. Remember, when going through old sewing boxes you may also find military buttons, Girl Scout insignia and badges, or other accessories that would have gone onto clothing. These may have additional value because of the organization represented. And then there are other items that get put into a sewing box, especially large boxes—lace and samplers being two of the more obvious. One woman actually found a gold ring sewn onto her grandmother's pincushion. So never carelessly discard a sewing basket or box without a thorough examination.

Clothing and Textiles. Clothing of the 1950s is now being bought from secondhand stores and worn as "fashions." The rebirth of the Jackie O look

You would probably expect these sewing machines to have value, but would you take the time to go through the sewing box? Many wonderful treasures have been found there. Photograph courtesy Garth's Auctions

will soon bring clothing from the 1960s out of the trunks and into the closets. Christie's and Sotheby's both feature designer clothing auction sales, and you have probably read about the prices paid for Hollywood stars' costumes in recent years. Museums feature period costumes and fashions as part of permanent and special exhibits. Clearly there is more interest in clothing and textiles in general—table linens, bedspreads, pillow shams, and so on—than ever before. However, condition is of utmost importance, as is design. The majority of old clothes and linens probably have little value if any, but look them over before casting them away. This might be the time to call your local historical society or the neighborhood little-theater group or college drama department!

Historically important as well as monetarily valuable, American Indian items are more often found in storage than on display in many homes. **Photograph courtesy John C. Hill, Phoenix, Arizona**

American Indian Items. With all the publicity about fine Early American Indian crafts, you might think everyone knows the value of these items. Most American Indian items that sell at auction fall in the hundred- and thousand-dollar range, but exceptional pieces have brought many thousands of dollars. Furthermore, where do many of these items come from? Basements and attics. There are so many Indian tribes within each of the geographical regions of our vast country that there is a wealth of variety within the broad category of American Indian arts. Each tribe preserved its culture in native crafts made from the natural resources of each area—pottery, carvings, textiles, and so on. The diversification and quality of the arts from tribe to tribe within each area also varied greatly. Because it takes a connoisseur of American Indian arts to easily recognize the subtleties, this is another area where expertise is crucial.

Office Equipment. The demand for typewriters, adding machines, and early computers is obviously not as great as that for antique or collectible household or kitchen items that can be used as accessories or conversation pieces. But here again, the collector does exist. Certain furnishings, such as lawyers' bookcases and glass-fronted units that can be stacked on one another, are now expensive and hard to find. The same is true for old post office mailboxes and dry-goods display cases. And if you've looked at any new office equipment today and noticed how expensive the fine-quality pieces are, you know there's a good secondhand market for attractive, sound desks, chairs, and file cabinets.

Fire and Police Collectibles. Insurance company firemarks, firemen's parade trumpets, convention medals, and firemen's and policemen's badges and insignia are collectible items with shops specializing in these goods. Local police and fire museums are always on the lookout for contributions of these mementos and accessories. You might consider these as a tax write-off if you can't find a buyer, as some may have considerable value. Remember also that many police and fire chief badges of the nineteenth and early twentieth century are sterling silver and high-karat gold. Speaking of police collectibles, newspaper articles and artifacts dealing with the 1930s gangsters are of interest, and one price guide even lists the value of "chain-gang collectibles."

Cast-iron banks, especially mechanical ones, are "hot" collectibles these days. Because there are so many reproductions, even a replaced screw is often cited in auction catalogs. **Photograph courtesy Garth's Auctions**

Toys. Every old toy in good condition has a value. Christie's, Sotheby's, Garth's, and numerous other auction houses now regularly schedule toy sales, and every year new records are set for each category. Until the middle part of the nineteenth century the majority of toys were made in Europe. The most valuable dolls are French and German, and even tea sets tended to be from England, Germany, or Japan rather than America. Of course later twentieth-century toys are predominantly American-made. Original condition is of prime importance in toys and—like furniture—repairs and restoration, even of the paint on metal model toys and soldiers, can decrease the value. Never attempt to restore or paint a toy until you learn if its value will be affected. Early cartoon toys are in great demand—yes, the Mickey Mouses and Plutos—and today's superheroes and space toys are already becoming obsolete as this year's model outdates last year's in sophistication and styling. Any time an original box or wrapping accompanies a toy or doll, the value increases immediately. Almost everyone knows, for example, that a fine 1959 Barbie doll in her original box will sell for approximately $1,000. When one woman asked me, "Why didn't someone tell me to save the boxes?" I assured

Cartoon toys never lose their charm. In fact, they grow more charming and more valuable as we and they "mature" together. These Popeye toys sold for $180. Photograph courtesy Savoia and Fromm

her that parents and children are throwing boxes away in 1989 as well, and in another twenty-five years someone in her family will ask an appraiser, "Why didn't someone tell me to save the boxes?" You should know that one of the hottest and fastest-growing categories is mechanical toys. Ones that sold for a few hundred dollars a couple of years ago are now selling in the thousands, and interest is only beginning, I am told. But beware; there have been fakes on the market for years, and even if you find one in an old trunk, it will be worth your time to establish its authenticity before spending your newfound cash. Meanwhile, before throwing away the Japanese robot toys you bought for your kids only a few years ago, it seems, you may want to consider, will this be the mechanical toy craze of the twenty-first century? I'd be willing to bet on it. But if you want to cash in now, rather than wait for the next generation to make the profit, you'll be excited as well as surprised to learn that some robot toys are now selling in the hundreds of dollars.

Why didn't someone tell me to keep the box? Obviously someone did *tell the former owner of this Moon Mullins and Kayo mechanical hand car and track that sold for $770 in 1987 at Savoia and Fromm!*

Jewelry. Deep down, we dream of finding a hidden treasure of gold or diamond jewelry. But if you do find one—how will you know if it's real? Appraisers know that often jewelry is not what it is thought or hoped to be and that pieces with value—if not really valuable—are tossed out. Roger Ponn, a premier appraiser of gemstones, states emphatically that your grandmother's ruby ring may not be a ruby after all. Synthetic rubies have been popular since the nineteenth century and are often set in gold with other precious stones. The larger the "red stone," the greater the chance that it will not be real. On the other hand, rhinestone jewelry is popular once again, so do not toss out your rhinestone pieces thinking they are worthless. Remember to check any silver mountings even of "fashion" jewelry, as sterling silver earrings, bracelets, necklaces, pins, and even shoe clips were commonplace from the nineteenth through the first half of the twentieth century. The stones may not be genuine, but why throw away sterling silver? On the other hand, the hardest item to resell is pearls. Further, many pearl necklaces are coated glass rather than natural or cultured pearls—even those belonging to your grandmother or great-grandmother. Ponn suggests that Art Nouveau, Art Deco, and designer jewelry is often overlooked when one is going through jewelry boxes "hoping to find the gemstone." Before throwing anything out, take the time to glance through some of the coffee table books on glamorous jewelry. True, you probably won't find any pieces comparable to those, but you may find some based on similar designs, and this will help you identify the otherwise overlooked Art Nouveau, Art Deco, or designer pieces. You may also find Victorian-style cameos—but imitation cameos were made in such quantities, how can you tell the real, carved cameo (shell, agate, carnelian, bloodstone, even sapphire) from the imitation? Tom Paradise, a jewelry appraiser, recommends seeking the advice of a gemologist. For example, if layers of glass have been assembled and cemented together to emulate a true cameo, the gemologist will detect this when the piece is viewed under magnification. If real, a cameo's value is established by an unusual motif (profiles are common, but mythological motifs, creatures, and places are more unusual), the height, or relief, of the carving, the shape (ovals are common, hexagons are rarer), and whether or not the cameo is signed (usually beneath the carving on the front or else on the reverse or back side). Further, the craftsmanship with which the cameo was carved and finished must always be considered. According to Paradise, cameos are miniature art forms, and the finer the execution of the details, the more valuable the piece. And of course the frame or mounting (gold or gold-filled, karat, workmanship, design, presence of stones such as pearls, garnets, or diamonds, and so on) affects the value. Finally, age is also of importance. During the second half of the nineteenth century, cameos in both Neoclassical (revival of classical Roman, Greek, or Egyptian motifs) and Victorian styles were made in all ranges of quality. During the first part of the twentieth century these motifs were continued, along with the Art Nouveau and Art Deco designs of the era. Fine craftsmanship, materials, and design will distinguish the "nice brooch" from the piece actively sought by the collector for its historical and artistic significance. Whether you are inquiring about diamonds, pearls, rhinestones,

Three cameos, circa 1920–1930, typical of those found in jewelry boxes in estates. The mountings will determine any ultimate value differences among these three.
Photograph courtesy Weschler's Auction Gallery

or cameos, there really is a tremendous markup in the price of retail jewelry over its fair market price. Ironically you may find that if you're selling you'll get almost as much for a few pieces of costume Disneyana jewelry from a collector as you'll get for a gold piece with small gemstones from a jeweler!

On the Other Hand . . .

Unfortunately there are some categories of items that are often assumed to be valuable but consistently hold more disappointments than rewards. Three of these are furs, fans, and violins. Now this doesn't mean yours won't be the exception, but before you get your hopes up, consider the following:

Furs.
- No matter what the fur (mink, fox, rabbit, or sable), if the leather is dried, cracking, or starting to peel, the item will have minimal value.
- If the leather is still supple and in good condition, check the fur for bald or worn spots or any tears.
- Check the color of the fur. A distinct reddish tint in dark-colored furs can be an indication of oxidation. Likewise a yellow tint on white furs can indicate discoloration, often a result of age or poor maintenance.
- Finally, remember that today's furs are fashion items, so even an excellent-quality fur in good condition, once its style is no longer "in," will have little value unless it can be restyled.

Fans. Few items evoke more romantic images than fans, whether European or Oriental. Along with the images is the realization that fans are handmade. In truth, by the nineteenth century fans were being mass-produced. Furthermore, the craft of fan decoration became popular among amateur artists during the second half of the nineteenth century. Thus, just as you find demitasse cups painted by your great-grandmother, so you might uncover a fan painted by a family member of an earlier generation. In all my years of appraising, I have yet to uncover a fan of substantial value, though I have

Fans, despite their charm, beauty, and romantic image, are often believed to be more valuable than they presently are. Photograph courtesy Skinner's

found many boxes filled with fans stored away in trunks. Because fans are made of fragile materials—textiles (silk, lace, and so on) and paper—many are in poor condition. Restoration, no matter how lovely the fan, may be prohibitively expensive. Some people believe that eighteenth- and early-nineteenth-century fans are one of the "sleepers" on the market, but it will be many years before the Oriental souvenir-type fans of the first half of the twentieth century come into their own.

Violins. I honestly wish I had ten dollars for every "Stradivarius" violin I've been asked about. I'd probably have enough money to buy, if not a Strad, a very fine Steinway piano.

Stradivarius violins were made in Italy in the late seventeenth and early eighteenth centuries by Antonio Stradivari and his two sons, Francesco and Omobono. Stradivari's instruments are so fine that they are given names (such as "Hellier," 1679; "La Pucelle," 1709; "Cessot," 1716; and so on). The instruments were made for royalty and the finest musicians in the world. Stradivari's method of making violins was so unique that with his death the secret of the special varnish he used was lost, never to be rediscovered. So why should everyone think his violin is a Stradivarius? Because at the turn of the century, Sears, Roebuck & Co. advertised a line of "Stradivarius" violins for only a few dollars each! If you have a violin with a "Stradivarius" label, ask yourself, "Would a seventeenth-century Italian craftsman have put a printed label, written in English, on his violin?"

So where does all of this lead? To one simple point: the objects in your attic and basement have value if they are in good condition, of sufficient quality, and if you can find a buyer.

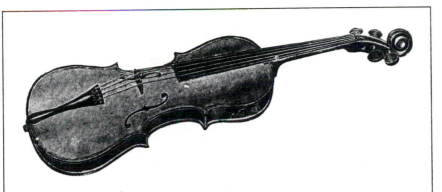

Our $2.45 Stradivarius Model.

No. 12R212 This violin is Stradivarius model, made of specially selected wood;
beautifully varnished, reddish color, highly finished. Possessing a tone very seldom
found in violins at very much higher prices. Such a violin as we offer herewith retails
everywhere at $8.00 to $10.00.
No. 12R212 Our special price $2.45

Our $6.95 Genuine Stradivarius Model.

No. 12R222 These violins are made expressly for us by one of the greatest
makers in Europe, and are offered at our one small percentage of profit as the
greatest value we can offer. It has a two-piece maple back, beautifully flamed, as
shown in illustration. Top of resonant spruce, especially selected; reddish brown varnish, beautifully shaded, in imitation of an old violin. Neck and scroll are made of
curly maple to correspond with the back and sides. The fingerboard, tailpiece and
pegs are of best quality solid ebony.
No. 12R222 Our special price $6.95

Before taking your million-dollar Stradivarius violin to the appraiser or—worse yet—spending the money to buy one, check out this Sears and Roebuck catalogue advertisement for 1902.

I believe in the search and the dream. My own favorite possessions are ones I have come upon unexpectedly. But researching every old thing you find packed away is like looking for a needle in a haystack. I have one hard-and-fast rule: First, know the value of the property you would have to account for if it were stolen, damaged, or destroyed; then, if you have the time, determine the worth of your Lionel train set or your great-grandfather's Union cavalry brass belt buckle. Who knows? It just might be valuable!

27

P.S. The Forgotten Essentials

Often when you make an appraisal or inventory you forget the most basic items—your refrigerator, stove, washer and dryer, even tools you use for hobbies or on the job. Sometimes you become so interested in insuring your antiques and expensive china and silver that you forget your basic household property.

For those of you who wish to have a thorough listing of your personal property, either photographic or written, here is a checklist for you to review:

All clothing, especially designer, Ultrasuede, and the like
Uniforms and sports clothes
All sporting equipment, including bicycles, skates . . .
Curtains and draperies
Blinds, shades, and interior shutters
Carpeting and rugs
Alarm and wall clocks
Kitchen utensils
Small kitchen appliances—irons, food processors, and so on
Large kitchen appliances—freezer, stove . . .
Cleaning items—brooms, mops, pails, and so forth
Painting items—ladders, brushes, and the like
Toys and hobby items
Tools—both hand and power tools, workbench, and so on
Luggage and storage trunks
Lawn and patio furniture
Garden and lawn tools—including trowels, rakes, and so on
Bathroom electrical appliances—shavers, toothbrushes, Water Piks, curling irons . . .
Any health-related items—humidifier, hospital bed, and so forth
All bed, bath, and kitchen linens
Home entertainment equipment—television, tape recorders, stereos, collections of records, musical instruments . . .
Expensive perfumes, wines, and liquors.

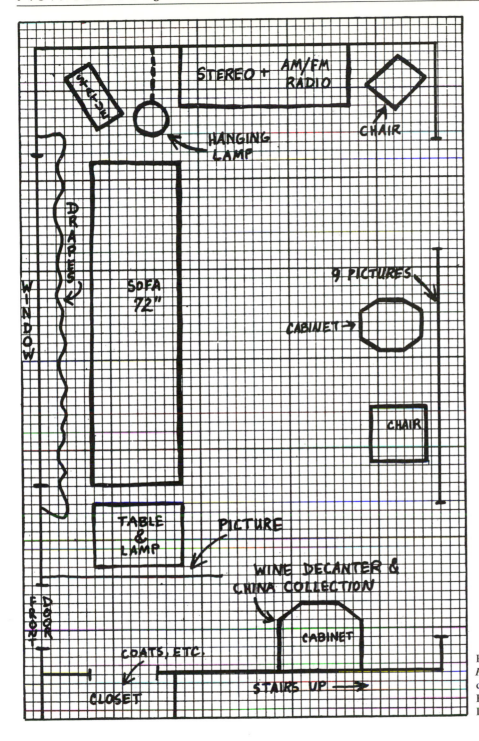

SKYLIGHT

STEREO + AM/FM RADIO

CHAIR

HANGING LAMP

DRAPES

WINDOW

SOFA 72"

9 PICTURES

CABINET →

CHAIR

TABLE & LAMP

PICTURE

WINE DECANTER & CHINA COLLECTION

CABINET

FRONT DOOR

COATS, ETC.

CLOSET

STAIRS UP →

Reprinted from the *Personal Property Inventory Booklet,* copyright 1975, Property Research Bureau, Chicago, Illinois

It is wise to make a skeletal list of these items—just in case. These necessities are so important that, when a family has to relocate after a disaster, many adjusters make their advance payment on the basis of the listing of appliances, washer, dryer, stove, and so on.

Warning: When taking expensive linens, designers clothes, furs, or leathers to be cleaned or repaired, have an accurate description and keep your receipt. Few laundries or repair shops carry insurance against loss or damage of *your* property. If anything happens, *you* may have to file with *your* insurance agent.

An excellent suggestion from the Property Loss Research Bureau of Chicago is to sketch out the room setup of your house or apartment with the arrangement of your furnishings on graph paper. Placing windows and closet doors in your drawing can also serve to jog your memory regarding draperies, clothes, and stored items.

Part Five

WHERE TO FIND OTHER ANSWERS

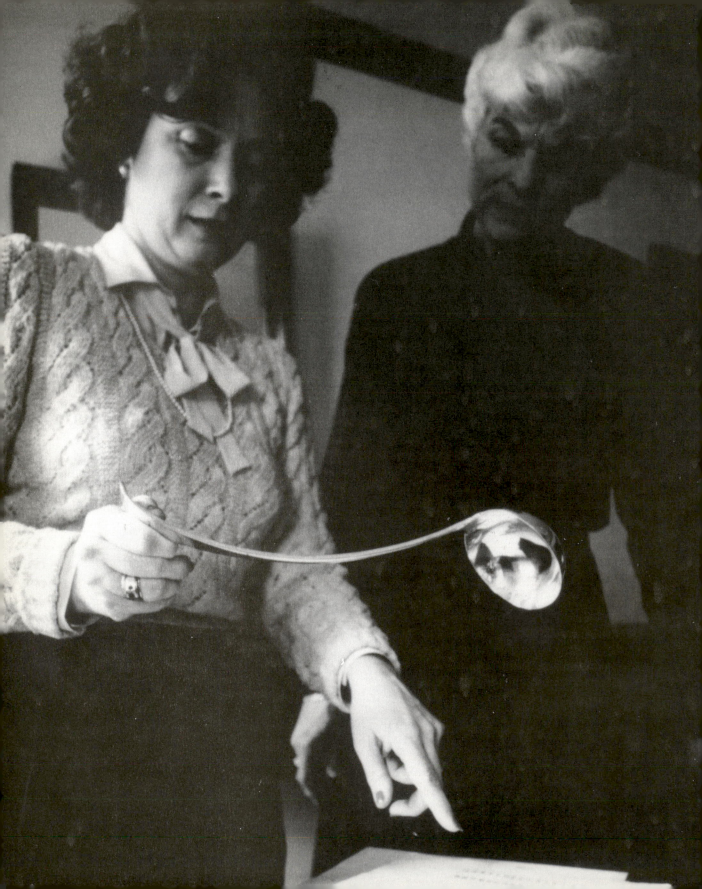

28

Finding an Appraiser

Finding a qualified, competent, and knowledgeable personal property appraiser can be difficult. There are an estimated 125,000 appraisers in the United States, according to the *New York Times,* but because there is no state or national certification, registration, or licensing program for appraisers (as there is for doctors, lawyers, and CPAs, for example), literally anyone can call himself or herself an appraiser.

This absence of licensing or any form of "policing" as to who can call him or herself an appraiser of personal property has greatly concerned me for years. The example I often use is that if a person wants to open a pet-grooming studio or salon he must get a license and list his place of business, Social Security number, and other vital information with the city and/or county and state. But to be an appraiser of personal property—to have access to a person's home, to learn when the person works, if the neighbors are home during the day, whether or not there are locks on the doors and windows, if the person may be hard of hearing or have poor sight, if there is a ready back exit from the house, and even where the owner keeps and hides his treasures—no license or other registration is required! I have not written this information to alarm you, but to make you cautious and perhaps to raise the public's consciousness about this truly negligent situation.

If you follow my suggestions about asking questions and checking references, you will undoubtedly be able to secure the services of a fine, honest, and reputable appraiser when you need one. The public naturally assumes that members of professional appraisal associations will automatically be qualified and responsible appraisers. However, because the demand for appraisers is greater than the number currently in existence, both unqualified appraisers and questionable appraisal societies have sprung up overnight. In fact, one way an appraiser can achieve instant respectability is by joining an appraisal association or organization. These organizations exist everywhere, and membership is often obtained simply by filling in a form and returning it with an accompanying check to "headquarters."

There are exceptions, of course; one is the American Society of Appraisers, which is recognized as this country's only multidisciplinary appraisal testing/ designation society. Membership in the ASA is not necessarily proof of ability. It does mean, however, that the ASA member has submitted his appraisals for examination by his peers, has taken and passed a multisection examination on ethics, appraisal principles, and his specialized area, and is experienced.

Because of the rigid requirements imposed on its members, the American Society of Appraisers is often referred to as the most prestigious of the appraisal organizations. The ASA and the International Society of Appraisers both have excellent educational programs conducted under college and university auspices. These two professional associations also grant their members different levels of professional proficiency as a result of successful course completion and/or testing. The Appraisers Association of America is also widely recognized, and applicants must submit appraisals and meet AAA requirements before they are accepted as members. The addresses of these and other appraisal groups are listed at the end of this chapter. Most will furnish a membership roster upon request or supply the name of a member in your area.

Locally, you may find personal property appraisers listed in the Yellow Pages, but if not, call your insurance agent, bank, attorney, or museum. A call to a college or university art department may be worthwhile. You can also check with antiques shops, interior decorators, or auction houses. They may offer appraisal services or refer you to an independent appraiser.

Appraisers are plentiful in metropolitan centers but are often scarce in less populous areas. Many appraisers will travel to accommodate clients who live in out-of-the-way areas.

But if finding an appraiser is difficult, getting the right appraiser is even more complicated.

"If I can't really trust some of the appraisal societies, how can I tell if I'm getting a qualified appraiser?" you may ask.

Unfortunately the ultimate responsibility does rest with you, but you can help yourself by asking the appraiser some specific questions:

- How long have you been an appraiser?
- What is your area of expertise?
- For whom have you worked, and what are your references?
  (Look for business references, names of banks, insurance companies, museums, and the like, and check these out. On the other hand, if the appraiser provides names of private individuals, *beware*. Would you want it known that *you* have objects of value? This is confidential information.)
- Do you belong to a professional appraisal group?
  (Even though this may be meaningless, it does tell you something about the appraiser's basic approach to his or her business.)
- How do you arrive at your values?
  (She or he should attend auctions, have an extensive library, attend conferences and lectures on antiques, subscribe to national antiques publications and auction catalogs, and have extensive current price indices at hand.)

Next, tell the appraiser your specific needs:

- What you need to have appraised.
  (One piece or a household—only furniture or several different categories, such as Oriental porcelain, English silver, Depression glass, and the like.)

- What the purpose of the appraisal is.

(Insurance coverage, moving damage, estate division, or other.)

Once you are satisfied that you and the appraiser can work together, learn what charges are involved. Some appraisers still charge a percentage of the value of the items they appraise. This practice is questionable at best, since the result is appraise high, fee high. Another questionable practice is charging contingent fees. This is so blatantly suspicious that the American Society of Appraisers' code of ethics calls it unethical, unprofessional, and self-serving. Contingent fees arise when an appraiser tells you she or he will appraise "high" an item that you want to sell or take as a tax donation in return for a share of the sale price or tax benefit. Or the reverse — he or she will appraise an item "low" for estate or tax purposes for a cut of the taxes saved.

The majority of good appraisers today charge on an hourly or daily basis, usually ranging from $35 to $150 an hour or $350 to $1,500 a day, plus expenses. Do not expect an appraiser who charges $50 an hour to walk into your home, spend an hour, then leave and send you an appraisal preparation. Appraisers also charge for research time and the appraisal preparation. Many send a contract to their clients explaining the exact expenses involved. If you do not receive such a contract, ask the appraiser to spell out the exact working terms before she or he comes to your house.

You may certainly ask for an estimate of what your appraisal will cost. For large jobs, appraisers often make a preliminary visit to your home and, for a fee, give you an estimate of the total cost. But if you honestly tell the appraiser what needs to be appraised, he or she can probably give you a fee range over the phone.

I have found that most people are extremely modest about the scope of their possessions when speaking to an appraiser for the first time. Don't be. Tell the appraiser what to expect.

"I have a seven-room house, approximately three thousand square feet, and a combination of antiques and reproductions that need appraising for insurance purposes. There will be approximately twenty-five pieces of furniture and numerous accessories around — probably about fifty or sixty, not including the silver. I have two sets of silver flatware, a cupboard full of silver hollowware, three sets of good china, and a collection of antique dolls."

This information tells the appraiser that she should plan to devote the better part of the day to making your appraisal. Based on $50 an hour, she then roughly calculates that your bill may be expected to run around $450 to $550 (higher or lower, depending on the appraiser's base rate). You now have a ballpark figure and can decide whether or not you want to hire an appraiser. This information can almost always be relayed in a telephone call. It is seldom either necessary or cost-effective for the appraiser to make a preliminary house call.

Now, what can you expect in return for your $450 to $550?

You should receive two copies of a professionally presented appraisal, listing each item you asked to have appraised. A full description of each piece will tell you, to the best of the appraiser's ability, the age, characteristics, physical condition, and, if possible or significant, the national origin of the piece. When the maker is known—whether company, craftsman, or artist—this will be included. Where pertinent, dimensions and silver weight will be stated. Numbers or sets will be included. Finally, each item or group will be assigned a value appropriate to the purpose of the appraisal—insurance, private sale, estate taxes, and so on. The date of the appraisal, purpose of the appraisal, and the appraiser's signature must always be present.

You should not accept a scribbled handwritten appraisal with incorrect spellings, scant listings, and inaccurate numbers. A professionally prepared appraisal that states "6 dining room chairs—$1,200" is meaningless.

The purpose of an appraisal is to establish rightful ownership of personal property, to identify the objects by describing their inherent characteristics, and to value the items based on known comparable objects in the market-place. Getting a sloppy or half-prepared appraisal can be likened to having a leaking fuel tank patched with sealing wax and string. You're throwing money away. Do not settle for less than a professionally presented and documented appraisal. Feel free to ask to see a sample appraisal before you hire an appraiser.

Study the example at the end of this chapter to become familiar with what constitutes an acceptable appraisal document.

What you cannot expect for $400 or $500 is to have every single piece in your house researched and authenticated. If you consider a particular item extremely rare or valuable, advise the appraiser of this beforehand. Explain that you want it authenticated, and ask if the appraiser has the expertise to do this. A good appraiser knows what he or she does *not* know. At this point the appraiser can either accept the job or refer you to someone more knowl-edgeable in this area.

You should now do the same thing you would do if you were making your own inventory. Take an overview of your property. Set up a system so that you are ready when the appraiser comes to your house.

- Gather together any earlier appraisals and all bills of sale or receipts. Place these on the appropriate items.
- Arrange your silver in groupings. Put all of one silver pattern together and count each specific piece—fifteen forks, seven soup spoons, and so on. Either label each grouping or make a list on a piece of paper. Example: "Chantilly, 15 forks, 7 soup spoons . . ." Do not mix patterns by placing all like pieces (forks, spoons, knives) together. Put all pieces of the same pattern together.
- Separate sterling silver hollowware and silver-plated objects into two distinct groups.
- Finally, arrange each of these two groups, sterling and silver plate, by like pieces—all water pitchers together, all meat platters together, all Revere bowls together, and so on.
- Match and count all china and crystal patterns. If sets are stored in boxes, closets, or cabinets, take out one of each piece and count the other pieces. The appraiser needs to see the items in your possession to

establish their existence and condition, but you can save him or her time and save yourself some money by counting the pieces in advance. China serving pieces are often stored separately, so remember these before the appraiser rings your doorbell.

- If you are having your linen appraised, organize this in clear sight as you have your china—a sample of each item set out with the quantity already counted.

I find many of my clients just do not know what to do while I am working. Certainly someone who knows about the personal property, either you or a housekeeper, should be within calling distance if the appraiser has questions. Unless you as a client want to spend your money talking to the appraiser, it is better to make yourself available and remain silent, except when you can add pertinent information. However, if you particularly wish to learn about specific pieces, tell the appraiser and ask to be present when those pieces are being examined. Good appraisers are anxious for their clients to know what they know and become more astute connoisseurs of the decorative arts.

Since I use a tape recorder, it is natural that clients want to listen to my descriptions of their pieces. They also often have questions I am more than happy to answer. The presence of others does not bother me, and I think most appraisers feel the same way. However, the constant query "What's this piece worth?" is worrisome. Appraisers seldom know the exact value of every item they are appraising on the spot.

Most appraisers assign prices to the pieces they are sure of at the time of the appraisal. On other pieces the appraiser notes a price range that may need narrowing. Finally, some pieces need more research or investigation before any value can be assigned, and here the appraiser will fill in the description (perhaps note where to find more information on the piece) but omit the price.

If you feel that the appraiser's figures or facts are inaccurate, ask how she or he arrived at these conclusions. You may wish to get a second opinion, or the appraiser may ask to bring in another expert to look at the piece.

Choose your appraiser carefully and examine the appraisal once it is in your hands.

Appraisal Societies and Associations

American Society of Appraisers
Dulles International Airport
P. O. Box 17265
Washington, D.C. 20041
703-478-2228
1-800-ASA-VALU

ASA Appraisal Profession Online
set your computer communication
program to dial 1-703-478-5502

Appraisers Association of America
60 E. 42nd Street, #2505
New York, NY 10165
212-867-9775

Canadian Association of Personal
    Property Appraisers
2 Briar Place
Halifax, Nova Scotia B3M 2X2
902-443-5698

International Society of Appraisers
16040 Christensen Road, #320
Seattle, WA 98188
206-241-0359
CompuServe address
75304, 3567

The Appraisal Document

Every appraisal document should clearly state
1. the appraiser's name and qualifications or professional designation
2. the appraiser's address
3. the purpose for which the appraisal is intended
4. the client's name
5. page number and total number of pages in the document
6. statement of disinterest in property
7. the appraiser's signature
8. the date the appraisal is signed
9. adequate description
10. appraised value

4 →

Personal property in the name of
Mrs. Gotrocks

1111 Main Street
Anytown, USA

5 →

Page 6 of 53

Qualified Appraiser

Antiques
Residential
Contents

← 1

ARTICLE	DESCRIPTION	APPRAISED VALUE
Dining room table.	Hepplewhite drop-leaf cherry dining table, of New England origin, having six tapering legs, two of which swing out to support the deep drop leaves. Measuring 29½″ high, 44″ deep, and 48″ long. C. 1800.	1,500.00
Tester bed.	Baker Furniture Company four-poster or tester Chippendale-style double bed with arched canopy, broken swan neck motif headboard, reeded posts, and blanket rail at the foot. Mahogany.	3,000.00
Dinner service.	English Johnson Brothers (a division of Wedgwood) ironstone dinner service, "Regency," consisting of 12 dinner plates, 12 coffee cups and saucers, 12 deep rimmed soup bowls, 12 bread and butter plates, 11 small fruit saucers, 1 gravy boat with separate tray, 1 coffeepot. All in excellent condition and currently available.	254.00

9 →

← 10

3 →

Appraisal for Insurance Purposes

P.O. Box 0000
Anytown, USA
100/222-3333

← 2

6 →

This appraiser has no present or future interest in the above property.

8 →

_____

Date

_____

Appraiser

← 7

29

Auction Houses:
The Best Show in Town

There really is no better place to learn about antiques than an auction house. Visitors at preauction viewings (usually held the week preceding the actual auction) are free to take out drawers, examine chair bottoms, scrutinize English silver hallmarks. In fact, there are even people there to answer your questions.

If you are only accustomed to the Friday night country auction held in the back room of a roadside store, you may be overwhelmed at both the sophistication and swiftness of a New York auction. The two most famous auction houses are Sotheby's and Christie's. There is seldom shouting or yelling from either the auctioneer or the audience, and often an item can be bid upon and sold without your ever knowing who was doing the bidding. But when an item sells for $1 million or so, the room may erupt with cheers and clapping.

Be forewarned. If you're going to bid at a New York auction, you won't have time to think about what you are doing. You must know how much you are going to bid ahead of time and act immediately. This is not the place for the timid, shy, or hesitant bidder. But while you may get passed by, you can also get caught up in the auction fever and overspend. Several dealer friends of mine never attend a sale. They visit presale viewings where they scrutinize each piece carefully. They leave their bids with the department head or bidding service provided by each house. Then they take their chances on whether they will get what they want or not. These are wise and astute buyers who do not want to be caught up in the auction fever.

Buying from an Auction House

The message to the auction buyer is *"Caveat emptor"*—"Let the buyer beware." Even though the major auction houses do all they can to guarantee that the item sold is authentic, they, too, can make mistakes, and they protect themselves by publishing their buy-back policy at the beginning of each catalog.

To correctly identify each piece they sell, auction houses carefully explain the terminology they use to identify the period, style, origin, date, and condition of each piece. For example, let's take a Chippendale chest of drawers and see how it is cataloged. Because you've read this book, you know that the Chippendale chest of drawers can either be a period chest of drawers from the eighteenth century, an old chest of drawers in the Chippendale style, or a recent reproduction. (The auction houses generally are not going to sell the new reproductions unless they are included in a house sale, in which case reproductions are clearly identified as such.) But to make the distinction between the period piece and the old reproduction in the Chippendale style, the catalog carefully describes the piece in bold-type heading.

An entry that reads **"Chippendale Mahogany Chest of Drawers, Philadelphia, Circa 1760–80"** designates that the chest is guaranteed by the auction house to be of the period.

However, if the heading for the chest of drawers reads "**Chippendale Mahogany Chest of Drawers**" *without any mention of the origin or the date,* the experts at the auction house consider the chest to date from the eighteenth century, but with too many later changes or restorations for it to be considered a period Chippendale chest.

And in the case of the old reproduction, the heading reads like this: **"Chippendale Style Mahogany Chest of Drawers."** Notice there are no dates or origin given. Further, the presence of the word "style" indicates that the chest of drawers is not of the period, but rather is in the style of the Chippendale period.

You must be particularly careful when buying at an auction antiques that you have not inspected personally. Not all pieces are in good condition.

Sotheby's notes that, because the majority of the items they sell have been used for an extended length of time, it will not assume responsibility for mentioning scratches, minor damage, age cracks, chips, and so forth.

A Christie's executive once remarked that the biggest shock the newcomer to the auction scene has is when he walks into a preauction showing and sees the condition of many of the items being sold. Veneer may be chipped, a desk leg may be gone, upholstery is often old and worn, and the silver may be unpolished. Although this scene is a far cry from the glamorous concept of the auction house, it also means that the astute buyer can pick up excellent bargains if he has the ways and means to restore the pieces to pristine condition.

A much debated question in the antiques world is, When you buy at auction are you paying full retail value or wholesale value? A few years ago the answer was simpler than it is today. In the past, the auction audience consisted almost totally of antiques dealers and interior decorators who were buying to stock their shops and furnish their clients' homes.

Naturally the dealers marked up the retail price of their auction purchases to cover their expenses of attending the auction, taking a day out of the shop for a buying trip, shipping the goods from the auction house to their shops, and the necessary cleaning and repairing of the pieces. In addition to covering these expenses, the dealer would, of course, add enough to make a profit.

But now auction houses have become popular hunting grounds for young families who are furnishing their homes. When the private individual bids against a dealer, he is willing to pay more for an item than the dealer is. Even if he pays more, the collector figures it's cheaper than if he bought the same piece from a dealer. Thus, he still feels that he has made a good buy.

In light of this change, with more private individuals buying at auctions, I asked experts at both Sotheby's and Christie's how *they* would insure a midvalue item purchased at an auction. I used as my examples a $500 chair or an $800 table. In both instances the experts replied that they would insure these items for at least two or three times what they had paid for them at the auction house. Thus the wholesale concept (in part) still holds true at the auction houses, even though the private collector is now an important bidder.

However, as the price paid for an item increases, the insurance or replacement markup decreases. In other words, if you paid $20,000 for a table at auction, a retail value of $40,000 or $60,000 may be unrealistically high. You see, it is not uncommon for a prestigious dealer to buy an exceptionally fine antique at auction for a specific customer. In these instances the dealer does not add a full 100 percent markup but charges the client a percentage to cover his services, sometimes as low as 10 percent.

At other times dealers will pay top dollar for a specific piece they can turn over quickly, even though they know that a 30 or 40 percent markup is the most the piece can bear. These last two examples are relevant only to expensive items; I would stick with the two- or threefold increase on the usual modest auction purchase.

Auction Houses As Appraisers

Sometimes an appraiser or dealer who is unable to identify a particular antique will suggest that you contact Sotheby's, Christie's, or another of the auction houses. This is fine for one item, but you can't handle a household that way. However, many auction houses have appraisal departments, and you may wish to inquire about these services.

If you are genuinely interested in selling a particular piece, have investigated its origin or value as thoroughly as you can locally, and wish to have a New York expert's opinion, you can write to the department of Sotheby's or Christie's that would handle your property, sending a photograph and all the information known about the particular piece. In your letter inquire if the auction house would be interested in selling the item and request a presale estimate of the piece. Don't expect a reply by return mail; the average reply time is ten days to three weeks. But if you have a potentially "hot" item, you may get a personal telephone call! When you do hear from the auction house, if you disagree with the opinion, seek another.

I recall taking an interesting glass decanter to New York for possible sale at one of the auction houses. I did not know its exact origin, but from what the owner could tell me, I felt it had potential auction sale value, and the owner needed money. One auction house said, *"Olé,"* meaning the decanter was from Mexico and worth about ten dollars. The other stated the decanter was American and was willing to sell it. In this instance, of course, a third opinion was needed. The majority decision concluded the decanter was Mexican.

Selling Through an Auction House

If you plan to sell property at an auction house, inquire about two major points:

1. The commission or percentage the house takes to cover the expense of selling the item. The figure will generally run between 10 and 25 percent, according to value of the piece (the higher the sale price, the lower the percentage commission charged) and the individual auction house's commission policy. Many houses have a 10/10 system whereby the seller pays 10 percent commission and the buyer pays 10 percent commission.

2. The "reserve," or confidential minimum price agreed upon by the auction house and the seller, below which the item will not be sold. A reserve protects the owner from having property sold below its projected value. For example, if you have an eighteenth-century needlework sampler that you wish to sell, the experts may tell you the preauction estimate is between $1,200 and $1,800. Discuss this estimate with the auction house expert, who may advise you not to sell the piece below $1,000. If the sampler does not sell for above $1,000, either it is returned to you or it can be held and reentered in a later auction. Some houses charge a commission on unsold lots; others do not. Hopefully the sampler will exceed the $1,800 top estimate—many items do.

Check the exact terms with each house and read all contracts carefully.

"My mother just died and left a house full of antiques, good reproductions, and fine-quality furnishings. I don't have time to sell the items to different dealers piecemeal, but I want to dispose of all of her property. Would any of the major auction houses be interested in coming in and having a house sale and getting it all over with?" This is a question I am often asked.

Brian Cole told me of several house sales that Christie's East has conducted, ranging from a five-room apartment on Park Avenue to a three-room apartment in Greenwich Village, and from a mansion in the Midwest to a six-room house in Atlanta. You don't have to live in a palatial home to have property of value these days, and the larger auction houses are often anxious to conduct lucrative house sales. A letter of inquiry and some photographs will draw a response from any auction house.

The key to finding the *right* auction house for your purposes is matching what you have to sell with an auction house that has sold these objects well in the past. If you are disposing of a "typical" estate, one having a combination of antiques and twentieth-century items—sterling and silver plate, antique and newer furniture, kitchen and laundry appliances, and a few interesting items, such as a mechanical bank, a crazy quilt, and a few World War II souvenir items—then you probably will be able to find a good local auctioneer who will advertise your sale and draw a good crowd.

On the other hand, if you have an outstanding collection of country items—crocks and stoneware, spatterware, two weathervanes, wonderful pine, cherry, and maple antiques, and a cupboard filled with early-nineteenth-century glass—and you live in the Pennsylvania-Ohio region, then you may want to investigate selling your collection through Garth's Auctions. Their highly successful auctions, particularly of country items, have brought bidders from across the country to their gallery to compete for these items.

But if you live in Massachusetts or Maine and have these items, you may wish to contact Bourne's, Skinner's, or Julia's. These, and several other well-known auction houses in the New England states, have also built strong national, as well as regional, followings by consistently selling fine merchandise through catalogs and brochures.

Let's say that you have inherited your aunt and uncle's collection of early- to mid-nineteenth-century high-style furniture. Their home is in eastern Virginia and you live in Illinois. What should you do?

If I knew absolutely nothing, I would call the headquarters of two or three of the appraisal associations and request names of several appraisers in the general region of my aunt and uncle's home. I would then call (don't write) these appraisers, describe the estate, explain the situation, and ask for their recommendations. You may learn that a local auctioneer recently held a highly successful auction of a similar estate, and you should call him. You may learn that there is no one conducting good-quality auctions in that region. And you may learn that the auction house currently drawing the highest prices for such a collection is Alford's in New Orleans.

I would also try to obtain copies of the most popular antiques publications that the collectors are reading in that region. Almost any antiques dealer will have these in his shop. A glance at the auction advertisements will give you a feel for the quality and types of items sold, as well as the individual auctioneer's quality of advertisement. Furthermore, if you see advertisements for auction houses outside that region—let's say you saw one for Alford's— then you would know that this auction house has a following in the area. This is very important, as collectors have their favorite auctioneers the same way they have their favorite antiques dealers. With the recommendations you have gathered, along with your own observations, you may now proceed with your investigation of how to receive the best service, as well as the best prices, for the estate.

Don't think that record prices are only made in the big-name New York galleries. Clearing House Auction Galleries in Wethersfield, Connecticut, only an hour's ride from Manhattan, is proof that dealers from across the country will join local collectors to bid for fine pieces. In well-advertised auctions, good pieces consistently bring high prices, as evidenced by the eighteenth-century matching highboy and lowboy that sold at Clearing House for $370,000.

There are two other points to remember. First, a lot of collectors are intimidated by the uptown Manhattan galleries and don't buy there. Second, the very fine, but not exceptional, piece may get "lost" in an auction that features exceptional items. But that same very fine piece may be the star at a regional auction and bring a very high price.

A few years ago everyone seemed amazed when California collectors flew to Asheville, North Carolina, to attend an auction conducted by Bunn's. But when bidding for the exceptional pieces soared, the message was clear—collectors go where the items are.

Here is a sampling of auction houses located throughout the United States. You can buy their catalogs, sell your things through them, or enjoy attending their sales.

California
Butterfield and Butterfield: 220 San Bruno Avenue at 15th Street, San Francisco, CA 94103

Connecticut
Arman Absentee Auctions: P.O. Box 4037, Woodstock, CT 06281
Clearing House Auction Galleries, Inc.: 207 Church Street, Wethersfield, CT 06109

District of Columbia
Adam A. Weschler & Son: 905 E Street, N.W., Washington, DC 20004

Illinois
Dunning's Auction Service, Inc: 755 Church Road, Elgin, IL 60123
Leslie Hindman Auctioneers: 225 West Ohio Street, Chicago, IL 60610

Indiana
Kruse Auction: Kruse Building, P.O. Box 190, Auburn, IN 46706

Kansas
Woody Auction Company: P.O. Box 618, Douglass, KS 67039

Louisiana
Neal Auction Company: 4038 Magazine Street, New Orleans, LA 70115

Maine
Julia's Auction Barn: Route 201, Skowhegan Road, Fairfield, ME 04937
Richard W. Oliver: P.O. Box 337, Kennebunk, ME 04043

Maryland
Richard Opfer Auctioneering, Inc.: 1919 Greenspring Drive, Timonium, MD 21093
C. G. Sloan and Company, Inc.: 4920 Wyaconda Road, N. Bethesda, MD 20852
Theriault's: P.O. Box 151, Annapolis, MD 21404

Massachusetts
Douglas Galleries: Routes 5 and 10, South Deerfield, MA 01373
Robert Eldred: P.O. Box 796, East Dennis, MA 02641
Willis Henry Auctions, Inc.: 22 Main Street, Marshfield, MA 02050
Robert W. Skinner, Inc.: 357 Main Street, Bolton, MA 01740

Michigan

Frank N. Boos Gallery: 420 Enterprise Court, Bloomfield Hills, MI 48013
DuMochelle Art Galleries Company: 409 East Jefferson Avenue, Detroit, MI 48226

New Hampshire

Withington, Inc.: RD2, Box 440, Hillsboro, NH 03244
Northeast Auctions: 694 Lafayette Road, Hampton, NH 03842

New Jersey

David Rago: 9 Main Street, Lambertville, NJ 08629

New York

Christie's: 502 Park Avenue, New York, NY 10022
Christie's East: 219 East 67th Street, New York, NY 10021
William Doyle Galleries: 175 East 87th Street, New York, NY 10028
Guernsey's: 108 East 73rd Street, New York, NY 10021
Mapes Auctioneers & Appraisers: 1729 Vestal Parkway West, Vestal, NY 13850
Phillip's: 406 East 79th Street, New York, NY 10021
Savoia & Fromm: Route 23, South Cairo, NY 12482
Sotheby's: 1334 York Avenue, New York, NY 10021

North Carolina

Robert S. Brunk Services: P.O. Box 18294, Asheville, NC 28814

Ohio

Garth's Auctions, Inc.: 2690 Stratford Road, P.O. Box 369, Delaware, OH 43015

Pennsylvania

Freeman Fine Arts of Philadelphia: 1808–1810 Chestnut Street, Philadelphia, PA 19103
Hake's Americana: P.O. Box 1444, York, PA 17405

Wisconsin

Milwaukee Auction Gallery: 4747 West Bradley Street, Milwaukee, WI 53223

30

Tag Sales

Though the auction has been the traditional way to dispose of an estate, today, every week in every town across the United States, thousands of tag sales are held in chic neighborhoods, studio apartments, high-rise condos, 1950s ranch-style homes, down country roads and along city streets, on patios and in backyards.

Actually these sales are called by many names—tag sales, estate sales, garage sales, house sales, rummage sales, patio sales, yard sales—but the results are the same. The items—from antiques to last year's lawn mower, even those things that only a few years ago you might have thrown or given away—are sold.

But there is a new professionalism emerging in these sales, especially in the true tag sale, where a knowledgeable appraiser/tag sale conductor carefully identifies each object and prices it according to its known market value. Thus, if you are considering disposing of an estate through a tag sale rather than an auction, you should know that there are many steps and procedures that can mean the difference between success and disaster.

Many people, faced with the need to empty out a house after a death or when the elderly are being moved to different quarters, assume that any antiques dealer can manage a tag sale. But the success of a tag sale depends not only on the items being sold, but on behind-the-scenes management as well.

Because a tag sale only lasts one to three days, whereas antiques shops are open week after week, year after year, the tag sale conductor must know about advertising, crowd control, cash control, even obtaining the right supplies unique to tag sales.

Thus, you have every right to ask the same sorts of questions of a tag sale conductor you would ask of an auctioneer or appraiser. Here are some suggested questions:

- Will I receive a clear financial agreement specifying the percentage commission charged and what it covers—for example, advertising, security, parking valet if necessary, and so on?
- What tasks will you, the seller, and I, the owner, be responsible for? Who pays for the insurance?
  What condition will the house be left in?
  When will prices be reduced?
  What happens to unsold items?
  How much security is needed inside and outside the residence?

- When and where will the sale be advertised? (Inquire about specific information on the size of ads and where they will be placed—local newspapers, antiques publications, fliers for distribution, and so forth.)
- How will you handle the traffic flow inside the residence to cut down on theft and breakage?
- Will I receive an inventory of the property prior to the sale? (This is absolutely essential.)
- When will the final accounting be due to the estate or owner? (Usually within fifteen to thirty days.)

This new "professionalism" among tag sale conductors also eliminates the image of buyers lined up ready to "crash the gates" at the crack of dawn. The successful conductors have eliminated the problems of crowd control, breakage, and other objectionable practices, just as professional auctioneers have developed techniques of advertising and auctioneering that usually insure an active, bidding audience.

But the question most frequently asked is, Which will make the most money—the tag sale or the auction? This is like asking, Which came first, the chicken or the egg? Because the same property cannot be sold both ways to find the answer, the question will be debated ad infinitum. Your decision may be based on how great a risk you are willing to take, along with the financial arrangements you are able to make with the auctioneer or tag sale conductor.

In many instances you will make your decision based on the reputation of a professional tag sale conductor or auctioneer in the area where the sale is to be conducted. But whether you elect to have a tag sale or an auction, the best prices are usually gotten when items are sold in the house, on the premises so to speak. Often auctioneers like to move entire estates to a gallery, perhaps to combine with another estate, and this is one point you must clarify ahead of time. If a family is well known or has been known to have very fine objects, things from other estates may be put into the same sale to ride piggyback on the reputation of the first estate. Avoid the combining of sales.

If you decide to have a tag sale, you will find that knowledgeable tag sale conductors carefully identify each item before pricing it. Then, if the more valuable or unusual items do not sell for the specified prices, they can be sent to a consignment shop or even to an appropriate auction for a second chance. Unless your auctioneer allows reserves on items, once an object is offered for sale it is sold to the highest bidder—regardless of the price. The difference, according to my associate, Joe Wilkinson, who has conducted house sales for attorneys and executors in several states, is that prices in a well-run tag sale are established by the knowledgeable professional, whereas prices in an auction are established by the audience. Obviously once a price is set on an object in a tag sale, you cannot expect to receive a higher bid. In an auction, two people can run the final price of a $10 item into the hundreds! But a $500 item can also sell for $10.

Before deciding whether you want to play it safe or take a chance, consider the following:

1. the specific commission each person will charge to hold the sale or auction;
2. exactly what services that commission includes;
3. the success of previous similar tag sales and auctions.

Remember, however, that if the auctioneer is working on the 10/10 concept (seller pays 10 percent, buyer pays 10 percent) you must be very sure what other expenses (photos, insurance, and so forth) you, the seller, are going to also be charged for. Also, the "broom clean" service of leaving a bare, clean house is often included in the tag sale conductor's contract, but seldom in an auctioneer's contract.

A couple of years ago tag sales would never have been included in a book like this. But with the success of tag sales, you should be aware of this alternate way of disposing of estates or even just cleaning out your own house. An informative book is, *How to Establish and Operate a Successful Tag Sale Business* available from Past Glories, 29 Gibson, North East, PA 16428.

TAG SALE CONDUCTORS

Alabama
Estate Services, Inc.
3716 Montrose Road
Birmingham, AL 35213

California
Roberta Ely
175 Beechtree Drive
Encinitas, CA 92024

Estate Sales Services
PO Box 3341
Lancaster, CA 93536

Ruth Geller Gold
Box 2151
Anaheim, CA 92804

Connecticut
Hughes & Hutnick
135 Highland Street
Wethersfield, CT 06109

Florida
Ina H. Baden
1210 99th Street NW
Bradenton, FL 33529

Patricia J. Hastings
Rt. 4 Box 3900
Citra, FL 32627

Diane Marvin
4738 NW 5th Place
Pompano Beach, FL 33063

Shirley L. Northern
PO Box 1008
Ponte Vedra Beach, FL 32082

The Professionals
900 Bay Drive #116
Miami Beach, FL 33141

Georgia
J & J Antiques
614 E. Main Street
Hogansville, GA 30230

Leslie Stephens Antiques
35 Peachtree Circle, NE #4
Atlanta, GA 30309

Shirley C. Stokes
127 Washington Avenue
Savannah, GA 31405

Indiana
Trash to Treasures
5505 N. Keystone Avenue
Indianapolis, IN 46220

Maryland
A. M. Sales
9900 Harrogate Road
Bethesda, MD 20817

Michigan
Golden Era Sales, Inc.
RR #2, Box 2365A
Grayling, MI 49738

New Hampshire
Corbe Morris Feeney Sales
Box 427
Rye, NH 03870

New Jersey
Country Girls Ltd.
34 Holly Drive
Saddle River, NJ 07458

New York
A Certain Ambiance
PO Box 325
Brookhaven, NY 11719

North Carolina
Butler & Associates
1325 Welcome Circle
Durham, NC 27705

301 Front Antiques
Box 470
Beaufort, NC 28516

Pat Thomas
501 North Street
Chapel Hill, NC 27514

S & J Associates
PO Box 12465
Raleigh, NC 27605

J. E. A. Wilkinson
PO Box 28164
Raleigh, NC 27611

Ohio
DK Estates Dales
10347 Lochcrest Drive
Cincinnati, OH 45231

Katie & Dee Tag Sales
1156 Lincoln Road
Columbus, OH 43212

John Wiedey
142 Highland Avenue
Wadsworth, OH 44281

Pennsylvania
August R. Fetcko
29 Gibson
North East, PA 16428

Barry S. Slosberg
232 North 2nd Street
Philadelphia, PA 19106

Texas
Assets Appraisal & Sales, Inc.
PO Box 121337
Forth Worth, TX 76116

Virginia
Langhorne Stokes House
1421 Main Street
Lynchburg, VA 24504

Wisconsin
Shannon Sales Inc.
645 North 36th Street
Milwaukee, WS 53208

31

Antiques Dealers

When I began writing this book I was tempted to call it *Everything You Wanted to Know About Antiques But Your Dealer Wouldn't Tell You.* Then, when I decided to include a chapter about dealers, good and bad, I was told I was taking my life in my own hands.

Really now! Antiques dealers are generally a pretty honorable group, no different from auctioneers, appraisers, interior decorators, dentists, bankers, lawyers, doctors, and ministers. There are the good and the bad. But because, like appraisers, they are an unregulated body, it is perhaps easier for an unscrupulous person to slip into the ranks of the scrupulous.

My purpose is to alert you to some of the practices, both appropriate and questionable, that distinguish the reputable dealers and expose the opportunists.

A certain disenchantment with some antiques dealers may be the result of the phenomenon of the group shop or mall concept. Businesswise, the concept makes sense. Lower overhead for rent and utilities, combined "shop tending" that allows more time for buying trips, higher customer traffic, and even complementary merchandise and services (a silver specialty shop, an interior design service, and a general antiques shop in one location) are only a few reasons for rapid growth of these malls.

But many collectors complain that the part-time antiques "booth" keeper cannot be compared with the independent shop owner who had to take higher risks to be successful. College students, housewives, professional engineers, even auctioneers can now have a small antiques business open full time to the public in an antiques mall. So though you can find convenient "one-stop shopping," a novice may not find the necessary guidance at a mall. Specialist dealers who are particularly interested in educating their customers still tend to be "independent souls" and keep separate shops.

Here, then, are some comments gathered from dealers themselves as to what they look for in other dealers:

- Will the dealer buy back, swap, or sell on consignment the items he has sold?

  Without question, each dealer put this as the number-one consideration that distinguishes both the knowledgeable and the honorable dealer from the one who is simply trying to get rid of merchandise at any price.

- Will the dealer give a refund if the items sold are found to be other than they were represented to be?

  This is a more direct way of making the first point. Your best protection is to get a bill of sale that fully and accurately describes the piece. If a chair labeled "eighteenth-century English Chippendale carved mahogany side chair" is written "Chair. $1,800" on your receipt, ask for a full description and learn the shop's policy on returns.

- Will the dealer let his items go out on approval?
  Most dealers felt that a reasonable length of time (three days to a week) was the mark of a dealer who has confidence in his objects and is looking to build a strong client-dealer relationship.

- Does the dealer have a research library?
  Because authentication and identification are so important, and there is so much to know, a working library of periodicals, books, and auction catalogs is considered essential to the serious dealer.

- Is each piece fully labeled with date, origin, maker, material, and so on?
  The ultimate accuracy of the information may challenge the dealer's statement, but few would intentionally mislabel an item. Once he has identified an object, sharing the information with his potential customers is a form of education. If an item has been mislabeled, the honest dealer will quickly correct his mistake—and probably change the price.

  On the other hand, never buy from a dealer who does not have a public price on his merchandise.

- Be wary of shops that have lots of signs around with such messages as "Do not handle" or "You break it, you buy it." One touch can tell you everything about some antiques (and dealers know it).

- Always inquire about delivery service and charges before making a purchase.

- Are reproductions mixed in with authentic antiques?
  This consideration brought mixed comments from dealers. Some feel that a "gift item" or "interior design" area separate from the antiques is both desirable and essential. Others felt that such a mixture indicates the dealer is a merchant and not a true antiques specialist.

There is little question that an honest and reputable dealer is the best source for the antiques collector. But you do not want to rely on just one dealer, if for no other reason than that one dealer cannot possibly buy everything. Different dealers have different sources and connections.

Perhaps one of the best bits of advice is to listen to what the dealer says when you are in his shop. Does he offer information readily? Does he point out differences between pieces? Does he point out repairs or restorations (after all, how many pieces survive one hundred years of life and more totally unscathed)? And always be wary if he begins talking about the "great buys." The moment a dealer says, "I could get twice the money for this [sofa, teapot, painting] in New York," you have to wonder what is wrong with it.

The other side of the story comes when you are selling and need to find a good dealer who will work openly and honestly with you. First of all, remember that the dealer has to make a profit, or he cannot stay in business. "I had one just like that that I sold for $75. The dealer who bought it sure did gyp me!" is a frequently heard comment. You then look at the object and see it is marked $125. Was the seller gypped?

Remember, the dealer has to have the $75 (cash) to pay the seller. Next he has to make enough profit from the eventual sale of the piece to pay his rent (or mortgage), telephone and utilities, inventory taxes, salespeople, advertising, and transportation costs, as well as make a living wage for himself. Furthermore, once he has bought the object from you, he can't return it if he doesn't sell it.

Whenever you are selling, if you think the offer is too low, you have the right to refuse it or name a higher price. In fact, your best protection is to offer the object for sale with an established price rather than asking the dealer what he will pay for it. Remember, you have many sources of what other, comparable pieces are selling for—from appraisers to price guides to your own observation in shops, auctions, and tag sales—to provide you with a price range for your object. But first, examine your piece carefully for condition and to be sure the object is what you believe it to be. You will be quite embarrassed if your rare Newport secretary is found to be an old reproduction with its label still in the drawer. Take the time to examine your objects before the dealer arrives.

Many dealers are dependent on consignment sales to maintain a positive cash flow. Further, entire shops of consignment merchandise are becoming quite popular, especially in larger cities. The secret, of course, is having a well-written, carefully filled in contract or consignment agreement. The paper must include the following:

- A full and accurate description of the object (or objects), including condition at the time of consignment
- The date the object is consigned and the length of time the dealer has to sell it
- The exact percentage commission the dealer charges (some as low as 20 percent, some as high as 35 percent)
- The price(s) the object(s) will be sold for and, if there is to be a reduction after a set time (usually sixty to ninety days), what the reduced price will be and when this lower price will go into effect
- Whether, if another offer is made, your right of acceptance or refusal is required or may be made by the consignment shop
- Insurance responsibility while the object(s) is in the shop
- Any other charges you will have to pay (pickup, delivery, advertising, whatever)
- How soon after the object has been sold you will receive your money (usually within thirty days)

Consignment selling has many advantages for both the dealer and the seller, but as in all business agreements, disappointments and even lawsuits can be avoided if each party has a clear concept of the terms from the outset.

Realize that these days there are numerous ways to sell your antiques, personal property, and collectibles. The chapters in this book on auction houses, antiques dealers, tag sales, appraisers, even price guides, are designed to awaken you to the many possibilities for getting the most money and the best service if you are selling your objects and getting the best prices and merchandise if you are buying.

32

Price Guides:
Bibles or Boondoggles?

A specialist may not need a price guide in his field of expertise. But almost every dealer, appraiser, and auctioneer uses some form of price guide at one time or another in his work.

The price guide may be written by the Kovels, Harry Rinker (editor in chief of *Warman's*), Robert Overstreet, or any of several authors whose guides appear as regularly as the New Year. Or the price guide may be an auction house catalog with estimated presale prices given for the items to be auctioned. After the auction, the houses send a printed follow-up sale price list. Or the price guide may be an actual retail price list provided by the manufacturer, listing specific prices of currently manufactured goods.

What do all three have in common? The prices stated in all three can and do fluctuate and can only be used as guides to prices.

For example, let's look at three objects and their prices as stated in the appropriate price guide or list.

Price Guide. An 11½-inch "Rose Medallion" punch bowl is quoted in one price guide as having a value of $775 and in another a value of $1,200.

Auction Catalog. A few years ago I bought two identical celestial globes at a Christie's sale. The first one sold for $480. The second one sold twenty seconds later for $380. These prices are now stated in the Christie's sale price list.

Manufacturer's List. A wing chair, which retails on the manufacturer's price list for $650, has a discounted sale ticket of $575, and the furniture dealer tells you that price is negotiable. He'll take $500.

The actual prices for all three examples—bowls, globes, and chair—have an obvious range: $775–$1,200, $380–$480, $500–$650. But the printed prices create a base from which the final price or value can be established.

No, price lists are not the final word. They are guides that either support or contradict your thinking. The mistake comes when a value is taken from one source or price guide and is considered the final word. There are just too many unknown facts about each individual item entered in a price guide to make *one price* taken from *one price guide* absolute.

But by taking the *price ranges* from several price guides, you get a base from which to work. Add to this base an understanding of all of the unknown factors that affect specific prices, and you will understand why price guides are what they say they are—price *guides*.

Take the 11½-inch "Rose Medallion" bowls, for example. Why is one $775 and the other $1,200? Both are the same size. Perhaps one bowl has some minor chips or a hairline crack that has lowered its value. Where is each being sold? "Rose Medallion" generally brings higher prices in the southern states than in New England. Is one bowl being sold in a more expensive shop than the other? What are the dates of each bowl? A "Rose Medallion" bowl dating from 1860 will bring more money than one dating from 1920. A price guide does not tell you about these variables.

What about my globes, which incidentally had presale price estimates in the Christie's catalog of $300 to $400 each? Why was one $100 more expensive to buy than the other? Who was in the audience that day? How much money had the other bidder already spent on other purchases that day? How much money was I willing to spend to get the globes? (I was willing to spend more than I did, in fact.) Even after the globes were sold to me, what are they really worth? Are auction prices wholesale or retail? (See chapter 29 on auction houses.)

And, finally, what about the newly manufactured chair? On his price list the manufacturer suggests that the chair be sold for $650, but if it goes from an eastern furniture manufacturer all the way to the West Coast, its quoted price will be even higher. On the other hand, if the chair is sold at a furniture discount house, its price can be substantially lower. And when inventory sale time comes around, a customer may even be able to buy the chair for its wholesale price.

The point is, once a price range is established by comparing two or more price guides, you can get a general concept of value. Price guides tell you that you probably cannot sell your 11½-inch "Rose Medallion" bowl for $5,000, but if you find one for $200, you'll be getting a super buy.

The auction house prices of my globes tell me that I would be foolish to sell them for $100 each, but I should not expect to sell them for $1,000 each (unless I luck out and find somebody who wants them more than I do).

The prices provided in this appraisal book do not establish *exact* values, but rather provide a range or a viable point of reference to help you get a realistic assessment of personal property values. Remember, too, that there can be considerable difference between fair market, estate, or sale values and replacement, insurance, or retail values.

Once you know that a wing chair made by a good middle-line furniture manufacturer is going to retail for $650, you recognize that you have a "steal" if you find a similar one in excellent condition in a house sale for only $150.

When you know what you are looking at (make sure the bowl really is antique "Rose Medallion" and not a five-year-old Oriental reproduction) and understand that price guides have limitations, you can use them to compile a range of values for some of your personal property.

And always remember that the mass-market price guide is going to be pretty useless in providing a value for a rarity such as a Paul Revere teapot, a Townsend-Goddard chest of drawers, or a Rembrandt portrait.

The exceptionally fine, rare, and valuable piece always needs to be authenticated and evaluated by an expert.

33

Collecting
for Investment Purposes

Each time the stock market dips or inflation starts up—and both happen on a cyclical basis—articles on alternative investments appear. Soon photos of celebrities buying antiques, collectibles, and art in pricey galleries are featured in newspapers and magazines. But are antiques, art, and collectibles true investments?

Glance at almost any investment book written today and you will find a chapter on art, antiques, and collectibles. Conversely, no book on antiques and personal property can be considered complete without a few words on investing and collecting. All along I have talked about the investments your parents, grandparents, or great-grandparents made when they bought their china, furniture, silver, or even your toys!

But I've also cited the times people have been disappointed when their possessions were not all they were thought to be. My purpose is not to paint a distortedly rosy or bleak picture, but to make you knowledgeable about what you already own and what you wish to buy—whether for pleasure or potential investment.

What should today's collector wishing to make a good investment do? There are three basic rules. Remembering that your grandparents probably did not consciously go out and invest in personal property for investment's sake, I would advise you to do exactly what they did:

> Buy what you like.
> Buy what you can afford.
> Buy the best you can afford.

Furthermore, do what successful investors do. When seeking advice about investing, turn to someone who has a proven track record in the investment world. One of America's best-known collectors is also one of America's best-known success stories on Wall Street. Richard Jenrette made his fortune on Wall Street at the helm of an investment firm, Donaldson, Lufkin and Jenrette. Jenrette's career in the often diverse, often similar, boardroom and auction gallery has been chronicled in scores of articles from the front page of the business section of the Sunday *New York Times* to *Town & Country*.

What does Jenrette have to say about investing in antiques?

"Antiques and old houses have been my best investments, but I can't qualify this. You really never know what your antiques are worth until you sell them. Right now the market is hot, and I'm certain my collection has appreciated a great deal in value. But if hard times came and I had to sell them, chances are the bids would be a lot lower. I personally don't think you should buy antiques solely for investment. To me this is a side benefit. The return on your investment comes in your personal enjoyment of the antique. If you happen to be able to sell it later at a gain, so much the better.

"There is another problem in selling antiques if you need to. I make the analogy in our business on Wall Street that on every stock there is a bid and an offer. The bid might be $25 a share and the offer $26 a share, which is a very narrow spread. But we've all had the experience of selling an antique to a dealer for $2,000 to $3,000 and coming back a week later to see it marked up to $12,000 or $15,000. This is a pretty wide spread."

Such words from an acknowledged business success and connoisseur of antiques should be well heeded by both investment and antiques novices.

But at the same time, Jenrette and many others are living proof that it is possible to make wise purchases in antiques, art, and collectibles. Thus, while you're buying what you like and can afford—be it Arts and Crafts furniture, Georgian silver, brand-new Waterford crystal, or 1950s movie posters—always buy the best examples of your choice that you can afford. In other words, buy the best quality that your pocketbook can stand. And do not buy damaged or broken pieces for investment—unless you have studied the subject carefully and have learned, for example, that some chipping is acceptable in eighteenth-century Delft or that some flaking of the original paint is permissible in exceptional mechanical banks.

The collector who wishes to make a conscious study of antiques, art, jewelry, or any specific area of personal property should follow these rules:

- Narrow your collection to as small an area as possible.
- Buy your first pieces from a fully established and reputable dealer who will help educate you in your chosen area.
- Study this one area until you become an expert yourself.

Let's say you like Victorian furniture and want to collect it. Victorian furniture dates from 1840 to 1900 and includes everything from whatnots to wardrobes. You will only become frustrated if you choose too large a field. Narrow your sights, choose a particular style of Victorian furniture—Eastlake or Renaissance, for example—and buy the best quality you can afford.

The same rule applies to each area. Rather than collecting "china," decide on one type of china—Satsuma, Minton, or Homer Laughlin—or try a specific item, such as demitasse cups and saucers or compotes. If you end up making an investment that pays off in a cash return, that's a bonus. But taste is so quixotic today that no one can positively guarantee what the next generation, or the next, will consider desirable.

And always remember when you read stories about collectors who have turned their collections into profit that they are no different from successful investors in the stock, commodities, real estate, or any other market. All devote a great deal of time to learning about their investments.

Even after considering these cardinal rules, the truly savvy potential investor might want to go one step farther. A few years ago Stephen Lash, senior vice president of Christie's, advised delving into firsthand experience as a way of "testing the waters." His recommendation—choose an object, buy an inexpensive sample, have it appraised, and then try to sell it. By taking a chance on an inexpensive object or as expensive an item as you can afford to lose money on, you may learn the economic realities of "investing" in an antiques and collectibles market that are never taught in Economics 101.

And so my ultimate message near the end of this book is the same as at the beginning. Look around you. You are already surrounded by valuable and in some instances rare and important antiques and personal property. I've written this book to help you protect your belongings while learning more about them. You may have had some disappointments, but you've also probably uncovered some unexpected treasures. Further, there are many undiscovered riches at every tag sale, auction, and antiques shop just waiting for the knowledgeable shopper. Recognize both and you'll be doubly rewarded.

34

Fakes Have Been Around Forever

In the antiques world, fakes are sometimes even more glamorous than the "real thing." From *The Maltese Falcon* to *Octopussy,* audiences have thrilled to the chase of uncovering a priceless work of art that may or may not be genuine.

In real life fakes abound. The question is, what is a fake? Chapter 13 explored the distinction between the reproduction and the fake. The purpose of this chapter is to alert you to the frequency with which objects—whether fakes (made with the distinct purpose to deceive) or reproductions (copies of an earlier style that simply are not as old or as valuable as you think)—are being sold as "valuable antiques" when they are not.

Warnings, stories, and hints on how to detect these "pretenders" are given here and in the chapters about specific objects. But if you can just learn always to be a little suspicious, you will be less likely to be disappointed later. So here are a few quotes, stories, and anecdotes to alert you to the preponderance of these objects in the marketplace.

William Hogarth warned in 1737 that there were already as many as forty fake Old Masters coming into England every day. This should pique your interest and make you most cautious. How many of these eighteenth-century fakes, assumed to be original fifteenth-, sixteenth-, and seventeenth-century original Old Master works, are exhibited in museums and private collections in the twentieth century?

In recent years Dwight Lanmon, director of the Corning Museum of Glass, has written extensively about glass known as the Mutzer group that was intentionally made to deceive Henry Francis du Pont (whose collection of American decorative arts housed at Winterthur is the world's greatest) and other collectors and experts in the 1920s and 1930s. At the end of his scholarly and convincing arguments, Lanmon states, "It seems an inescapable conclusion that the entire Mutzer group was made secretly in limited quantities and planted for sale as rare early-nineteenth-century glass."

The 1920s and early 1930s in America was a time when many objects were both intentionally faked and simply copied to meet the increasing demand for "antiquities." In 1925 Ellen D. Wangner wrote this "message" in the March *Garden Magazine & Home Builder*:

Time was, a few years ago, when to be valued such furniture must be labeled "antique" and, because there could not possibly be enough old furniture to meet the demand, there grew up a widespread business of manufacturing fake antiques. To those with a reverence for the work and the workers of by-gone days, this was desecration. It was not revivifying the past—it was killing it. It was then that the earnest cabinetmakers of our own times boldly discarded antiquity as such and with fine discrimination began to reproduce as *strictly twentieth-century furniture and furnishings* the best of the housewares of those earlier days when men loved the work of their hands and often put years into the making of one piece of furniture. It is these men who are keeping alive the traditions of the past, striving as creators, not as mere copyists, to adapt these furnishings to the life of the vigorous present.

From Wangner we learn two important points the serious collector must always remember:

- There was a large fake antiques trade around the turn of the century.
- Many excellent copies of period pieces were made in the 1920s and 1930s.

Just imagine what has happened to those faithfully created copies. First, they are sixty to seventy years old now. Metals have rusted, oxidized, and become pitted over the years. Wood surfaces have mellowed and built up a natural patina. China and glass have become chipped and aged by usage. The result—many of these items *appear* to be much older than they are.

Add to these natural aging processes the family stories: "This came from my grandparents' house," the septuagenarian tells us, and quickly the younger generation is led to believe these objects date from the eighteenth or early nineteenth century. Sometimes even experts are deceived, and it takes a combination of gut reaction and luck to prove the true age of these items.

A well-known museum had received a pair of andirons along with several other gifts about which there was no question of age and authenticity. But the andirons were literally driving me crazy. I couldn't put my finger on why, but they just weren't right. All of my intellectual arguments—wear, proportion, design, and so on—were successfully argued down by the curators. Then late one afternoon while relaxing at home, I was looking through a group of 1920s magazines. There, in the gift suggestions of a 1920 *House Beautiful* magazine, were the "faithful copies" made for the Christmas season. The lesson for you to learn from this story is that looking through old magazines of the 1910s through the 1950s is an enjoyable and painless way to learn about the reproductions of those eras.

But don't stop with antiques. As a student of eighteenth- and nineteenth-century antiques, I have trained myself to look for signs of workmanship and quality. Fine craftsmen in the eighteenth century took pride in the finished product—inside and out. The most obvious proof of fine craftsmanship is the

Everything about this bisque cupid appears appropriately "Victorian." Could those be the crossed-swords marks of the famous German factory Meissen that made wonderful pieces in the nineteenth century? And look—there are even signs of wear at the raised "touch" points—the wing, the rounded buttocks, and heel. But this style of crossed swords and this type of gold numbers are immediately recognized by the knowledgeable person as those used on Japanese reproductions.

A 1970s copy of a 1920s piece! And how will it be sold in 2070? As a 1920s original or a 1970s copy?

detail of measured and precise dovetailing the connoisseur expects to find in furniture of the period. Imagine then my surprise when I had the privilege of closely examining a Rietveld chair at a New York museum exhibit and discovered unfinished surfaces and even traces of dripped paint that had dried where it was assumed the casual eye would not detect it.

When lack of finish and care was evident, why was I so surprised when a friend showed me his Rietveld chair—one built for another museum exhibition—not by Rietveld in the 1920s, but by another craftsman in the 1970s! This chair will undoubtedly be purchased in the future as something it is not.

Sam Pennington, editor of *Maine Antiques Digest,* often writes about and includes articles on fakes in his highly acclaimed antiques publication. And the catalog he wrote for the 1988 April Fool exhibit of fakes at the Hirschl and Adler Folk Gallery will be a twentieth-century testament of fakery in American folk art. Pennington takes the sting out of past mistakes made (by you and me) when he writes, "No matter what the field, the collector who hasn't bought a fake is either kidding himself or he hasn't bought very aggressively."

You see, aggressive collectors are willing to spend money and take a chance on items being rare or "undiscovered." On the other hand, the conservative collector seeks out the "safe" buy that has been carefully authenticated. The area of folk art has long been rife with fakes and copies.

The individuality of folk art makes it particularly easy to fake because there is no established criterion of quality as there is, for example, when judging an eighteenth-century Philadelphia Chippendale chest of drawers.

Advice: The Wrong Kind and the Right Kind

Several years ago I was wandering through an antiques shop when I spied in a darkened corner a rather large carved wooden eagle. I knew of the work of Wilhelm Schimmel, a Pennsylvania carver with an alcoholic bent whose mid-nineteenth-century work has sold for thousands of dollars. Might it be? I wondered. The price was certainly low enough that the eagle could be bought for a decorative item—if you like eagles. Since it was in a dark corner I decided it would probably roost there a few days longer and I would have a chance to research it further.

Obviously I wasn't obsessed by the eagle the way a true folk art aficionado would be, because I didn't begin my research immediately. But when I ran into a knowledgeable dealer a couple of days later, I did recall the eagle and asked innocently, "What would you do if you found a large carved eagle that might possibly be a Schimmel?"

"Sign it," was his instant reply.

With this anecdote under your belt, you might heed Pennington's advice on how to avoid "expensive mistakes":

1. Work with reputable dealers. The old axiom is, "If you don't know your antiques, know your antiques dealer."
2. Get a written guarantee as to what you are buying. Remember that auction purchases are often "as is."
3. If you see something at auction that catches your fancy, you may be able to commission a good dealer to buy it for you unless he already has an interest of a commission. For an extra 10 percent or so, you get his guarantee.
4. Do your homework. Read, go to museums, study, study, study. Collecting is a field that rewards knowledge.
5. Ask yourself, Could this piece really have been done when and where the seller says it was? Does it have the proper tool marks? Check out things like ships' names.
6. Avoid the "just like." If what you are offered is exhibited somewhere, check out the original. Ask yourself, What are the chances of another turning up?
7. Look at a portrait as art. The best folk portraits were done quickly and freely by real artists. The faces may be stylized, but they have a vitality and look like real people. Copies are much more laborious and often show it.
8. Always look for provenance. Where did the object come from? Who owned it? It's no accident that the biggest prices at auction come when the family history is known.
9. Be wary of bargains unless you know exactly what you are doing.

Extraordinary sleeping black duck—by A. Elmer Crowell, East Harwich, Massachusetts, with crossed wing carving and large oval Crowell stamp on bottom. Condition: this beautiful decoy is in nearly mint condition with only minor flaking of paint on neck and bill. Photograph courtesy William Doyle Galleries

10. Buy something and try to sell it for more than you paid for it. You'll learn more than any of us can ever teach you.

And always remember, "If it's too good to be true, it probably is."

To alert you to just a few of the areas where fakery and reproduction are particularly hard to detect, here is a partial list of frequently encountered problems:

Decoys. With decoys selling for thousands, tens of thousands, and even hundreds of thousands of dollars, you can be sure there are fakes around. Though these are usually offered for fairly modest prices—in the hundreds— they are still fakes. The test decoy dealers use is to fill the kitchen sink with water. A decoy is made for floating in the water. Fakers seldom take the time to make their decoys seaworthy. If your newly purchased duck rolls, lists, or sinks, it is a fake.

All varieties of glass. The warnings both at the beginning of this chapter and from Gladys Taber in chapter 14, along with all the information on reproductions in price guides, should suffice.

Orientalia, especially porcelain, cinnabar, jade, and ivory. The problem with Oriental objects is twofold. First, Oriental cultures traditionally imitate objects of the past, including marks, thereby making it difficult for the unknowledgeable person to distinguish the original from copies that may be centuries old themselves. Second, because Oriental objects are not part of our native culture, they may seem rare and unusual when seen for the first time. In reality the objects may be mass-produced and commonplace. My advice is that you take the time to visit the Chinatowns in New York, Seattle, San Francisco, and Vancouver and the shops in smaller metropolitan areas that sell new Oriental objects. I cannot tell you how many times I have been shown resin-type composition figurines and told they were "ivory" or how

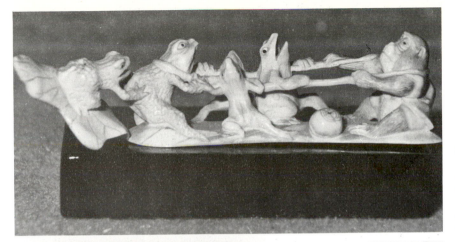

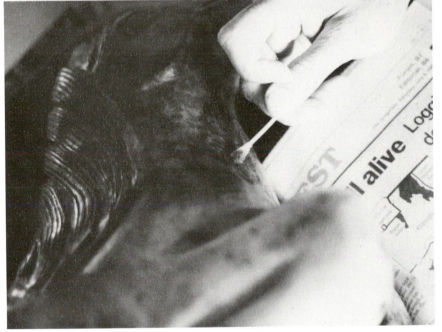

This appealing carved-ivory group sold for $275, but for every piece of genuine ivory we are brought, we have to tell another person his pieces are not genuine ivory. Photograph courtesy Savoia and Fromm Auction Services

A little paint remover immediately revealed the false coloring used to create an "aged" appearance on this sculpture. Sold for several thousand dollars as an eighteenth-century jade piece, the horse was neither eighteenth century nor jade. An identical figure was offered for sale in San Francisco's Chinatown for $950.

many softstone carvings I've seen that were purchased as "jade." If there is one area I would stay away from, it is Orientalia. This doesn't mean that you may not make a wonderful find, but experience has shown me that disappointments far outnumber discoveries.

Limited edition prints. Refer to chapters 2 and 25 for a review. Then remember that hundreds of thousands of lithographic copies of well-known prints (Currier & Ives and Audubon, in particular) have been made over the years. To tell the difference between a photolithograph and an engraving, you must be able to identify true rag bond paper and know what an impressed engraving looks like.

Furniture. Many clues are given in the furniture chapter and throughout this book. But a succinct hint is that the more desirable the form, the greater the likelihood a piece may not be what it purports to be. For every true eighteenth-century Chippendale chair, there are thousands of old, nineteenth-century copies, custom-made reproductions, and even twentieth-century "made-up" chairs purporting to date from the eighteenth century. On the other hand, I have yet to see a fake Eastlake chair—not a very popular style. Also, be particularly wary of European pine pieces that "look like new" but are said to be antique. Pine is such a soft wood, how could any one-hundred-year-old piece look as clean as most of these "antique" pine pieces being sold in America today? And before you invest in English antiques, you need to be sure the "Georgian" piece you are buying is not an Edwardian piece about one hundred years younger.

How can I avoid being duped? Everyone wants to know. Sometimes, as Sam Pennington suggests, you can't. But if there were just one piece of advice I would give everyone, it is to use your head, not your heart. Remember all those hours you spent in history class. Now is the time to put some of the knowledge you gained to work for you.

I've given you benchmarks to use in dating objects and hints and clues that tell you how to distinguish the real from the reproductions, copies, and fakes. But brushing up on a little history can be most helpful, especially when you're getting ready to write a check for an antique.

A few years ago a lovely young hostess proudly showed me to my bedroom for the night. I would have the privilege of sleeping in a room furnished with a French seventeenth- or early-eighteenth-century bedroom suite, probably from a royal château, she said. The twin beds were carved with garland swags. The matching chest of drawers and dressing table were also exquisitely carved, and the pièce de résistance was the eight-foot-tall armoire with mirrored doors, I was told.

If my hosts had only reviewed a little history, they would have learned that "suites" of bedroom furniture with so many matching pieces were not around in the seventeenth and eighteenth centuries, not even in French royal châteaus. Furthermore, twin beds like hers came into existence at the turn of the century, when American society doctors told their wealthy clients that they could avoid bad colds and flu if they slept in separate beds. Finally, the technology to cut a piece of glass to be made into a seven- or eight-foot-tall mirror did not exist until the second half of the nineteenth century. In reality, the French eighteenth-century bedroom suite, though most impressive, had been made in Grand Rapids, Michigan, in the 1920s.

A little history never hurts.

35

Books:
Your Best Source of
Knowledge

The novice antiquer asked, "I want to buy an antique. What should I do?" "Buy a book on antiques," was the reply.

It has been estimated that over twenty thousand books have been written on antiques and collectibles. Glance at the magazine shelf and count the number of life-style publications, each having at least one article on antiques and collectibles. There are probably fifty or more newspaper-type monthly antiques publications across the country at the moment. With so much knowledge available, why are people duped day in and day out?

Romance, sentiment, impulse buying, passion, greed, lust, chance—there are as many reasons as there are different personality types.

Ironically, I've even seen fakes, reproductions, and "pretenders" in homes where I was envious of the owners' extensive library on antiques—including books on fakes! This observation long ago led me to the conclusion that you have to do more than buy the books. You have to read them!

Knowledge is not transmitted by osmosis. Knowledge is gained by long hours of reading, wading through, weeding out, and gleaning the information you need. For this reason, I have departed from the standard procedure of putting the bibliography at the end of the book. Perhaps this will serve as a reminder when you pick up this book that if the answer isn't here, it is somewhere in another book.

One of my favorite quotes comes not from a book on antiques, but from one on modern business, *Megatrends* by John Naisbitt. "We are drowning in information but starved for knowledge," Naisbitt writes. It is the popular view that we of the late twentieth century are living in an "information revolution." But perhaps the most revealing comment on acquiring knowledge, not just information, about antiques comes not from the twentieth century, but from the eighteenth century, when James Boswell quoted Dr. Samuel Johnson: "Knowledge is of two kinds: we know a subject ourselves, or we know where we can find information upon it." One book that is an invaluable source for additional information on multiple specialty areas is *Maloney's Antiques & Collectibles Resource Directory,* third edition (Antique Trader Publications).

The following list represents only a few of the thousands of resources available. The sheer volume of information on the limitless field of "antiques, collectibles, and personal property" may also serve as a reminder: choose an area and become a specialist. At any rate, refer to these pages as often as you do any in this book.

The books listed are arranged by categories—collectibles, silver, and so on—and those referred to in the text itself are included. However, many books are no longer in print and cannot easily be plucked from the shelves of your favorite bookstore. A visit to the library (especially one with a loan agreement with other libraries) will produce excellent results. But remember that colleges, universities, and art museums also have extensive collections of books on the decorative arts. A wonderful source for adding books to your personal library is the deaccessioning sales these libraries often hold once or twice a year. Then there are the invaluable used-book stores, both the walk-in and the specialized mail-order out-of-print book services; these often have the books you need at reduced prices.

Finally, while you're searching through the bins and shelves of the community-sponsored bargain box for the Rookwood vase or sterling silver Jensen pin, don't forget the books!

AMERICAN FURNITURE

Bjerkoe, Ethyl Hall. *The Cabinetmakers of America.* Exton, Pennsylvania: Schiffer Ltd., 1978.

Butler, Joseph T. *Field Guide to American Antique Furniture.* New York: Roundtree Press-Facts on File Publications, 1985.

Comstock, Helen, ed. *The Concise Encyclopedia of American Antiques.* New York: Hawthorn Publishers, Inc., 1984.

Downs, Joseph. *American Furniture in the Winterthur Museum.* New York: Macmillan Publishing Co., 1952.

Fairbanks, Jonathan L., and Elizabeth B. Bates. *American Furniture: 1620–Present.* New York: Richard Marek Publishers, 1981.

Fitzgerald, Oscar P. *Three Centuries of American Furniture* Englewood Cliffs, New Jersey: Prentice-Hall, Inc., 1982.

Kirk, John T. *The Impecunious Collector's Guide to American Antiques.* New York: Alfred A. Knopf, 1977.

Kovel, Ralph and Terry H. *American Country Furniture: 1780–1875.* New York: Crown Publishers, Inc., 1965.

Marsh, Moreton. *The Easy Expert in Collecting and Restoring American Antiques.* Philadelphia and New York: J. P. Lippincott, 1978.

Montgomery, Charles F. *American Furniture: The Federal Period 1788–1825.* New York: Bonanza Books, 1978.

Moses, Michael. *Master Craftsmen of Newport.* Tenafly, New Jersey: MMI Americana Press, 1984.

Sack, Albert. *Fine Points of American Furniture: Early American.* New York: Crown Publishers, Inc., 1982.

Smith, Nancy. *Old Furniture: Understanding the Craftsman's Art.* Boston: Little, Brown and Company, 1975.

ART

Currier & Ives: A Catalogue Raisonné. Detroit, Michigan: Gale Research Co., 1984.

Currier, William T. *Currier's Price Guide to American Artists 1645–1945 at Auction.* Brockton, Massachusetts: Currier Publications, 1987.

Falk, Peter H., ed. *Who Was Who in American Art.* Madison, Connecticut: Sound View Press, 1985.

McClain, Craig. *Currier & Ives: An Illustrated Value Guide.* Lombard, Illinois: Wallace-Homestead Books, 1987.

Meyer, George H., ed. *Folk Artists Biographical Index.* Detroit, Michigan: Gale Research Co., 1987.

Nutting, Wallace. *The Wallace Nutting Expansible Catalog.* Maple Glen, Pennsylvania: Diamond Press, 1987.

Schnessel, S. Michael, and Mel Karmel. *The Etchings of Louis Icart.* Exton, Pennsylvania: Schiffer Publishing Ltd., 1982.

Theran, Susan. *The Official Price to Fine Art.* New York: The House of Collectibles, 1987.

CANADA

Cathcart, Ruth. *Jacques & Hay 19th Century Toronto Furniture Makers.* Erin, Ontario: Boston Mills Press, 1986.

Guyette, Dale and Gary. *Decoys of Maritime Canada.* Exton, Pennsylvania: Schiffer Publishing Ltd., 1983.

Hearn, John. *Collector's Items—A Guide to Antique Hunting Across Canada.* Scarborough, Ontario: Van Nostrand Reinhold Ltd., 1981.

King, Thomas B. *Glass in Canada.* Erin, Ontario: Boston Mills Press, 1987.

Palardy, Jean. *The Early Furniture of French Canada.* Toronto: Macmillan Publishing Co., 1965.

Shackleton, P. *The Furniture of Old Ontario.* Toronto: Macmillan Publishing Co., 1973.

COLLECTIBLES

Anderson, Scott. *Check the Oil.* Lombard, Illinois: Wallace-Homestead, 1986.

Barlow, Ronald. *The Antique Tool Collector's Guide to Value.* El Cajun, California: Windmill Publishing Co., 1985.

Bergerin, Al. *Tobacco Tins and Their Prices.* Lombard, Illinois: Wallace-Homestead, 1986.

Bowers, Q. David. *The Moxie Encyclopedia.* Vestal, New York: The Vestal Press, 1985.

Conway, Shirley, and Jean Wilson. *Steiff Teddy Bears, Dolls and Toys with Prices.* Lombard, Illinois: Wallace-Homestead Books.

Crittenden, Alan. *Hidden Treasures.* Novato, California: Union Square Books, 1985.

Fellows, Paul. *Doll Auction Prices.* Lombard, Illinois: Wallace-Homestead Books, 1985.

Florence, Gene. *Kitchen Glassware of the Depression Years.* Paducah, Kentucky: Collectors' Books, 1987.

40's and 50's Collectibles For Fun and Profit. Tucson, Arizona: H. P. Books, Inc., 1985.

Fraley, Tobin. *The Carousel Animal.* Berkeley, California: Zephyr Press, 1983.

Franklin, Linda C. *Three Hundred Years of Kitchen Collectibles.* Florence, Alabama: Books Americana, 1981.

Gardiner, Gordon, and Alistair Morris. *The Price Guide to Metal Toys*. Woodbridge, Suffolk, England: Antique Collectors' Club, 1980.

Haskins, Bud. *Avon Bottle Encyclopedia*, 10th ed. Ft. Lauderdale, Florida: Avon Res., 1984.

Hill, Deborah G. *Wallace-Homestead Price Guide to Coca-Cola Collectibles*. Lombard, Illinois: Wallace-Homestead Books, 1985.

Holiner, Richard. *Collecting Barber Bottles*. Paducah, Kentucky: Collectors' Books, 1986.

Hugeons, Thomas. *Official Guide to Paper Collectibles*. Orlando, Florida: The House of Collectibles, Inc., 1986.

Huxford, Bob and Sharon. *The Collector's Encyclopedia of Fiesta*. Paducah, Kentucky: Collectors' Books, 1987.

Irick-Nauer, Tina. *The First Price Guide to Antique & Vintage Clothing*. New York: E. P. Dutton, 1983.

Jones, Susan, ed. *Collectibles Market Index Guide to Plates, Figurines, Bells, Graphics, Steins and Dolls*, 5th ed. West Chester, Pennsylvania: Schiffer Publishing Ltd., 1988.

Kaduck, John M. *Rare and Expensive Postcards, Book I*, rev. ed. Des Moines, Iowa: Wallace-Homestead Books.

Kaduck, Margaret and John. *Rare and Expensive Postcards, Book II*. Lombard, Illinois: Wallace-Homestead Books, 1979.

Kelley, Lyngerda, and Nancy Schiffer. *Costume Jewelry: The Great Pretenders*. West Chester, Pennsylvania: Schiffer Publishing Ltd., 1987.

Kennett, Frances. *The Collector's Book of Fashion*. New York: Crown Publishers, 1983.

Ketchum, William. *The New and Revised Catalog of American Collectibles*. New York: Gallery Books, 1984.

Kirsch, Francine. *Christmas Collectibles*. Lombard, Illinois: Wallace-Homestead Books, 1985.

Kovel, Ralph and Terry. *The Kovels' Collector's Guide to American Pottery*. New York: Crown Publishers, Inc., 1974.

Kovel, Ralph and Terry. *Kovels' Depression Glass & American Dinnerware Price List*, 3rd ed., rev. New York: Crown Publishers, Inc., 1988.

Kovel, Ralph and Terry. *Kovels' Know Your Collectibles*. New York: Crown Publishers, Inc., 1982.

Kovel, Ralph and Terry. *The Kovels' Collectors' Source Book*. New York: Crown Publishers, Inc., 1983.

Kovel, Ralph and Terry. *Advertising Collectibles*. New York: Crown Publishers, Inc., 1986.

Lynnlee, J. L. *All That Glitters*. West Chester, Pennsylvania: Schiffer Publishing Ltd., 1986.

Mackey, William J., Jr. *American Bird Decoys*. Exton, Pennsylvania: Schiffer Publishing Ltd., 1979.

Malouff, Sheila. *Collectible Clothing*. Des Moines, Iowa: Wallace-Homestead Books, 1983.

Mannis, William, Peggy Shank, and Marianne Stevens. *Painted Ponies*. Millwood, New York: Zon International Publishing Co., 1986.

McCullough, Lou. *Paper Americana: A Collector's Guide*. San Diego, California: A. S. Barnes & Co., Inc., 1980.

McCumber, Robert L. *Toy Bank Reproductions & Fakes*. Self-published: 102 Carriage Drive, Glastonbury, Connecticut, 1970.

McMorris, Penny. *Crazy Quilts*. New York: E. P. Dutton, 1984.

Miller, Robert W. *Clock Guide Identification with 1986–1987 Prices*. Lombard, Illinois: Wallace-Homestead Books, 1986.

Miller, Robert W. *Wallace-Homestead Price Guide to Dolls: 1986–1987 Prices*. Lombard, Illinois: Wallace-Homestead Books, 1986.

Opie, James. *British Toy Soldiers, 1893–1932*. New York: Harper & Row, 1985.

Pollak, Emil and Martyl. *A Guide to American Wooden Planes and Their Makers*, 2nd ed. Morristown, New Jersey: The Astragal Press, 1987.

Russell, Martin, and Ron Lockton. *Price Guide to Collectable Cameras*. Available from Seven Hills Books, Cincinnati, Ohio, 1986.

Safford, Carleton L., and Robert Bishop. *America's Quilts and Coverlets*. New York: Weathervane Books, 1974.

Schwartz, Jeri. *Tussie Mussies*. Self-published: P. O. Box 271, Hartsdale, New York 10530.

Scroggins, Clara J. *Hallmark Keepsake Ornaments: A Collector's Guide,* 2nd ed. Lombard, Illinois: Wallace-Homestead Books, 1985.

Selman, Laurence. *Collectors' Paperweights*. Rutland, Vermont: Charles Tuttle, 1986.

Smith, Wayne. *Ice Cream Dippers*. Self-published: P. O. Box 418, Walkersville, Maryland 21793, 1986.

Sroufe, Ted. *Midway Mania*. Gas City, Indiana: L-W, Inc., 1985.

Uden, Grant. *Understanding Book Collecting*. Woodbridge, Suffolk, England: Antique Collectors' Club, 1986.

Viel, Lyndon C. *The Clay Giants, Book 3*. Lombard, Illinois: Wallace-Homestead Book Co., 1987.

Vogelzang, Vernagene, and Evelyn Welch. *Granite Ware, Book II*. Lombard, Illinois: Wallace-Homestead, 1986.

von Hoelle, John. *Thimble Collector's Encyclopedia, New International Edition*. Lombard, Illinois: Wallace-Homestead Books, 1986.

Zeder, Audrey B. *British Royal Commemoratives*. Lombard, Illinois: Wallace-Homestead Books, 1986.

ENGLISH FURNITURE

Andrews, John. *Price Guide to Antique Furniture*. Woodbridge, Suffolk, England: Antique Collectors' Club, 1978.

Cescinsky, Herbert. *English Furniture from Gothic to Sheraton*. New York: Dover Publications, 1968.

Chinnery, Victor. *Oak Furniture, The British Tradition*. Woodbridge, Suffolk, England: The Antique Collectors' Club, 1979.

Edwards, Ralph. *The Dictionary of English Furniture*. Three volumes. Woodbridge, Suffolk, England: Antique Collectors' Club, 1983.

Fastnedge, Ralph. *English Furniture Styles, 1500–1830*. New York: A. S. Barnes & Co., 1964.

Macquoid, Percy. *A History of English Furniture*. Woodbridge, Suffolk, England: Antique Collectors' Club, 1987.

Macquoid, Percy. *The Age of Oak and Walnut*. Woodbridge, Suffolk, England: Antique Collectors' Club, 1987.

Macquoid, Percy. *The Age of Mahogany and Satinwood*. Woodbridge, Suffolk, England: Antique Collectors' Club, 1987.

Watson, Sir Francis. *The History of Furniture*. New York: William Morrow and Company, 1976.

FAKES AND REPRODUCTIONS

Bly, John, ed. *The Confident Collector*. New York: Prentice-Hall Press, 1986.

Cescinsky, Herbert. *The Gentle Art of Faking Furniture*. New York: Dover Publications, 1967.

Goodrich, Donald L. *Art Fakes in America*. New York: Viking Press, 1973.

Hammond, Dorothy. *Confusing Collectibles: A Guide to Identification of Contemporary Objects*. Des Moines, Iowa: Wallace-Homestead Co., 1979.

Kaye, Myrna. *Fake, Fraud, or Genuine?* New York: Little, Brown and Company, 1987.

Mills, John Fitzmaurice. *How to Detect Fake Antiques*. New York: Desmond Elliott Publisher Ltd., 1980.

Mills, John F., and John M. Mansfield. *The Genuine Article*. London: British Broadcasting Corp., 1979.

Peterson, Harold L. *How Do You Know It's Old?* New York: Charles Scribner's Sons, 1975.

Savage, George. *Forgeries, Fakes, and Reproductions: A Handbook for the Art Dealer and Collector*. New York: Praeger, 1963.

Yates, Raymond F. *Antique Fakes and Their Detection*. New York: Gramercy Publishing Co., 1950.

GENERAL BOOKS AND TERMINOLOGY

The Best of Antique Collecting. Woodbridge, Suffolk, England: Antique Collectors' Club, 1981.

Boger, Louise A. *Furniture Past and Present*. New York: Doubleday and Co., 1986.

Cameron, Ian, et. al, ed. *Random House Collector's Encyclopedia. Victoriana to Art Deco*. New York: Random House, 1974.

Complete Color Encyclopedia of Antiques. New York: Hawthorn Books, Inc., 1975.

Cowle, Donald, and Keith Henshaw. *Antique Collector's Dictionary*. New York: Arc Books, Inc., 1969.

Doane, Ethyl. *Antiques Dictionary*. Portland, Maine: The Anthoensen Press, 1949.

Dreppard, Carl W. *A Dictionary of American Antiques*. Boston, Massachusetts: Charles T. Branford Co., 1952.

Edwards, Ralph, and L.G.G. Ramsey. *The Connoisseur's Complete Period Guides*. New York: Bonanza Books, 1968.

Kovel, Ralph and Terry H. *Know Your Antiques*. New York: Crown Publishers, Inc., 1981.

The Random House Encyclopedia of Antiques. New York: Random House, Inc., 1973.

Revi, Albert C. *The Spinning Wheel's Complete Book of Antiques*. New York: Grosset and Dunlap, 1977.

GLASS

Bogess, Gill and Louise. *American Brilliant Cut Glass*. New York: Crown Publishers, Inc., 1977.

Florence, Gene. *The Collector's Encyclopedia of Depression Glass*. Paducah, Kentucky: Collectors' Books, 1977.

Florence, Gene. *Elegant Glassware of the Depression Era*. Paducah, Kentucky: Collectors' Books, 1983.

Hartung. *Carnival Glass Books 1–10*. Self-published: 718 Constitution Street, Emporia, Kansas 66801.

Klamkin, Marian. *The Collector's Guide to Carnival Glass*. New York: Hawthorn Books, Inc., 1976.

McClinton, Katharine M. *Introduction to Lalique Glass*. Des Moines, Iowa: Wallace-Homestead Book Co., 1978.

McKearin, Helen and George. *Two Hundred Years of American Blown Glass,* rev. ed. New York: Crown Publishers, Inc., 1966.

Miller, Robert W. *Wallace-Homestead Guide to Pattern Glass,* 11th ed. Lombard, Illinois: Wallace-Homestead Books, 1986.

North, Jacquelyne. *Perfume, Cologne and Scent Bottles.* West Chester, Pennsylvania: Schiffer Publishing Ltd., 1986.

Padgett, Leonard E. *Pairpoint Glass.* Des Moines, Iowa: Wallace-Homestead Book Co., 1979.

Presznick, Rose M. *Carnival Glass, Books 1–6.* Self-published: 7810 Avon Lake Road, Lodi, Ohio 44254, 1966.

Pullin, Anne G. *Glass Signatures, Trademarks and Trade Names.* Lombard, Illinois: Wallace-Homestead Books, 1986.

Revi, Albert C. *American Cut and Engraved Glass.* Exton, Pennsylvania: Schiffer Publishing Ltd., 1982.

Revi, Albert C. *American Art Nouveau Glass.* Exton, Pennsylvania: Schiffer Publishing Ltd., 1981.

Sloan, Jean. *Perfume and Scent Bottle Collecting.* Lombard, Illinois: Wallace-Homestead Books, 1986.

Spillman, Jane. *Glass—Volumes I and II.* New York: Alfred A. Knopf, Inc., 1982.

Swan, Martha L. *American Cut and Engraved Glass.* Lombard, Illinois: Wallace-Homestead Books, 1986.

MAKING MONEY IN ANTIQUES AND COLLECTIBLES

Baker, Robert and Cynthia. *How to Manage Estate Sales.* Niles, Michigan: Acorn Press, 1985.

Barlow, Ronald S. *How to Be Successful in the Antiques Business,* rev. ed. New York: Charles Scribner's Sons, 1981.

Gilbert, Anne. *Investing in the Antiques Market.* New York: Grosset and Dunlap, 1980.

Grotz, George. *Double Your Money in Antiques in Sixty Days.* New York: Doubleday, 1986.

Johnson, Bruce E. *How to Make $20,000 a Year in Antiques & Collectibles Without Leaving Your Job.* New York: Rawson Associates, 1986.

Persky, Robert S. *ARTnews Guide to Tax Benefits.* New York: ARTnews Books, 1987.

Pohl, Irma and R. A. *Rummage, Tag and Garage Sales for Profit and Fun.* Garden City, New York: Doubleday, 1984.

Rinker, Harry L. *How to Make the Most of Your Investments in Antiques and Collectibles.* New York: Arbor House, 1988.

Sommer, Elyse. *How to Make Money in the Antiques-and-Collectibles Business.* Boston, Massachusetts: Houghton-Mifflin Co., 1979.

NINETEENTH- AND TWENTIETH-CENTURY FURNITURE

Andrews, John. *Price Guide to Victorian, Edwardian & 1920's Furniture.* Woodbridge, Suffolk, England: Antique Collectors' Club, 1980.

Ayars, Marcy and Walter. *Larkin Oak.* Summerdale, Pennsylvania: Echo Publishing, 1984.

Brooks, H. Allen. *Frank Lloyd Wright and the Prairie School.* New York: George Brazilier, 1984.

Darling, Sharon. *Chicago Furniture.* New York: Norton, 1984.

Dubrow, Eileen and Richard. *American Furniture of the 19th Century, 1840–1880.* Exton, Pennsylvania: Schiffer Publishing, 1983.

Duncan, Alistair. *Art Nouveau Furniture.* London: Thames and Hudson Ltd., 1982.

Duncan, Alistair. *American Art Deco.* New York: Abrams, 1986.

Edwards, Robert, ed. *The Arts and Crafts Furniture of Charles Limbert.* Catalog reprint. Watkins Glen, New York: American Life Foundation, 1982.

Garner, Philippe. *20th Century Modern.* New York: Van Nostrand Reinhold, 1980.

Garner, Philippe. *Twentieth Century Style & Design: Nineteen Hundred to the Present.* New York: Van Nostrand Reinhold, 1986.

Gray, Stephen, and Robert Edwards, eds. *The Collected Works of Gustav Stickley.* Catalog reprint. New York: Turn of the Century Editions, 1981.

Gray, Stephen, ed. *Lifetime Furniture.* Catalog reprint. New York: Turn of the Century Editions, 1981.

Gray, Stephen, ed. *Limbert's Holland Dutch Arts and Crafts Furniture.* Catalog reprint. New York: Turn of the Century Editions, 1981.

Gray, Stephen, ed. *Roycroft Furniture.* Catalog reprint. New York: Turn of the Century Editions, 1981.

Hanke, David. *The Decorative Designs of Frank Lloyd Wright.* New York: E. P. Dutton, 1979.

Mackinson, Randell. *Greene and Greene: Architecture As a Fine Art.* Salt Lake City, Utah: Peregrine Smith Books, 1977.

Mackinson, Randell. *Greene and Greene, Furniture and Related Designs.* Salt Lake City, Utah: Peregrine Smith Books, 1982.

McNerney, Kathryn. *Victorian Furniture . . . Our American Heritage.* Paducah, Kentucky: Collectors' Books, 1981.

Ormsbee, Thomas H. *Field Guide to American Victorian Furniture.* New York: Bonanza Books, 1962.

Payne, Christopher. *Price Guide to 19th Century European Furniture.* Woodbridge, Suffolk, England: Antique Collectors' Club, 1985.

Schaefer, Herwin. *Nineteenth Century Modern*. New York: Praeger, 1970.

Schwartz, Marion D., Edward J. Stanek, and Douglas K. True. *The Furniture of John Henry Belter and the Rococo Revival*. New York: E. P. Dutton, 1981.

Stickley Craftsman Furniture Catalogs. Gustav Stickley 1910 catalog and L. & J. G. Stickley 1912 catalog reprint. New York: Dover Publications, 1979.

Swedberg, Robert and Harriett. *American Oak Furniture Styles and Prices*. Book I, rev. ed. Lombard, Illinois: Wallace-Homestead Book Co., 1986.

Swedberg, Robert and Harriett. *Victorian Furniture Styles and Prices*. Book II, rev. ed. Lombard, Illinois: Wallace-Homestead Book Co., 1986.

Swedberg, Robert and Harriett. *Furniture of the Depression Era*. Paducah, Kentucky: Collectors' Books, 1987.

Thonet Bentwood and Other Furniture: The 1904 Illustrated Catalogue. New York: Dover Publications, 1980.

Yates, Raymond F. and Marguerite W. *A Guide to Victorian Antiques*. New York: Gramercy Publishing Co., 1969.

ORIENTAL RUGS

Aschenbrenner, Erich. *Oriental Rugs Volume 2: Persian*. Oriental Textile Press, Inc., 1981. Distributed by Antique Collectors' Club.

Bennett, Ian. *Oriental Rugs Volume 1: Caucasian*. Oriental Textile Press, Inc., 1981. Distributed by Antique Collectors' Club.

Dilley, Arthur U. *Oriental Rugs and Carpets*. New York: Scribner's, 1931.

Edwards, A. Cecil. *The Persian Carpet*. London: Duckworth, 1953.

Eiland, Murray L. *Chinese and Exotic Rugs*. Boston, Massachusetts: Little, Brown and Co., 1979.

Eiland, Murray L. *Oriental Rugs: A New Comprehensive Guide*. Boston, Massachusetts: Little, Brown and Co., 1981.

Erdmann, Kurt. *Seven Hundred Years of Oriental Carpets*. Berkeley, California: University of California Press, 1970.

Jacobsen, Charles W. *Check Points on How to Buy Oriental Rugs*. Rutland, Vermont: Charles Tuttle, 1969.

Lewis, C. Griffin. *The Practical Book of Oriental Rugs*. Philadelphia, Pennsylvania: Lippincott, 1911.

Mumford, John K. *Oriental Rugs*. New York: Scribner's, 1925.

Parsons, R. D. *Oriental Rugs Volume 3: The Carpets of Afghanistan*. Oriental Textile Press, Inc., 1983. Distributed by Antique Collectors' Club.

von Bode, W., and E. Kuhnel. *Antique Rugs from the Near East*. London: 1970.

Yetkin, S. *Early Caucasian Carpets in Turkey*. London: Oguz Press, 1978.

POTTERY AND PORCELAIN

Alden, Aimee, and Marian K. Richardson. *Early Noritake China with Value Guide*. Lombard, Illinois: Wallace-Homestead Book Co., 1987.

Andacht, Sandra. *Treasury of Satsuma*. Lombard, Illinois: Wallace-Homestead Book Co., 1981.

Bondhus, Sandra V. *Quimper Pottery*. Self-published: P. O. Box 203, Watertown, Connecticut 06795, 1981.

Cameron, Elisabeth. *Encyclopedia of Pottery & Porcelain 1800—1960*. New York: Facts on File Publications, 1986.

Cunningham, Jo. *American Dinnerware*. Paducah, Kentucky: Collectors' Books, 1982.

Cushion, J. R. *Handbook of Pottery & Porcelain Marks*. London: Faber & Faber, 1980.

Degenhardt, Richard K. *Belleek*. Huntington, New York: Portfolio Press, 1978.

Evans, Paul. *Art Pottery of the United States, An Encyclopedia of Producers and Their Marks*. New York: Charles Scribner's Sons, 1974.

Gallo, John. *Nineteenth and Twentieth Century Yellow Ware*. Richfield Springs, New York: Heritage Press, 1985.

Garner, F. H., and Michael Archer. *English Delftware*. London: Faber & Faber, 1972.

Godden, Geoffrey. *Encyclopedia of British Pottery & Porcelain Marks*. Exton, Pennsylvania: Schiffer Publishing Ltd., 1983.

Godden, Geoffrey. *British Pottery—An Illustrated Guide*. New York: Abner Schram Ltd., 1983.

Godden, Geoffrey. *Godden's Guide to Mason's China and the Ironstone Wares*. Woodbridge, Suffolk, England: Antique Collectors' Club, 1981.

Godden, Geoffrey. *Ridgway Porcelains*. Woodbridge, Suffolk, England: Antique Collectors' Club, 1985.

Godden, Geoffrey. *Victorian Porcelain*. London: Herbert Jenkins, 1961.

Gordon, Elinor. *Collecting Chinese Export Porcelain*. New York: Main Street Press, 1977.

Gordon, Elinor. *Treasures from the East*. New York: Main Street Press, 1984.

Henzke, Lucile. *Art Pottery of America*. Exton, Pennsylvania: Schiffer Publishing Ltd., 1982.

Hotchkiss, John F. *Hummel Art*. Des Moines, Iowa: Wallace-Homestead Books, 1981.

Jacobson, Gertrude T. *Haviland China Volumes I & II.* Des Moines, Iowa: Wallace-Homestead Book Co., 1979.

Kirsner, Gary, and Jim Gruhl. *The Stein Book.* Coral Springs, Florida: Glentiques Ltd., 1985.

Kovel, Ralph and Terry H. *The Kovels' Collectors' Guide to American Art Pottery.* New York: Crown Publishers, Inc., 1974.

Kovel, Ralph and Terry H. *The Kovels' Illustrated Price Guide to Royal Doulton,* 2nd ed. New York: Crown Publishers, Inc., 1984.

Kovel, Ralph and Terry H. *New Dictionary of Marks.* New York: Crown Publishers, Inc., 1986.

Lehner, Lois. *American Kitchen and Dinner Wares.* Des Moines, Iowa: Wallace-Homestead Books, 1980.

Leibowitz, Joan. *Yellow Ware.* Exton, Pennsylvania: Schiffer Publishing, 1985.

May, Harvey. *The Beswick Collectors Handbook.* Available from Seven Hills Books, Cincinnati, Ohio, 1986.

Miller, Robert L. *The No. 1 Price Guide to M. I. Hummel.* Huntington Press, 1983.

Oates, Joan C. *Phoenix Bird Chinaware Books 1, 2, and 3.* Self-published: 5912 Kingsfield, West Bloomfield, Michigan 48033, 1984, 1985, 1986.

Palmer, Arlene M. *A Winterthur Guide to Chinese Export Porcelain.* New York: Crown Publishers, 1976.

Pearson, Kevin. *The Character Jug Collectors Handbook,* 3rd ed. Available from Seven Hills Books, Cincinnati, Ohio, 1986.

Peck, Herbert. *The Book of Rookwood Pottery.* New York: Crown Publishers, 1968.

Pottery and Porcelain: The Knopf Collectors' Guides to American Antiques. New York: Alfred A. Knopf, Inc., 1983.

Rebert, M. Charles. *American Majolica, 1850–1900.* Des Moines, Iowa: Wallace-Homestead Books, 1981.

Rontgen, Robert E. *Marks on German, Bohemian and Austrian Porcelain: 1710 to the Present.* Exton, Pennsylvania: Schiffer Publishing, 1981.

Schiffer, Herbert, Peter, and Nancy. *Chinese Export Porcelain.* Exton, Pennsylvania: Schiffer Publishing, 1975.

Schiffer, Herbert, Peter, and Nancy. *China for America.* Exton, Pennsylvania: Schiffer Publishing, 1980.

Schiffer, Nancy. *Japanese Porcelain.* Exton, Pennsylvania: Schiffer Publishing, 1986.

Schlegelmilch, Clifford J. *Handbook of Erdmann and Reinhold Schlegelmilch Prussia-Germany and Oscar Schlegelmilch German Porcelain Marks.* Self-published: Whittmore, Minnesota, 1973.

Schleiger, Arlene. *Two Hundred Patterns of Haviland China.* Self-published: Omaha, Nebraska, 1974.

Sikota, Gyozo. *Herend.* Budapest: Kossath Printing House, 1973. Available from Puski Covin, New York.

Van Patten, Joan F. *The Collector's Encyclopedia of Nippon Porcelain.* Paducah, Kentucky: Collectors' Books, 1979.

Walcha, Otto. *Meissen Porcelain.* New York: Putnam, 1981.

Williams, Howard Y. *Gaudy Welsh China.* Des Moines, Iowa: Wallace-Homestead Books, 1978.

Wonsch, Lawrence L. *Hummel Copycats with Values.* Lombard, Illinois: Wallace-Homestead Book Co., 1987.

Worth, Veryl M., and Louise M. Loehr. *Willow Pattern China,* 3rd ed. H. S. Worth Co., 1986.

SILVER

Banister, Judith, ed. *English Silver Hallmarks.* London: W. Foulsham, 1970.

Bly, John. *Discovering Hallmarks on English Silver,* rev. ed. London: Shire Publishing Ltd., 1974.

Bradbury, Frederick. *Bradbury's Book of Hallmarks.* Sheffield, England: J. W. Northend Ltd., 1980 (1987 edition distributed by Seven Hills Books).

Brett, Vanessa. *The Sotheby's Directory of Silver 1600–1940.* New York: Sotheby's Publications, Harper & Row, 1986.

Carpenter, Charles H., Jr. *Gorham Silver 1831–1981.* New York: Dodd, Mead & Co., 1982.

Carpenter, Charles H., Jr., and Mary G. *Tiffany Silver.* New York: Dodd, Mead & Co., 1978.

Chaffers, William. *Chaffers' Handbook to Hallmarks.* Revised by Cyril Bunt. London: William Reeves Bookseller Ltd., 1969.

Culme, John. *The Dictionary of London Gold & Silversmiths and Allied Traders 1838–1914.* Woodbridge, Suffolk, England: Antique Collectors' Club, 1987.

Darling, Sharon. *Chicago Metalsmiths.* Chicago, Illinois: Chicago Historical Society, 1977.

Ensko, Steven G., and Edward Wenham. *English Silver: 1675–1825.* New York: Arcadia Press, 1980.

Green, Robert A. *Marks of American Silversmiths.* Self-published: Shawnee Trail, Harrison, New York 10528, 1977.

Hagan, Tere. *Silverplated Flatware: An Identification and Value Guide.* Paducah, Kentucky: Collectors' Books, 1981.

Hogan, Edmund P. *The Elegance of Old Silverplate.* Exton, Pennsylvania: Schiffer Publishing Ltd., 1980.

Jackson, Charles J. *English Goldsmiths & Their Marks.* Woodbridge, Suffolk, England: Antique Collectors' Club, 1987.

Jewelers' Circular Keystone Sterling Flatware Pattern Index, 2nd ed. Radnor, Pennsylvania: Chilton Co., 1978.

Kovel, Ralph and Terry H. *Kovels' American Silver Marks.* New York: Crown Publishers, 1989.

Luddington, John. *Starting to Collect Silver.* Woodbridge, Suffolk, England: Antique Collectors' Club, 1984.

The Meriden Britannia Silver Plate Treasury. New York: Dover Publications, Inc., 1982.

Okie, Howard P. *Old Silver & Old Sheffield Plate.* Garden City, New York: Doubleday and Co., Inc., 1928.

Osterberg, Richard F., and Betty Smith. *Silver Flatware Dictionary.* San Diego, California: A. S. Barnes & Co., Inc., 1981.

Les Poinçons de Garantie Internationaux pour l'Argent. Tardy, 21, rue des Boulangers, Paris, France, 1980.

Rainwater, Dorothy T. *Encyclopedia of American Silver Manufacturers,* 3rd ed., rev. Exton, Pennsylvania: Schiffer Publishing Ltd., 1986.

Rainwater, Dorothy T., and Donna H. Felger. *American Spoons, Souvenir and Historical.* Nashville, Tennessee: Thomas Nelson, Inc.; and Hanover, Pennsylvania: Everybody's Press, 1968.

Robertson, R. A. *Old Sheffield Plate.* London: Ernest Benn Ltd., 1957.

Scroggins, Clara J. *Silver Christmas Ornaments.* San Diego, California: A. S. Barnes & Co., Inc., 1980.

Turner, Noel D. *American Silver Flatware, 1837–1910.* Cranbury, New Jersey: A. S. Barnes & Co., Inc., 1972.

Waldron, Peter. *The Price Guide to Antique Silver,* 2nd ed. Woodbridge, Suffolk, England: Antique Collectors' Club, 1982.

Wardle, Patricia. *Victorian Silver & Silverplate.* New York: Universe Books, 1963.

Wyler, Seymour B. *The Book of Old Silver.* New York: Crown Publishers, 1937.

TWENTIETH-CENTURY DECORATIVE ARTS

The Book of the Roycrofters. Roycroft Shop Catalog: 1919 and 1926. Catalog reprint. East Aurora, New York: House of Hubbard, 1977.

Catley, Bryan. *Art Deco and Other Figures.* Woodbridge, Suffolk, England: Antique Collectors' Club, 1978.

Clark, Robert Judson, ed. *The Arts and Crafts Movement in America 1876–1916.* Princeton, New Jersey: Princeton University Press, 1972.

Evans, Paul. *Art Pottery of the United States,* 2nd ed. New York: Feingold and Lewis Publishing Corp., 1987.

Johnson, Bruce. *The Official Identification and Price Guide to Arts and Crafts.* New York: House of Collectibles, 1988.

Waddell, Robert. *The Art Nouveau Style.* New York: Dover Publications, Inc., 1977.

Weber, Eve. *Art Deco in America.* New York: Exeter Books, 1985.

36

Questions and Answers

The following questions are representative of those I am constantly asked both in private homes and at public talks. They cover specific and general areas of personal property and antiques.

General

1. *I have just inherited a house full of personal property. What can I do to find out what I've got?*

Consult an outside person who has no sentimental attachment to the property and who also is knowledgeable about personal property values today. A good personal property appraiser should be able to tell you about the majority of items in a household and refer you to other experts for those pieces she does not know about. Most appraisers can also give you guidelines as to how to dispose of pieces you no longer wish to keep. Tax benefits are available to donors of personal property whether it goes to the Salvation Army, a church bazaar, or a restoration or museum. However, do not expect the appraiser to purchase pieces being appraised, as this is a direct conflict of interest.

The alternative is to call in an antiques dealer who can tell you about the items and their value and offer to purchase pieces or take them on consignment to sell in his or her shop. An auctioneer performs a role similar to the dealer.

If you already know which items you wish to keep and which you wish to dispose of, then an antiques dealer or auctioneer can handle the job for you. However, if you are baffled about values, the best course is to hire an appraiser.

2. *I bought a chair from a reputable antiques dealer twenty years ago. Now I want to sell it. Should I ask the dealer to buy it back?*

Yes. Many dealers are extremely anxious to buy back pieces they sold in the past. Dealers complain that every year it is getting harder to find quality pieces. Therefore, if your chair is of fine quality, the dealer will almost always be pleased to put it back into stock. In fact, advertisements in antiques journals and magazines boast, "We have just repurchased these items and are happy to offer them once again." Sometimes owners worry about whether the dealer will pay enough if he buys the chair back. Remember that the dealer must make a profit, thus he cannot pay you full retail value for your chair. However, because the dealer did sell you the chair in the past, he cannot come in and tell you the chair is not what you think it is; after all, *he* sold it to *you* as a specific piece and charged you according to its quality, condition, age, and so on. Some dealers offer to buy back pieces for the same prices you paid for them. Others are willing to make allowances for inflation and increased values.

3. *We're getting ready to go on vacation, and our neighborhood has had several break-ins. What should we do to protect ourselves?*

The answer to this question seems so obvious, but it is often overlooked. First, do not "broadcast" your vacation. Gossip columns in newspapers and idle talk at country clubs and hairdressers can reach the wrong people. Consider using a timer on lights so there appears to be some movement in the house. If you are leaving a car at home, park it partway down the driveway so a van or strange car cannot pull all the way up to the house, where it would be unnoticed from the street. Tell a trusted neighbor that you are leaving and have him or her check the house for packages and other deliveries that make it obvious the house is unoccupied.

Also, ask a neighbor to check the doors in the front and back on occasion to make sure they are locked and that there has been no attempted or successful forced entry. In some instances, glass has been knocked out and homes have been broken into by burglars who intend to return to take more out of the house. In such cases, an alert neighbor's call to the police or the owners has prevented further theft.

Of course you may wish to consider storing or hiding particular items. Thieves know where to look, but you can certainly make the job of robbing your house more difficult if you use ingenuity in selecting your hiding places. In other words, the thief who can walk in and open up a single drawer and empty all of your silver has a much better chance of getting in and out in a hurry than one who has to look in ten or fifteen different places to find the items you have hidden. However, you also have to remember where you have put these pieces when you wish to take them out of storage or hiding. There is always the danger of vandalism if everything is put away. For this reason, it is often suggested that, if you're going to store a lot of personal property, you leave out enough for the burglar to be satisfied with what he is getting. This means you should leave out items that are easily replaceable but hide or store your more prized and antique pieces.

4. *I have some fine antiques, but the time has come to sell them. I don't want a lot of dealers coming in and picking the good things first, and I don't want an auction. Should I consider a tag sale to sell my antiques?*

If you have a professional tag sale conductor in your region, this may be an excellent solution. Review chapter 30 on tag sales and seek out a reputable person who fits the criteria established there. If one cannot be located, you may want to have your pieces appraised (tell the appraiser the purpose of the appraisal—private sale). Then offer the pieces to your friends and acquaintances based on the values established by the appraiser. But remember—the appraiser may not buy items he has valued.

5. *What sort of markups do antiques dealers put on items in their shops?*

It depends entirely on what the piece is and how much the dealer had to pay for it. I have even seen dealers sell a piece for what it cost them. Many times an antiques dealer will pay a great deal for a piece just to have it in stock, knowing that he has paid full retail value for the item when he bought it. Dealers will pay top dollar for one item in order to get a group of other pieces at very low prices. This happens especially when the dealer is buying from a private individual who tells him exactly what he wants for each piece. On the other hand, if the dealer buys a real sleeper, he can then put it into his shop at several hundred percent markup.

You must remember that dealers are running a business. They have to pay overhead and employees, inventory, and income taxes the way any business does. The dealer is entitled to make a profit on his merchandise.

6. *I found out my antique is not an antique after all. What can I do? Do I return it to the dealer?*

The best way to face this problem is to avoid it. If you can't be more knowledgeable than the antiques dealer (and few people can be without spending a lifetime studying antiques), you need to protect yourself by getting a full description of the item on the bill of sale. Don't settle for a bill of sale that says "Chair—$395." Request a written description that tells the kind of chair, its age, and its condition. Then ask the dealer if this item is returnable should you find it to be other than stated on the bill of sale. If the dealer says no, be wary. On the other hand, if the dealer is reputable, he *should be* willing to take back any item that is other than what he has stated. Although some antiques dealers violently oppose this practice, I do not see it as being any different from a retail store accepting the return of merchandise found to be faulty.

7. *Where do I find the best buys?*

Generally speaking there are two places. One is from the dealer who specializes in a category and has pieces of the finest quality. These are considered "best buys" because they will continue to increase in value, are often rare, and are highly desirable as investments. Such pieces are also authenticated and sold in auction houses. (Remember, the elite dealer or auction house "provenance" adds glamour and eventual monetary worth to a piece.)

You can also find the best buys whenever *you* know more about an object than the person selling it. This seldom happens if the seller is an expert. However, it can happen if you are able to buy silver from the Oriental rug specialist who had to buy silver items in an estate sale in order to get the rugs or if you are lucky in a shop or flea market stall where the dealer specializes but has an odd piece or two with which you are more familiar.

8. *I want to invest in some personal property for my portfolio. What should I do?*

The objects most commonly suggested for investment holdings today are Oriental rugs, diamonds, and fine-quality silver from the nineteenth and early twentieth centuries. However, before investing be aware that there are fakes and overpriced pieces in every category of personal property from gems to paintings to stamps to autographs to furniture. My first recommendation is that you protect what you have already by knowing what you own and what its value is. Then consider adding to your personal property portfolio.

9. *How do you know?*

This is one of the most often asked questions, and the answer is both simple and tremendously important.

There are three steps to the appraiser's thought process. (a) First of all, he or she must know what the piece is, whether it is period, a reproduction, a forgery, or a fake. Once she has determined what the piece is, then she must consider the quality of the piece as compared with the finest and the worst of its type. Next, she must note the condition of the piece. (b) Once she has properly identified the item, determined its quality, and noted its condition, she must know the market value of the piece. (c) Finally, she must understand the different levels of appraisal evaluation. She must be familiar with the differences between estate values, fair market values, retail values, insurance or replacement values, and projected growth values (when looking at personal property for investment potential). You know by thoroughly investigating and researching your piece or by having an appraiser do so.

Appraisals

1. *How do I find a licensed appraiser?*

First, there is no such thing as a licensed appraiser. Granted, some belong to professional organizations and societies, which shows their professional approach to appraising. However, appraisers are not certified or licensed by any governmental group. And unfortunately many insurance agencies will accept almost any appraiser's figures. But as personal property becomes more valuable and the insurance companies become more knowledgeable, good insurance companies are looking at the credentials of each appraiser. You, too, should ask for an appraiser's credentials and references. And if an appraiser tells you he or she *is* licensed, watch out.

2. *I want to donate some things to a museum. Will they give me an appraisal I can use for my taxes?*

When donating items to museums, you must first be sure that the pieces are appropriate for the museum's collection. Often acquisition committees will not accept donations because they are inappropriate (not the right age, not of adequate quality, in poor condition, and so forth). At other times museums are happy to accept almost any item a person wishes to donate, if the donation is made without any strings attached. This means that the museum can exhibit the piece, put it into a study collection (which means it may never be seen in an exhibit but is important to the research of the museum staff), or keep the property only until the museum decides to sell it. (Incidentally, pieces sold by museums usually bring more money than sales of comparable pieces from private estates because of the museum provenance.) The sale money is then put toward purchasing an item needed or deemed more important by the museum's acquisition committee.

If the museum does accept your gift, generally they should not give you an appraisal of the piece. It is not considered lawful or ethical for museum curators or staff to appraise contributions to their collections. Most museums require that the donor himself acquire an independent appraisal of the contribution for his own tax purposes. In this case the financial burden of the appraisal rests with the donor; however, this is a professional expense and is tax deductible.

3. *My mother has just died. We've got to divide her property three ways. Can an appraiser help us?*

When the family does not know the value of the property or has sentimental attachment to some items and not to others, and the children cannot agree on how to divide the pieces, an appraiser can be of great benefit. The appraiser is objective and looks at the property from an unbiased standpoint. Seldom can an estate be divided within a penny's equal share, but once monetary values are determined, the heirs have specific information that will guide them in their decisions.

4. *I need a low appraisal for tax purposes. Will you do that?*

Good appraisers understand the different types of appraisals that are needed at different times—such as the insurance appraisal, the private sale appraisal, and the estate appraisal. There is a difference between an estate or tax appraisal and a replacement or insurance appraisal. However, the appraiser is a professional who determines the value of the pieces. Any attempt to tell an appraiser how to value an item is an insult to his or her professional integrity.

5. *I've just had a fire. Can an appraiser help me?*

Because the appraiser begins each job with a fresh perspective, she can be helpful. The appraiser who has had a lot of experience in fire claims can help the owner remember items that he may even have forgotten. My experience has shown that insurance companies will more carefully evaluate the merits of an appraisal when it has been prepared by an outside objective expert rather than by the owner, who may not even know what he has lost, much less the value of the pieces.

6. *Why will some dealers make appraisals and others not?*

Some believe that a conflict of interest exists when a dealer makes an appraisal and then offers to buy the piece for that amount of money. Such dealers prefer to leave appraising to appraisers, and then, if offered items that have been previously appraised, they can either accept or reject the appraised value. If the dealer rejects the appraiser's value, which he is free to do, he can then make an offer to buy. This is not an appraisal, but simply his offer of how much he will pay for the item. Another reason some dealers will not make an appraisal is that they are not equipped to handle the work involved.

7. *I don't know if I need an appraisal. Is it possible to find out whether or not I really need one before I make the investment?*

Before you engage an appraiser's services you should have a thorough discussion with the appraiser, usually by telephone. The appraiser spends all his time dealing with personal property and knows what is in people's homes. He or she can usually get a feeling for your property by discussing it with you. After the discussion, the appraiser may say "Yes, you definitely need an appraisal" or "No, an appraisal is not needed at this time." Remember, appraisers are selling their time and their services, and most are so heavily booked that they do not want to become involved in an unprofitable or unnecessary job. However, when necessary most appraisers are willing to go to your home or apartment for a minimum fee, take a look at your property, and at that point determine whether or not an appraisal is genuinely needed. If there is a long distance between the appraiser's office and your property, you can send photographs of the pieces so she or he can make a judgment as to whether or not an appraisal is justified. An appraisal cannot be made from the photographs, but the photos will at least show what you have.

8. *I had an appraisal made two years ago. Now I've been robbed. Should I contact the appraiser, and will she be able to help me? And what about the values given two years ago? I know some things are more valuable now than then.*

Always contact the appraiser when you have a loss. If the appraiser has also worked for the insurance company, she can probably save both you, the victim, and the insurance company time and problems. Whether or not you will receive *full* compensation for your items two years or more after the appraisal was made depends upon the kind of insurance policy you have. Some have escalating clauses. Others lock you into a specific amount. Ask your agent about this when the policy is first written. If you do not receive sufficient compensation from your insurance, you may be able to deduct the loss from your income taxes. Check with a CPA or tax expert for guidance. But even an out-of-date appraisal is much better than none at all.

9. *What does an appraiser do when his client insists that his furniture belonged to a famous person but has no concrete proof?*

The appraiser gently explains that value is established by the *quality* of the object, not who owned it. For example, a really poor quality twentieth-century kitchen chair that might have been in President Roosevelt's home will be nowhere near as valuable as a fine Chippendale-style chair owned by his unknown neighbor.

China

1. *My plate has "22-karat gold" written on the back of it. Is it valuable?*

The value of the piece lies in its quality, manufacturer, design, and age. The use of gold on a plate may make it more expensive to purchase; however, gold in itself does not make the plate more valuable. This particular notation was used on a lot of china made in the United States in the twentieth century. Most of the china that bears this marking is not considered valuable by today's standards.

2. *My complete set of china for twelve—cups, saucers, dinner plates, and so on—was dropped in a recent move. Several pieces were broken. I believe the entire set should be replaced because the pattern is no longer being made, and it does me no good to have four cups, ten saucers, and seven dinner plates. Am I right?*

Some people will want to take the time to locate replacements for those broken pieces through the various replacement services. On the other hand, it may be less expensive to purchase a new, comparable set than to replace the broken pieces. Your adjuster will undoubtedly make his decision based on the type of policy you have rather than your wishes. It may work to your advantage to present both options. If you will take a new china service, explain to the adjuster or agent that finding the other pieces will be expensive and troublesome.

Silver

1. *My silver is monogrammed. Does that make it less valuable?*

For insurance purposes, silver has a specific value determined by the pattern and condition. If you have to replace silver with a monogram on it, getting the new silver monogrammed will add to its expense. On the other hand, it is easier to sell silver that does not have a monogram on it because the new owner may wish to add his own or leave it unmonogrammed. However, you will not find that a monogram will affect the price of estate silver as a rule.

2. *Will it hurt the value of my silver to have it replated?*

If yours is true Sheffield silver from the eighteenth or very earliest part of the nineteenth century, then it should not be replated, regardless of its condition. However, the silver plate of the later nineteenth century and that of the twentieth century may be replated without damaging its value. Copper showing through the silver plate is called "bleeding." Many people consider the contrast between the copper and the silver attractive and desirable, even on semiantique pieces. Others want their silver in pristine condition. Before replating a piece, consider whether or not it is worth the expense. To find out, check with an appraiser or jeweler and learn the price of a comparable piece in perfect condition and compare that with the price of having the piece replated.

3. *My mother's apartment has been burglarized. She really does not know if her stolen pieces were sterling silver or silver plate. What should she do?*

Remember, sterling silver has always been expensive. Large pieces are usually silver plate. I suggest making out a list from memory first—stating the object, its size, and whether she believes it to be sterling or silver plate. Then refer back to the chapter on silver. The information in this book may serve to jog her memory and clarify whether some pieces were indeed sterling silver or silver plate. Review the maker's marks and see if these help, and then use the illustrations and glossary to write accurate descriptions of the pieces on your insurance claim.

Glass

1. *My collection of nineteenth-century pressed glass was displayed on special shelves in my living room window. A disaster occurred, and almost all the pieces were damaged or broken. How do I get this claim settled quickly and easily?*

Of course, the claim will be settled based on your insurance company's policy against breakage. Was the collection included on a fine arts policy? If so, there should be little problem. But if not, it may be necessary to have an appraisal made. Dimensions, approximate age, and whether or not any of the glass was colored should be included on the appraisal, even though the items are broken.

2. *I have several hundred pieces of Depression glass. Should I insure the collection separately?*

Absolutely! You will want to discuss the type of coverage with your agent, but regardless of whether you put the collection on a separate rider or simply increase your policy value to include the collection, be certain that the collection is covered for breakage.

Furniture

1. *My mother-in-law says her Chippendale dining room suite is eighteenth century. Is this possible?*

Large suites of furniture, or matching pieces—table, chairs, buffet or sideboard or bed, dressing table, chest, mirror, and so on—were not common until the mid- to late nineteenth century. Your mother-in-law's suite is most likely an early-twentieth-century reproduction. But remember, age alone does not determine value. Her dining room suite may be worth a great deal, depending on its style, condition, and quality.

2. *Does veneer indicate the quality of furniture?*

Yes and no. Fine-quality veneer enhances the beauty of furniture and can be extremely expensive. Many fine-quality Hepplewhite case pieces, such as sideboards, secretaries, breakfronts, and the like, are veneered and inlaid. On the other hand, inexpensive, poor-quality veneer is often used as a cost-reducing material by low-end manufacturers. Such cheap veneers were commonly used in 1920s to 1940s reproductions.

3. *My early-nineteenth-century table had a leg broken off. The table had been appraised for $5,200. The repairs will cost almost $700. Should I also claim depreciation?*

Absolutely! The breaking-off of and replacement or extensive repair to a table leg is considered major restoration. The table's potential sale value or investment possibilities has been reduced by at least 25 percent.

4. *The marble top to my Victorian chest of drawers was dropped in moving. What do I do?*

For years I have said that movers forget that marble is both heavy and fragile. Without the original top the chest has lost a substantial portion of its value. Further, replacing the marble can be time-consuming, expensive, and often unsatisfactory. Check your options: (a) replacement of the top (claim some depreciation as well) and (b) cash settlement so you can purchase a comparable chest. Your decision may well be determined by whether you have sentimental attachment to this particular piece or not. But remember, you can't put a price on sentiment.

ACKNOWLEDGMENTS

To everyone who has helped to put this book together by supplying information, photographs, especially Sue Hall Waldron for many illustrations, ideas, and inspiration, a heartfelt thank you. And to everyone who has generously shared wonderful treasures, both inherited and purchased, with me over the years, thank you for adding to my knowledge and understanding of our material objects that say so much about craftsmanship, culture, and history.

Special thanks to Janella Smyth, Carolyn Samet, Joe Wilkinson, Michael Rulison, August Fetcko, Joyce Johnson, Hazel Buchanan, Tom Norris, Steve Minor, David Maloney, and my family for loyalty and help that can never be repaid.

And thank you to my agent, Susan Urstadt, to Helen Pratt, Ralph and Terry Kovel, Bruce Johnson, Ann Cahn, and to my editor, Sharon Squibb for so selflessly sharing their knowledge, experience, and encouragement.

Index